Walking with Jesus Christ

EVANGELICALS AND CATHOLICS IN DIALOGUE II

WALKING WITH JESUS CHRIST

Catholic *and* Evangelical Visions *of the* Moral Life

edited by
Steven Hoskins *and* Christian D. Washburn

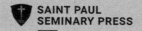

SAINT PAUL, MINNESOTA • 2024

Cover design by Judy Gilats

© 2024 Steven Hoskins and Christian D. Washburn
Saint Paul Seminary Press is a registered trademark
of The Saint Paul Seminary.
All rights reserved

Published 2024 by
Saint Paul Seminary Press
2260 Summit Ave., Saint Paul, Minnesota 55105

Library of Congress Control Number: 2024931809
LC record available at https://lccn.loc.gov/2024931809

ISBN 978-1-953936-08-0 (paperback)
ISBN 978-1-953936-58-5 (ebook)

spspress.com

Dedicated to Bonn Clayton and Bishop Arthur Kennedy

Contents

Foreword   ix
Bishop David D. Kagan and Rev. Bruce Cromwell, PhD

Dialogue in Pursuit of the Moral Life: xii
A Testimony of Ecumenical Friendship
Dr. Steven Hoskins and Dr. Christian D. Washburn

Abbreviations   xvii

SECTION I. Norms Governing the Moral Life   1

1.0   Common Statement on Norms Governing the Moral Life   3

BACKGROUND PAPERS

1.1   Theological Sources for Morality: Scripture, Tradition, and the Magisterium   5
Dr. Christian D. Washburn

1.2   Classical Natural Right and the Origins of Natural Law Doctrine as a Source of the Moral Life   37
Dr. William B. Stevenson

1.3   The Role of the Decalogue in Protestant and Catholic Catechisms   49
Dr. Daniel A. Keating

1.4   The Wesleyan Quadrilateral and Norms of the Moral Life   67
Rev. Bruce Cromwell, PhD

1.5   Preliminary Sketch of a Method for Reformed Ethics   83
Dr. Dennis W. Jowers

SECTION 2. Sexual Ethics 103

2.0 Common Statement on Sexual Ethics ... 105

BACKGROUND PAPERS

2.1 Marriage within the Economy of Salvation:
An Introduction to the Catholic Teaching on Marriage ... 109
Dr. David P. Fleischacker

2.2 Fruitful Married Love: The Catholic Church's Teaching
on Marriage, Abortion, and Contraception ... 129
Dr. Christian D. Washburn

2.3 A Catholic Understanding of Homosexual Relations:
The Biblical Foundations ... 155
Dr. Daniel A. Keating

2.4 A Quasi Conservative-Progressive Approach to
Homosexuality: A Vineyard Approach to Engaging
the Biblical, Theological, and Pastoral Issues ... 172
Luke T. Geraty, MA, MDiv

SECTION 3. Social Ethics 189

3.0 Common Statement on Social Ethics ... 191

BACKGROUND PAPERS

3.1 Catholic Social Teaching: Orientation and Overview ... 193
Dr. Daniel A. Keating

3.2 "Absurd Equality": The Church's Condemnation
of Socialism in *Rerum novarum* ... 210
Dr. William B. Stevenson

3.3 An Evangelical Perspective on Social Ethics ... 230
Dr. Glen Menzies

3.4 Social Issues and Wesleyan Evangelicals   256
 Dr. Steven Hoskins

SECTION 4. Moral Life and Eschatology   279

4.0 Common Statement on Moral Life and Eschatology   281

BACKGROUND PAPERS

4.1 "What must I do to be saved?": The Power of Grace, the Moral Life, and Eschatology in Catholic Doctrine and Theology   283
 Dr. Christian D. Washburn

4.2 Our Moral Life Determines Our After Life: Catholic Notes on the Relationship of the Moral Life to the Last Things   304
 Dr. David P. Fleischacker

4.3 The Way to Heaven: Wesleyan Ecclesial Ethics and Eschatology   312
 Rev. Bruce Cromwell, PhD and Dr. Steven Hoskins

Contributors   331

Index of Names   335

Index of Subjects   339

Foreword

IN THE FOREWORD of the first book published by the national Evangelical-Catholic dialogue, *Justified in Jesus Christ*, my predecessor as Catholic chair of the dialogue, Bishop John Gaydos, and the Evangelical chair, Mr. Bonn Clayton, began by recalling "In the early 1980s, several Christian groups were promoting moral and ethical issues in the Minneapolis, MN area. Interestingly, almost all the participants in these groups were either Evangelicals and Catholics." Subsequent to a thorough reflection upon the nature of soteriology and justification in its first formal round, the second round of conversations brought the group of Catholic and Evangelical scholars back to those same issues which gathered them together in the first place. The volume you hold in your hand is the product of prayerful reflection, scholarly research, and rigorous dialogue about Christian ethics between Evangelical and Catholic theologians who are committed to being of service to Christians across denominational boundaries here in the United States.

We read in the first letter of John, "Children, let us love not in word or speech but in deed and truth" (3:18). This text is an invitation from some of the brightest minds in Catholic and Evangelical communities to walk with Jesus Christ. It was an abundant blessing to witness their commitment to the Lord Jesus as they shared the wisdom of their faith traditions with each other. All of them share a common concern for the good of our society, fidelity to the Lord, and the salvation of souls. Despite those moments when there were clear differences of opinion expressed, a spirit of deep respect and fraternity prevailed over all of the dialogue meetings. Each session was an experience of Christian community that included prayer, laughter, and serious study. It was a sheer joy to participate in the meetings.

The authors of this book wrote with the hope that our Christian communities might come closer together so that more of us might be able to experience the joy of walking together with Jesus Christ. In a society which seems to be moving away from what we hold in common in regard to morals and ethical values, the work of Christian unity has become more urgent than ever.

The concerns addressed in this volume will not only aid the reader in understanding the ways of thinking that inform Evangelical and Catholic moral principles, but also touch on some of the most discussed issues of our age, including social responsibility, human sexuality, and the implications of our moral living for our eternal destiny. Undoubtedly, an engaging reading experience awaits anyone fortunate enough to pick it up.

While reading the text itself will give one a deeper understanding of Evangelical and Catholic views on these matters, I would urge you to go a step further. The convergences described were formulated as a result of serious dialogue and at times intense discussions. This book is an opportunity to continue the conversation. It can be used as a tool to facilitate further dialogue in a variety of contexts. Should you find it useful, perhaps you would consider introducing it to your congregation? Perhaps an inspired reader might start a book discussion group, deliberately seeking out both Catholics and Evangelicals to join. This book could also be shared with local ecumenical clergy associations for discussion. There are many ways in which one could continue the conversations that were begun during the dialogue and culminated in this book.

Just as with the last volume, this text gains its authority exclusively from the knowledge, experience, and reputations of the authors themselves. None of them intended to speak in an official capacity for their churches/faith communities/institutions, nor have their churches given any type of public endorsement of this book. These pastors, theologians, and scholars speak for themselves. Nevertheless, the wisdom they bring to these conversations speaks for itself and is undoubtedly most valuable.

There were many hands that went into the completion of this text who should be recognized and thanked. We are grateful to Archbishop

Hebda of St. Paul and Minneapolis for his encouragement and hospitality. Msgr. James P. Shea and the University of Mary in Bismarck, North Dakota, kindly offered space and support for many of the meetings of the dialogue. The generosity of St. Paul Seminary School of Divinity in St. Paul, Minnesota, and its Rector Rev. Joseph Taphorn, provided a space and support for our last meeting and also the gifts of its publishing house for this text. We are also indebted to Erika Zabinski, Maggee Hangge, Judy Gilats, and Gretchen K. Washburn for their patience and skill as editors of the final text.

May the good Lord bless all of those who contributed to the dialogue and this text so that we might witness a deepening of unity between Christians and a society that embraces the call of Christ for us to love one another as He has loved us.

Bishop David D. Kagan
Bishop of Bismarck
United States Conference of Catholic Bishops

Rev. Bruce N. G. Cromwell, PhD
Superintendent
Great Plains and Mid-America Conferences
Free Methodist Church USA

Dialogue in Pursuit of the Moral Life: A Testimony of Ecumenical Friendship

"CHRISTIAN DIALOGUE, especially ecumenical dialogue, is a testament to friendship."[1] So began the first book that published the efforts of the National Evangelical-Catholic Dialogue sponsored by the United States Council of Catholic Bishops (2004–present). That book, *Justified in Jesus Christ*, served to give a short history of the dialogue and its proceedings, underscored by the intellectual friendship—in spirit and structure—that emerged in its meetings.

The dialogue began with informal meetings in the mid-1990s and took on official status with the USCCB in 2004. *Justified in Jesus Christ* reflected the gains of the dialogue that had been achieved through a series of preliminary meetings on matters doctrinal from 2003–2013 (Scripture, Atonement, the Church, etc.) that led to a four-year round of dialogues on the topic of Justification (2014–2017). This topic was completed as the 500th anniversary of the Protestant Reformation was observed.

This book, *Walking with Jesus Christ: Catholic and Evangelical Visions of the Moral Life*, is composed in the same format as its predecessor and offers the work of the National Evangelical-Catholic Dialogue during its round on the moral life (2017–2021), completed in 2021 at the University of St. Thomas in St. Paul, MN. Sessions were held each year on the following topics. In 2017, the dialogue discussed the norms governing the moral life. In 2018, the dialogue discussed sexual ethics. In 2019, the dialogue discussed social ethics. Finally,

---

1. Steven Hoskins, "A Dialogue in Testament to Friendship," 5–10 in *Justified in Jesus Christ: Evangelicals and Catholics in Dialogue*, eds. Steven Hoskins and David Fleischacker (Bismarck, ND: University of Mary Press, 2017), 5.

in 2021 the dialogue discussed the relationship of the moral life to eschatology. At each of the annual meetings, members presented background papers that formed the basis of that meeting's discussion and served as starting points for constructing a common statement. These common statements and background papers from dialogue participants on both sides make up this book.

The Catholic essays offered during the round of the dialogue begin with the contributions of Catholic theologians Daniel Keating, William Stevenson, and Christian D. Washburn, who examine the various norms for Catholic moral theology, including the role of Scripture, tradition, magisterium, and natural law (2017). David Fleischacker, Daniel Keating, and Christian D. Washburn then examine the morality of marriage, contraception, abortion, and homosexual acts (2018). Daniel Keating and William Stevenson next discuss social ethics, including Catholic social teaching and socialism (2019). Finally, David Fleischacker and Christian D. Washburn discuss the relationship of the moral life to our final beatific end (2021).

The Evangelical essays presented to the group begin with the contribution of Evangelical theologians Bruce Cromwell and Dennis Jowers, who explore the norms of Protestant ethics (2017). Luke Geraty discusses sexual ethics from the pastoral perspective of the Vineyard USA Church (2018). Glen Menzies and Steve Hoskins then evaluate approaches to Evangelical social ethics from Pentecostal and Wesleyan points of view (2019). Finally, Bruce Cromwell and Steve Hoskins discuss the notions of eschatology and ethics from a Wesleyan viewpoint (2021).

A few notes about the book are in order. The book includes the listing of those who participated in the dialogue sessions during 2017–2021. The Catholic participants were chaired by The Most Reverend David Kagan, Bishop of the Diocese of Bismarck, North Dakota. The Evangelicals were chaired by Bonn Clayton, a representative of the Conservative Congregational Christian Conference, with participants coming from a variety of churches and communions throughout the United States.

The meetings during this round of the dialogue also saw some necessary internal reorganizing of matters related to presentation and leadership. Some of those changes included the creation of best practices for the dialogue agreed upon by both sides and the selection of Co-Chairs to assist the Chairs and the dialogue in its meetings. Father Walter Kedjierski, Executive Director of the Secretariat of Ecumenical and Interreligious Affairs for the USCCB and The Reverend Bruce Cromwell, PhD, Superintendent of the Great Plains Conference for the Free Methodist Church, were chosen as Co-Chairs for the respective sides of the dialogue. This round of the dialogue also held its first virtual meeting in 2021 during the days of the Covid-19 pandemic, a difficult time for all of our churches, that brought with it significant challenges to the dialogue.

This book, and the changes noted above, are indicative of the dialogue's maturation as it has pursued the ideal inherent in its efforts since its genesis: a growing together of the mind and spirit that reaches toward understanding. The papers and common statements are indicative of ecumenical friendship. They do not spend much time on polemics or doctrinal triumphalism, the enemies of ecumenical work. Rather, they represent the highest ideals of an "ecumenical consciousness" that moves beyond polemics and into a respectful dialogue of shared beliefs, teachings, and confessions based on the pursuit and love of truth and signified by genuine friendship.[2] In doing so, this account of the dialogue is a testimony of the moral life required of all Christians, explored through a range of schools of thought in the Christian tradition, and it fulfills the charge of the Apostle Paul to "encourage one another and build one another up" as we live together in Christ (1 Thess 5:10-11).

This kind of friendship, and the moral life it demands, exists for those whose lives are oriented toward to the highest good. That good is God and God's revelation in Jesus Christ. It is in the pursuit of that good that we are met by God and grow in understanding of him and one another. Love for the truth that is God, the demands of witness

---

2. Albert Outler, "The Idea of 'Development' in the History of Christian Doctrine: A Comment," 7-14 in *Schools of Thought in the Christian Tradition*, ed. Patrick Henry (Philadelphia: Fortress, 1984), 11; Cardinal Avery Dulles, "The Travails of Dialogue," 221-33 in *Church and Society: The Laurence J. McGinley Lectures, 1988-2007* (New York: Fordham University Press, 2008), 221.

and imitation of God's action in Christ, and the pursuit of the Christian moral life together are all necessary components of true dialogue. The members of the dialogue offer this book in that spirit and hope this book will provide a fruitful starting point for future conversations between Evangelicals and Catholics.

In this, we are indebted to those who began the work of this dialogue. The roots of the National Evangelical Dialogue reach back to meetings of ecumenical friends in Minneapolis-Saint Paul, MN sometime during the mid-1990s around a table where food and doctrine were shared by friends. The friends who chaired those earliest meetings and gathered their friends for the conversations were The Most Reverend Arthur Kennedy, now Retired Auxiliary Bishop of Boston, Massachusetts, and Bonn Clayton. It is to them that we dedicate this work.

Steven Hoskins, PhD
  Trevecca Nazarene University

Christian D. Washburn, PhD
  Saint Paul Seminary School of Divinity
  University of St. Thomas

Abbreviations

AB	Anchor Bible
ACW	Ancient Christian Writers
ANF	Ante-Nicene Fathers, ed. Alexander Roberts, James Donaldson, and A. Cleveland Coxe (Buffalo, NY: Christian Literature Publishing Co., 1885)
CCC	*Catechism of the Catholic Church*, 2nd ed. (New York: Doubleday, 1997)
CCT	*Catechism of the Council of Trent*
CDF	Congregation for the Doctrine of the Faith
Compendium	Pontifical Council for Justice and Peace, *Compendium of the Social Doctrine of the Church* (June 29, 2004) (Vatican City: Libreria Editrice Vaticana, 2004)
CSEL	Corpus Scriptorum Ecclesiasticorum Latinorum
CST	Catholic social teaching
DH	Heinrich Denzinger, Peter Hünermann, Helmut Hoping, Robert L. Fastiggi, and Anne Englund Nash, eds., *Compendium of Creeds, Definitions, and Declarations on Matters of Faith and Morals*, 43rd ed. (San Francisco: Ignatius, 2012)
DS	Denzinger-Schönmetzer, *Enchiridion Symbolorum, definitionum et declarationum de rebus fidei et morum* (1965ff)
ESV	English Standard Version
FaCh	Fathers of the Church
GCS	Griechischen christlichen Schriftsteller der ersten drei Jahrhunderte
HC	*Heidelberg Catechism*
LCD	Lutherans and Catholics in Dialogue

NAB	New American Bible
NET	New English Translation
NFP	Natural Family Planning
NPNF	A Select Library of Nicene and Post-Nicene Fathers of the Christian Church, ed. Philip Schaff and Henry Wace (Buffalo, NY: Christian Literature Publishing Co., 1894)
NRSV	New Revised Standard Version
PG	Patrologia Graeca, ed. Jacques-Paul Migne (Paris: J.-P. Migne, 1857–66)
PL	Patrologia Latina, ed. Jacques-Paul Migne (Paris: J.-P. Migne, 1841–55)
RST	Reformationsgeschichtliche Studien und Texte
RSV	Revised Standard Version
RSVCE	Revised Standard Version, Catholic Edition
SC	Sources chrétiennes
ST	*Summa Theologiae* (Thomas Aquinas)
USCCB	United States Council of Catholic Bishops
Vg.	Vulgate
WLC	*Westminster Larger Catechism*
WSA	Works of Saint Augustine (Hyde Park, NY: New City Press, 1997–)

SECTION I.
Norms Governing the Moral Life

1.0. Common Statement on Norms Governing the Moral Life

1. Evangelicals and Catholics agree that the Sacred Scripture functions as the infallible rule for faith and conduct (i.e. moral life). Both Catholics and Evangelicals have made use of the Decalogue as fulfilled in Christ and as taught in the Sermon on the Mount to teach the norms of the moral life.

2. Catholics and Evangelicals agree that God's will and design are evident in the natural world. God has given us the light of understanding so we can discern the wisdom of the order in that world, but because our knowledge is obscured by sin, the testimony of Sacred Scripture is necessary to understand God's full plan for the moral life. This natural order has normative value for human beings. However...
   a. Catholics tend to speak in terms of the natural law, which "is nothing other than the light of understanding infused in us by God, whereby we understand what must be done and what must be avoided. God gave this light and this law to man at creation" (*Veritatis Splendor*, 40).
   b. Evangelicals, while not opposed to the language of natural law, tend to speak using scriptural language (e.g., Psalm 19:1–3, "the heavens declare the glory of God ... speaking without words").

3. Evangelicals and Catholics draw from their own traditions for understanding and shaping the norms of the moral life.
   a. Catholics hold that God's revelation is not only contained in the Sacred Scriptures but also in what is called "Apostolic

Tradition." This Tradition is to be held with equal respect alongside Sacred Scripture. Catholics also hold that there are authoritative traditions that are not part of divine revelation.
   b. Evangelicals value and respect their own traditions but they are always subject to the authority of Sacred Scripture for the norms of the moral life.

4. Evangelicals and Catholics agree that the Church has the duty to proclaim and apply whatever God has revealed regarding the moral life.
   a. Catholics hold that the magisterium (the Church's teaching authority) is not a source of this revelation but rather its servant and authoritative interpreter. Catholics also hold that the magisterium under certain conditions can infallibly interpret this revelation, even concerning concrete moral norms. Catholics hold that the magisterium can also authoritatively interpret the natural law.
   b. Evangelical teaching authorities are called to be faithful interpreters of revelation but Evangelicals do not consider fellowships or communions as infallible and believe they may even apostatize.

5. Catholics and Evangelicals agree that experience and conscience play an essential role in the apprehension, discernment, and application of moral norms, but do not in the first place constitute moral norms. Catholics and Evangelicals also agree that for proper moral discernment, the Word of God must inform the human conscience.

1.1. Theological Sources for Morality: Scripture, Tradition, and the Magisterium

Dr. Christian D. Washburn

JESUS CHRIST, *perfectus homo*, is the principal norm of the moral life for the Catholic Church. His life, death, and resurrection are the supreme illumination of the path to human flourishing. To guide his Church, he gave to her Sacred Scripture "for reproof, for correction, and for training in righteousness, that the man of God may be complete, equipped for every good work" (2 Tim 3:16–17).[1] To continue his salvific work Christ founded a living Church and invested certain men with authority to proclaim and to guard God's Word, guiding all men in a path of righteousness that leads to salvation. This paper will be a primer on the doctrinal sources that are normative in the Catholic Church's teaching on the moral life. To this end, this paper will examine the authoritative nature of the Word of God as expressed in both Sacred Scripture and Apostolic Tradition. It will then discuss the magisterium of the Church in its role as the "servant" of the Word of God and its role as teacher. From here, this paper will treat the question of who can teach authoritatively as part of the magisterium and the various levels of authority of magisterial teaching. Finally, it will discuss some basic rules for interpreting magisterial documents.

---

1. All scriptural references in the text are to the *ESV Study Bible* (Wheaton, IL: Crossway, 2008).

The Word of God as Contained in Scripture and Apostolic Tradition

The Church teaches that God "chose to reveal himself and to make known to us the hidden purpose of his will by which through Christ, the Word made flesh, man might in the Holy Spirit have access to the Father and come to share in the Divine Nature."[2] The Father gathered a chosen people to himself, teaching them to confess him as "the one living and true God, provident Father and just judge, and to wait for the Savior promised by him."[3] Finally, the Father sent his Son, who reveals the Father:

> To see Jesus is to see his Father. For this reason Jesus perfected revelation by fulfilling it through his whole work of making himself present and manifesting himself: through his words and deeds, his signs and wonders, but especially through his death and glorious Resurrection from the dead and final sending of the Spirit of truth.[4]

God the Father sent the Son as the fulfillment of revelation, and his "gospel . . . is the source of *all saving* truth and moral teaching."[5] This public revelation ended with the death of the last apostle. Therefore, "we now await no further new public revelation."[6]

---

2. Second Vatican Council, *Dei verbum* (November 18, 1965), §2. Trans. Heinrich Denzinger, Peter Hünermann, Helmut Hoping, Robert L. Fastiggi, and Anne Englund Nash, eds., *Compendium of Creeds, Definitions, and Declarations on Matters of Faith and Morals*, 43rd ed. (San Francisco: Ignatius, 2012), §4202 (hereafter DH followed by paragraph number; where applicable, the second number after the slash is a reference to the older DS).
3. Second Vatican Council, *Dei verbum*, §3 (DH 4203).
4. Second Vatican Council, *Dei verbum*, §4 (DH 4204).
5. Second Vatican Council, *Dei verbum*, §7 (DH 4207, emphasis added).
6. Second Vatican Council, *Dei verbum*, §4 (DH 4204). The Council of Trent clearly implied that revelation was closed when it stated that the apostles handed on the "fontem omnis veritatis salutaris." DH 1501/783. The First Vatican Council taught, "For the Holy Spirit was not promised to the successors of Peter so that they might disclose a new doctrine by his revelation, but rather that, with his assistance, they might reverently guard and faithfully explain the revelation or deposit of faith transmitted by the apostles." DH 3070/1836. Finally, Saint Pius X also condemned the following view of the Modernists: "Revelation, constituting the object of the Catholic faith, was not completed with the apostles." DH 3421/2020.

The Gospel, "the source [*fontem*] of all saving truth and norms of conduct," was "promulgated" by Christ, who commanded the apostles to "preach" it to all creatures. This Gospel is preserved "in written books and unwritten Traditions."[7] According to Catholic doctrine, there are two sources of divine revelation: Sacred Scripture and Apostolic Tradition. All that is revealed, whether in Scripture or Apostolic Tradition, make up the "deposit of faith." God is the principal author of the seventy-three books of the Old and New Testament. The inspired writers of the Old and New Testaments were also authors but only in such a way that they "consigned to writing everything and *only* those things that he wanted."[8] The consequence of this divine inspiration is that the Scriptures are inerrant.[9]

The second source of revelation is Apostolic Tradition. Apostolic Tradition must be distinguished from what is called ecclesiastical tradition, such as the writings of the Fathers of the Church or conciliar documents.[10] Apostolic Tradition is a source of revelation distinct

---

7. DH 1501.

8. Second Vatican Council, *Dei verbum*, §11 (DH 4215).

9. "For all the books which the Church receives as sacred and canonical are written wholly and entirely, with all their parts, at the dictation of the Holy Spirit; and so far is it from being possible that any error can coexist with inspiration, that inspiration not only is essentially incompatible with error, but excludes and rejects it as absolutely and necessarily as it is impossible that God Himself, the supreme Truth, can utter that which is not true. This is the ancient and unchanging faith of the Church . . ." Leo XIII, *Providentissimus Deus* (November 18, 1893), pp. 37–62 in *The Scripture Documents: An Anthology of Official Catholic Teachings*, ed. Dean P. Béchard (Collegeville, MN: Liturgical Press, 2002), §20. Vatican II teaches, "Therefore, since everything asserted by the inspired authors or sacred writers must be held to be asserted by the Holy Spirit, it follows that the books of Scripture must be acknowledged as teaching solidly, faithfully and without error that truth which God, for the sake of our salvation, wanted put into sacred writings." Second Vatican Council, *Dei verbum*, §11 (DH 4216); *Catechism of the Catholic Church* (Vatican City: Libreria Editrice Vaticana, 2000), 107 (Hereafter cited as *CCC* followed by paragraph number.); CDF, *Doctrinal Commentary on the Concluding Formula of the Professio Fidei*, §11. Pablo T. Gadenz, "Magisterial Teaching on the Inspiration and Truth of Scripture: Precedents and Prospect," *Letter & Spirit* 6 (2010): 67–91.

10. "Tradition is to be distinguished from the various theological, disciplinary, liturgical, or devotional traditions, born in the local churches over time. These are the particular forms, adapted to different places and times, in which the great Tradition is expressed. In the light of Tradition, these traditions can be retained, modified or even abandoned under the guidance of the Church's magisterium." CCC 83.

from Scripture. The Church teaches that Apostolic Tradition is to be accepted with "an equal affection of piety" (*pari pietatis affectu*) with Sacred Scripture.[11] The Catholic Church finds evidence for the existence of this Apostolic Tradition in the Scriptures themselves. Saint Paul writes, "So then, brothers, stand firm and hold to the traditions that you were taught by us, either by our spoken word or by our letter" (2 Thess 2:15), and "Now we command you, brothers, in the name of our Lord Jesus Christ, that you keep away from any brother who is walking in idleness and not in accord with the tradition that you received from us" (2 Thess 3:6).

Magisterium as the Servant of the Word of God

According to Catholic doctrine, the "deposit of faith" is fundamentally binding on the Church, such that whatever is taught by the

---

11. DH 1501. An early draft of Trent's decree on Scripture and tradition read, "This truth [of the Gospel] is contained *partly* [*partim*] in written books, *partly* [*partim*] in unwritten traditions." This formulation clearly suggested that neither Scripture nor Tradition was by itself sufficient as a source of revelation since each contained merely part of revelation. The *partim-partim* formulation was changed in the final decree to a simple *et*: the Gospel is preserved "in written books and (*et*) unwritten traditions." Unfortunately, it is not known why this change was made. Post-Tridentine theologians down to the twentieth century held a two-source theory of revelation. In the mid-twentieth century Joseph R. Geiselmann argued that the council's decree had been fundamentally misunderstood. Geiselmann argued that when Trent chose the term *et*, it had intended to leave the question open. He then proposed the theory that Scripture is materially sufficient, but not formally sufficient. This attempt to reread the Council of Trent met with staunch opposition from theologians like Charles Boyer, SJ and Heinrich Lennerz, SJ. See Geiselmann, *Die Heilige Schrift und die Tradition: zu den neueren Kontroversen über das Verhältnis der Heiligen Schrift zu den nichtgeschriebenen Traditionen* (Freiburg: Herder, 1962); Charles Boyer, SJ, "Non-Written Apostolic Traditions," *Unitas* 15 (1963): 243–57; Boyer, "The Council of Trent and the Question of the Insufficiency of Sacred Scripture," *Unitas* 16 (1964): 159–70; Boyer, "Traditions apostoliques non écrites," *Doctor Communis* 15 (1962): 5–21; Heinrich Lennerz, SJ, "Notulae Tridentinae: Primum Anathema in Concilio Tridentino," *Gregorianum* 27 (1946): 136–42; Lennerz, "Scriptura sola?" *Gregorianum* 40 (1959): 38–53; Lennerz, "Sine scripto traditiones," *Gregorianum* 40 (1959): 624–35; Lennerz, "Scriptura et traditio in decreto 4. Sessionis Concilii Tridentini," *Gregorianum* 42 (1961): 517–22; Christian D. Washburn, "The Theological Importance of the Council of Trent and Vatican I for Catholic Theology," 630–650 in *Oxford Handbook of Catholic Theology* (Oxford: Oxford University Press, 2019), 632–33.

Church must be in conformity with the Word of God.[12] It must be noted that the juridical use of the term "deposit" implies that it is "not the property of the guardian but of the consignor who has handed it over to him to keep it in a safe state. The deposit of faith has come from God and is entrusted to those to whom a special assistance of the Holy Ghost is assured (2 Tim. 1:14)."[13] The deposit was entrusted to the apostles, who "handed on what they had received from the lips of Christ, from living with him, and from what he did or what they had learned through the prompting of the Holy Spirit."[14] The apostles left bishops as their successors, "'handing over' to them 'the authority to teach in their own place.'"[15] This teaching office is called the magisterium. According to Catholic doctrine, this authoritative "teaching office is not above the Word of God, but serves it [*ministrat*], teaching only what has been handed on, listening to it devoutly, guarding it scrupulously, and explaining it faithfully in accord with a divine commission and with the help of the Holy Spirit."[16]

There are several fundamental differences between God's Word as expressed in Sacred Scripture and magisterial statements, whether papal, conciliar, or episcopal. First, the Sacred Scriptures are immediately revealed by God, whereas magisterial decrees are not. The human authors of Scripture were inspired by an immediate revelation that

---

12. Pius XII admonished bishops that they "ought time and again to meditate on what the Apostle Paul said of his preaching of the Gospel: 'For I give you to understand, brethren, that the Gospel which was preached by me is not of man. For I did not receive it from man, nor was I taught it; but I received it by a revelation of Jesus Christ' (Gal. 1. 11–12)." *Ad sinarum gentem* (October 7, 1954), pp. 4:265–70 in *The Papal Encyclicals*, 5 vols., ed. Claudia Carlen, IHM (Wilmington, NC: McGrath, 1981), §19.

13. Pietro Parente, Antonio Piolanti, and Salvatore Garofalo, *Dictionary of Dogmatic Theology* (Milwaukee: Bruce, 1951), 74.

14. Second Vatican Council, *Dei verbum*, §7 (DH 4207).

15. Second Vatican Council, *Dei verbum*, §7 (DH 4208).

16. "Quod quidem Magisterium non supra verbum Dei est, sed eidem ministrat, docens nonnisi quod traditum est, quatenus illud, ex divino mandato et Spiritu Sancto assistente, pie audit, sancte custodit et fideliter exponit, ac ea omnia ex hoc uno fidei deposito haurit quae tamquam divinitus revelata credenda proponit." Second Vatican Council, *Dei verbum*, §10 (DH 4214).

caused them to write the words of God himself.[17] Through this divine inspiration, God caused the sacred writers either to reveal that which was previously unknown or to write down the things which they had seen and heard. Second, God's inspiration so moved the sacred writers that they were not required to investigate the matter. Popes and councils, on the other hand, are morally obligated to study and to discuss thoroughly the subject matter prior to formulating their doctrinal decrees.[18] Third, the Scriptures are inerrant in everything they assert.[19] The only parts of magisterial decrees that necessarily do not contain error, on the other hand, are solemn definitions concerning faith and morals for the universal Church.[20] Other parts of magisterial statements can contain error.[21] Fourth, every word of Scripture requires the assent of faith, whereas only a solemn definition of a revealed truth by the magisterium requires the assent of faith.[22] From the foregoing, one can clearly see that God's revealed Word is fundamentally superior to magisterial decrees.

Ultimately, the Church is not the judge of Sacred Scripture as has sometimes been alleged. The Church cannot decide whether this or that proposition contained in the Scriptures is true or false. If it could do this, then the Church's authority would clearly be higher than that of the Sacred Scriptures. In the sixteenth century, Bellarmine assured his readers that "no matter what the heretics say, the Church has never taught this." Instead, the Church judges whether a particular interpretation of Scripture is consistent with the truth of Scripture. Moreover, Bellarmine is quite clear that the Church's judgment does not add any truth value to the Scriptures; instead the Church's judgment provides certainty of whether an individual Christian's interpretation

---

17. Robert Bellarmine, *Disputationes Roberti Bellarmini Politiani Societatis Jesu, de Controversiis Christianae Fidei, adversus hujus temporis Haereticos*, 4 vols. (Paris: Triadelphorum, 1613), 4.2.12, vol. 2, col. 86.

18. Bellarmine, *De Controversiis*, 3.4.2, vol. 1, cols. 794–95; 4.2.12, vol. 2, col. 87.

19. Bellarmine, *De Controversiis*, 1.1.4, vol. 1, col. 18.

20. Bellarmine, *De Controversiis*, 4.2.12, vol. 2, col. 87. Christian D. Washburn, "St. Robert Bellarmine on the Infallibility of General Councils of the Church," *Annuarium Historiae Conciliorum* 42 (2010): 186–92.

21. Bellarmine, *De Controversiis*, 3.4.2, vol. 1, col. 793; 4.2.12, vol. 2, col. 87.

22. Bellarmine, *De Controversiis*, 1.1.15, vol. 1, col. 43.

is true.[23] Therefore, according to Bellarmine, "the judge of the true sense of Scripture and of all controversies is the Church, that is, the pope with the council, in which all Catholics agree, and that this doctrine is taught explicitly in the Council of Trent."[24] *Dei verbum* is clear that the task of authoritatively interpreting Scripture has been entrusted "exclusively to the living teaching office of the Church, whose authority is exercised in the name of Jesus Christ."[25]

Why Does the Magisterium Teach Authoritatively?

The first and most important reason that the magisterium teaches authoritatively is to proclaim the Gospel for the salvation of men.[26] The Second Vatican Council states that "among the principal duties of bishops" is "the proclamation of the Gospel,"[27] in order to fulfill the Church's universal mission to bring "all humanity and all its possessions back to its source in Christ, with him as its head and united in his Spirit."[28] The task of preaching the Gospel cannot be a mere repetition of the Word of God but must assist the faithful so that they may know what is to be believed and how to live this faith (*fidem credendam et moribus applicandam*).[29]

---

23. Bellarmine, *De Controversiis*, 1.3.10, vol. 1, col. 158. See also Christian D. Washburn, "St. Robert Bellarmine on the Authoritative Interpretation of Sacred Scripture," *Gregorianum* 94 (2013): 55–77.

24. "Nos enim existimamus, hunc Spiritum, etsi multis privatis hominibus saepe conceditur, tamen certò inveniri in Ecclesia, id est, in Concilio Episcoporum confirmato à summo Ecclesiae totius Pastore, sive in summo Pastore cum Concilio aliorum Pastorum: non enim disputare volumus hoc loco de summo Pontifice & Conciliis, an solus Pontifex possit rem definire, & an solum Concilium, de hoc enim suo loco agemus. Sed hîc in genere dicimus, iudicem, veri sensus Scripturae & omnium controversiarum, esse Ecclesiam, id est, Pontificem cum Concilio, in quo omnes Catholici conveniunt; & habetur expressè in Concilio Tridentino sess. 4." Bellarmine, *De Controversiis*, 1.3.3, vol. 1, col. 138.

25. Second Vatican Council, *Dei verbum*, §10 (DH 4214).

26. Second Vatican Council, *Ad gentes* (December 7, 1965), §1.

27. Second Vatican Council, *Lumen gentium* (November 21, 1964), §25 (DH 4149); *Christus Dominus* (October 28, 1965), §12.

28. Second Vatican Council, *Lumen gentium*, §13 (DH 4133).

29. Second Vatican Council, *Lumen gentium*, §25 (DH 4149).

While the magisterium cannot add to the deposit of faith, the magisterium issues new doctrinal decrees for three principal reasons: 1. to reconfirm a teaching of the Church, 2. to solve new questions, and 3. to guard a doctrine which has come under attack.[30] These three often appear concomitantly in the order of intention and execution. First, the magisterium intervenes when it wishes to reconfirm a teaching contained in Sacred Scripture or in previous expressions of Tradition. Pope Saint Pius V and Saint John Paul II promulgated, respectively, the *Catechism of the Council of Trent* (1566) and the *Catechism of the Catholic Church* (1992) to reconfirm the authoritative teachings of the Church.[31]

Second, the magisterium sometimes intervenes to solve new questions that pertain to doctrine in some respect. This is seen most clearly in recent magisterial interventions on sexual and biomedical issues. In *Humanae vitae* (1968), for example, Paul VI responded to the "new questions" raised by the introduction of the birth control pill in the mid-twentieth century.[32] Some Catholic theologians had argued that the pill was not really a form of contraception but rather a natural method of birth control like natural family planning (NFP). Paul VI answered the new question by excluding abortion, sterilization, and "any action which either before, at the moment of, or after sexual intercourse, is specifically intended to prevent procreation—whether as an end or as a means."[33]

Third, the magisterium also sometimes intervenes to *guard* "scrupulously" the deposit of faith and to remove "errors that threaten the flock."[34] In the sixteenth century, for example, some Protestants had argued that divorce and remarriage for the Christian was morally

---

30. CDF, *Mysterium ecclesiae* (June 24, 1973) (Washington, DC: United States Catholic Conference, 1973), §5.

31. The apostolic constitution *Fidei depositum* makes clear that the *Catechism of the Catholic Church* was intended as a confirming act. CCC 5.

32. Paul VI, *Humanae vitae* (July 25, 1968), pp. 4:223–33 in *The Papal Encyclicals*, 5 vols., ed. Claudia Carlen, IHM (Wilmington, NC: McGrath, 1981), §3.

33. Paul VI, *Humane vitae*, §14.

34. Second Vatican Council, *Dei verbum*, §10 (DH 4539); *Lumen gentium*, §25 (DH 3069).

permissible. The Council of Trent guarded the teaching of revelation (Luke 16:18) on the immorality of divorce and remarriage by reaffirming that marriage is both intrinsically indissoluble, i.e., it cannot be dissolved by the couple, and extrinsically indissoluble, i.e., it cannot be dissolved by any other human power such as the Church or the state.[35] Anabaptists, Luther, and Melanchthon also permitted simultaneous polygamy.[36] In response, the Council of Trent solemnly condemned "anyone [who] says that it is lawful for Christians to have several wives at the same time, and that it is not forbidden by any divine law (Matt 19:4f)."[37] When Anglicans broke with the tradition of two thousand years on the prohibition of contraception, Pius XI in *Casti connubii* guarded the deposit of faith by defining:

> any use whatsoever of matrimony exercised in such a way that the act is deliberately frustrated in its natural power to generate life is an offense against the law of God and of nature, and those who indulge in such are branded with the guilt of a grave sin.[38]

This last reason is perhaps the most common reason for authoritative "interventions" in the history of the Church. The Church usually does not solemnly define a doctrine until an error arises; or as Newman pithily said, "No doctrine is defined till it is violated."[39]

As can be seen from these examples, the magisterium has an obligation to teach on morals as well as doctrine. There are three major

---

35. DH 1807. E. Christian Brugger, *The Indissolubility of Marriage & the Council of Trent* (Washington, DC: Catholic University of America Press, 2017). Christian D. Washburn, Review of *The Indissolubility of Marriage & the Council of Trent*, by E. Christian Brugger, *Nova et Vetera* 18 (2020): 731–40.

36. Bellarmine, *De Controversiis*, 12.1.10, vol. 3, cols. 1323–1324.

37. DH 1802.

38. DH 3717.

39. John Henry Newman, *An Essay on the Development of Christian Doctrine* (Westminster, MD: Christian Classics, 1968), 151; Henry Edward Manning, *The Oecumenical Council and the Infallibility of the Roman Pontiff: A Pastoral Letter to the Clergy, &c.* (London: Longmans, Green, and Co., 1869), 40; Joseph Fessler, *The True and the False Infallibility of the Popes: A Controversial Reply to Dr. Schulte* (London: Burns and Oates, 1875), 18; Herbert Vaughan, *Submission to a Divine Teacher: Neither Disloyalty nor the Surrender of Mental and Moral Freedom. A Pastoral Letter* (New York: Catholic Publication Society, 1875), 31.

reasons for the necessity of the magisterium to teach on moral matters. First, Christ founded the magisterium to teach all that he had commanded, and part of his teaching concerns moral truths. Second, since revelation contains both general principles of morality and concrete moral norms, the Church must be able to teach on the range of its content in order to expound the Word of God authoritatively. Third, it is necessary and possible for the Christian to keep the commandments of God and his Church; therefore, the Christian must know how to live according to God's plan for man so that he might avoid hell and grow in holiness and merit eternal life.[40]

Included in its obligation to teach morals is the natural law. There are four reasons for this. First, Christ constituted the apostles and their successors as the authoritative interpreters of the whole moral law, including "the law of the Gospel" and the natural law. Second, the observance of the natural law is necessary for salvation, so the Church must be able to teach on it so men can reach their end.[41] Third, while "the moral order, as established by the natural law, is in principle accessible to human reason,"[42] human reason is capable of only an imperfect knowledge of the moral law due to the darkening of the intellect.[43] Fourth, the whole moral law, as John Paul II noted, including those truths known by the light of natural reason, is contained in revelation.[44]

---

40. DH 1535–39. Germain Gabriel Grisez, *The Way of the Lord Jesus* (Chicago: Franciscan Herald Press, 1983), 1:914.

41. Paul VI, *Humanae vitae*, §4.

42. John Paul II, *Veritatis splendor*, pp. 674–771 in *The Papal Encyclicals of John Paul II*, ed. J. Michael Miller (Huntington, IN: Our Sunday Visitor, 1996), §74.

43. John Paul II, *Veritatis splendor*, §74. On this see also Lawrence Welch, "Redeemed Reason, Natural Law, and the Competency of the Magisterium," 85–100 in *Reason and the Rule of Faith: Conversations in the Tradition with John Paul II*, ed. Christopher J. Thompson and Steven A. Long (Lanham, MD: University Press of America, 2011).

44. John Paul II, *Veritatis splendor*, §72. Francis Sullivan admits that his view is contrary to John Paul II. Francis Sullivan, "Infallible Teaching on Moral Issues? Reflections on *Veritatis splendor* and *Evangelium vitae*," 77–89 in *Choosing Life: A Dialogue on Evangelium Vitae*, ed. Kevin Wm. Wildes and Alan C. Mitchell (Washington, DC: Georgetown University Press, 1997), 83.

The Subject of the Magisterium of the Church

The "subject" of the magisterium of the Church concerns those who possess the right to teach authoritatively in the Catholic Church. According to Catholic doctrine, Christ constituted the apostles "after the manner of a college or stable group, over which he placed Peter chosen from among them."[45] Bishops have succeeded to the place of the apostles as shepherds of the Church,[46] and they consequently receive from the Lord the mission to teach all nations and to preach the Gospel to every creature. The bishops collectively make up the college of bishops that has the pope as its head on earth. This college has succeeded the apostolic college. There are two conditions necessary to be part of this college. The first condition is episcopal consecration, which confers the office of teaching on the *ordinandi*.[47] The second is the necessity of those who have received episcopal consecration to be in hierarchical communion with the pope and the other members of the college.[48]

The magisterium or teaching authority of the Church can be exercised either individually or collectively. The individual bishop speaks on matters of faith and morals "with the authority of Christ."[49] The pope's power to teach authoritatively is at its root a type of "episcopal" power.[50] Groups of bishops gathered together in synods or councils can also authoritatively teach the faithful. There are four basic types of councils: diocesan, provincial, national, and general or ecumenical.[51] Each of these types of councils can teach authoritatively,

---

45. Second Vatican Council, *Lumen gentium*, §19 (DH 4142).
46. Second Vatican Council, *Lumen gentium*, §20.
47. Second Vatican Council, *Lumen gentium*, §21. *Nota explicativa praevia* (DH 4353).
48. Second Vatican Council, *Lumen gentium*, §21. *Nota explicativa praevia* (DH 4353).
49. Second Vatican Council, *Lumen gentium*, §25 (DH 4149).
50. "Docemus proinde et declaramus, Ecclesiam Romanam, disponente Domino, super omnes alias ordinariae potestatis . . . obtinere principatum, et hanc . . . Romani Pontificis iurisdictionis potestatem, quae vere episcopalis est, immediatam esse." DH 3060.
51. There are other divisions of councils. Cano, following Gratian in part, divides councils into three types: general, provincial, and episcopal. Melchior Cano, OP, *De Locis Theologicis Libri Duodecim* (Salamanca: Mathias Gastius, 1563), 5.2, 169. Dominico

but with different levels of authority depending on the type of council.

In the nineteenth century, episcopal conferences were founded as "permanent institutions whereby bishops in a nation or other territory jointly exercise pastoral functions in the church."[52] This raised new questions about the teaching authority of these conferences. In *Apostolos suos* (1999), John Paul II clarified the nature of the teaching authority of these conferences,[53] expressly denying that the doctrinal decrees of organs of the conference, such as its doctrinal commission or executive committee, have authority except under certain limited conditions.[54] The letter also reaffirms the doctrinal competence granted in canon law to episcopal conferences to produce catechisms or translations of Sacred Scripture, for example.[55] When the bishops of an episcopal conference unanimously approve a doctrinal decree, these decrees are authoritative for the faithful of the territory of the conference.[56] If a doctrinal decree is not unanimously approved, the bishops of a conference must approve it by at least two-thirds of the bishops and it must receive the *recognitio* of the Holy See for it to be published.[57] These restrictive criteria imply a denial that episcopal conferences as such have a *mandatum docendi*.[58]

Within the college of bishops, the bishop of Rome has a special ministry as head of the college of bishops. The college of bishops has

---

Jacobatius divides councils into four types: general, provincial, episcopal, and religious. Dominico Jacobatius, *De Concilio tractatus*, in *Sacrosancta concilia ad Regiam editionem exacta: quae nunc quarta parte prodit auctior* (Paris: Impensis Societatis Typographicae Librorum Ecclesiasticorum jussu Regis constitutae, 1903), 0:3.

52. William J. Collinge, "Episcopal Conferences," *Historical Dictionary of Catholicism* (Lanham, MD: Scarecrow Press, 2012), 149–50.

53. In a footnote at the very beginning of the document, John Paul II distinguished episcopal conferences from the synods of bishops in Eastern churches, making it clear that the latter are not affected by this document.

54. John Paul II, *Apostolos suos* (May 21, 1998), §23.

55. John Paul II, *Apostolos suos*, §21. Cf. *Code of Canon Law*, c. 775, §2; *Code of Canon Law*, c. 825.

56. John Paul II, *Apostolos suos*, §22.

57. John Paul II, *Apostolos suos*, §22.

58. Francis A. Sullivan, SJ, "The Teaching Authority of Episcopal Conferences," *Theological Studies* 63 (2002): 472–93, at 491.

no authority unless it is understood to act together with the Roman Pontiff, the successor of Peter, as its head.[59] The pope, on the other hand, has the supreme teaching authority by himself. *Lumen gentium* repeats the assertion of *Pastor aeternus* that the pope's doctrinal decisions have a validity "of themselves, and not from the consent of the Church."[60] The pope's doctrinal decrees, therefore, "need no approval from others, nor do they allow an appeal to any other judgment."[61]

Since the magisterium is limited only to those with episcopal consecration who are in hierarchical communion with the pope, this excludes two groups. First it excludes those bishops who are not in hierarchical communion with the pope, such as the bishops of the Society of St. Pius X or the Orthodox bishops. Second, it also excludes all those without episcopal consecration such as priests, deacons, and laity. For some years after the Second Vatican Council, it was customary to argue that theologians were members of a sort of parallel magisterium based on the distinction (found for example in Saint Thomas) between the *magisterium cathedrae pastoralis* of the bishop and the *magisterium cathedrae magistralis* of the university theologian.[62] As the CDF's instruction *Donum veritatis* notes, "these texts do not give any support to this position, for St. Thomas was absolutely certain that the right to judge in matters of doctrine was the

---

59. Second Vatican Council, *Lumen gentium*, §22.

60. Second Vatican Council, *Lumen gentium*, §25 (DH 4149); see also First Vatican Council, *Pastor aeternus* (July 18, 1870), §4 (DH 3074).

61. Second Vatican Council, *Lumen gentium*, §25 (DH 4149).

62. Thomas Aquinas, *Quodlib*. III, q. 4, a.1 (9), ed. Marietti (Marietti Editori Ltd., 1956; reprint, Nuova Oflito s. r. l., Mappano, Torino, 1986), 46–47; Glenn W. Olsen, "The Theologian and the Magisterium: The Ancient and Medieval Background of a Contemporary Controversy," *Communio* 7 (December 1, 1980): 292–319; Richard John Neuhaus, "In Response to Glenn W. Olsen and J. Brian Benestad," *Communio* 16 (1989): 552–57; Avery Dulles, "The Two *Magisteria*: An Interim Reflection," *CTSA Proceedings* 35 (1980): 155–69; Avery Dulles, *Magisterium: Teacher and Guardian of the Faith* (Naples, FL: Sapientia Press of Ave Maria University, 2007), 36; Yves Congar, "A Semantic History of the Term 'Magisterium'," 297–313 in Charles E. Curran and Richard A. McCormick, eds., *The Magisterium and Morality* (New York: Paulist, 1982); Yves Congar, "A Brief History of the Forms of the Magisterium and Its Relations with Scholars," 314–31 in *The Magisterium and Morality*.

sole responsibility of the 'officium praelationis.'"[63] While theologians perform an important function for the life of the Church and are often called upon to assist the magisterium, they are not members of the magisterium. Their authority is simply the authority of their arguments.[64]

A member of the magisterium, however, does not always act in his capacity as a member of the magisterium. The pope can teach and write as a private theologian. In this capacity his writings have no magisterial authority. Pope Benedict XVI, for example, wrote a trilogy entitled *Jesus of Nazareth*. In the first volume, Benedict XVI states that the book "is in no way an exercise of the magisterium, but is solely an expression of my personal search 'for the face of the Lord'." He goes on to say, "everyone is free, then, to contradict me."[65] This is also true for bishops who, like Pope Benedict, often have expertise in various areas of theology.

The Fathers of the Church

One needs to distinguish between the theological use of the term "Fathers" and the merely historical use of the term. Theologically, Fathers are those who: 1. lived between the first and sixth centuries, 2. lived holy lives, 3. were theologically orthodox, and 4. meet ecclesiastical approval. Thinkers such as Origen, Tertullian, Lactantius, and Eusebius are considered merely ecclesiastical writers. The Fathers of the Church were not simply early Christian witnesses but were for the most part also members of the magisterium, and as such their teaching has further dogmatic implications for the theologian.[66]

The binding character of the Fathers' teaching on both doctrine

---

63. CDF, *Donum veritatis*, note 27, *L'Osservatore Romano* (July 2, 1990): 1. See also Bellarmine, *De Controversiis*, 1.3.10, vol. 1, col. 158.

64. Bellarmine, *De Controversiis*, 4.1.16, vol. 2, col. 33. Cano, *De Locis Theologicis*, VIII, 266, 268.

65. Benedict XVI, *Jesus of Nazareth*, vol. 1, *From the Baptism in the Jordan to the Transfiguration*, trans. Adrian Walker (New York: Doubleday, 2007), xxiii.

66. Joseph Clifford Fenton, *The Concept of Sacred Theology* (Milwaukee: Bruce Publishing Co., 1941), 134; l. Salaverri, *Sacrae Theologiae Summa*, 4th ed. (Madrid: Biblioteca de Autores Cristianos, 1967), 1: 768.

and scriptural interpretation has a long history and has been repeatedly affirmed by the magisterium. The Council of Trent and the First Vatican Council are clear that "no one . . . shall dare to interpret the . . . Sacred Scripture . . . contrary to the unanimous consent of the Fathers."[67] The Fathers' interpretation is a theological locus when certain conditions are met. The Fathers' agreement must be morally (not numerically) unanimous on a biblical interpretation, the interpretation must concern a matter of faith or morals, and the Fathers must consider the doctrine as divinely revealed.[68] Leo XIII taught that the Fathers of the Church

> are of supreme authority, whenever they all interpret in one and the same manner any text of the Bible, as pertaining to the doctrine of faith or morals; for their unanimity clearly evinces that such interpretation has come down from the Apostles as a matter of Catholic faith.[69]

The Object of the Magisterium

The "object" of magisterial teaching is those truths over which Christ has given the magisterium authority. The object of the magisterium is strictly circumscribed to those doctrines pertaining to faith and

---

67. DH 1507, 3007. Bellarmine explains, "Etsi enim errauerint aliqui Patrum in quibusdam dogmatibus, nunquam tamen omnes simul in eodem errore conuenerunt: proinde cùm ostendimus, omnes conuenire in traditionibus non scriptis asserendis, satis efficaciter probamus, in eo illos non errasse." Bellarmine, *De Controversiis*, 1.4.7, vol. 1, col. 178.

68. Franc. X. De Abarzuza, OFM Cap., *Manuale Theologiae Dogmaticae*, 2nd ed. (Madrid: Ediciones Studium, 1956), 1:481–88; R. P. Hermann, *Theologia Generalis*, vol. 1 of *Institutiones Theologiae Dogmaticae*, 7th ed. (Paris: Emmanuelem Vitte, 1937), 539–40 J. M. Hervé, *Manuale Theologiae Dogmaticae*, 16th ed. (Westminster, MD: The Newman Bookshop, 1943), 1:565–75; H. Hurter, SJ, *Theologiae Dogmaticae Compendium*, 12th ed. (Oeniponte: Libraria Academica Wagneriana, 1908), 1:155–57; Salaverri, *Sacrae Theologiae Summa*, 1:765; Adolphe Tanquery, *Manual of Dogmatic Theology*, trans. John J. Byrnes (New York: Desclée Co., 1959), 1:179n1; Adolphe Tanquery, *Synopsis Theologicae Dogmaticae* (Paris: Desclée et Socii, 1953), 1:739–48; G. Van Noort, *The Sources of Revelation and Divine Faith*, vol. 3 of *Dogmatic Theology*, trans. John Castelot and William Murphy (Westminster, MD: The Newman Press, 1961), 174.

69. DH 3284.

morals.⁷⁰ The magisterium has no competence in matters that are strictly scientific, economic, political, or historical. It only has competence in these disciplines insofar as particular topics touch on matters pertaining to faith and morals.⁷¹ The term "faith" here refers to those doctrines that are of a speculative nature such as doctrines concerning the Trinity or the real presence. In contemporary usage the term "morals" refers to those doctrines which concern the goodness or badness of a human action, such as the immorality of contraception.

The "direct object" or "primary object" of the magisterium concerns divine revelation. The primary object includes 1. the canon of Scripture, 2. the true meaning of a passage in Scripture, 3. the extent of Apostolic Tradition, 4. the meaning of Apostolic Tradition, 5. the selection of terms in which revealed truth is presented, 6. those doctrines opposed to revealed truth. This includes therefore any moral matters found in Sacred Scripture or Apostolic Tradition.

The Church also holds that it is competent to teach on "secondary objects," which are those doctrines not directly found in divine revelation but are in such contact with revelation that the deposit of faith cannot be guarded, expounded, and defended without them.⁷² This includes dogmatic facts, canonizations of saints, theological conclusions, moral precepts, and natural truths of the natural order.

---

70. Francisco A. P. Sola, SJ, "De sacramentis vitae socialis christianae seu de sacramentis Ordinis et Matrimonii," 4:573–824 in Iosepho A. de Aldama, SJ, Richardo Franco, SJ, Severino Gonzalez, SJ, Francisco A. P. Sola, SJ, Iosepho F. Sagüés, SJ, *Sacrae Theologiae Summa*, 4th ed. (Madrid: Biblioteca de Autores Cristianos, 1967), 4:714.

71. Piet Fransen, "A Short History of the Meaning of the Formula 'Fides et mores,'" 287–318 in *Hermeneutics of Councils and Other Studies*, ed. H. E. Mertens and F. de Graeve (Leuven: Leuven Univ. Press, 1985); David Stagaman, "Piet Fransen's Research on Fides et Mores," *Theological Studies* 64 (2003): 69–77; Maurice Bevenot, "Faith and Morals in Vatican I and in the Council of Trent," *Heythrop Journal* 3 (1962): 15–30; John Mahoney, *The Making of Moral Theology* (Oxford: Clarendon, 1987), 116–74; Johann Beumer, "Res fidei et morum: Die Entwicklung eines theologischen Begriffes in den Dekretem der drei letzten Okumenischen Konzilien," *Annuarium Historiae Conciliorum* 2 (1979): 112–34; Teodoro López Rodriguez, "'Fides et mores' en Trento," *Scripta Theologica* 5 (1973): 175–221; Marcelino Zalba, SJ, "'Omnis et salutaris veritas et morum disciplina': Sentido de la expresión 'mores' en el Concilio de Trento," *Gregorianum* 54 (1973): 679–715.

72. Henry Edward Manning, *The Vatican Council and Its Definitions: A Pastoral Letter to the Clergy* (London: Longmans, Green, and Co., 1870), 78.

Most Catholic theologians hold that the object of the magisterium also includes the assignment of theological notes or censures to propositions.[73] Theological notes signify positively the degree of doctrinal certainty that a particular doctrine has.[74] Common theological notes are *de fide divina, fidei proxima, fides ecclesiastica,* and *theologice certa.*[75] Theological censures, on the other hand, characterize the degree to which a proposition is contrary to Catholic doctrine.[76] Common theological censures of propositions are: *haeretica, falsos, scandalosa, temeraria, piarum aurium offensive,* and *male sonans.* The major censures *haeretica* and *falsos* concern the truth of a proposition, while minor censures such as *temeraria, piarum aurium offensive,* and *male sonans* concern the ethical nature of a proposition. Some propositions, even if true, simply should not be said because they show disrespect to that which is holy. The following prayer is often given as a prayer that is offensive to pious ears (*piarum aurium offensive*): "Magdalena, the harlot, Matthew, the usurer and covetous, Peter, the perjurer and the apostate, pray for us."[77] Theological censures were the principal way that the papacy intervened in theological controversies in the seventeenth and eighteenth centuries.[78]

The object of the magisterium also includes the content of the natural law, as explained above. The magisterium has consistently taught that it has authority to teach on the natural law.[79] Pius XII affirmed, "The power of the Church is not bound by the limits of

---

73. Manning, *The Vatican Council and Its Definitions*, 67, 73–74, 76. John Henry Newman, *Letters and Diaries of John Henry Newman* (Oxford: Clarendon Press, 1976), 22:262.

74. Parente, *Dictionary of Dogmatic Theology*, 45.

75. On theological notes, see Claudius Ludovicus Montaigne, *De Censuris, seu notis theologicis, et de sensu propositionum*, in *Theologiae cursus completus* (Paris: Migne, 1853) 1:1409–1549; Sixtus Cartechini, *De valore notarum theologicarum et de criteriis ad eas dignoscendas* (Rome: Gregorian University, 1951).

76. Parente, *Dictionary of Dogmatic Theology*, 45.

77. John Cahill, *The Development of the Theological Censures after the Council of Trent (1563–1709)* (Fribourg: University Press, 1955), 189.

78. Bruno Neveu, *L'erreur et son juge: remarques sur les censures doctrinales à l'époque moderne* (Naples: Bibliopolis, 1993).

79. Pius IX, *Qui pluribus*, 16. Pius XI, *Casti connubii*. John XXIII, *Mater et magistra*, 30, 108. John C. Ford and Germain Grisez, "Contraception and the Infallibility of the Ordinary Magisterium," *Theological Studies* 39 (1978): 258–312.

'matters strictly religious,' as they say, but the whole matter of the natural law, its foundation, its interpretation, its application, so far as their moral aspects extend, are within the Church's power."[80]

The magisterium also teaches on truths in the philosophical order insofar as they pertain to faith and morals. The Church has a duty to indicate the elements in a philosophical system which are incompatible with her own faith. As John Paul II asserted, "in the light of faith, therefore, the Church's Magisterium can and must authoritatively exercise a critical discernment of opinions and philosophies which contradict Christian doctrine."[81] This is necessary since many philosophical opinions directly touch on revealed truths, such as those concerning God, the human being, and ethical behavior. The magisterium has issued interventions on philosophical issues such as the pre-existence of the soul, the idolatry and superstition found in astrological speculations, and certain claims of Latin Averroism.[82] There have also been several magisterial condemnations of the following philosophical systems: Fideism, radical Traditionalism, Rationalism, and Ontologism.[83]

The magisterium has also repeatedly affirmed its right to teach authoritatively on economic and political issues insofar as they bear a certain relation to faith and morals.[84] There are two reasons for the Church's authority in these matters. First, the foundation of the Church's social doctrine is "in biblical revelation and in the tradition

---

80. Pius XII, *Magnificate Dominum*, in *The American Ecclesiastical Review* 132 (1955): 58. Paul VI, for example, stated that "no member of the faithful could possibly deny that the Church is competent in her magisterium to interpret the natural moral law." Paul VI, *Humanae vitae*, §4.

81. John Paul II, *Fides et ratio* (September 14, 1998), in *On the Relationship between Faith and Reason: Fides et Ratio* (Washington, DC: United States Conference of Catholic Bishops, 1998), §55.

82. (pre-existence of the soul) DH 403; (astrological speculations) DH 205, 459–60; (Latin Averroism) DH 1440.

83. (Fideism) DH 2751–56, 2765–69; (radical Traditionalism) DH 2811–14; (Rationalism) DH 2828–31, 2850–61; (Ontologism) DH 2841–47.

84. Pius XI stated in *Quadragesimo anno* (May 15, 1931): "Yet before proceeding to explain these matters, that principle which Leo XIII so clearly established must be laid down at the outset here, namely, that there resides in Us the right and duty to pronounce with supreme authority upon social and economic matters." *Quadragesimo anno*, pp. 3:415–41 in *The Papal Encyclicals*, 5 vols., ed. Claudia Carlen, IHM (Wilmington, NC: McGrath, 1981), §41.

of the Church."[85] Second, the Church's social doctrine is "aimed at guiding people's behavior,"[86] i.e., judging whether contemporary social realities are in "conformity with or divergence from the lines of the Gospel teaching on man and his vocation."[87] Therefore, the Church's social doctrine has "the same dignity and authority as her moral teaching."[88] The magisterium, however, recognizes that there are limits to its teaching on economic issues, as the CDF makes clear that "it is not the Church's task to set forth specific political solutions—and even less to propose a single solution as the acceptable one—to temporal questions that God has left to the free and responsible judgment of each person."[89] Historically, magisterial interventions on economic matters have covered a range of issues, from the right to ownership and property, to the trade unions, to the right to a just wage.[90] Magisterial documents also include interventions

---

85. Pontifical Council for Justice and Peace, *Compendium of the Social Doctrine of the Church* (June 29, 2004) (Vatican City: Libreria Editrice Vaticana, 2004), §74 (hereafter *Compendium*).

86. *Compendium*, §73.

87. *Compendium*, §72.

88. *Compendium*, §80.

89. CDF, *Doctrinal Note on Some Questions Regarding the Participation of Catholics in Political Life* (November 24, 2002) (Washington, DC: United States Catholic Conference, 2004), §6. *Gaudium et spes* states, "Let the layman not imagine that his pastors are always such experts, that to every problem which arises, however complicated, they can readily give him a concrete solution, or even that such is their mission. Rather, enlightened by Christian wisdom and giving close attention to the teaching authority of the Church, let the layman take on his own distinctive role. Often enough the Christian view of things will itself suggest some specific solution in certain circumstances. Yet it happens rather frequently, and legitimately so, that with equal sincerity some of the faithful will disagree with others on a given matter. Even against the intentions of their proponents, however, solutions proposed on one side or another may be easily confused by many people with the Gospel message. Hence it is necessary for people to remember that no one is allowed in the aforementioned situations to appropriate the Church's authority for his opinion. They should always try to enlighten one another through honest discussion, preserving mutual charity and caring above all for the common good." Second Vatican Council, *Gaudium et spes* (December 7, 1965), §43 (DH 4343). Dulles argues that when bishops endorse debatable policy solutions to specific problems, "they stir up opposition to themselves within the church and undermine their own authority to teach and govern." Avery Dulles, "Religion and the Transformation of Politics," *America* 167, no. 12 (1992): 296–301, at 297.

90. (property) DH 3133, 3265; (trade unions) DH 4773; (just wage) DH 3269, 3271, 3734.

concerning political realties, such as the incompatibility of socialism with Christian dogma, the judgment that "communism is intrinsically wrong,"[91] and the moral duty of men and societies toward the true religion and toward the one Church of Christ.[92] The object also includes the conditions for a just war[93] and the intrinsically immoral nature of wars of aggression.[94]

How the Magisterium Authoritatively Teaches

There are different ways that the magisterium teaches authoritatively. The first way is through the ordinary magisterium (*magisterium ordinarium*), which is simply the teaching office of the pope and the bishops exercised in their daily teaching. This is what most individual Catholics will encounter on a day-to-day basis in sermons, homilies, and catechetical instructions. We find the pope's ordinary magisterium exercised in such things as encyclical letters, Wednesday audiences, decisions of the Roman congregations, and *editiones typicae* for universal use of the liturgical prayers and practices of the Church. We find the bishops' ordinary magisterium exercised in the writings of the Fathers of the Church, pastoral instructions of bishops, approved catechisms, and approved theological texts. The doctrinal decrees of ecumenical councils, when not engaged in a solemn definition, are simply part of the ordinary magisterium, although they are extraordinary events in the life of the Church.

The highest level of authority with which the magisterium can teach is with infallibility. "Absolute infallibility" is properly only an attribute of God; such infallibility does not belong to the Church, as

---

91. Pius XI referred to Pius IX's "solemn condemnation," which he "directed against 'that infamous doctrine of so-called Communism which is absolutely contrary to the natural law itself, and if once adopted would utterly destroy the rights, property and possessions of all men, and even society itself.'" *Divini redemptoris* (March 19, 1937), pp. 3:537–54 in *The Papal Encyclicals*, 5 vols., ed. Claudia Carlen, IHM (Wilmington, NC: McGrath, 1981), §4. John Paul II also mentioned the authentic interventions on communism in *Fides et ratio*, 67. See also John XXIII, *Mater et magistra* (May 15, 1961), §34.
92. Second Vatican Council, *Dignitatis humanae* (December 7, 1965), §1.
93. CCC 2309. *Compendium*, §500.
94. *Compendium*, §500.

Bishop Vincent Gasser (1809–1879) made clear in his *Relatio* for the First Vatican Council.[95] There is no limit on God's infallibility, which is threefold: he is infallible in being, knowing, and teaching.[96] Ecclesiastical infallibility, on the other hand, is less than God's infallibility and is confined to matters pertaining to faith and morals. The term infallibility means "immunity from error."[97] It is common to use the term "infallible" to refer to the teaching office,[98] e.g., the "pope's infallible magisterium"; whereas the result of an exercise of that office is referred to as irreformable, e.g., "irreformable definitions."

There are essentially two main ways that the magisterium can teach infallibly: through the extraordinary magisterium and through the ordinary universal magisterium. The extraordinary magisterium teaches infallibly through a "defining act," i.e., through a solemn definition that determines in a definitive way a doctrine of faith or morals that must be held by all the faithful. The term "definition" has two senses, "the one forensic and narrow, the other wide and common."[99] The narrow sense of the term simply means "the logical act of defining by genus and differentia," whereas the wide sense of the term is "an authoritative termination of questions which have been in doubt and debate."[100] It is in this latter sense that the term "definition" is used with respect to definitions by the magisterium.

There are only two agents that can teach in an extraordinary way: 1. the pope alone; or 2. the pope and the college of bishops gathered in an ecumenical council. In each case there are several conditions that must be met for an act to be infallible. An exercise of the infallible papal magisterium requires that the pope: 1. teach a doctrine

---

95. Gasser, *Relatio*, in *The Gift of Infallibility* (San Francisco: Ignatius, 2008), 49.

96. Augustinus Reding, *Theologiæ Scholasticæ in Primam Partem (-in Primam, Secundæ, -in Tertiam Partem, -in Secundam Secundæ) Divi Thomæ Ad Normam Theologorum Salisburgensium Tomus I.(-X.)* (Einsiedeln: Typis Monasterii Einsidlensis, 1687), vol. 9, col. 2.

97. Avery Dulles, "Infallibility: the Terminology," 69–80 in *Teaching Authority & Infallibility in the Church*, ed. Paul C. Empie, T. Austin Murphy, and Joseph A. Burgess, LCD 6 (Minneapolis: Augsburg, 1980), 71.

98. Dulles, *Magisterium*, 66.

99. Manning, *The Vatican Council and Its Definitions*, 93.

100. Manning, *The Vatican Council and Its Definitions*, 93–94.

that pertains to faith or morals, 2. with supreme authority, 3. to be held definitively, 4. by the universal Church.[101] For an extraordinary act of an ecumenical council, one would add to these conditions: 5. The council must act in union with the pope, the supreme head of the Church, and with the college of bishops. If any one of these conditions is missing from a decree, then the decree, while perhaps still authoritative, cannot be said to be an infallible act of the magisterium.

While acts of the extraordinary magisterium are always infallible, the ordinary magisterium is sometimes infallible and sometimes not infallible, depending on whether certain conditions are met. When the ordinary magisterium is infallible, it is called the ordinary universal magisterium. The ordinary universal magisterium teaches infallibly through a "non-defining act," which is to teach authoritatively without making a solemn definition. The ordinary universal magisterium's teaching is infallible when the following five conditions are met: 1. the magisterium teaches a doctrine that pertains to faith or morals, 2. although dispersed throughout the world, the bishops are in communion with one another and with the pope, 3. the bishops teach authoritatively, 4. they agree in one judgment, and 5. they propose this as something to be held definitively by the faithful.[102] There are a number of difficulties in the practical order in identifying those "non-defining acts." The universality of the teaching must be established synchronically, but it must also be shown to have been universally held diachronically.[103] Therefore, one must sift through the various acts of the ordinary magisterium in order to determine if there is an ordinary universal teaching. There are currently two proposals by theologians that seek to discern whether an act is infallible without recourse to this long and arduous task. First, Francis Sullivan proposes that the consensus of theologians and the *consensus fidelium* are signs that something has been proposed by the ordinary universal

---

101. DH 3074.
102. Second Vatican Council, *Lumen gentium*, §25.
103. Francis Sullivan, *Creative Fidelity: Weighing and Interpreting Documents of the Magisterium* (New York: Paulist, 1996), 106.

magisterium.¹⁰⁴ Second, Brian Ferme has proposed that one can look for confirming acts of the papal magisterium.¹⁰⁵

According to Catholic theologians, both popes and councils are capable of teaching doctrinal error when not teaching infallibly. There are only two basic categories of magisterial teachings: when a pope or a council infallibly defines a doctrine, and everything else, which is subject to error.¹⁰⁶ Members of the magisterium are men with free will who can refuse the divine assistance given to them and teach in ways that are contrary to revealed truth. Popes Innocent III (r. 1198–1216), Innocent IV (r. 1243–1254), and Paul IV (r. 1555–1559) affirmed that popes are able to err.¹⁰⁷ Medieval theologians and canonists did not seem particularly bothered by the tension between the fact that a pope could, when certain conditions were met, be infallible and that he could also fall into formal heresy in any other capacity. In the sixteenth century, however, a few early modern theologians, such as Augustin von Alfeld, OFM (1480–c. 1535), Albert Pigge

---

104. Sullivan argues that if at some point theologians no longer have consensus, then "it would seem necessary to conclude that this was not the kind of constant consensus that points to infallible teaching." Sullivan, *Creative Fidelity*, 104. This, of course, would essentially mean that one could never determine whether something has been taught by the ordinary universal magisterium. It is always possible that that which was previously taught could be questioned by a significant number of theologians at some future point. This is precisely what has happened in almost every doctrinal controversy in the history of the Church: a doctrine accepted by a consensus of theologians was no longer accepted by a consensus of theologians. The Church then had to await a "defining act." Sullivan therefore has rendered useless the ordinary universal magisterium.

105. Brian Ferme, "The Response of the Congregation for the Doctrine of the Faith to the *Dubium* Concerning the Apostolic Letter *Ordinatio Sacerdotalis*: Authority and Significance," *Periodica* 85 (1996): 701–10.

106. Christian D. Washburn, "Conciliar Infallibility and Error in the Thomistic Ecclesiology of St. Robert Bellarmine, S.J.," *The Journal of Early Modern Christianity* 8 (2021): 251–73.

107. "In tantum mihi fides necessaria est, ut quum de ceteris peccatis solum Deum judicem habeam, propter solum peccatum, quod in fide committitur, possem ab ecclesia judicari. Nam qui non credit, jam judicatus est." Innocent III, *Sermo II in consecratione pontificis maximi* (PL 217:656). James Moynihan, *Papal Immunity and Liability in the Writings of the Medieval Canonists* (Rome: Gregorian University Press, 1961), 115; Pope Paul IV, *Cum ex apostolates officio* in *Bullarum, diplomatum et privilegiorum sanctorum romanorum pontificum taurinensis* (Augustae Taurinorum: Seb. Franco et Henrico Dalmazzo editoribus, 1857), 6:551.

(c. 1490–1542),[108] and Bellarmine, began to propose a new theory that a pope could not fall into *formal* heresy even when not teaching infallibly.[109] This can only be considered a "pious opinion."

The Levels of Authority of Magisterial Teaching

This distinction in the way that the magisterium can teach authoritatively entails that there are various levels of authoritative teaching. The *Professio fidei* (1989) and the CDF's instruction *Donum veritatis* (1990) together indicate four levels of magisterial teaching, each with a corresponding degree of required assent. These four levels have particular importance since the magisterium has given the first three levels the force of law in the current *Code of Canon Law,* with corresponding canonical penalties for violating them.[110] These levels of magisterial teaching should not be confused with the hierarchy of Catholic doctrine, which is intended to explain the relationship that a particular authoritative teaching has to the core of the Christian faith.[111] These four levels reflect the degree of certitude that the

---

108. Hubert Jedin, *Studien über die schriftstellertätigkeit Albert Pigges* (Münster in Westfalen: Aschendorff, 1931), 136. For a bibliography of Pigge's works, see Wilbirgis Klaiber, comp., *Katholische Kontroverstheologen und Reformer des 16. Jahrhunderts*, RST 116 (Münster in Westfalen: Aschendorff, 1978), 230–31. On Pigge's ecclesiology, see Remigius Bäumer, "Das Kirchenverständnis Albert Pigges. Ein Beitrag zur Ekklesiologie der vortridentinischen Kontroverstheologie," 306–22 in *Volk Gottes. Zum Kirchenverständnis der katholischen, evangelischen und anglikanischen Theologie. Festgabe für Josef Höfer*, ed. Remigius Bäumer and Heimo Dolch (Freiburg: Herder, 1967).

109. Christian D. Washburn, "Three 16th Century Thomist Solutions to the Problem of a Heretical Pope: Cajetan, Cano, and Bellarmine," *The Thomist* 83 (2019): 547–88.

110. *Code of Canon Law*, c. 1364 for denial of a revealed truth; c. 1371 for rejection of a non-revealed definitive truth, and any other non-infallible and merely authentic teaching. See also Pope John Paul II, Address to the Congregation for the Doctrine of the Faith (November 24, 1995), English trans. "Magisterium Exercises Authority in Christ's Name," *L'Osservatore Romano*, English Edition (November 29, 1995): 3.

111. One must note that the term "doctrine" appears two times in the first clause of the celebrated passage of *Unitatis redintegratio*: "In comparandis doctrinis meminerint existere ordinem seu «hierarchiam» veritatum doctrinae catholicae, cum diversus sit earum nexus cum fundamento fidei christianae." Second Vatican Council, *Unitatis redintegratio* (November 21, 1954), pp. 90–112 in *Acta Apostolicae Sedis* 57 (1965), §11. See also *CCC* 90; and CDF, *Mysterium ecclesiae*, §4. Recall that the hierarchy of truths

Church has about a particular authoritative teaching rather than the truth of the teaching.

The first level of magisterial teaching consists of definitive declarations of revealed truth (aka the primary object of infallibility or dogma). These teachings, contained within the two sources of revelation, namely, Scripture and Tradition, have been formally revealed by God and proposed definitively as such by the Church to the faithful, who have the obligation of believing it. This is generally thought to include all those things that pertain directly to divine revelation. Examples of primary objects, as identified by theologians, include: decisions on the canon of Scripture, the true meaning of a passage in Scripture, decisions on the extent of Apostolic Tradition, decisions on the meaning of Tradition, decisions on the selection of terms in which revealed truth is presented, and decisions on doctrines which are opposed to revealed truth.[112] Finally, *Donum veritatis* asserts that it is a doctrine of the Catholic faith that moral teachings which are contained in revelation and which *per se* could be known by natural reason can be infallibly taught by the magisterium.[113] Therefore, this degree also includes matters of the natural law.

The second degree is definitive declarations of non-revealed truth (the secondary object of infallibility), and it extends "to those matters without which that deposit cannot be rightly preserved and expounded."[114] After the Second Vatican Council all relevant magisterial documents assert that the Church's infallibility extends beyond primary objects.[115] The question today is not whether there are sec-

---

is concerned with doctrinal truths and not with truths of the natural order. Thus Ratzinger and Schönborn noted that "the hierarchy of truths is a principle of organic structure." It simply means that the different doctrinal truths are "organized" around a center. Joseph Ratzinger and Christoph von Schönborn, *Introduction to the Catechism of the Catholic Church* (San Francisco: Ignatius, 1994), 42.

112. Hermann, *Theologia Generalis*, 390; Hervé, *Manuale Theologiae Dogmaticae*, 1:506; Salaverri, *Sacrae Theologiae Summa*, 1:714–20; Tanquery, *Synopsis Theologicae Dogmaticae*, 1:617–18; Van Noort, *The Sources of Revelation and Divine Faith*, 108–10.

113. CDF, *Donum veritatis*, §16. Vatican I, *Dei Filius*. DH 3005.

114. CDF, *Mysterium ecclesiae*, §3.

115. What has given rise to some controversy is the various ways in which the magisterium has formulated the extent of the secondary object. *Lumen gentium* stated that this infallibility "extends as far as the deposit of Revelation extends, which must be

ondary objects of infallibility but what is the extent of these secondary objects of infallibility. Traditionally, the list of possible secondary objects included such things as theological conclusions, truths of the natural law, the legitimacy of the election of the Supreme Pontiff, the legitimacy of an ecumenical council, the canonizations of saints, and dogmatic facts.[116] An example of an infallibly defined dogmatic fact is the declaration on the invalidity of ordinations carried out according to the Anglican rite, issued by Pope Leo XIII in the apostolic letter *Apostolicae curae*.[117]

There are several concrete moral norms which the magisterium claims it has taught infallibly as either primary or secondary objects through the ordinary universal magisterium, including the immorality of contraceptive acts,[118] of simultaneous polygamy,[119] of prostitu-

---

religiously guarded and faithfully expounded." Second Vatican Council, *Lumen gentium*, §25 (DH 4149). This phrase does not restrict the object to the deposit of faith and includes those things that are required to guard and expound the deposit, as was made clear by the official explanation that accompanied the text. Sullivan, *Magisterium: Teaching Authority in the Catholic Church* (New York: Paulist, 1983), 132. *Mysterium ecclesiae* states that infallibility extends "also to those matters without which that deposit cannot be rightly preserved and expounded." CDF, *Mysterium ecclesiae*, §3. The *Catechism of the Catholic Church* says that infallibility "extends to all those elements of doctrine, including morals, without which the saving truths of the faith cannot be preserved, explained, or observed." CCC 2035. Finally, the CDF's commentary includes those things which are "... connected with revelation by a logical necessity." CDF, *Doctrinal Commentary on the Concluding Formula of the Professio Fidei* (June 29, 1998), pp. 116–19 in *Origins* 32 (1998), §11.

116. De Abarzuza, *Manuale Theologiae Dogmaticae*, 1:449–56; R. P. Hermann, *Theologia Generalis*, 390–97; Hervé, *Manuale Theologiae Dogmaticae*, 1:507–18; Hurter, *Theologiae Dogmaticae Compendium*, 1:314–18; Salaverri, *Sacrae Theologiae Summa*, 1:720–37; Tanquery, *Synopsis Theologicae Dogmaticae*, 1:618–25; Van Noort, *The Sources of Revelation and Divine Faith*, 110–18.

117. CDF, *Doctrinal Commentary on the Concluding Formula of the Professio Fidei*, §11. DH 3315–19. This claim seems to demand modification of the "Catholic Reflections" in Paul C. Empie, T. Austin Murphy, and Joseph A. Burgess, eds., *Teaching Authority & Infallibility in the Church*, LCD 6 (Minneapolis: Augsburg, 1980), 51.

118. Pontifical Council for the Family, "Vade mecum for Confessors Concerning Some Aspects of the Morality of Conjugal Life," *Origins* 26 (March 13, 1997): 617–25; Ford and Grisez, "Contraception and the Infallibility of the Ordinary Magisterium."

119. Trent: "If anyone says that Christians are permitted to have several wives simultaneously, and that such a practice is not forbidden by any divine law (MT 19:4–9): let him be anathema." DH 1802/972.

tion,[120] of fornication,[121] of homosexual acts,[122] of the direct and voluntary killing of an innocent life,[123] of abortion,[124] and of euthanasia.[125]

The third degree of magisterial teaching is non-definitive obligatory teachings. These are teachings regarding truths of faith or morals proposed by the magisterium but not necessarily to be responded to with divine faith or definitive assent.

The fourth degree of magisterial teaching concerns prudential judgments, which are applications of Christian doctrine or admonitions for a particular time and place.[126] In these instances, the magiste-

---

120. CDF, *Doctrinal Commentary on the Concluding Formula of the Professio Fidei*, §11.
121. CDF, *Doctrinal Commentary on the Concluding Formula of the Professio Fidei*, §11.
122. CDF, "Notification Regarding Sister Jeannine Gramick, SSND, and Father Robert Nugent, SDS," 488–91 in *Documenta inde a Concilio Vaticano Secundo expleto edita (1966–2005)* (Vatican City: Libreria Editrice Vaticana, 2006), 491. See also Richard R. Gaillardetz, "The Ordinary Universal Magisterium: Unresolved Questions," *Theological Studies* 63 (2002): 447–71, at 454.
123. John Paul II, "Therefore, by the authority which Christ conferred upon Peter and his Successors, and in communion with the Bishops of the Catholic Church, I confirm that the direct and voluntary killing of an innocent human being is always gravely immoral. This doctrine, based upon that unwritten law which man, in the light of reason, finds in his own heart (cf. Rom. 2:14–15), is reaffirmed by Sacred Scripture, transmitted by the Tradition of the Church and taught by the ordinary and universal Magisterium." *Evangelium vitae* (March 25, 1995), pp. 792–894 in *The Papal Encyclicals of John Paul II*, ed. J. Michael Miller (Huntington, IN: Our Sunday Visitor, 1996), §57.
124. John Paul II, "Therefore, by the authority which Christ conferred upon Peter and his Successors, in communion with the Bishops—who on various occasions have condemned abortion and who in the aforementioned consultation, albeit dispersed throughout the world, have shown unanimous agreement concerning this doctrine—I declare that direct abortion, that is, abortion willed as an end or as a means, always constitutes a grave moral disorder, since it is the deliberate killing of an innocent human being. This doctrine is based upon the natural law and upon the written Word of God, is transmitted by the Church's Tradition and is taught by the ordinary and universal Magisterium." *Evangelium vitae*, §62.
125. John Paul II, "Taking into account these distinctions, in harmony with the Magisterium of my Predecessors and in communion with the Bishops of the Catholic Church, I confirm that euthanasia is a grave violation of the law of God, since it is the deliberate and morally unacceptable killing of a human person. This doctrine is based upon the natural law and upon the written word of God, is transmitted by the Church's Tradition and taught by the ordinary and universal Magisterium." *Evangelium vitae*, §65.
126. I think it is unclear as to whether this represents a distinct fourth degree or if it is simply a subset of the third degree.

rium intends to warn the faithful of "dangerous opinions which could lead to error" and therefore intervenes "in questions under discussion which involve, in addition to solid principles, certain contingent and conjectural elements. It often only becomes possible with the passage of time to distinguish between what is necessary and what is contingent."[127] Here would be included many of the decisions of the Pontifical Biblical Commission in the early part of the twentieth century. The declaration of the Holy Office on the "Johannine Comma" (1927), for example, was clearly not intended to "prevent catholic writers from investigating the subject more fully" but to ensure that theologians were "ready to abide by the judgment of the Church."[128]

It must be recalled that degrees of Church teaching concern the Church's current certainty about the authority of these teachings. Because of the development of doctrine, the magisterium may at some future point be able to discern more clearly the certainty which the Church has about a given doctrine.[129] Having said this, those teachings in level one, for example, will always remain in level one, since they are revealed truths that are definitively taught and are, as such, irreformable. Thus prior to the First Vatican Council, for example, it was generally held by theologians that the doctrine of papal infallibility was infallibly taught; what was at stake at the council was the determination that the teaching was revealed and not merely a theological conclusion. In the future, the teaching of *Ordinatio sacerdotalis* may come to be proposed as divinely revealed.[130] So a teaching that is known to be defined as a secondary object may become a primary object in the future, but a secondary object could never become a level three teaching. Those truths in the second degree may move up but not down, and those in levels three and four may move up or down.

---

127. CDF, *Donum veritatis*, §24.
128. DH 3682.
129. CDF, *Doctrinal Commentary on the Concluding Formula of the Professio Fidei*, §7.
130. CDF, *Doctrinal Commentary on the Concluding Formula of the Professio Fidei*, §11.

Infallible Teaching as Irreformable

In the past, theologians tended to use the term "immutable" or "definitive" as frequently as "irreformable" for infallible decisions.[131] Both the First Vatican Council and the Second Vatican Council affirmed that definitive declarations are "irreformable."[132] The term "irreformable" means simply that the doctrine cannot be transformed or metamorphosed into a new doctrine with some other meaning. The First Vatican Council was clear that

> the doctrine of faith which God revealed has not been handed down as a philosophic invention to the human mind to be perfected, but has been entrusted as a divine deposit to the Spouse of Christ, to be faithfully guarded and infallibly interpreted. Hence, also, that understanding of its sacred dogmas must be perpetually retained, which Holy Mother Church has once declared; and there must never be recession from that meaning under the specious name of a deeper understanding.[133]

The council then quoted Saint Vincent of Lerins, who maintained that doctrine must remain "with the same sense and the same understanding,"[134] even when there is doctrinal development.

Subsequent magisterial interventions were equally clear that the meaning of an infallible doctrine is irreformable. In the midst of the modernist crisis, Saint Pius X required an oath to be taken by all

---

131. Bellarmine, *De Controversiis*, 4.2.8, vol. 2, col. 90. Louis Billot, *De immutabilitate traditionis contra modernam haeresim evolutionismi* (Rome: Gregorian University Press, 1929), 38. Giuseppe Agostino Orsi, *De irreformabili Romani Pontificis: in definiendis fidei controversiis judicio* (Rome: Typis Sacrae Congregationis de Propaganda Fide, 1739). Cardinal Manning stated that irreformability means that "no future acts will retouch them. This is the meaning of irreformable." *Petri Priviligium: Three Pastoral Letters* (London: Longmans, Green, and Co., 1871), 40.

132. DH 3074; Second Vatican Council, *Lumen gentium*, §25. *Proclaiming the Truth of Jesus Christ: Papers from the Vallombrosa Meeting* (Washington, DC: United States Catholic Conference, 2000), 61.

133. DH 3020. See also Canon 3: "If anyone says that, as science progresses, at times a sense is to be given to dogmas proposed by the Church different from the one that the Church has understood and understands, let him be anathema." DH 3043.

134. DH 3020.

clergy, pastors, confessors, preachers, religious superiors, and professors in philosophical-theological seminaries which included: "I entirely reject the heretical misrepresentation that dogmas evolve and change from one meaning to another different from the one which the Church held previously."[135] The CDF's instruction *Mysterium fidei* asserts that "there is no doubt that, according to these texts of the Council, the *meaning* of dogmas which is declared by the Church is determinate and unalterable."[136]

Some contemporary theologians have questioned whether one may speak of an irreformable doctrine even with respect to the meaning of the doctrine,[137] but this is contrary to the sense of the magisterium. Other theologians prefer the terms "definitive" or "irreversible,"[138] since "irreformable'" suggests that no development is possible. But the use of terms such as "irreformable" or "immutable" was never intended to suggest that no development could take place. In the sixteenth century, Bellarmine, for example, who commonly used the term "immutable," clearly recognized that in some cases the wording

---

135. DH 3541.

136. CDF, *Mysterium ecclesiae*, §5.

137. A contemporary theologian argues that "Dogmatic statements are teachings judged by the church to be faithful and trustworthy mediations of God's offer of salvation revealed to us in Christ by the power of the Spirit. Consequently, dogmatic continuity may not reside in some eternal and immutable core of transient meaning but in the saving praxis to which a dogma calls us. In this view, the central insight in the Church's claim regarding the irreversible and definitive nature of dogma would appear to be that no dogma could so change or develop as to lead us away from the path to salvation." Richard R. Gaillardetz, *Teaching with Authority: A Theology of the Magisterium in the Church* (Collegeville, MN: Liturgical Press, 1997), 108. First, the author's language is here somewhat obscure: "eternal and immutable core of transient meaning." One is not quite sure how immutable and transient can be used simultaneously. Clearly, both the First Vatican Council and *Mysterium ecclesiae* assert that dogmas of the Church are immutable in meaning. It was Modernists who seemed to shift the significance of dogmas from their intellectual meaning to being guides to action. Hence Pius X condemned the following Modernist proposition: "The dogmas of the Faith are to be held only according to their practical sense; that is to say, as perceptive norms of conduct and not as norms of believing." Pius X, *Lamentabili* (July 3, 1907), §26 (DH 3426).

138. Sullivan, *Magisterium*, 81. Francis Schüssler Fiorenza and John P. Galvin, *Systematic Theology: Roman Catholic Perspectives* (Minneapolis: Fortress, 2011), 104.

of an infallible decree could have been better.[139] Since irreformability is confined to the doctrine's meaning and not the terms in which it is presented, it does not exclude reformulation.[140] Moreover, doctrines taught by the magisterium are taught sometimes "in terms that bear traces of the changeable conceptions of a given epoch."[141] Some reformulation of the terms in which a doctrine is expressed may be necessary precisely to preserve the meaning of the doctrine. Reformulation, however, only pertains to the "mode of expression" and not to the content or meaning of the statements.[142]

Another condition for an authoritative teaching of the magisterium is that the declaration must be in conformity with those previous teachings that are fundamentally binding on the Church. During the Second Vatican Council, for example, Pope Paul VI proposed inserting into *Lumen gentium*, §22 the principle that the pope *qua* pope is answerable only to God. The pope's suggestion was rejected by the theological commission, which explained, "The Roman Pontiff is also bound to revelation itself, to the fundamental structure of the Church, to the sacraments, to the definitions of earlier councils, and other obligations too numerous to mention."[143] This consideration does not just apply to the pope and his magisterium but to the entire teaching office of the Church. This submission is seen perhaps most clearly formulated in John Paul II's apostolic letter, *Ordinatio sacerdotalis*. The central assertion of the apostolic letter is not primarily a sacramental claim; it is an ecclesiological claim asserting that "the Church has no authority whatsoever to confer priestly ordination on women."[144] Clearly, infallible

---

139. Bellarmine, *De Controversiis*, 4.2.12, vol. 2, col. 87.

140. One must distinguish between "the substance of the ancient doctrine of the deposit of faith . . . and the way in which it is presented." John XXIII, *Opening Speech to the Vatican II Council* (October 12, 1962), pp. 786–96 in *Acta Apostolicae Sedis* 54 (1962), p. 791. English translation from *The Documents of Vatican II*, ed. Walter Abbott, trans. Joseph Gallagher (New York: Guild Press, 1966), pp. 710–19, at 715.

141. CDF, *Mysterium ecclesiae*, §5.

142. Avery Dulles, "Infallibility: the Terminology," 75.

143. Cited in Dulles, "Moderate Infallibilism," 81–100 in *Teaching Authority & Infallibility in the Church*, 87.

144. John Paul II, *Ordinatio sacerdotalis* (May 22, 1994) (Washington, DC: United States Catholic Conference 1994), §4. Ratzinger notes that "with the new document,

declarations are binding not only on the whole Church but even on the pope, who cannot retract them[145] precisely because these decrees are "irreformable."

Infallibility is a property that belongs to the whole Church and not just to the magisterium; and all the members of the Church participate in the gift of infallibility but in different ways. This infallibility is manifest when the whole Church "from the bishops down to the last of the lay faithful" agree universally in matters of faith and morals.[146] This *ecclesia discens* does not have an *infallibilitas activa in docendo* but rather an *infallibilitas passiva in credendo*. While some theologians have bemoaned this distinction, I think that their dislike of this distinction is misplaced for two reasons. First, *Lumen gentium* is clear that the subject of this infallibility is the whole Church with both the faithful and the hierarchy together. Therefore, the hierarchy first stands in a fundamental position of receptivity, like the rest of the faithful, to the Word of God as it has been handed on. Second, this receptivity precedes the magisterium's teaching activity and is a condition binding on its teaching activity since whatever it teaches must be in conformity with the faith of the Church.

Conclusion

At its heart, the Church's teaching authority is not primarily about power; it has been given to the Church in the service of God and mankind. The Church's magisterium stands below God's Word and is in service to it. This teaching authority is confined to those matters which pertain to faith and morals. Matters not touching on faith and morals are outside the Church's competency.

---

the pope does not wish to impose his own opinion but precisely to verify the fact that the Church cannot do whatever she wants and that he, indeed precisely he, cannot do so. Here it is not a question of hierarchy opposed to democracy, but of obedience opposed to autocracy. In matters of faith and the sacraments, the church cannot do what she wants." Joseph Cardinal Ratzinger, "The Limits of Church Authority," *L'Osservatore Romano* 26, English Edition (June 29, 1994): 7.

145. Bellarmine, *De Controversiis*, 4.2.11, vol. 2, col. 85.
146. Second Vatican Council, *Lumen gentium*, §12 (DH 4130).

1.2. Classical Natural Right and the Origins of Natural Law Doctrine as a Source of the Moral Life

Dr. William B. Stevenson

If the doctrine of the natural moral law is among the most enduring contributions to the Western Catholic tradition from the great writers of late antiquity, it has also proven to be among the most subject to reformulation, revision, and outright controversy. Karl Barth famously regarded it as nothing less than an idol of human rationality, erected in opposition to the God of revelation. Barth's critique which itself implicitly opposes the God of creation to the God of revelation may be open to the charge of crypto-Marcionism, but it is hard to deny its basic kinship to other critiques which have appeared at intervals throughout the Church's history, especially after the Reformation. The doctrine has lately suffered neglect even amongst Catholics. The *Catechism of the Catholic Church* addresses it thematically in a niggardly six paragraphs, far fewer than its treatment of social justice. This latter concept, the bastard child of modern rights theory, is generously given its own chapter. At a typical Catholic university in the United States, it is common to have a variety courses on the theme of social justice, without a single offering devoted to the natural law, even within the theology department. Outside Christian circles the idea of a natural law doesn't even arouse serious academic opposition, even if its defenders, academic and otherwise, are ever the objects of cultural and social opprobrium.[1] Still, the teaching

---

1. "One safe sign of the disfavor into which [natural law] has fallen is that few of its detractors feel the need to attack it any more, either because they no longer regard it

that nature prescribes laws for human thinking and acting which are discoverable by reason appears to be as intractable as nature herself. The supposed demise of the natural law has been celebrated at intervals throughout Christian and post-Christian history by those who would either restrict moral norms to what has been divinely revealed or those who would dispense with any such normativity altogether. But natural law, like the bad penny, reliably turns up just when this or that New Day was scheduled to dawn.[2]

Admittedly, in the very first centuries of Christian thought the place of natural law theory was far from secure, due to the uncertainty surrounding the relationship of Jerusalem to Athens[3] and the

---

as a force to be contended with or because they find little with which to quarrel in the bland and emasculated versions that are now being offered of it, the majority of which retain only those elements of the original synthesis that are not in open conflict with the currently most fashionable notions of justice and right." Ernest L. Fortin, "Natural Law and Social Justice," *The American Journal of Jurisprudence* 30 (1985): 1–20, at 1. My own essay is greatly indebted to the pioneering work of Fortin, as well as to other students of Leo Strauss.

2. Cf. M. B. Crowe, *The Changing Profile of the Natural Law* (The Hague: Martinus Nijhoff, 1977), ix; ibid., 246: "It (the natural law) has been declared dead, never to rise again from its ashes; but it has risen livelier than ever and buried its undertakers. It is commonplace to observe that the funeral orations for the natural law have always been premature." Also A. P. d'Entrèves, *Natural Law*, 2nd ed. (London: Hutchinson of London, 1970), 13.

3. Tertullian, *De Praescriptione Haereticorum* VII: "Fuerat Athenis et istam sapientiam humanam affectatricem et interpolatricem ueritatis de congressibus nouerat, ipsam quoque in suas haereses multipartitam uarietate sectarum inuicem repugnantium. Quid ergo Athenis et Hierosolymis? quid academiae et ecclesiae? quid haereticis et christianis? Nostra institutio de porticu Solomonis est qui et ipse tradiderat Dominum in simplicitate cordis esse quaerendum. Viderint qui Stoicum et Platonicum et dialecticum christianismum protulerunt. Nobis curiositate opus non est post Christum Iesum nec inquisitione post euangelium. Cum credimus, nihil desideramus ultra credere. Hoc enim prius credimus non esse quod ultra credere debeamus" (PL 2:19–21). ["He had been at Athens, and had in his interviews (with its philosophers) become acquainted with that human wisdom which pretends to know the truth, whilst it only corrupts it, and is itself divided into its own manifold heresies, by the variety of its mutually repugnant sects. What indeed has Athens to do with Jerusalem? What concord is there between the Academy and the Church? what between heretics and Christians? Our instruction comes from 'the porch of Solomon,' who had himself taught that 'the Lord should be sought in simplicity of heart.' Away with all attempts to produce a mottled Christianity of Stoic, Platonic, and dialectic composition! We want no curious disputation after

fact that the early Fathers did not clearly distinguish between natural and supernatural orders. Ultimately, however, Augustine's appropriation of the view that there exists a moral law derivable proximately from nature and serviceable for guiding human acts virtually guaranteed its permanent place in the subsequent intellectual tradition of the West. In the Middle Ages, Thomas Aquinas, reacting to the strict Aristotelianism of his Islamic precursors, provided the tradition with the definitive reformulation of Augustine's doctrine. That reformulation finds its final expression in Questions 90–97 of the *Prima Secundae* of the *Summa Theologiae*. The very definitiveness of the so-called "treatise on law," however, has willy-nilly led to a general forgetfulness about the actual origins of natural law doctrine and thus of the original question "whether the existence of such a law can be defended on the basis of reason alone or whether it is ultimately dependent on revealed religion."[4] It is in fact the contention of this essay that the doctrine of the natural law, while indebted to the classical doctrine of natural right, represents a radical alteration of that teaching and, further, depends upon divine revelation for its intelligibility.

Plato, Aristotle, and Natural Right

Although it is not uncommon for scholars to regard Plato and Aristotle as progenitors of natural law theory, neither philosopher evinces anything close to what Catholics understand by natural law. Plato does indeed use the expression, but only twice: once in the *Timaeus*, as a biological principle for explaining the purging of bodily fluids,[5] and another time in the *Gorgias*, in which the champion of the law of nature is none other than Callicles, who, like Thrasymachus in the *Republic*, identifies it with the advantage that the stronger exercise

---

possessing Christ Jesus, no inquisition after enjoying the gospel! With our faith, we desire no further belief. For this is our palmary faith, that there is nothing which we ought to believe besides" (trans. Peter Holmes, ANF 3:246).]

4. Ernest L. Fortin, "Augustine, Aquinas, and the Problem of Natural Law," in *Classical Christianity and the Political Order: Reflections on the Theologico-Political Problem*, vol. 2 of *Ernest Fortin: Collected Essays*, ed. Brian Benestad (Lanham, Maryland: Rowman & Littlefield, 1996), 199–222, at 200.

5. Plato, *Timaeus* 83e.

over the weaker. By his reckoning, all men without exception naturally desire pleasure and would pursue it without serious concern for the good of others. But the state of nature posited by Callicles cannot of itself serve as a foundation for the political life which alone makes that pursuit possible. This would necessarily mean that political justice, which protects the weaker but many against the stronger but few, is a convention that is opposed to the natural order of things.[6] It hardly needs to be said that this sort of natural law bears no resemblance to that found in Catholic moral teaching.

Socrates responds to Callicles by demonstrating that the pleasurable is distinct from the good, and that justice, so far from being a useful fiction, is actually desirable in its own right. And while his argument is based on an appeal to what is right according to nature, this natural right does not have the character of a universally binding law. Fr. Ernest Fortin describes the difference between natural right and natural law in this way:

> If, from a purely juridical point of view, the two terms are closely related and often used interchangeably in the later tradition, philosophically they remain dichotomous and reflect two notably different conceptions of justice. It is one thing to claim that an action is intrinsically right, insofar as it accords with the demands of right reason, and quite another to contend that its goodness derives from its conformity to a universal law whose injunctions can never be infringed with impunity. One may be correct in assuming that a life of reason and virtue generally leads to greater happiness than a life of unreason and vice, but this is still a far cry from asserting that crime never pays and that in the end the only people who are happy are the ones who deserve to be happy. The Platonic dialogues know of no law of the cosmos certifying that justice will necessarily prevail in human affairs. In the light of the later, non-Platonic natural law teaching, one could say that the choice is between a morally lawful universe in which all evils are eventually set straight and a universe in which morality, however important it may be in other respects, is left without any cosmic or suprahuman support other than that which takes the form of a myth.[7]

---

6. Plato, *Gorgias* 482c–484c.
7. Fortin, "Augustine, Aquinas, and the Problem of Natural Law," 201.

Classical Natural Right and the Origins of Natural Law Doctrine 41

With regard to the last point, it should be emphasized that the suggestion of an "amoral" cosmos does not make Plato the purveyor of an exoteric virtue teaching by which he artfully conceals an esoteric nihilism. According to the doctrine of natural right the intrinsic superiority of a life of virtue may be established on the basis of reason alone—that is, independently of divine or cosmic sanctions.

It would be reasonable to suppose that Plato's most famous student came closer to propounding a natural law doctrine, mostly because of *his* most famous student. But Aristotle's writings simply do not bear this out. Aristotle is so closely associated with Aquinas, the wish to see in his *oeuvre* the classic account of the natural law has proven for many Thomists a temptation too great to withstand. In the teeth of the evidence, Aristotle is routinely transformed, *mirabile dictu*, into the Greek proto-Aquinas. It is most telling, however, that the very book in which one might expect to find a natural moral law, the *Nicomachean Ethics*, not only has nothing to say on the subject, but knows nothing at all of moral obligation. Yet Aristotle is not completely silent on the matter of a moral law rooted in nature. In fact, it appears in the *Rhetoric*, a book whose subject requires the serious student to have acquired some knowledge of the natures of his potential hearers. But the immediate context of the discussion of "what is lawful by nature" is peculiar.[8] Aristotle does not provide his own illustrations of the natural law, but instead relies upon key texts from Sophocles, Empedocles, and Alcidamas. This is not unusual for Aristotle, who clearly delights in illuminating important points by drawing on his preternaturally encyclopedic knowledge of Greek authors, major and minor. But the texts of these three authors—a tragic poet, a pre-Socratic philosopher, and a favorite disciple of the Sophist Gorgias—represent views which are nearly impossible to square with Aristotle's teaching elsewhere. Take, for instance, the example found in his citation from Alcidamas's *Messeniacus*: "the god has left everyone free; nature has made no one a slave." Such an illustration of the natural law is curious in light of Aristotle's own detailed treatment of natural slavery in the first book of the *Politics*. Moreover,

---

8. Aristotle, *Rhetoric* 1373b 1–25.

Empedocles's unqualified insistence that it is naturally unjust to slaughter "anything with the breath of life in it," with its corresponding categorical imperative to veganism, represents an extreme which has no place in Aristotle or any other classical philosopher. It seems safe to assume, then, that in the context of the *Rhetoric*, Aristotle is simply giving the promising politician examples of what some writers have claimed to be just by nature, which is why he could refrain from making judgments about the plausibility or relative merits of these claims. In other words, natural law is incidental to Aristotle's main concern in the *Rhetoric*.

Cicero and Augustine

Since neither Plato nor Aristotle teach a moral law grounded in nature, one is left to search out its origins in later antiquity. Despite scholarly efforts to locate the origins of natural law doctrine in the Stoics,[9] it appears that the first figure to speak unambiguously of a natural moral law is Cicero. But since Cicero understands himself to be following closely in the footsteps of both Plato and Aristotle, it is hard to see why he would introduce a teaching that departs so dramatically from that of his masters. Serious clues to the answer, however, may be found in Cicero's dialogue *De re publica*.

In Book III of that dialogue, the reader meets a figure that is quite nearly the Roman counterpart to the Callicles of the *Gorgias*. This is Philus, who declares that the mother of justice is weakness and that if the old Romans had been just, they would still be living in the humble huts of the city originally founded by Romulus. By Philus's account, the Romans rightly disregarded the dictates of conventional justice

---

9. Cf., Helmut Koester, "*NOMOS PHYSEÓS:* The Concept of Natural Law in Greek Thought," 521–41 in *Religions in Antiquity: Essays in Memory of E.R. Goodenough*, ed. J. Neusner (Leiden: Brill, 1968). Koester's work is a virtual education in the difficulty of tracing the genealogy of ideas. One wishes to emphasize that while "it appears" in the main text to reassure the skeptical reader that, despite the evidence, the older Stoics are almost certainly not the creators of the natural law doctrine, that fact does not amount to apodictic certitude about this essay's claim concerning Cicero. Nevertheless, it does contribute to the "antecedent probability" that he is indeed the first to develop a theory of a natural law in the order of human morals.

in order that they might enjoy the fruits of conquest. The best crimes do, and should, pay.

The shocking immorality of Philus is countered by the upstanding jurist Laelius, who argues, not altogether convincingly, that Rome's conquests have been in accordance with "a true law, namely, right reason, which is in accordance with nature, [applying] to all men, and which is unchangeable and eternal. By its commands it summons men to the performance of their duties, and by its prohibitions it restrains them from doing wrong." This law, according to Laelius, is given by God, who is the "common master and ruler of men." Pious Laelius declares that any individual or nation which transgresses the divinely ordained law of nature will, whether or not they are tried before men, suffer a just sentence: "The man who will not obey it will abandon his better self, and, in denying the true nature of a man, will thereby suffer the severest of penalties, though he has escaped all the other consequences which men call punishment."[10]

Of course, the reader is impressed more by Laelius's piety than by his stubborn contention that Rome always acted justly.[11] This, one supposes, is partly why Cicero later has Scipio modify Laelius's defense of a divinely promulgated natural law. Scipio takes the *via media* between the *Realpolitik* of Philus and the idealism of Laelius. His speech acknowledges the hard fact that political orders never, or hardly ever, come into being by just means. Foundings are necessarily bloody and unjust affairs.[12] Be that as it may, it makes all the difference whether an established polity cultivates laws that conduce to

---

10. Cicero, *De re publica*, trans. G. H. Sabine and S. B. Smith, *Marcus Tullius Cicero: On the Commonwealth* (Indianapolis: Bobbs-Merrill, 1929), 3.22.

11. Cf., Lactantius, *Divinae institutiones* 5.16.12, regarding the persuasiveness of Philus's claims: "Clearly these arguments are subtle and ensnaring; indeed, Cicero could not refute them. For though he makes Laelius answer Philus and present the case for justice, Cicero left all the objections unrefuted, as if they were traps. The result is that Laelius appears as the defender not of natural justice, which had been subjected to the charge of being mere stupidity, but rather of political justice, which Philus had admitted to be prudent, though it was not just." Trans. Sabine and Smith, in *Marcus Tullius Cicero: On the Commonwealth*, p. 207.

12. In the main, Scipio agrees with the political teaching of the Old Testament, wherein the first political founder is also the first murderer. Cf., Genesis 4.

the virtue of its members, or whether it panders to the baser passions of comfortable self-preservation. The Ciceronian doctrine of natural law, concerned as it is with foreign policy and the architectonic good of political life, may be best understood as a practical response to the excesses to which Rome was perennially susceptible. Did Cicero actually believe it? God knows.

With Augustine, however, the doctrine of a natural moral law comes finally into its own as a properly ethical, rather than largely political, teaching. The *locus classicus* for his discussion of natural law is in the first book of his dialogue *De libero arbitrio*, an early work written largely as a challenge to the determinism of the Manichees. Book I opens with Augustine's friend Evodius asking whether God is the cause of evil. Augustine explains that because God is all good, he could not be either the proximate or remote cause of evil or injustice. The evil that exists in the world is due solely to the sin of human beings. Moreover, they are culpable for the evil choices that they make because they are endowed with the ability to distinguish good and bad, and the freedom to choose one or the other. Such ability is the source of the human laws that govern the actions of all civilized men. But obedience to these laws is insufficient to make men truly good and happy, because the laws of the city are concerned only with external behavior and address themselves more to man's fear of punishment than to any inborn desire for the just or the good for its own sake. Mere legal justice cannot be equated with justice *simpliciter*.

The limitations of human or temporal law point beyond themselves to an eternal or natural law that serves as their foundation and as the standard of the most fully human life. Speaking in his own voice, Augustine finally asks,

> What of that law called supreme reason, which must always be obeyed, whereby the wicked merit an unhappy life and the virtuous a happy life and by which, ultimately, that law which we called "temporal" can be justly enacted and justly changed? Can any thinking person fail to see that this law is changeless and eternal? Could it ever be unjust that the wicked should be unhappy, while the good are happy . . . ?[13]

---

13. Augustine, *De libero arbitrio*, trans. Robert Russell, FaCh 59 (Washington, DC: The Catholic University of America Press, 1968), 1.6.15.

Like Plato and Aristotle, Augustine distinguishes between nature and convention—the distinction on which philosophy turns—but unlike them, he posits a teleology in which the universe is moral. However, a world in which the bad must finally be wretched and the good happy requires an eternal legislator. The discovery of the natural law *as* law is coextensive with a belief in a just and personal God.[14]

Yet while Augustine proposes an eternal law, that law, inasmuch as it is natural, cannot of itself make a person happy. Sin hobbles man's efforts to arrive at the happiness that is the object of his deepest longings: "If man were good, he would be other than he in fact is. But since he is the way that he is, he is not good, and does not have the ability even to be good—either because he does not see what he is supposed to be, or because he does, yet doesn't have the power to become what he sees he ought to be."[15] The natural or eternal law is of itself powerless to deliver on the promise of happiness which man discerns in it.

Thomas Aquinas

Augustine never saw a need to advance a full-blown theory of the natural law. The appeals he makes to it, scarce as they are, seem to arise from a need to combat the Manichean dualism that regards material nature as incorrigibly evil.[16] Thomas Aquinas would be the Christian teacher to develop the natural law teaching that came to characterize Catholic moral teaching from the thirteenth century onwards. Contrary to what one might expect, Thomas does not rely upon Aristotle as an authoritative source for his treatise on law. Rather, he looks to Cicero and Augustine as his principal guides in the matter. But his teaching is no mere elaboration of his ancient masters. His is, as we noted above, a reformulation of Augustine's doctrine. This becomes clear in the distinction he makes between the kinds of law. Whereas Augustine posits two laws, the natural or eternal and the temporal or human, Aquinas makes a fourfold division: the eternal, the natural,

---

14. Augustine, *De libero arbitrio*, 1.7.57.
15. Augustine, *De libero arbitrio*, 3.18.174.
16. E.g., the *Contra Faustum*.

the human, and the divine.[17] What is most noteworthy, of course, is the distinction between the natural and the eternal laws, which, in Augustine's thought, are convertible. This suggests that, while Aristotle does not provide Aquinas with a natural law doctrine, he does exercise a decisive influence on him by way of his treatment of nature in the *Physics*:

> Independently of Revelation and prior to the infusion of divine grace, man has access to the most general principles of moral action and, to the extent to which his will has not been corrupted by sin, finds within himself the power to act in accordance with them. There is thus constituted a specifically natural order apart from, though obviously not in opposition to, the higher order to which human nature is elevated through grace. For the single whole in the light of which man's final end had been discussed by Augustine, two complete and hierarchically structured wholes have been substituted, of which the lower or natural whole possesses its own intrinsic perfection and is capable of operations that do not of themselves require the aid of divine or properly supernatural grace. The issue was not without far-reaching practical implications. Speaking figuratively, Augustine had warned that one cannot safely appropriate the spoils of the Egyptians, that is to say, pagan learning and philosophy without first observing the Passover. Without much exaggeration, one could say that Thomas shows a greater willingness to postpone the celebration of the Passover until the Egyptians have been properly despoiled and, indeed, until such time as the whole land of Canaan has been annexed.[18]

It should be emphasized that Thomas does not propose a "two-story universe" or a mere overlapping of the spheres of nature and grace, such as could be illustrated by a Venn diagram. The natural law is a particular expression of the eternal law, which is the ground of all law properly so-called: "it is evident that all things partake in some way in the eternal law, insofar as, namely, from its being imprinted

---

17. Thomas Aquinas, *Summa Theologiae* (hereafter *ST*) I-II, q. 91. English translations of the *ST* in this chapter are taken from *Summa Theologica*, 3 vols., trans. Fathers of the English Dominican Province (New York: Benziger, 1947).

18. Fortin, "Augustine, Aquinas, and the Problem of Natural Law", 210.

on them, they derive their respective inclinations to the proper acts and ends."[19]

That Aquinas allows nature its own proper perfections in a way Augustine never did may be partly attributable to the fact, previously adverted to, that Augustine's teaching on nature is found almost exclusively in his occasional polemics against the Manichees. His concern was with defending man's rational nature and freedom in a universe that is both good and intelligently ordered. Thomas, on the other hand, considers law within the broader context of the extrinsic principles of acts.[20] His treatise is directly applicable to the various political orders of the Christian West at the height of the so-called medieval synthesis.[21] It may be said that Aquinas was navigating a middle way between Augustine, who in the waning years of late Roman antiquity tended to see all things in the light of their highest ends, and the radical Aristotelianism of the Islamic philosophers of the eighth through eleventh centuries, whose political writings could be broadly characterized as an attempt to establish the rule of philosophy over a religion that took the form of a comprehensive and divinely revealed body of laws. More particularly, inasmuch as Thomas allows for perfections that are proper to the natural order, he provides a foundation for the city's relative independence from ecclesiastical rule, even as its Christian citizens will make use of the natural goods secured by political life for the working out of their salvation.

Jerusalem and Athens

It seems that such an enterprise was possible only within Christianity. One might say the peculiar nature of the Christian religion made its appearance very nearly inevitable. Unlike both Judaism and Islam, which come to sight as divinely revealed legislations, governing every

---

19. *ST* I-II, q. 91, a. 2.
20. *ST* I-II, q. 90, prologue.
21. Indeed, the subsequent history of political thought of the fourteenth century is inconceivable apart from Aquinas's transformation of Augustine's teaching on nature. See, e.g., Dante's *De monarchia*.

detail of public and private life, Christianity always understood itself first and foremost as a faith, or *sacra doctrina*, wherein belief is primary. A defining mark of Christianity is that it has ever put orthodoxy before orthopraxy. The Gospel provides believers with the loftiest principles by which to form their thinking and guide their actions, but leaves them free to determine prudentially how those principles are to be applied under the varied circumstances of their lives. Jesus commands his followers to love their enemies, but he does not specify the virtually infinite number of ways in which such love ought to express itself. In the absence of a divine law code, Christianity requires the cultivation and exercise of right reason. This fact goes a long way toward explaining the unique relationship Christianity has always had with philosophy. If philosophy has always been regarded with suspicion, if not outright hostility, by Judaism and Islam, it found something of a home within the Church, almost from the beginning of its history. Tertullian famously asked, "What indeed has Athens to do with Jerusalem?" In fact, the discovery of nature that occurred in fourth- and fifth-century Athens would be decisive in every aspect of Christianity's growth and the development of its foundational teachings. What the first philosophers discovered was ultimately perfected by the biblical doctrine of creation. "Nature" was effectually baptized by the Church and, in the event, the teleological understanding of the cosmos became emphatically moral.

1.3. The Role of the Decalogue in Protestant and Catholic Catechisms

Dr. Daniel A. Keating

Here, then, we have the Ten Commandments, a summary of divine teaching on what we are to do to make our whole life pleasing to God. They are the true foundation from which all good works must spring, the true channel through which all good works must flow.[1]
    Martin Luther

The moral law is summarily comprehended in the ten commandments, which were delivered by the voice of God upon Mount Sinai, and written by him in two tables of stone; and are recorded in the twentieth chapter of Exodus. The four first commandments containing our duty to God, and the other six our duty to man.[2]
    Westminster Larger Catechism

Since, then, the Decalogue is a summary of the whole Law, the pastor should give his days and nights to its consideration, that he may be able not only to regulate his own life by its precepts, but also to instruct in the law of God the people committed to his care.[3]
    Catechism of the Council of Trent

---

    1. Martin Luther, *The Large Catechism of Martin Luther*, trans. Robert H. Fischer (Philadelphia: Fortress, 1959), 51.
    2. *Westminster Larger Catechism*, Q. 98. https://prts.edu/wp-content/uploads/2013/09/Larger_Catechism.pdf.
    3. *Catechism of the Council of Trent for Parish Priests*, trans. John A. McHugh and Charles J. Callan (New York: Joseph F. Wagner, 1923), 357.

Introduction and Preliminaries

In view of our topic, "norms governing the moral life," I thought it would be instructive to revisit the practice, found in both Protestant and Catholic catechisms, of teaching the Decalogue as the primary means of grounding (and so norming) the moral life of the Christian. The fact that the most authoritative Protestant and Catholic catechisms look to the Ten Commandments as the "teacher" of the moral life is often overlooked. Doctrinal disputes and differences gather most of the attention, while the strikingly parallel treatments of the moral life go unrecognized. It is my aim in this paper to show the substantial agreement between Catholics and Protestants on moral teaching, both in method and in content, but at the same time to identify notable points of difference and disagreement that appear.

I have chosen to examine three catechisms of Protestant origin (Luther's *Large Catechism*, the *Heidelberg Catechism*, and the *Westminster Larger Catechism*) and two of Catholic provenance (*Catechism of the Council of Trent* and the recent *Catechism of the Catholic Church*). I have chosen these five because all of them have played (or are playing) a significant role in the life of the churches from which they sprang. All these catechisms carry weight in their respective traditions and have shaped (or are shaping) the moral culture of their churches. Rather than conduct a detailed comparison between one catechism from each camp, I thought it more useful to recognize common patterns and points of difference among a wider set of catechisms.

A word on the numbering of the Ten Commandments. There are two primary traditions, the first of Latin origin stemming from Augustine, the second of Greek origin. In the Latin tradition, the commandments against coveting another's wife and his goods are distinguished as two separate commands. This entails folding the material on graven images into the first commandment. In the Greek tradition, the commands on coveting are received as one commandment, while the command against making graven images becomes a distinct and second commandment. Lutherans followed the Latin numbering while the Reformed and other Protestants followed the Greek numbering. It is deeply ironic that the two traditions—the

Eastern Orthodox and Reformed—that adopt the Greek numbering and so identify the command against graven images as a distinct commandment are at opposite ends of the debate on the use of images in worship. Interestingly, the contemporary Jewish ordering agrees with elements of both traditions, joining graven images to the first commandment and combining the commands on coveting into one. In the Jewish ordering, the number ten is reached by counting the so-called prologue as a distinct "commandment." This approach is grounded in the conclusion that the scripture speaks of ten "words," not specifically ten "commandments," and that the first "word" is the declaration, "I am the Lord your God, who brought you out of the land of Egypt, out of the house of bondage" (Exod 20:1, RSV).

Summary of the Common Ground

Before examining each of the catechisms in turn, I will summarize what I found to be the significant common ground among all the catechisms, as well as identifying areas where differences appear most prominently. The first agreement is that the moral law *for the Christian* is deemed best taught by direct and extended exposition of the Decalogue. On examination, this is not surprising given the attention to the Decalogue in the New Testament. Jesus refers to the commandments on several occasions as expressing God's will, and Paul too upholds the commandments (see Matt 5:19; 19:17; Mark 10:19; Luke 18:20; Rom 13:9; 1 Cor 7:19). All the catechisms agree, as would be expected, that Christians must fulfill the Decalogue by the power of the Spirit and according to the twofold commandment of love (Matt 22:40; Mark 12:28; Rom 13:9). That is to say, Christians are to observe the Ten Commandments as fulfilled in Christ. Nonetheless, these specific commandments retain their authority to reveal and teach the main outlines of the Christian moral life.

Second, there appears to be broad agreement on how Christians should evaluate the law given under the Old Covenant, as divided into three categories: the ceremonial law, the judicial (or civil) law, and the moral law. This traditional way of dividing the Law harks back to an ancient tradition, found for example in Thomas Aquinas (*ST* I-II, 98).

The threefold division of the Law appears in several early Protestant Confessions, where there is agreement that only the moral law (as fulfilled in Christ) remains binding upon Christians. For instance, the *Second Helvetic Confession* (1566), when expounding the normativity of the Decalogue, explains:

> For the sake of clarity we distinguish the moral law which is contained in the Decalogue or Two Tables and expounded in the books of Moses, the ceremonial law which determines the ceremonies and worship of God, and the judicial law which is concerned with political and domestic matters.[4]

The *Second London Confession* (1677), of Baptist origin, distinguishes the "ceremonial" and "judicial" laws that were given only for a season and are no longer binding, from the moral law: "The moral law doth forever bind all, as well justified persons as others, to the obedience thereof.... Neither doth Christ in the Gospel any way dissolve but much strengthen this obligation."[5] The *Thirty-Nine Articles of the Church of England* (1571 edition) adopts the same stance:

> Although the Law given from God by Moses, as touching ceremonies and rites, does not bind Christian men, nor the civil precepts thereof, ought of necessity to be received in any commonwealth, yet, notwithstanding, no Christian man whatsoever is free from the obedience of the commandments, which are called moral.[6]

Third, the emphasis in Catholic teaching on the Decalogue as a revealed summary of the *natural* moral law finds an echo in select Protestant sources. For example, the *Second Helvetic Confession*, written by Heinrich Bullinger, speaks of the "law of nature" in these terms: "And this law was at one time written in the hearts of men by the finger of God (Rom 2:15), and is called the law of nature . . . and at another it was inscribed by his finger on the two Tables of Moses,

---

4. *The Second Helvetic Confession*, Chapter XII, in *Reformed Confessions of the 16th Century*, ed. Arthur C. Cochrane (Philadelphia: Westminster, 1966), 247–48.

5. *The Second London Confession*, Chapter XIX, 1–5, in William L. Lumpkin, ed., *Baptist Confessions of Faith* (Valley Forge: Judson Press, 1969), 276–77.

6. *Thirty-Nine Articles of the Church of England*, 7, in Mark A. Noll, ed., *Confessions and Catechisms of the Reformation* (Grand Rapids: Baker, 1991), 216.

and eloquently expounded in the books of Moses."⁷ John Wesley says much the same thing in his commentary on the Decalogue in Exodus: "This law God had given to man before, it was written in his heart by nature; but sin had so defaced that writing, that it was necessary to revive the knowledge of it."⁸ At this point a difference emerges, at least in emphasis. For the Protestant writers, even if the Decalogue expresses what had already been "revealed" in the natural law, sin has made access to the knowledge of the natural law difficult if not impossible. Catholic teaching firmly maintains the ability of fallen man to perceive the natural law. Still, a long-standing tradition, enshrined in the recent *Catechism of the Catholic Church*, acknowledges that because of sin, knowledge of the natural law is difficult to attain, and so it was fitting that it be made clear through divine revelation: "The Decalogue contains a privileged expression of the natural law.... The commandments of the Decalogue, although accessible to reason alone, have been revealed. To attain a complete and certain understanding of the requirements of the natural law, sinful humanity needed this revelation."⁹

Fourth, and for our purposes most importantly, all the catechisms view each commandment as an entire heading for part of the moral life. That is to say, the commandment is much broader and deeper than just the single item commanded; each governs a *sphere* of the moral life and together they teach and convey the *whole* of the moral life. As we will see through examples, this means that not only is a single action forbidden (e.g., thou shalt not commit adultery), but other actions related to it directly are also forbidden. There is normally a further or more distant extension to other acts that fall within the sphere of the commandment. Notably, all the catechisms identify the

---

7. *The Second Helvetic Confession*, Chapter XII, in Cochrane, *Reformed Confessions*, 247.

8. John Wesley, *Explanatory Notes upon the New Testament* (London: Bowyer, 1755), at Exod 20:1.

9. *Catechism of the Catholic Church*, 2nd ed. (New York: Doubleday, 1997), §2064–65. The *Catechism* cites Irenaeus to support the view that the Decalogue expresses the natural moral law and cites Bonaventure in support of the view that sin has made necessary the revealing of this moral law through the Decalogue.

positive goal and duties that each commandment requires. The commandments do not only forbid, they also enjoin, and to keep the commandments is to follow the *positive* duties they require. Finally, each of the catechisms—some more, some less—relates the commands to corresponding virtues. To keep the commandment requires inculcating and acting from the requisite virtues that provide the inner power to the commandment. In other words, these catechisms, both Protestant and Catholic, apply a similar catechetical method to the Decalogue in the conviction that from within these prescriptions the entire moral life of the Christian can be unfolded.

When we turn to compare what the catechisms teach about the specific actions forbidden and enjoined, there is significant agreement amidst areas of sharp disagreement. When it comes to things like adultery, homicide, perjury, blasphemous language, and so on, there is solid agreement—these were not areas of dispute between Protestants and Catholics. Disagreements arise between Catholic and Protestant—and between Protestant and Protestant—just where we would expect them: the wisdom and legality of monastic vows, the making of images used in worship, the taking of civic oaths, etc. These are well known differences and appear just where we would expect them. Notably, I found no references in any of the sixteenth or seventeenth century catechisms to abortion, euthanasia, or contraception, and only very fleeting references to homosexual activity. The moral issues that unite (and divide) us today were either assumed or were simply not at issue at that time. The contemporary Catholic Catechism is the exception, as it offers detailed treatment of each of these issues.

Brief Commentary on the Catechisms

MARTIN LUTHER'S *LARGE CATECHISM*

The occasion for Luther composing his *Small* and *Large Catechisms* was a request from his prince to visit and evaluate the spiritual state of the local churches in the region. Luther, appalled by what he found, resolved to address the problem by composing a catechism, first for young people themselves (*Small Catechism*), and then a longer treatment aimed at parents and especially pastors (*Large Catechism*, first edition 1531, final edition 1538). In the preface to the *Large Catechism*, Luther exhorts his readers to follow his example of daily reading of the Catechism: "I must still read and study the Catechism daily, yet I cannot master it as I wish, but must remain a child and pupil of the Catechism, and I do it gladly.... Let all Christians exercise themselves in the Catechism daily, and constantly put it into practice."[10]

Unlike the pattern of catechisms both before and after, Luther places the exposition of the Decalogue in *first* position, with the commentary on the Creed following. According to Mark Noll, placing the Law first emphasizes "Luther's conviction that the primary purpose of God's Law is to drive the sinner to Christ."[11] While undoubtedly true, Luther's praise of the Decalogue, and his lengthy exposition, seems to recognize in it more than a mere instrumental role in driving us to the Gospel. He spends nearly fifty pages expounding the details of the commandments, a length that equals his treatment of the Creed, the Lord's Prayer, and the Sacraments combined. And he grants that knowledge of the Decalogue brings about great things:

> This much is certain: anyone who knows the Ten Commandments perfectly knows the entire Scriptures. In all affairs and circumstances he can counsel, help, comfort, judge, and make decisions in both spiritual and temporal matters. He is qualified to sit in judgment upon all doctrines, estates, persons, laws, and everything else in the world.[12]

This high praise of the value of the Decalogue in its own right is repeated at the close of Luther's treatment:

> From all this it is obvious once again how highly these Ten Commandments are to be exalted and extolled above all order, commands, and works which are taught and practices apart from them.... Therefore, we should prize and value them above all other teachings as the greatest treasure God has given us.[13]

---

10. Luther, *The Large Catechism*; Fisher, 3, 5.
11. Noll, *Confessions and Catechisms of the Reformation*, 60.
12. Luther, *The Large Catechism*; Fisher, 5.
13. Luther, *The Large Catechism*; Fisher, 54–55.

Without going into detail, we can recognize that Luther follows the standard method of viewing each commandment as an entire heading that covers a sphere of moral activity. So for example when treating the command against killing, he writes: "Not only is murder forbidden, but everything that may lead to murder."[14] And again, when speaking of the command against adultery, "This commandment applies to every form of unchastity, however it is called. Not only is the external act forbidden, but also every kind of cause, motive, and means."[15] In his concluding remarks, Luther acknowledges that keeping the commandments of the Decalogue is beyond human power to fulfill. Nonetheless, he urges the faithful to apply themselves to observe them: "Just concentrate upon them and test yourself thoroughly, do your very best, and you will surely find so much to do that you will neither seek nor pay attention to any other works or other kind of holiness."[16]

THE *HEIDELBERG CATECHISM*

The *Heidelberg Catechism* (*HC*) was commissioned by Frederick III in order to bring about greater unity between Lutheran and Reformed churches in his territory. Published in 1563, with Zacharius Ursinus as the primary author, this catechism became the standard exposition of faith for the Dutch Reformed churches. According to Mark Noll,

> With most other Reformed statements of Christian faith, teaching on the Ten Commandments comes after an exposition of the Apostles' Creed . . . . With this arrangement, the Reformed were stressing the Law as part of a Christian's joyful service to Christ, where Lutherans characteristically described it as the force that drives the sinner to Christ.[17]

The statement of the first commandment displays the broad interpretation of the commandments that we saw in Luther. Here it is in full:

---

14. Luther, *The Large Catechism*; Fisher, 34.
15. Luther, *The Large Catechism*; Fisher, 36.
16. Luther, *The Large Catechism*; Fisher, 52.
17. Noll, *Confessions and Catechisms of the Reformation*, 135.

What does the Lord require in the first commandment? That I must avoid and flee all idolatry, sorcery, enchantment, invocation of saints or other creatures because of the risk of losing my salvation. Indeed, I ought properly to acknowledge the only true God, trust in him alone, in humility and patience expect all good from him only, and love, fear, and honor him with all my heart. In short, I should rather turn my back on all creatures than do the least thing against his will.[18]

Notice that idolatry and *all related acts* are viewed as forbidden (and for the Reformed this includes invoking the saints!), but the positive goods that are required receive equal attention: acknowledgement of God as God, trust in him alone, and fear and love of God. The language here has a resemblance to Moses' moral exhortations in Deuteronomy.

In the command against killing, the *HC* moves from homicide to accompanying actions and inner states, following the example of Jesus in the Sermon on the Mount. But then it details the positive duties required: "When God condemns envy, hatred, and anger, he requires us to love our neighbor as ourselves, to show patience, peace, gentleness, mercy, and friendliness toward him, to prevent injury to him as much as we can, and also to do good to our enemies."[19] In a similar way, the command against adultery extends to "all unchaste actions, gestures, words, thoughts, desires, and whatever may excite another person to them,"[20] while the command against bearing false witness requires positively "that I work for the good of my neighbor wherever I can and may, deal with him as I would have others deal with me, and do my work well so that I may be able to help the poor in their need."[21]

The conclusion contains a significant comment on the attitude we should have when seeking to keep the fullness of the commands of God. The *HC* states that no Christian can keep the commandments perfectly: "For even the holiest of them make only a small beginning

---

18. *HC*, Q. 94; Noll, *Confessions and Catechisms of the Reformation*, 157.
19. *HC*, Q. 107; Noll, 160.
20. *HC*, Q. 109; Noll, 160.
21. *HC*, Q. 111; Noll, 161.

in obedience in this life."[22] The obvious follow-up question is then asked: *Why, then, does God have the Ten Commandments preached so strictly since no one can keep them in this life?* The answer:

> First, that all our life long we may become increasingly aware of our sinfulness, and therefore more eagerly seek forgiveness of sins and righteousness in Christ. Second, that we may constantly and diligently pray to God for the grace of the Holy Spirit, so that more and more we may be renewed in the image of God, until we attain the goal of full perfection after this life.[23]

The answer is twofold, and both purposes drive us to Christ and his grace: the first, to seek forgiveness for our failures and find our righteousness in Christ; the second, to ask for the Holy Spirit so as to grow in the image of God. There is hope and expectation for moral progress but not for keeping the law in its fullness. As we shall see, this answer is notably different than that found in the *Catechism of the Council of Trent*.

THE *WESTMINSTER LARGER CATECHISM*

The *Westminster Larger Catechism* (*WLC*) was drawn up and published in 1647, and adopted officially by the Church of Scotland in 1648, as a commentary on the Westminster Confession of Faith. Along with the *Westminster Shorter Catechism*, this longer version was intended to provide a more detailed and exact commentary on the faith, akin to Luther's *Short* and *Large Catechisms*. The *WLC* is clearly arranged according to what is to be believed (the creed), what is to be done (the commandments), including the means of grace (word and sacrament), and how we are to pray (the Lord's Prayer). The section on the commandments occupies just over one third of the whole Catechism.

The *purpose* of the moral law for Christians is summarily described at the beginning of the treatment of the Decalogue:

> Q. Of what use is the moral law to all men? A. The moral law is of use to all men, to inform them of the holy nature and the will of God, and

---

22. *HC*, Q. 114; Noll, 161.
23. *HC*, Q. 115; Noll, 161.

of their duty, binding them to walk accordingly; to convince them of their disability to keep it, and of the sinful pollution of their nature, hearts, and lives: to humble them in the sense of their sin and misery, and thereby help them to a clearer sight of the need they have of Christ, and of the perfection of his obedience.[24]

Though put in different words, this purpose lines up with the statement found in the *Heidelberg Catechism*. In good scholastic fashion, the *WLC* offers eight rules for rightly observing the Decalogue as Christians. The first rule states that the moral law is perfect and must be kept in its fullness: "That the law is perfect, and binds everyone to full conformity in the whole man unto the righteousness thereof, and unto entire obedience forever; so as to require the utmost perfection of every duty, and to forbid the least degree of every sin."[25] The remaining seven rules express in detail the pattern we have found in all the catechisms: how the individual command extends to all related offenses, how the command requires positive duties and obligations, and how the law reaches into the heart and enjoins the fullness of godly character and the fruits of the Spirit.

What follows is a highly patterned exposition of each commandment: first the positive duties are enumerated and then the list of actions forbidden is given. Leaving nothing to chance, the *WLC* provides in fine detail the specific actions that are enjoined and prohibited. One example, from the command against adultery, will show the pattern used throughout.

> Q. What are the duties required in the seventh commandment? A. The duties required in the seventh commandment are: chastity in body, mind, affections, words, and behavior; and the preservation of it in ourselves and others; watchfulness over the eyes and all the senses; temperance, keeping of chaste company, modesty in apparel; marriage by those that have not the gift of continency, conjugal love, and cohabitation; diligent labor in our callings; shunning all occasions of uncleanness, and resisting temptations thereunto.

---

24. *WLC*, Q. 95.
25. *WLC*, Q. 99.

Q. What are the sins forbidden in the seventh commandment? A. The sins forbidden in the seventh commandment, besides the neglect of the duties required, are, adultery, fornication, rape, incest, sodomy, and all unnatural lusts; all unclean imaginations, thoughts, purposes, and affections; all corrupt or filthy communications, or listening thereunto; wanton looks, impudent or light behaviour, immodest apparel; prohibiting of lawful, and dispensing with unlawful marriages; allowing, tolerating, keeping of stews [brothels], and resorting to them; entangling vows of single life, undue delay of marriage, having more wives or husbands than one at the same time; unjust divorce, or desertion; idleness, gluttony, drunkenness, unchaste company; lascivious songs, books, pictures, dancings, stage plays; and all other provocations to, or acts of uncleanness, either in ourselves or others.[26]

The *WLC* concludes with a similar statement on the inability of Christians to keep the moral law in its fullness: "Is any man able perfectly to keep the commandments of God? A. No man is able, either of himself, or by any grace received in this life, perfectly to keep the commandments of God but doth daily break them in thought, word, and deed."[27] On the one hand, a distinction between the gravity of sins is recognized: "Are all transgressions of the law of God equally heinous in themselves, and in the sight of God? A. All transgressions of the law of God are not equally heinous; but some sins in themselves, and by reason of several aggravations, are more heinous in the sight of God than others."[28] But on the other hand, this distinction in the gravity of sins does not affect our status in Christ or the efficacy of his atoning sacrifice for all sins: "What doth every sin deserve at the hands of God? A. Every sin, even the least, being against the sovereignty, goodness, and holiness of God, and against his righteous law, deserves his wrath and curse, both in this life, and that which is to come; and cannot be expiated but by the blood of Christ."[29]

---

26. *WLC*, QQ. 138–39.
27. *WLC*, Q. 149.
28. *WLC*, Q. 150.
29. *WLC*, Q. 152.

THE *CATECHISM OF THE COUNCIL OF TRENT*

The Council of Trent met in three sessions (1545–1557, 1551–1552, 1562–1563), and called for the production of a catechism that would communicate the teaching of the Council to a new generation. After a period of preparation and revision (including a change in the intended audience), the *Catechism of the Council of Trent* (*CCT*), also known as the *Roman Catechism*, was promulgated in 1566 by Pope Pius V.[30] The third main section is entitled simply, "The Decalogue"; the authority of Augustine is cited for this law being the sum and epitome of all laws, as fulfilled in the twofold law of love. Notably, the *CCT* teaches that the Decalogue remains authoritative for Christians, not because it was given by Moses, but because it expresses the inspired summary of the natural moral law that pertains to human life for all time: "It is most certain that we are not bound to obey the Commandments because they were delivered by Moses, but because they are implanted in the hearts of all, and have been explained and confirmed by Christ our Lord."[31]

Among the motives offered by the *CCT* for obeying the commandments, the most striking is that the observance of the commandments is not difficult or burdensome.[32] This judgment is based on the authority of Scripture (1 John 5:3) and on the testimony of the saints. "But should anyone plead human infirmity to excuse himself for not loving God, it should be explained that He who demands our love pours into our hearts by the Holy Ghost the fervor of His love; and this good Spirit our heavenly Father gives to those that ask him."[33]

---

30. McHugh and Callan, "Introduction," *Catechism of the Council of Trent*, xxv. McHugh and Callan (xxviii) offer evidence for the existence of many local or regional catechisms in the high Middle Ages, including two in the period just before Luther's own activity: *Fundamentum Aeternae Felicitatis*, *Discipulus de Eruditione*. Both of these catechisms follow the same fourfold order of the *Catechism of Council of Trent*: the Creed, the Sacraments, the Decalogue, and the Lord's Prayer.

31. *CCT*; McHugh and Callan, 359.

32. Among the other motives for keeping the commandments are: (1) God is the author of this law; (2) the commandments were proclaimed with great solemnity; (3) the observance of the commandments is necessary; (4) keeping the commandments is attended by many blessings; and (5) God's goodness invites us to keep his commandments.

33. *CCT*; McHugh and Callan, 360.

There is no mention of the Old Testament Law as pedagogue in this context, driving us to Christ. The *CCT* is not treating the law here in its dispensational role in salvation history but as the perennial purpose of God for the human race, now empowered by the gift of the Spirit.

The *CCT* follows the tradition of dividing the Decalogue into two tables, defined by the two commands of love. The structure for treating each commandment also follows the traditional pattern of asking what is positively commanded (and this usually comes first) and what is negatively prohibited. Notably, the positive command is often given greater weight even though the commandment is stated in the negative. So for instance regarding the first commandment: "The (mandatory part) contains a precept of faith, hope and charity . . . . The (negative) part of the Commandment is comprised in these words: *Thou shalt not have strange gods before me*."[34] Parallel to the practice of several of the Protestant catechisms, the command to honor father and mother is extended to all rightful authorities:

> The application of this Commandment is of very great extent. Besides our natural parents, there are many others whose power, rank, usefulness, exalted functions or office, entitle them to parental honor . . . . We are bound to honor not only our natural parents, but also others who are called fathers, such as bishops and priests, kings, princes and magistrates, tutors, guardians and masters, teachers, aged persons and the like, all of whom are entitled, some in a greater, some in a less degree, to share our love, our obedience, and our assistance.[35]

The commands in the second table follow this same pattern, each one providing a heading for an entire area of the moral life. Thus, "every species of immodesty and impurity are included in this prohibition of adultery."[36] This includes all outward behaviors but also every thought of the heart, and we are enjoined to cultivate the virtues of continence, chastity, and temperance.[37]

---

34. *CCT*; McHugh and Callan, 368.
35. *CCT*; McHugh and Callan, 408–9; 414.
36. *CCT*; McHugh and Callan, 432.
37. *CCT*; McHugh and Callan, 433, 437.

Significantly, the *CCT* considers that virtues are "included" in the keeping of the commandments, and a crucial part of teaching the commandments is the inculcation of virtue. So, the virtue of charity is paramount in keeping the commandment "Thou shalt not kill": "In his instruction on the precept [the pastor] should exhort the faithful as much as possible to the practice of this virtue [charity], since it is especially included in this precept."[38] By extension, we are also commanded to practice the virtues of patience, beneficence, and kindness in the fulfillment of this commandment.

THE *CATECHISM* OF THE *CATHOLIC CHURCH*

The contemporary *Catechism of the Catholic Church* (*CCC*, second edition, 1997), is the chronological exception in this study, but it helpfully provides an account of the normativity of the Decalogue in Catholic teaching for today. Much could be profitably said about the third part of the *CCC* entitled "Life in Christ," but for our purposes I will limit myself to observations that show continuity and difference with the *Catechism of the Council of Trent*.

First, the treatment of the moral life is much broader in extent in the *CCC* than in the *CCT*. The *CCT* covers the Decalogue alone; the *CCC* embeds its treatment of the Decalogue within a wider discussion that includes: a basic theological anthropology, a discussion of the Beatitudes and the Sermon on the Mount, an account of Christian freedom, the moral life, and conscience, an examination of the moral and theological virtues, a discussion of sin, an overview of social justice and participation in civil society, and a treatment of the moral law, grace, and justification. Still, the examination of the Decalogue in detail (120 pages) occupies the central frame of the third part of the *CCC*:

> In fidelity to Scripture and in conformity with the example of Jesus, the tradition of the Church has acknowledged the primordial importance and significance of the Decalogue . . . . Ever since St. Augustine, the Ten Commandments have occupied a predominant place in the catechesis of baptismal candidates and the faithful . . . . The

---

38. *CCT*; McHugh and Callan, 426.

catechisms of the Church have often expounded Christian morality by following the order of the Ten Commandments.[39]

The *CCC* consciously follows both Trent and Vatican II in upholding the obligatory nature of the Decalogue: "The Council of Trent teaches that the Ten Commandments are obligatory for Christians and that the justified man is still bound to keep them; the Second Vatican Council confirms [this]."[40]

Second, the *CCC* follows the pattern of the other catechisms, both Protestant and Catholic, by viewing each command as defining an entire sphere of moral life and activity. And so after identifying the core meaning of the first commandment as "God's first call and just demand . . . that man accept him and worship him," the exposition turns quickly to the importance of the theological virtues for keeping this commandment: "The first commandment embraces faith, hope, and charity."[41] The subheadings that follow show the *extension* and *positive application* of the commandment: adoration, prayer, sacrifice, promises and vows, and religious freedom. This pattern is followed variously in each of the commandments, as this summary of the command against adultery displays: "The tradition of the Church has understood the sixth commandment as encompassing the whole of human sexuality."[42]

Third, the *CCC* teaches concrete moral truths that are worthy of our attention. On the command to keep the sabbath holy, the *CCC* provides a profound theology of the Sabbath and the Lord's Day, showing the distinction between the two theologically, but showing how the fulfillment of a day of worship and rest is reasonably transferred in the Church from the Sabbath to the Lord's Day. The command to honor father and mother, following a broad tradition, is applied to all rightful authorities, not only in the family but in the Church and society. The commands against killing and adultery specifically address sins that were not named in the catechisms of the

---

39. *CCC* 2064–65.
40. *CCC* 2068 (citing *Lumen gentium*, §24).
41. *CCC* 2084, 2086.
42. *CCC* 2336.

sixteenth and seventeenth centuries: abortion, euthanasia, masturbation, contraception, and pornography. For obvious reasons due to our society and culture, these require a full treatment today.

Fourth, the *CCC* strikes a similar note to the *CCT*, when it says that Christians are called to live a life worthy of the Gospel of Christ, and "that they are made capable of doing so by the grace of Christ and the gifts of his Spirit, which they receive through the sacraments and through prayer."[43] Strengthened by the Holy Spirit and granted the grace of filial adoption, the Christian is made "capable of acting rightly and doing good," and through union with Christ "the disciple attains the perfection of charity which is holiness."[44] The emphasis here falls on the *ability*, not the *incapability*, of keeping the commandments and living a way of life pleasing to Christ. The *CCC* does not deny that Christians often fall into what are called "light" or "venial" sins, citing Augustine to this effect,[45] but the emphasis is on the graced ability to fulfill the law of God and live by the charity poured into our hearts through the Spirit.

Conclusions

A comparison of Protestant and Catholic treatments of the Decalogue reveals significant common ground that we can build on together. The Decalogue, as fulfilled in the twofold law of love and lived by the power of the Spirit, remains authoritative for Christians. The commandments, in their full explication, continue to teach the faithful the "way of life" pleasing to God in Christ. Much of the specific content of the commandments, especially of the second table, we hold in common. The various lists of what is forbidden and enjoined by the commandments yields a great deal of common ground for those who continue to regard the Decalogue in its traditional exposition as still in force. There is also a method of viewing the commandments (the extension of the commandment, the application to the heart,

---

43. *CCC* 1692.
44. *CCC* 1709.
45. *CCC* 1863.

the corresponding virtues and positive duties) that we would do well to recapture. While avoiding a legalistic approach to the commands, which the *CCC* makes great pains to avoid, the kind of catechesis offered in all of these catechisms would serve the faithful well in our gnostic, antinomian, individualistic culture, a culture that deeply impacts the life of our churches.

This comparison of the respective catechisms also points to certain notable differences between Protestant and Catholic approaches to the Decalogue (and the moral life). Most obvious are disagreements regarding concrete acts or practices, for example, monastic vows or the use of images in worship. Many of these arise from different ways of construing the first table of the law, though differences exist with respect to the second table as well. We should note that several disagreements appear here *between* Protestants as well. I have also drawn attention to what is at the very least a significant difference in emphasis: how capable are Christians, renewed in the Spirit, of keeping the law? The Reformation catechisms emphasize the inability to keep the law in its fullness; the Catholic catechisms (while not holding to a doctrine of "entire sanctification") underline the capability of keeping the law and of fulfilling the command to love God and neighbor.

Together we face enormous challenges given the powerful currents in our culture. Plainly, living according to the commandments is becoming increasingly difficult. But even more alarming is the widespread dismissal of the requirement to keep the commandments *in their fullness* across our churches. And so we face the formidable challenge of conveying that there are moral norms in the first place, and of communicating that God has revealed a "way of walking" that leads to life, and that he has given the Spirit to enable us to walk in that way of life by his grace.

1.4. The Wesleyan Quadrilateral and Norms for the Moral Life

Rev. Bruce Cromwell, PhD

The Norming Method of the Wesleyan Quadrilateral

I recently travelled to Nepal to visit several churches which my congregation in Michigan supports and has brought into greater connection with the Free Methodist Church. Warmly welcomed and received with wonderful hospitality, I shared numerous times in numerous places about the denomination, about our polity, about our doctrines. I preached a dozen times, shared numerous illustrations, read chapters of Scripture, prayed literally for hours, and simply sat together with other sisters and brothers on the journey of faith, connected by the convictions we share and not primarily by the countries we inhabit or the cultures we portray. And whether speaking in the expansive city of Kathmandu, in the poverty-stricken plains at the Beldangi refugee camp, or in the remote jungle village of Gorkha, I was asked consistently how a Free Methodist was supposed to live. "What does this mean for us as followers of Jesus?"

It's the same question I get asked by the Nepalese speakers who attend my church in the United States. It's the same question the persons from Central Africa who speak Swahili ask me on Sunday mornings, the same question raised by the Karenni people from Myanmar and the French-Creole speakers from Haiti. And for that matter, it's the same question asked by the persons working through one of our 12 Step Groups, by the persons trying to re-enter society from prison, and by the persons who perhaps have been raised in the Church and have heard such teaching and preaching all their life. It's the question Saint Paul asked after his Damascus Road experience. "What should I do, Lord?" "How are we supposed to live?" And in our postmodern age of increasing religious relativism, equally frequent is the more foundational question, "How do we know that's the truth?"

These questions speak directly to the issue of method. They seek guidance as to the norms for the moral life. In this paper I will attempt to demonstrate the Methodist reliance on what is frequently termed the "Wesleyan Quadrilateral," and how it is used when it comes to establishing and determining norms for life. I will then investigate some of John Wesley's thought, particularly within his "General Rules" for the Methodist societies, to illustrate how early Methodist practice and preaching continues to influence contemporary Methodist discipline and lifestyle.

In his sermon on "The Promise of Understanding," John Wesley preached that "it is the Divine Spirit 'who worketh in us both to will and to do of his good pleasure,' of this, experience, and reason, and Scripture convince every sincere inquirer."[1] This is part, Wesley claimed, of God's "particular methods of working."[2]

John Wesley has been described as "a technically competent theologian with a remarkable power of creative simplification."[3] As Mildred Bangs Wynkoop explains within *A Theology of Love*, this is due to the hermeneutic of love which flows throughout all of Wesley's works.[4] This does not mean he was without a systematic theology[5] or

---

1. John Wesley, "The Promise of Understanding," *The Bicentennial Works of John Wesley*, ed. Frank Baker et al. (Nashville: Abingdon, 1984ff), 4:284. References to Wesley's works all come from the *Bicentennial Edition* unless otherwise noted and will be referred to hereafter simply as *Works*.

2. John Wesley, "The Promise of Understanding," *Works*, 4:284.

3. Albert Outler, "John Wesley: Folk Theologian," *Theology Today* 34, no. 2 (1977): 150–60, at 150.

4. Mildred Bangs Wynkoop, *A Theology of Love* (Kansas City: Beacon Hill, 1972), 11.

5. See Randy L. Maddox, "Responsible Grace: The Systematic Nature of Wesley's Theology Reconsidered," *Wesleyan Theological Journal* 19, no. 2 (1984): 7–22; H. Ray Dunning, "Systematic Theology in a Wesleyan Mode," *Wesleyan Theological Journal* 17, no. 1 (1982): 15–22. Also consult the Wesleyan theological collections of Richard Watson, *Theological Institutes*, 2 vols. (New York: Lane & Scott, 1851); William Burt Pope, *Compendium of Christian Theology*, 3 vols., 2nd ed. (New York: Phillips & Hunt, 1880); and H. Orton Wiley, *Christian Theology*, 3 vols. (Kansas City: Beacon Hill, 1940).

without significant contributions to Christology, salvation, and the process of sanctification.[6] But it does mean that his methodology was first and foremost geared toward what Albert Outler called a "folk theology."[7] It was meant to be understood so that it could be lived.

The so-called "Wesleyan Quadrilateral" is a model of how Wesley saw this method of theology. It emphasizes the authority of Scripture, understood in the light of tradition, reason, and experience. Such thinking can be found in several places within Wesley's writings, including the early part of *The Doctrine of Original Sin*, within his *Appeals*, and most clearly in his sermon "On Sin in Believers."[8]

Albert Outler coined the term "Wesleyan Quadrilateral" in the late 1960s and chose the concept for its familiarity with both Anglican and Episcopal churches. The Lambeth Quadrilateral had been ratified in 1886 and spoke to the steps needed for a unified Christianity, articulating the fundamentals of the Anglican Communion's doctrine and serving as a reference point for ecumenical discussions with other Christian denominations. It affirmed Scripture as the guide and grounding for the Christian faith, but also emphasized the Apostles' and Nicene creeds as summaries of the faith, the necessity of the sacraments of baptism and the Lord's Supper, and the important role and rulings of the Church historic, particularly the episcopate.

The substance of the Wesleyan Quadrilateral is slightly different from this. Moreover, it is not intended to be seen as a balanced geometric figure, with each "leg" carrying equal weight. In fact, near the end of his life Outler said that he regretted having coined the term, for it was misused and widely misconstrued. As he explained,

---

6. See John Deschner, *Wesley's Christology* (Grand Rapids: Zondervan, 1988); Kenneth J. Collins, *Wesley on Salvation: A Study in the Standard Sermons* (Grand Rapids: Zondervan, 1989); and Harald Linström, *Wesley and Sanctification* (Grand Rapids: Zondervan, 1983).

7. Outler, "John Wesley: Folk Theologian," 12.

8. John Wesley, "On Sin in Believers," *Works*, 1:318–19. Wesley also listed Scripture, reason, and experience as doctrinal norms within "The Repentance of Believers," and Scripture, reason, and Christian antiquity within the preface to his collected works, published in 1771. For more analysis see Donald Thorsen, *The Wesleyan Quadrilateral* (Grand Rapids: Zondervan, 1990), and Charles Yrigoyen, *John Wesley: Holiness of Heart and Life* (Nashville: Abingdon, 2010).

It was intended as a metaphor for a four-element syndrome, including the four-fold guidelines of authority in Wesley's theological method. In such a quaternity Holy Scripture is clearly unique. But this in turn is illuminated by the collective Christian wisdom of other ages and cultures between the Apostolic Age and our own. It also allows for the rescue of the Gospel from obscurantism by means of the disciplines of critical reason. But always, Biblical revelation must be received in the heart by faith: this is the requirement of "experience".[9]

Though *sola Scriptura* has long been esteemed as the shibboleth for faithful, evangelical theology, the reality is that no one uses a single religious authority, and Evangelicals are no exception. Scripture certainly has primacy. But primacy does not mean exclusivity. Indeed, Scripture alone, tradition alone, reason alone, or even experience alone doesn't fully satisfy the contemporary demand for a more comprehensive and relevant Christianity. As Don Thorsen has pointed out, even commitment to two or three of these elements does not satisfy the need for a more catholic or universal treatment of both the content and the vitality of Christianity. "The model of the Wesleyan quadrilateral seeks to satisfy the need for greater evangelical catholicity in theology."[10]

Wesley himself was solidly orthodox in his Christianity. He often distinguished mere personal opinion from what he considered to be the essentials of theology. And since most of the conflicts that existed among Christians (then and now) were of the former, Wesley chose to emphasize catholicity and unity rather than exclusivity and diversity. He allowed a wide spectrum of theological opinion on many issues, choosing intentionally to avoid dogmatic extremes. "Evangelical" was not the catchword in eighteenth-century theology that it is today, but Wesley would certainly have been comfortable with the most inclusive attributes of it.

As Outler explains, "Wesley's theological pluralism was evangelical in substance (firm and clear in its Christocentric focus) and irenic in

---

9. Albert C. Outler, "The Wesleyan Quadrilateral in John Wesley," *Wesleyan Theological Journal* 20, no. 1 (1985): 7–18, at 11.

10. Thorsen, *The Wesleyan Quadrilateral*, 230.

its temper ('Catholic spirit')."[11] Wesley incorporated Scripture, tradition, reason, and experience with the explicit hope of presenting the Christian faith in a way that adhered to the orthodox understanding of scriptural truth while affirming a spiritually transformed life. Let us briefly consider Scripture, tradition, reason, and experience, then, in turn.

Scripture: There is great power and clarity within the Reformation slogan *sola Scriptura*. It cautions against authoritarian claims of anything counter to the revealed word of God, and its simplicity allows Evangelical Christians (and all Christians, for that matter) to understand the basis on which our claims of truth are made. As I've heard believers sing in multiple languages, "Jesus loves me, this I know, for the Bible tells me so."

Though written seventy years after Wesley's death, the words to that song would have been consistent with Wesley's life. When challenged on matters of doctrine, he appealed to Holy Scripture as the primary justification for his teachings. Early in his ministerial career he famously referred to himself as *homo unius libri*, a man of one book.[12] Forty-one years later he used the phrase yet again when reviewing the beginnings of the Methodist movement.

> From the very beginning, from the time that four young men united together, each of them was *homo unius libri*, a man of one book. God taught them all to make his word a lantern unto their feet, and a light in all their paths. They had one, and only one rule of judgment, with regard to all their tempers, words and actions, namely, the oracles of God. They were one and all determined to be Bible-Christians. They were continually reproached for this very thing; some terming them in derision Bible-bigots; others, Bible-moths, feeding, they said, upon the Bible as moths do upon cloth. And indeed unto this day it is their constant endeavor to think and speak as the oracles of God.[13]

---

11. Outler, "The Wesleyan Quadrilateral in Wesley," 9. See also Larry R. Shelton, "The Trajectory of Wesleyan Theology," *Wesleyan Theological Journal* 21, no. 2 (1986): 159–75.

12. See Scott J. Jones, "The Rule of Scripture," 39–62 in *Wesley and the Quadrilateral: Renewing the Conversation* (Nashville: Abingdon, 1997) for a more detailed analysis of Wesley's emphasis on the word of God for all matters of doctrine and faith.

13. John Wesley, "On God's Vineyard," *Works*, 7:203.

To understand Wesley's method of determining the norms for the Christian life, one must begin with Scripture. Wesley is crystal clear on this point. The authority of Scripture is understood in light of tradition, reason, and experience, but Scripture alone is the ultimate authority for Christian faith and practice. It serves as the final court of appeal.[14]

Stephen Gunter has noted that Wesley, as an Anglican, viewed the authority of Scripture from a perspective significantly different from that of the non-Anglican Evangelicals of the eighteenth century, especially the Dissenters, the eighteenth-century descendants of the Puritans.[15] Though all saw Scripture as authoritative, all did not see it the same way. The Dissenters, in broad terms, used Scripture as the authority for all things in life. Anglican Evangelicals, however, emphasized its authority for issues related to salvific knowledge. Its authority rested primarily in communicating all that is necessary for salvation.

Tradition: Wesley's Anglican Evangelicalism also caused him to view tradition in a different manner than many of his Puritan neighbors. In Wesley's day, many within the Puritan tradition exhibited a strong tendency to place value on Christian history, but only from the time of the Protestant Reformation launched by Luther in 1517. In time the theological influence of John Calvin eclipsed anything Luther contributed to the conversation. Wesley, as with most Anglicans, found great value in the entirety of the Church historic. And though Calvinism certainly left its mark on Anglican theology, in Wesley's day there was plenty of room to be thoroughly Anglican and yet not thoroughly Calvinist. It was in this theological space that Wesley roamed.

Though Wesley claimed to be a man of one book, barely five paragraphs after that declaration we find him quoting from Homer's *Iliad*, and in the original Greek, no less! Wesley was a firm student of

---

14. See Thomas C. Oden, *John Wesley's Teachings, Volume 1: God and Providence* (Grand Rapids: Zondervan, 2012), for a more thorough analysis of Wesley's theological method.

15. Stephen W. Gunter, "The Quadrilateral and the 'Middle Way,'" 17–38 in *Wesley and the Quadrilateral: Renewing the Conversation* (Nashville: Abingdon, 1997), 17–18.

history and tradition. In his sermon "On Sin in Believers" he attacked what he saw as inadequate theology by claiming that "it is contrary to the whole tenor of Scripture; secondly, because it is contrary to the experience of the children of God; thirdly, because it is absolutely new, never heard of in the world till yesterday; and lastly, because it is naturally attended with the most fatal consequences, not only grieving those whom God hath not grieved, but perhaps dragging them into everlasting perdition."[16] He attempted to teach people in a manner that was "agreeable, I hope, to Scripture, reason and Christian antiquity."[17]

When he used the term "antiquity," Wesley said he was referring to "the religion of the primitive church, of the whole church in its purest ages," with special reference to "Clemens Romanus, Ignatius, and Polycarp . . . Tertullian, Origen, Clemens Alexandrinus,[18] and Cyprian[19]. . . Chrysostom,[20] Basil,[21] Ephrem Syrus,[22] and Macarius.[23]"[24] Ted Campbell, in his excellent work *John Wesley and Christian Antiquity: Religious Vision and Cultural Change*, further details Wesley's adherence to and appreciation of Christian tradition, and goes into much greater explanation and example than we have the time for here.[25]

---

16. John Wesley, "On Sin in Believers," *Works*, 1:325.

17. Wesley's preface to the 1771 edition of his works, quoted by Thomas Jackson, *The Works of John Wesley: Complete and Unabridged* (March 1771), 1:4.

18. For other references to Clement of Alexandria, see John Wesley, *Works*, 2:327–28, 342, 387; 3:586; 4:402; 5:43, 197; 6:129; 9:31.

19. For Wesley's extensive references to Cyprian see John Wesley, *Works*, 1:277, 323; 2:320, 333–37, 361, 373, 387, 416; 2:263, 2:461–62; 3:196–97, 450–51, 458–59, 469–70; 4:97.

20. For further references to John Chrysostom, see John Wesley, *Works*, 1:155–59, 381–453; 2:113; 3:586; 4:402; and also K. Steve McCormick, "John Chrysostom and John Wesley" (Ph.D. diss., Drew University, 1983), for a comparative study of John Chrysostom and John Wesley.

21. John Wesley, *Works*, 4:176; 11:8.

22. John Wesley, *Works*, 1:276, 279, 284–85, 294–95; 3:284; 4:457–59.

23. John Wesley, *Works*, 1:254; 2:387.

24. John Wesley, "On Laying the Foundation of the New Chapel," *Works*, 3:586.

25. Ted Campbell, *John Wesley and Christian Antiquity: Religious Vision and Cultural Change* (Nashville: Kingswood, 1991). See especially his Appendix 2, which lists references to ancient Christian works in John Wesley's corpus.

Reason: When it comes to the role of reason, a few brief examples from Wesley should suffice. He urged persons to not despise or lightly esteem reason, knowledge, or human learning. "To renounce reason is to renounce religion," he said, for "all irrational religion is false religion."[26] Religion is stripped of its vitality and victory when reason is neglected, for "it is impossible, without reasoning, either to prove or disprove anything."[27]

Reason, Wesley simply believed, is a gift from God. On July 6, 1781, he preached a sermon entitled "The Case for Reason Impartially Considered." "In all the duties of common life," Wesley said, "God has given us our reason for a guide. And it is only by acting up to the dictates of it, by using all the understanding which God hath given us, that we can have a conscience void of offence towards God and towards man."[28]

But whereas many reduce what they choose to believe to what they clearly can understand and perceive, Wesley was quick to highlight reason's shortfalls. "First," he cautioned, "reason cannot produce faith. Although it is always consistent with reason, yet reason cannot produce faith in the scriptural sense of the word."[29] Moreover, reason cannot produce hope. "If reason could have produced a hope full of immortality in any child of man, it might have produced it in that great man whom Justin Martyr scruples not to call, 'a Christian before Christ'. For who that was not favoured with the written Word of God ever excelled, yea, or equaled Socrates? In what other heathen can we find so strong an understanding, joined with so consummate a virtue? But had he really this hope?"[30] Only Socrates can answer that, Wesley concluded. Reason cannot.

Wesley drew his argument to a climax by addressing what he saw as the pinnacle of the virtues. "Reason, however cultivated and

---

26. John Wesley to Dr. Rutherforth, March 28, 1768, in *Works of John Wesley*, ed. Frank Baker (Nashville: Abingdon, 1984), 29:364.
27. John Wesley, "A Dialogue between an Antinomian and His Friend," *Works*, 19:267.
28. John Wesley, "The Case of Reason Impartially Considered," *Works*, 2:592.
29. John Wesley, "The Case of Reason Impartially Considered," *Works*, 2:593.
30. John Wesley, "The Case of Reason Impartially Considered," *Works*, 2:596.

improved, cannot produce the love of God."[31] And since reason "cannot give either faith, hope, love, or virtue, so it cannot give happiness, since separate from these there can be no happiness for any intelligent creature."[32]

Experience and the Norms of the Moral Life: This is important to Wesley, and as we said at the beginning of this paper, it's important to women and men around the world today. The *Works of John Wesley* (so far as I know) are not translated into Nepalese. They certainly were neither readily available nor widely read among the Christians whom I visited in Nepal. But many had read the *Westminster Catechism*. And many asked, in one form or another, that first famous question with which the Catechism begins: "What is the chief end of humanity?"

Within his sermon "The Unity of the Divine Being," Wesley answers, saying:

> The answer is, "To glorify and enjoy [God] for ever." This is undoubtedly true; but is it quite clear, especially to men of ordinary capacities? Do the generality of common people understand that expression, "to glorify God"? No, no more than they understand Greek. And it is altogether above the capacity of children, to whom we can scarce ever speak plain enough. Now is not this the very principle that should be inculcated upon every human creature, "You are made to be happy in God," as soon as ever reason dawns? ... In this plain and familiar way a wise parent might many times in a day say something of God; particularly, insisting, "He made you; and he made you to be happy in him; and nothing else can make you happy." We cannot press this too soon. If you say, "Nay, but they cannot understand you when they are so young;" I answer, No, nor when they are fifty years old, unless God opens their understanding. And can he not do this at any age?[33]

Wesley insisted that just "as there is but one God, so there is but one happiness, and one religion,"[34] which is summed up in the Great Commandment, love of God and love of neighbor. "It is, in two words, gratitude and benevolence: gratitude to our Creator and supreme

---

31. John Wesley, "The Case of Reason Impartially Considered," *Works*, 2:598.
32. John Wesley, "The Case of Reason Impartially Considered," *Works*, 2:598.
33. John Wesley, "The Unity of the Divine Being," *Works*, 4:64.
34. John Wesley, "The Unity of the Divine Being," *Works*, 4:70.

Benefactor, and benevolence to our fellow-creatures. In other words, it is the loving God with all our heart, and our neighbor as ourselves."[35]

Rebekah Miles, in her excellent chapter within the *Cambridge Companion to John Wesley* entitled "Happiness, Holiness, and the Moral Life in John Wesley,"[36] explains that such active goodwill to others, especially to others not like us, is born from gratitude to God and is the "wellspring of the moral life and of human happiness."[37] As Wesley preached, "The love of Christ constrains us, not only to be harmless, to do no ill to our neighbour, but to be useful, to be 'zealous of good works', 'as we have time to do good unto all men', and be patterns to all of true, genuine morality, of justice, mercy, and truth. This is religion, and this is happiness, the happiness for which we were made."[38]

The Norming Ideal of Wesley's Three Rules

What, then, does this mean? How should we measure our experiences in the light of tradition and reason, all interpreted through the lens of Scripture? How do we focus on living a moral life? How do we ensure that our experiences, our actions, align with God's good and perfect will?

For Wesley, life cannot be separated into "sacred" parts and "secular" parts. The moral life cannot be separated out from the rest of life. Any belief system, any personal piety which is not focused on an

---

35. John Wesley, "The Unity of the Divine Being," *Works*, 4:66–67.
36. Rebekah L. Miles, "Happiness, Holiness, and the Moral Life in John Wesley," 207–24 in *The Cambridge Companion to John Wesley*, ed. Randy L. Maddox and Jason E. Vickers (New York: Cambridge University Press, 2010). Much of the work in this section under "Experience and the Norms of the Moral Life" is heavily indebted to Miles's work.
37. Miles, "Happiness, Holiness, and the Moral Life in John Wesley," 207.
38. John Wesley, "The Unity of the Divine Being," 67. For various perspectives on Wesley's teleological understanding of humanity, see H. Ray Dunning, *Reflecting the Divine Image: Christian Ethics in Wesleyan Perspective* (Eugene, OR: Wipf & Stock, 2003); Albert C. Outler, *Evangelism and Theology in the Wesleyan Spirit* (Nashville: Discipleship Resources, 2003); Ron Stone, *John Wesley's Life and Ethics* (Nashville: Abingdon, 2001); and D. Stephen Long, *John Wesley's Moral Theology: The Quest for God and Goodness* (Nashville: Kingswood, 2005).

active love of both God and neighbor is, in Wesley's mind, a false and failing religion. Loving one's neighbor is not just an important part of the rule of faith. In conjunction with loving God, it is the very heart thereof.

We genuinely begin to live the way Christ Jesus calls us to live, Wesley preached, when

> we begin to know God, by the teaching of his own Spirit. As soon as the Father of spirits reveals his Son in our hearts, and the Son reveals his Father, the love of God is shed abroad in our hearts; then, and not till then, we are happy. We are happy, first, in the consciousness of his favour, which indeed is better than life itself; next, in the constant communion with the Father, and with his Son, Jesus Christ; then in all the heavenly tempers which he hath wrought in us by his Spirit; again, in the testimony of his Spirit that all our works please him; and, lastly, in the testimony of our own spirit that "in simplicity and godly sincerity we have had our conversation in the world." Standing fast in this liberty from sin and sorrow, wherewith Christ hath made them free, real Christians "rejoice evermore, pray without ceasing, and in everything give thanks." And their happiness still increases as they "grow up into the measure of the stature of the fullness of Christ."[39]

The happiness and holiness expected as fruit in a Christian's life, including moral holiness of heart and life, are only possible as the follower of Jesus is engaged and transformed by divine love into the divine image.

To help nurture some growth in holiness and love, Wesley encouraged persons to join together with others in small groups within the Methodist societies. Within *The Nature, Design, and General Rules of the United Societies*, he described such gatherings as a company of persons "'having the form, and seeking the power of godliness', united in order to pray together, to receive the word of exhortation, and to watch over one another in love, that they may help each other to work out their salvation."[40]

---

39. John Wesley, "The Unity of the Divine Being," *Works*, 4:67.
40. John Wesley, "The Nature, Design, and General Rules of the United Societies in London, Bristol, Kingswood, and Newcastle upon Tyne," *Works*, 9:69.

And the bar for joining such Methodist societies was set fairly low, too. The initial requirement for membership was simply "a desire to flee from the wrath to come, to be saved from their sins."[41] But as one would expect from a man as methodical as Wesley, there were expectations for continuing to participate in and benefit from these groups. Continued evidence of a "desire of salvation" should be seen in and through the daily practices of each person.

To help people understand and develop these norms of the moral life, Wesley formulated a specific set of guidelines, dividing his General Rules around three guiding principles: (1) doing no harm, (2) doing good, and (3) attending upon all the ordinances of God. But he was equally careful to instruct his followers that simple adherence to the practice of the General Rules was not the essence or the dynamic of the holy life. Strict adherence to religious practices without fellowship with the Triune God would become nothing more than the religion of the world. And the religion of the world, Wesley said,

> implies three things: first, the doing of no harm, the abstaining from outward sin, at least from such as is scandalous, as robbery, theft, common swearing, drunkenness; secondly, the doing good, the relieving the poor, the being charitable, as it is called; thirdly, the using the means of grace, at least the going to church and to the Lord's Supper. He in whom these three marks are found is termed by the world a religious man. But will this satisfy him who hungers after God? No. It is not food for his soul. He wants a religion of a nobler kind, a religion higher and deeper than this. He can no more feed on this poor, shallow, formal thing, than he can "fill his belly with the east wind." True, he is careful to abstain from the very appearance of evil. He is zealous of good works. He attends all the ordinances of God. But all this is not what he longs for. This is only the outside of that religion which he insatiably hungers after. The knowledge of God in Christ Jesus; "the life that is hid with Christ in God"; the being "joined unto the Lord in one Spirit"; the having "fellowship with the Father and the Son"; the "walking in the light as God is in the light"; the being "purified even as he is pure", this is the religion, the righteousness he thirsts after. Nor can he rest till he thus rests in God.[42]

41. John Wesley, "General Rules," *Works*, 9:70.
42. John Wesley, "Sermon on the Mount, II," *Works*, 1:496–97.

The General Rules, then, were not commended by Wesley simply as a way to identify early Methodists as distinct and separate from other persons. They also were not intended to be a simple strategy for mere moral improvement. They were to be seen as normative behaviors of persons who had encountered and continued to be in fellowship with God the Father, God the Son, and God the Holy Spirit.

Doing No Harm: Under the first heading of the General Rules, Methodists are to demonstrate their desire for salvation and transformation into the likeness of Christ by "avoiding evil in every kind, especially that which is most generally practiced."[43] "Evil in every kind" is obviously a very broad descriptor and is open to all sorts of interpretations, but Wesley did offer some specific things to avoid. Such things included doing work on the Lord's day, drunkenness, fighting, uncharitable conversation (especially speaking evil of ministers or those in authority), doing to others as we would not want them to do to us, doing what we know is not for the glory of God, and singing songs or reading books that do not "tend to the knowledge or love of God."[44] They were to avoid the "putting on of gold or costly apparel," in part because it might lead the wearer toward pride of appearance and, more significantly, it was poor stewardship and lack of Christian charity to spend money for luxuries that might have been spent providing necessities for the poor.

Such advice regarding apparel continued within Free Methodism well into the twentieth century, and unfortunately (as is often the case), what started as a good regulation for the benefit of the Body became a measuring stick by which the self-assured sanctified could judge who was holy and who was not. As recently as 1960 Free Methodist pastors were enjoined "on the rules concerning dress. This is no time to give encouragement to superfluity of apparel. Therefore, receive none into the church until they have left off superfluous ornaments. In order to do this: 1. In visiting the classes be very mild but very strict. 2. Allow no exempt case; better one suffer than many."[45] This

---

43. John Wesley, "General Rules," *Works*, 9:70.
44. John Wesley, "General Rules," *Works*, 9:71.
45. *Free Methodist Book of Discipline*, 1960 (Winona Lake, IN: Free Methodist Publishing House, 1961), Paragraph 82.

was actually a softening of the original regulations, which included the counsel that "every one who has charge of society shall read Mr. Wesley's sermon on dress at least once a year in every society."[46]

Doing Good: Under the second heading, Methodists were encouraged to do good, "by being in every kind merciful after their power, as they have opportunity doing good of every possible sort and as far as is possible" to all people.[47] Like the first, this rule is extremely broad and could include limitless numbers of things, but, again like the first, Wesley once more offered specifics. Methodists were instructed to give food to the hungry and clothe the naked, to visit those who are sick and in prison. They were encouraged to instruct, reprove, and exhort others, and to do good to others, especially others within the "household of faith."[48]

Once again, Wesley is clear to avoid any suggestion that the holy life is defined solely in terms of staying pure. For Wesley, true holiness is revealed as much in what one does as in what one avoids. Holiness should be part and parcel of one's whole life, and in all of one's relationships. And so whereas he appreciated the benefit of select times of spiritual retreat and withdrawal from society, he placed loving engagement with others, especially at the point of their need, at the center of his depiction of the Methodist ideal.[49]

Attending upon the Ordinances: The third way in which Wesley counseled Methodists to show evidence of their desire for salvation was "by attending upon all the ordinances of God."[50] In his sermon "The Means of Grace" Wesley defined ordinances as the "means ordained of God as the usual channels of his grace."[51] He went on to highlight prayer, study of Scripture, and the Lord's Supper as among these ordained means. Within the General Rules he expanded the list

---

46. *Free Methodist Book of Discipline*, 1931 (Winona Lake, IN: Free Methodist Publishing House, 1931), Paragraph 71.
47. John Wesley, "General Rules," *Works*, 9:72.
48. John Wesley, "General Rules," *Works*, 9:72.
49. We find this particularly within John Wesley, "The Character of a Methodist," *Works*, 9:30–46 and John Wesley, "Sermon on the Mount, IV," *Works*, 1:531–49.
50. John Wesley, "General Rules," *Works*, 9:73.
51. John Wesley, "The Means of Grace," *Works*, 1:378.

even further, including public worship of God, the ministry of the Word, the Supper of the Lord, family and private prayer, searching the Scriptures, and fasting.[52]

The Norm of Wesleyan Social Ethics For Ecumenical Dialogue

It is important to recognize that, although the General Rules did not make up the whole or the heart of religion, they were considered essential among early Methodists. They were not just friendly advice for the optional consideration of members. They were clear requirements for membership and continuation in the Methodist societies. The last paragraph of the General Rules is very clear about the consequences of serious, ongoing infractions: "If there be any among us who observe them not, who habitually break any of them, let it be made known unto them who watch over that soul, as they who must give account. We will admonish him of the error of his ways. We will bear with him for a season. But if then he repent not, he hath no more place among us."[53]

This was not an empty threat. Members of early Methodist societies were often expelled, sometimes many of them at once. And the causes of such expulsion could be as diverse as Sabbath-breaking, quarrelling, or carelessness. This may seem harsh, and indeed, might perhaps be so but for some mitigating factors. To begin with, nearly all of the members of the earliest Methodist societies were baptized members of another church, most typically an Anglican communion. Those expelled from Methodist societies could still attend worship and receive Holy Communion with the Anglicans. Additionally, expulsion from a society did not mean permanent estrangement or excommunication. Persons were regularly given opportunities to return. The early Methodists even set up special groups known as penitential bands for people who had fallen away and now desired to return to the society.

---

52. John Wesley, "General Rules," *Works*, 9:73.
53. John Wesley, "General Rules," *Works*, 9:73.

The practice of expelling members from the society must ultimately be seen in light of the perceived consequences. The General Rules were valued not as rules for rules' sake, but as rules for the sake of a greater goal. The rule of faith existed to nurture holiness in oneself and in others. The dialogue among Scripture, tradition, reason, and experience was foundational to helping persons achieve such holiness.

Part and parcel of any ecumenical dialogue is the consideration of how each tradition is different from the next. With regards to the norms of the moral life, I'd suggest that we differ because we have different perspectives on the "analogy of faith." We have slightly different orientations when it comes to how we interpret Scripture, tradition, reason, and experience. For Methodists, the orientation at some level is always soteriological.

And as we continue to dialogue ecumenically, we continue to interpret and be interpreted by the Quadrilateral. Perhaps more accurately, the interrelationship of these components is "quadrilogical," in that they are all in conversation with each other. Tradition, reason, and experience help us understand and explain Scripture. And yet at the same time we humble ourselves and are obedient to Scripture's critique of tradition, reason, and experience, for I doubt any of us would presume to have heard all that Scripture, the normative source of God's self-revelation, is saying to us.

1.5. Preliminary Sketch of a Method for Reformed Ethics

Dr. Dennis W. Jowers

This essay constitutes an explanation and defense of one method that Reformed Christians employ to resolve questions about what Christians should do when ethical circumstances render their obligations ambiguous. The essay consists, specifically, in three main sections: one that explains the method, a second that clears it of certain misapprehensions, and a third that presents its theological rationale. The method, admittedly, does not command the assent of every Reformed believer in every detail. Its faithfulness to the teaching of Scripture and the great confessional documents of the Reformed tradition, its consonance with views consistently expressed by Reformed ethicists of all stripes, and its affinity with the ethical practice of most Reformed Christians, nonetheless, render it sufficiently representative of the Reformed tradition to serve as a basis for dialogue with other traditions about ethics.

The Method Itself

In order to resolve a specific question about what one should do when one's obligations are in doubt, one should take at least the following five steps. First, one ought carefully to consider individual passages of Scripture that appear to be relevant to the question at hand, availing oneself of whatever uninspired aids to interpretation one deems necessary or useful. Second, one should measure one's interpretation of these texts against the analogy of faith: sc., the teaching of Scripture as a whole. In prosecuting this task, it is frequently useful to consult systematic expositions of this teaching such as one finds in the *Gallican Confession*, the *Westminster Confession* and *Catechisms*, and the *Three Forms of Unity* or, on a grander scale, Calvin's *Institutes* or Amandus Polanus's *Syntagma theologiae Christianae*. Having refined one's interpretation of the individual texts of Scripture with which one begins and supplemented one's interpretation with additional insights derived from the analogy of faith, one ought, third, to elicit from one's findings general imperatives relevant to the issue under discussion. If, upon reflection, the evidence one has gathered appears insufficient to warrant such general imperatives, one should repeat the first three steps, this time taking into consideration a broader array of scriptural texts and plumbing the analogy of faith more deeply.

Once one has obtained relevant, well-grounded imperatives, then, one should, fourth, consider extra-scriptural information that might modify the appropriate application of these general imperatives to the matter in dispute. Especially significant in this regard are the consequences for stakeholders that might ensue upon the various courses of action one might choose. Fifth and finally, one ought to determine what, if any, action the general imperatives derived in the third step imply that the party or parties concerned should take. If one finds the evidence one possesses inadequate to justify a firm conclusion about this, one should repeat the fourth step and, if this yields no fruit, the entire process until one reaches a clear verdict.

The Theological Rationale for Our Method

The method of resolving moral quandaries outlined above is relatively simple; establishing its suitability for this task appears correspondingly straightforward. If one assumes conventional evangelical beliefs about biblical inspiration and hermeneutics, it seems, one can demonstrate the method's adequacy on the strength of two premises: viz., that God requires all human beings to obey his law and that this law consists in the commandments at least implicitly revealed in Scripture.

I. TWO MISAPPREHENSIONS

Before offering our theological rationale for this method, we should like to counter two misapprehensions of our position, which, if left unaddressed, might prevent readers from according the method proposed here the serious consideration it deserves.

a. Presumption? First, it might appear presumptuous for anyone to suppose that Scripture could supply comprehensive guidance about ethics. In order to see why this objection is mistaken, one must realize that those who follow and advocate the method of resolving ethical quandaries proposed here do not claim that it enables one to calculate one's duty precisely in every instance. In some circumstances persons cannot deduce their obligations from Scripture (or, one might add, from the natural law) and must determine their duty by applying a suprarational moral sense. One can increase the likelihood of this moral sense's accurately discerning one's duty by reading and meditating on Scripture, cultivating the virtues commended therein, and praying for divine assistance. Scripture does not promise to eliminate ambiguity from Christians' moral lives.

What Scripture promises its readers and hearers, instead, is knowledge sufficient for salvation: "the holy Scriptures, which are able to make you wise unto salvation" (2 Tim 3:15; cf. Rom 10:17; Jas 1:21; 1 Pet 1:23).[1] Since God saves human beings not only from sin's punishment, but also from sin itself, this promise implicitly guarantees wide-ranging ethical guidance. In other words, if "the unrighteous will not inherit the kingdom of God" (1 Cor 6:9); if "faith without works is dead" (Jas 2:26); and if only those whose righteousness exceeds that of the scribes and Pharisees will enter the kingdom of heaven (Matt 5:20), justification requires a high standard of moral conduct, at least as its consequent condition. This high standard of conduct is not, of course, an antecedent condition, i.e., a prerequisite, of justification. It is rather justification's consequent condition: sc., its inevitable concomitant.

The wisdom unto salvation supplied by Scripture, therefore, must include ethical guidance sufficient for the attainment of that high

---

1. All translations of the Bible in this essay are those of the author.

standard: "the holiness without which no one will see the Lord" (Heb 12:14). In fact, inasmuch as: (a) "by God's power all things necessary for life and godliness have been given to us through the knowledge of him who calls us to his own glory and virtue" (2 Pet 1:3); and (b) most of the saints, being incapable of serious philosophical reflection, must necessarily receive ethical guidance primarily from Scripture, whether immediately from Scripture's pages or mediately through the Church's instruction; Scripture must, it seems, supply virtually all of the information one requires to keep God's law perfectly.

The commands to love God with all of one's heart, soul, and mind and one's neighbor as oneself, after all, seem implicitly to contain all other divine commandments within themselves. "On these two commandments," says Jesus, "depend all the Law and the Prophets" (Matt 22:40). Since "this is the love of God, that we keep his commandments" (1 John 5:3; cf. 2 John 6), moreover, the first of the two great commandments implicitly contains the second. If the commandments referred to in 1 John 5:3 consist in the imperatives laid down in Scripture, then, Scripture must at least implicitly state all of the obligations one must fulfill in order to render God perfect obedience. It is reasonable, therefore, to expect Scripture to provide readers who persevere in studying Scripture as a whole in a reverent, thoughtful, and prayerful manner whatever ethical guidance is indispensable to the attainment of that "holiness without which no one will see the Lord" (Heb 12:14). That is the ethical guidance that Reformed Christians expect from the Bible: that and nothing more.

b. Voluntarism? Second, the method of resolving moral dilemmas sketched above neither presupposes nor implies a voluntaristic theory of morality that attributes the moral law to God's arbitrary fiat. It is true that the method's practitioners seek to derive rules from a text and, initially at least, do not take more general theories of the intrinsically good or just into account. This is not, however, because they hold with Euthyphro that just conduct is just simply because it is "dear to the gods" and, therefore, disdain philosophical reasoning about ethical matters. Reformed thinkers' privileging of exegesis over philosophical reflection, rather, springs from two concerns.

First, although Reformed theologians differ considerably in their opinions as to the measure in which the Fall weakened human beings' powers of reason, they all agree that the foolish heart of postlapsarian human beings has been darkened (Rom 1:21) and that God has given the human race over to a depraved mind (Rom 1:28). The Reformed, therefore, typically hold with Pius XII (*Humani generis*, §3), the fathers of Vatican II (*Dei verbum*, §6), and the authors of the *Catechism of the Catholic Church* (§38) that "divine revelation must be considered morally necessary so that [even] those religious and moral truths which are not of their nature beyond the reach of reason in the present condition of the human race, may be known by all people."[2] This insight, when transposed into a Reformed horizon of understanding, amounts to the claim that, although recourse to the Bible may be unnecessary in some instances for the resolution of a moral quandary, human beings in their present debilitated condition should seek ethical guidance first and primarily from Scripture.

Second, all theologians loyal to Scripture recognize that human beings' obligations to God extend well beyond what anyone, before or after the Fall, could conceivably deduce from reflection on God's creation. It is true, admittedly, that God's "invisible attributes, his eternal power and deity, since the creation of the world have been clearly seen, being understood through the things he made" (Rom 1:20). Even before the Fall, however, God required Adam and Eve to obey more than the natural law. God, in particular, required Adam and Eve to obey a positive command of incalculably great importance: "Of every tree of the garden, you may eat; but of the tree of the knowledge of good and evil you may not eat, for on the day in which you eat of it, you will surely die" (Gen 2:16–17). Subsequent to the Fall, God commanded human beings to obey numerous positive commands: commands, that is to say, that, although consistent with the natural law's dictates, require human beings to perform acts that the natural law does not prescribe. God commanded Noah, for example, to build

---

2. The quote here is from Pius XII, *Humani generis* (August 12, 1950) (New York: Paulist, 1950), §3. For *Dei verbum* see Second Vatican Council (November 18, 1965), *Word of God: Dei Verbum* (New York: Ignatius, 2004), §6, and for the *Catechism of the Catholic Church*, 2nd ed. (Washington, DC: United States Council of Catholic Bishops, 2019), no. 38.

the ark (Gen 6:14–16), Abraham to circumcise his male progeny (Gen 17:10–14), Moses to return to Egypt and deliver his people (Exod 3:7–10), Amos to prophesy in Samaria (Amos 7:14–15), Matthew to follow Jesus (Matt 9:9 par), and Paul to evangelize the Gentiles (Acts 22:21; Gal 2:7). God commanded his people formerly to observe the Mosaic Law's ceremonial ordinances (Deut 12:32). God commands his people now to believe in the Lord Jesus Christ unto salvation (Mark 1:15; John 6:29; 10:38; 12:36; 14:1, 11; 1 John 3:23), to feed on the "wordy milk" of Scripture (1 Pet 2:2), to enter the Church through baptism (Acts 2:38; 10:48; 22:16), and to proclaim their Savior's death until he comes by partaking of the Eucharist (1 Cor 11:25–26).

In certain cases, it seems, one can scarcely do justice to the gravity of divinely imposed obligations that transcend the natural law by categorizing them as positive commands. For the category of positive law encompasses all manner of arbitrary, trivial regulations. One does not believe in the Lord Jesus Christ, undergo baptism, partake of the Eucharist, and study Scripture assiduously, however, merely because one believes that God has instructed one so to do. One performs such tasks also and primarily because, in the economy of salvation that God has instituted, each of these acts is an existential necessity. He who performs these tasks by the Spirit's empowerment reaps righteousness, peace, and joy in the Holy Spirit (Rom 14:17), and he who omits them, insofar as he omits them, starves his soul of the one thing needful (Luke 10:42) and calls into question his own salvation.

Insofar, then, as one learns of certain obligations, whose fulfillment is indispensable to the attainment of salvation, through Scripture rather than nature, any serious inquirer into human beings' duties must devote sustained attention to Scripture. If and insofar as one can derive at least a rudimentary knowledge of human beings' obligations under the natural law by studying Scripture, furthermore, it seems only reasonable to pursue insight into human beings' obligations first and primarily through the study of Scripture.

This conclusion does not imply that philosophical reflection on the natural law is dispensable to a thorough understanding of the moral life. It would be foolhardy, in any event, not to avail oneself of the full range of insights available from special and general revelation.

Nor does our conclusion that one should seek ethical guidance first and primarily from Scripture entail a voluntaristic theory of morality that reduces the moral law to a product of divine caprice.

c. Conclusion. In sum, the method of ethical inquiry defended here does not presuppose a voluntaristic conception of morality, according to which God might render, say, blasphemy or rape, cardinal virtues.[3] The moral law does not derive from God's whim; rather, by virtue of divine simplicity, the moral law is identical with his being and, correspondingly, necessary and immutable. Reformed thinkers do not claim, moreover, that the procedure for resolving moral quandaries proposed here or others like it eliminate the occasional necessity of making decisions of deep moral import on grounds other than cold calculation. No method of rational decision-making can unburden the human race of moral uncertainty.

2. GOD REQUIRES OBEDIENCE TO HIS LAW

That God requires all human beings to obey his law appears from three considerations. First, Scripture declares obedience to God's commandments indispensable to authentic love for God. "If you love me," Jesus says, "you will keep my commandments" (John 14:15). Likewise, he asserts, "Whoever has my commandments and keeps them, he it is who loves me" (John 14:21); and, "If anyone loves me, he will keep my word" (John 14:23). Jesus' love commandments themselves (Matt 22:36–40; Mark 12:28–31; Luke 10:25–8; cf. Jas 2:8) constitute law: indeed, Old Testament law (Deut 6:5 and Lev 17:18). We have already seen, moreover, that John identifies the love of God with obedience to God's commandments (1 John 5:3; 2 John 6). It seems clear, accordingly, that Scripture declares obedience to God's law mandatory for all human beings.

Second, the apostle Paul, his strenuous advocacy of justification by faith alone notwithstanding, unmistakably affirms that human beings ought to observe God's law. In 1 Corinthians 9:21, for example, he declares himself "not . . . outside the law of God, but under the law

---

3. For a refutation of accusations that Calvin grounded morality in God's arbitrary fiat, cf. Paul Helm, *John Calvin's Ideas* (Oxford: Oxford University Press, 2004), 347–60.

of Christ." In Romans 7:25, he states, "I myself serve the law of God with my mind." It is "the mind of the flesh," Paul avers in Romans 8:7, that "does not submit to the law of God": not the mind of the Spirit, which God graciously bestows on his children. Paul cites the Old Testament law repeatedly as an authority on ethical questions (1 Cor 9:8–10; 14:34; 1 Tim 5:17–18) and even tells Christians to love their neighbors, because this love fulfills the law (Rom 13:8–10; Gal 5:13–14). Instead of annulling the law by preaching grace, Paul believes that he confirms the law. "Do we then overthrow the law by this faith?" he asks in Romans 3:31. "By no means! On the contrary, we uphold the law." Paul, accordingly, is no antinomian; he too directs human beings to "fulfill the law of Christ" (Gal 6:2).[4]

Third, God's law must continue to bind human consciences, because otherwise human beings could not continue to sin. For, as Paul observes, "sin is not imputed where there is no law" (Rom 5:13). "Where there is no law," he writes, "there is no transgression" (Rom 4:15). Sin, indeed, is inconceivable without law. "Everyone who commits sin is guilty of lawlessness; sin is lawlessness" (1 John 3:4). Evidently, moreover, Christians continue to sin. "If we say we have no sin, we deceive ourselves, and the truth is not in us" (1 John 1:8). Christians, therefore, remain duty-bound to obey God's law.

3. ALL ARE BOUND TO OBEY THE DICTATES OF SCRIPTURE IN ITS ENTIRETY

That God mandates obedience to precisely that law articulated by Scripture as a whole appears from Jesus' Great Commission: "Go therefore and make disciples of all nations, baptizing them in the name of the Father and of the Son and of the Holy Spirit, teaching them to observe all that I have commanded you" (Matt 28:19–20a). This remark alone, owing to Jesus' deity and the consequent inerrancy and authority of his words, suffices to establish that Jesus'

---

4. We are aware, naturally, of passages such as Rom 7:1–6; 10:4; Gal 3:10–13, 19–25; 4:3–5; and Eph 2:11–15 that might seem to suggest otherwise. For discussions of each of these texts by an orthodox Reformed exegete, cf. Patrick Fairbairn's *The Revelation of Law in Scripture* (Edinburgh: T&T Clark, 1869), 247–51, 391–403, 425–33, 442–46, and 453–62.

teachings constitute a binding rule for human beings. Christ's statement, moreover, constitutes an implicit endorsement of the entire Old Testament's authority as an ethical norm. For he declares in Matthew 5:17-19:

> Do not suppose that I have come to abolish the Law or the Prophets; I did not come to abolish, but to fulfill. For, amen I say to you, until heaven and earth pass away, not one iota or one serif will pass from the Law until all things are accomplished. Whoever then annuls one of the least of these commandments and teaches men to do thus, will be called least in the kingdom of the heavens; but whoever does and teaches them, that one will be called great in the kingdom of the heavens.

This statement and especially Christ's pronouncement as to who will be least and great in the kingdom of heaven show that he expects the Old Testament law to retain its authority *mutatis mutandis* permanently.

The fate of the ceremonial law. This is not to say, naturally, that new covenant saints should imitate their fathers in the faith who lived before Christ's resurrection and ascension by adhering to the ritual provisions of the Mosaic Law. For, first, Scripture not only allows Christians to refrain from observing the Mosaic Law in its ceremonial aspects; it positively commands them to refrain from so doing.

The ceremonial law's precepts cannot be obligatory for the saints of today, because Scripture explicitly teaches otherwise. In the council of Acts 15, for example, Peter rebukes those who insist that Gentile believers must undergo circumcision and fulfill the Mosaic Law's provisions thus (Acts 15:10): "Why do you tempt God by placing a yoke on the neck of the disciples, which neither our fathers nor we have been able to bear?" Paul specifically forbids the Christians of Colossae from observing the ceremonial law, moreover, in Colossians 3:16-17: "Let no one judge you in a matter of food, or drink, or a feast, or a new moon, or Sabbaths. These are shadows of things coming, but the body is Christ's." In Galatians 4:8-11, in fact, Paul explains that by observing the Mosaic Law's ceremonial provisions, the Gentile Christians of Galatia are, in effect, reverting to paganism.

> Then [i.e., before their conversion] you were slaves to beings who were not by nature gods. But now that you know God, or rather are known by God, how can you turn again to the weak and beggarly elements, which you again desire to serve as slaves? You are observing days and months and seasons and years; I fear lest I have perhaps labored for you in vain.

In their misguided zeal to obey the God of Moses, it seems, the straying Galatians turned from Moses' God to the elemental powers that had previously enslaved them and now were enslaving them again by donning the guise of Moses (cf. 2 Cor 11:14).

The abrogation of the ceremonial law as a rule of conduct for God's people followed necessarily, moreover, from the replacement of the Aaronic priesthood, whose offerings foreshadowed the one, effectual sacrifice of Christ, with the sole priesthood of Christ, who intercedes for the saints at his Father's right hand. "When the priesthood is changed," observes the author of Hebrews, "there is of necessity a change of the law" (Heb 7:12). This change of the law, nonetheless, constitutes not a repudiation of the Old Testament's laws, but an inevitable concomitant of God's fulfillment of promises he made to his people: promises for the sake of whose fulfillment God instituted the laws originally. The same Old Testament that contains the Mosaic Law's regulations, that is to say, also at least implicitly promises that a divine-human Redeemer will perform the acts of atonement and cleansing that the Mosaic Law's ceremonies merely foreshadow and thereby render all of the Old Testament's strictly ceremonial observances obsolete.

The promise that David's Lord would become a priest after the order of Melchizedek (Ps 110:4), in particular, constitutes a guarantee that a new kind of priest would one day supersede the exclusively Aaronic priesthood. By predicting that God would one day take of the Gentiles priests and Levites (Isa 66:21), Isaiah also foretells the exclusively Aaronic priesthood's demise. The very repetition of the animal sacrifices that the Aaronic priests offered, furthermore, indicates that they were ineffectual and hence provisional. "The law," explains the author of Hebrews:

having a shadow of the good things to come and not the very image of them, can never with the same annual sacrifices that they offer in perpetuity perfect those who come to them. Otherwise, would they not have ceased to be offered, because the worshippers, having once been cleansed, would no longer have had any consciousness of sin? But in these there is remembrance of sins annually; for the blood of bulls and goats cannot take away sins (Heb 10:1–4).

Admittedly, the author of Hebrews here speaks only of the high priest's offering on the Day of Atonement. That the author deems no animal sacrifices capable of cleansing from sins, however, appears from his remarks in Hebrews 10:11: "Every priest stands daily ministering and offering frequently the same sacrifices, which can never take away sins." The animal sacrifices prescribed in the Pentateuch, therefore, never served to expiate anyone's sins. The evidence on the basis of which Hebrews' author reached this conclusion, i.e., the unending, mandatory repetition of the sacrifices and perhaps also general revelation, was available to Scripture's readers long before Christ's Incarnation. One may thus reasonably consider the animal sacrifices' impotence for the purpose of satisfying God's justice implicitly revealed in the Old Testament and perhaps also general revelation, jointly considered.

Anyone aware of the sacrifices' impotence to secure the remission of sins, moreover, could reasonably have inferred that in the wake of whatever sacrifice God would use to appease his wrath against his people, the practice of animal sacrifice would become obsolete. "Where remission of these is, there is no longer (οὐκέτι) offering for sin" (Heb 10:18). For, being impotent to propitiate God's wrath against his people's sins, the animal sacrifices prescribed in the Pentateuch could have served at best to prefigure the effectual sacrifice to come. Of this sacrifice, whose priest and victim would be God's suffering servant, God informed his people through the prophet Isaiah:

> Who has believed our report?
>
> And the arm of Yahweh, to whom has it been revealed?
> For he arose like a shoot before him

and like a root out of dry ground;
he had no form or majesty that we should look upon him,
and no beauty that we should take pleasure in him.
He was despised and abandoned by men,
a man of pains and acquainted with illness;
and as if men had hidden their faces from him,
he was despised, and not esteemed.

Nevertheless, he has borne our illnesses
and carried our pains
although we esteemed him stricken,
beaten by God, and humiliated.

Yet he was pierced for our crimes;
he was crushed for our misdeeds;
The chastisement of our peace was upon him,
and by his wounds we are healed.
All we like sheep have gone astray;
we have turned—each of us—to his own way;
and Yahweh has laid on him
the iniquity of us all (Isa 53:1–6).

The Old Testament, considered apart from the New, thus at least implicitly teaches (a) that the animal sacrifices prescribed in the Pentateuch could not possibly have satisfied God's righteous wrath against his people; and (b) that these sacrifices, therefore, must have served merely to foreshadow the one effectual sacrifice whereby God would reconcile his people to himself. This second consideration implies, furthermore, that after the accomplishment of the prophesied effectual sacrifice, the animal sacrifices offered to foreshadow that sacrifice would become not only superfluous, but counterproductive. For continuing to offer God the corpses of beasts after Christ's offering of the one, effectual sacrifice would be tantamount to denying that this sacrifice had occurred. The faith that God would supply a suffering servant, whose sacrifice would propitiate God's wrath against his people, the very faith that previously warranted the offering of animal sacrifices, thus now requires God's people to cease offering animal sacrifices lest they imply by their deeds that the suffering servant has not yet come.

At this juncture, a sympathetic critic might grant that the Old Testament implies that the sacrifices it mandates would eventually become obsolete and even sacrilegious on account of the accomplishment of the effectual sacrifice that they foreshadowed. That sacrifice, a sympathetic critic might concede, abundantly suffices to warrant the abandonment of the animal sacrifices, whose offering supplied the *raison d'être* of the Aaronic priesthood, and hence the quashing of the Aaronic priesthood itself. The arguments adduced thus far, the critic might contend however, hardly justify discarding the manifold regulations in the Mosaic Law that relate tangentially if at all to the superannuated animal sacrifices. The Old Testament, the critic might charge, does not so much as hint that the dietary laws, the mandate to circumcise, and the fasts and feasts instituted by Moses will ever become obsolete.

In order to see that, quite to the contrary, the Old Testament does lead one to expect a new order to supersede the Mosaic covenant with its numerous ritual ordinances, one need merely take three considerations into account. First, the ceremonial law's most burdensome provisions relate directly or indirectly to the offering of animal sacrifices by Aaronic priests. Specifically, each of the biblical feasts, with the sole exception of Purim, derives much of its significance from the sacrifices appointed to be offered in connection with it.[5] One who contracted impurity by touching a dead body, or a human being's bone, or a grave, or even by entering a tent in which a dead body lay, required for his cleansing, among other things, to be sprinkled with water that contained ashes from the burnt offering of the red heifer (Num 19:14–20). A woman who bore a child of either sex, likewise, required for her cleansing, among other things, to present to a priest before the Tabernacle's entrance a lamb[6] for a burnt offering and a pigeon or turtledove for a sin offering (Lev 12:6–7). In order to regain the ritual purity she lost when she menstruated, a woman

---

5. Cf. the accounts of the sacrifices to be offered on these occasions in Lev 23:4–43 and Num 28:16–29:39.

6. The law permitted a woman who could not afford a lamb to offer as a burnt offering to offer instead either a pigeon or a turtledove in addition to the pigeon or turtledove presented for a sin offering (Lev 12:8).

needed on the eighth day after her monthly menstruation to present two pigeons or turtledoves to the priest before the Tabernacle, one for a burnt and the other for a sin offering (Lev 15:29–30). A man who suffered a discharge needed to do the same on the eighth day after his discharge's cessation in order to end his state of impurity (Lev 15:14–15). In order to regain his ritual purity, in fact, one who recovered from any of a range of skin diseases that went by the name of צָרַעַת needed to offer through a priest before the Tabernacle either two male lambs and one yearling ewe or, if he was poor, one male lamb and two pigeons or two turtledoves (Lev 14:10, 21). One cannot reasonably maintain, therefore, that the laws of ritual purity and the biblical feasts relate only tangentially to the practice of animal sacrifice.

It is true, admittedly, that Israelites could be cleansed from ritual impurity without offering animal sacrifices in certain instances. In most of these instances, however, the ritual impurity in question is only secondary impurity: impurity, that is to say, contracted by touching or being touched by something rendered unclean by a source of primary impurity: e.g., a dead body, an unnatural discharge, menstruation, childbirth, a severe skin disease, or various objects that have come into contact with persons who have contracted primary impurity. There can be no secondary impurity, consequently, in the absence of primary impurity. Most of the laws of primary impurity, as we have seen, are intricately bound up with animal sacrifices, the Aaronic priesthood, and the Tabernacle. Without these three, there is no clear way to regain purity after contracting primary impurity. Without these three, more importantly, the laws of primary impurity in question lose at least the lion's share of their religious value, which consists precisely in connecting important life events with sacrifice by means of the Aaronic priesthood before the Tabernacle. It would seem quite reasonable to expect even before the event, therefore, that when the Aaronic priesthood, its animal sacrifices, and the Tabernacle themselves perished, the laws of impurity discussed here would perish with them.

Second, the Old Testament predicts that at some unspecified point in the future, God will open his kingdom to the Gentiles. The Hebrew Bible promises, that is to say, that the Jewish people will eventually lose their virtual monopoly on the saving grace that one receives through trusting in Yahweh's promise of salvation through a Redeemer. Then, the first testament of Scripture assures us, God's promises that in Abraham (Gen 12:12; 18:18), in his seed (Gen 22:18), and in the seed of Isaac (Gen 26:4) and Jacob (Gen 28:14) all nations will be blessed, will finally come to fruition.

Throughout the Old Testament, one reads time and again variations on and elaborations of this prediction. In Habakkuk 2:14, for example, the prophet testifies that the geographical bounds of God's kingdom will become co-extensive with the earth's: "the earth will be filled with the knowledge of the glory of Yahweh as the waters cover the sea." Zephaniah, likewise, predicts that in the future God "will restore to the peoples a pure language that all of them might call on the name of Yahweh and serve him with one accord" (Zeph 3:9). At that time, writes the same prophet, foreigners "will worship him [i.e., Yahweh], each from his own place, all the isles of the Gentiles" (Zeph 2:11). Employing more extravagant imagery, God himself testifies in Malachi 1:11: "From the rising of the sun to its setting, my name will be great among the Gentiles, and in every place incense will be offered to my name and a pure offering, for my name shall be great among the Gentiles."

Isaiah, likewise, speaks of a day when "Yahweh will be known to Egypt, and the Egyptians will know Yahweh. Then they will serve him with sacrifices and offerings; they will vow vows to Yahweh and pay them" (Isa 19:21) On that day, writes Isaiah, "Israel will be third to Egypt and Asshur, a blessing in the midst of the earth, because Yahweh of hosts will bless him: 'Blessed be my people, Egypt, and the work of my hands, Asshur, and my inheritance, Israel" (Isa 19:24–5). In Zechariah 2:11, in fact, one reads that many nations will become God's people: "Many nations will join themselves to Yahweh on that day, and they will be my people." In the future, prophesies Jeremiah, many Gentiles will forsake their ancestral religions and turn instead to the God of Israel. "Yahweh, my refuge, my stronghold, and my sanctuary in the day of distress," he writes, "to you nations will come from the ends of the earth, and they will say, 'Surely, we have inherited lies from our fathers, vanity, things in which there is no profit'" (Jer 16:19).

The book of Psalms, moreover, fairly brims with testimonies to the future conversion of the Gentiles to Yahweh. In Psalm 22:7 (Masoretic Text 22:8), for instance, David asserts, "all the ends of earth will remember and turn to Yahweh." Addressing the Almighty in Psalm 86:9, David writes, "All nations that you have made will come and bow down before you, O Lord, and they will glorify your name." "The Gentiles," writes the author of Psalm 102, "will fear the name of Yahweh and all the kings of the earth your glory" (Ps 102:15; Masoretic Text 102:16).

The Old Testament's God thus plainly manifested his intention at some unspecified point in the future to incorporate Gentiles *en masse* into his kingdom. The dietary laws of the Pentateuch, however, i.e., precisely those aspects of the ceremonial law that seem most remote from the Aaronic priesthood and the sacrificial cult, seem both to presuppose and to reinforce the separation of Jews from Gentiles. As God himself explains in Leviticus 20:24-6:

> I am Yahweh your God who has separated you from the peoples. Therefore, you will separate between the clean beast and the unclean beast and between the unclean bird and the clean bird, and you shall not render yourselves detestable by beast, by bird, or by anything which creeps on the ground that I have separated from you as unclean. And you shall be holy to me, for I Yahweh am holy, and I have separated you from the peoples to be mine.

Because he, Yahweh, has separated Israel from the Gentiles, God explains, the Israelites should also separate clean from unclean beasts and birds and avoid polluting themselves by consuming that which is unclean. God instituted the dietary laws, therefore, because he separated the Jews from the Gentiles, presumably to heighten Israel's consciousness of her duty to remain separate.[7] When God's mandate that Israel separate herself from the Gentiles expired, accordingly, the principal reason for the dietary laws' institution expired with it. Circumcision also served as a means of distinguishing Jews from Gentiles. It too, therefore, seems purposeless if not outright dangerous

---

7. So reasons Jacob Milgrom (*Leviticus*, AB 3-3a [New York: Doubleday, 1991, 2000], 1:724-6 and 2:1398), for example.

if and when God merges his people of Jewish and Gentile descent into a single, multi-ethnic community. That circumcision and the dietary laws would eventually expire, then, should have been perceptible long before Christ's coming to anyone who both (a) grasped the rationale that originally warranted the institution of circumcision and the dietary laws; and (b) foresaw that God would one day engraft the Gentiles into the vine of God's people (Rom 11:17–24).

One might object to all this, admittedly, that Scripture sometimes states that Gentile servants of Yahweh will stream into Jerusalem to worship Yahweh (Isa 2:2–3; Jer 3:17; Mic 4:1–2; Zech 8:20–22), offer sacrifice (Isa 56:7), and even observe the Feast of Tabernacles (Zech 14:16–19). In order to defuse this objection, one need merely observe that when the prophets predicted that large numbers of Gentiles would come to worship Yahweh, they understandably depicted the Gentiles' worship in terms of the worship with which their audience was familiar. The employment of imagery that does not exactly correspond to that which the imagery represents is commonplace in all literature and pre-eminently in the genre of prophecy, and it is in the prophetic books that each of the texts in question appears. A few scattered texts, regardless, do not suffice to overthrow the thrust of those large chunks of Scripture that presage the supplanting of Israel's ceremonial observances by a new and more spiritual form of worship.

That the Old Testament does portend the ceremonial law's eventual obsolescence appears, third, from God's promise to replace the Mosaic covenant with a new covenant in Jeremiah 31:31–4:

> Behold, days are coming—it is an oracle of Yahweh—in which he will cut with the house of Israel and the house of Judah a new covenant. It will be not like the covenant, which I cut with their fathers on the day when I took them by their hands and brought them out of the land of Egypt, because they broke my covenant, although I married them. It is an oracle of Yahweh. For this is the covenant, which I will cut with the house of Israel after those days. It is an oracle of Yahweh. I will put my law within them, and on their hearts I will write it; I will be to them God, and they will be to me a people. And they will not teach any more, a man to his neighbor and a man to his brother, saying, "Know Yahweh"; for all of them shall know me from the least of them to the

greatest of them. It is an oracle of Yahweh. For I will forgive them, and their sins I will remember no more.

In this passage, admittedly, God supplies few details about how his people under the new covenant will worship him corporately or honor him individually in their everyday lives. Nevertheless, insofar as God will commune intimately with his new covenant children, one can reasonably surmise that elaborate ritual obligations will not figure prominently in the new covenant. God does promise, moreover, that the new covenant will not simply supplement the old, but replace it. God explains that he will make this covenant with Israel, which will not be like the old, precisely "because they broke [הֵפֵרוּ] my covenant, although I married them."

The Israelites, that is to say, nullified the old covenant; they invalidated it, rendered it inoperative. God does not superimpose one covenant atop another, therefore. He replaces the old, which the people of Israel themselves nullified, with the new; "he takes away the first that he might establish the second" (Heb 10:9). One should not presuppose, therefore, that ritual commandments remain in force if Jesus and the apostles do not explicitly abrogate them. The burden of proof, rather, falls on him who maintains that new covenant believers must abide by the commands, say, to affix tassels to the corners of their garments (Num 15:38–39; Deut 22:12) or to refrain from consuming any tree's fruit until the fourth year of the tree's existence (Lev 19:23). Since the old covenant is obsolete in its entirety, one can justify the observance of Old Testament precepts now only by showing the precepts in question to be at least virtually implicit in either: (a) the natural law; or (b) the directions that Christ and his apostles gave to the Church.

4. CONCLUSION

Notwithstanding the seemingly antinomian tenor of certain statements by the apostle Paul, his own words and the testimony of Scripture as a whole indicate that God's law retains its authority even after Christ's death and resurrection. Given conventional Reformed assumptions about Scripture's sufficiency and perspicuity, therefore, the Church and individual Christians possess abundant reason for confidence that responsible exegesis of Scripture, when coupled with careful consideration of the circumstances in which it is to be applied, will yield accurate conclusions as to Christians' duty in the Church and the world.

Conclusion

Now that we have surveyed the method of Reformed ethics proposed here and its theological rationale, it seems desirable to outline a few ways in which Reformed convictions about ethics diverge from Catholic views of the same subject. First, the Reformed take the first and second commandments to forbid the rendering of any religious honor to any mere creature. Second, the Reformed do not consider even the best redeemed human beings capable of performing works of supererogation by which they might merit rewards *de condigno* from God. For God requires the utmost possible righteousness of each human being, including those whom he has not endowed with the gift of continence outside of marriage (Matt 19:11). Regardless of any special capacities with which God might endow a mere human being, no one can do better than loving God with all of his heart, soul, and strength, which is what God demands of all (Deut 6:5; Matt 22:37). Even the perfect man, therefore, is only an unprofitable servant (Luke 17:10).

Third, the Reformed do not acknowledge the existence of light matter: i.e., trivialities too insignificant to constitute the matter of serious sin. God does not exempt human beings from the requirement to love him with all their heart, soul, and strength in matters they consider inconsequential. Scripture teaches, rather, that "whoever keeps the whole law, but offends in one point, is guilty of all" (Jas 2:10). Fourth, the Reformed regard concupiscence, i.e., instinctive urges to do or acquire what is forbidden, as sin in the strictest sense of the term. For Paul asserts that the tenth commandment informed him of what sin is. "I did not know sin except through the law; for I would not have known lust [Vg. *concupiscentiam*] if the law had not said, 'You shall not covet [Vg. *concupisces*].'" Fifth and finally, the Reformed hold that, although God sanctifies everyone whom he justifies (Rom 8:29; Phil 2:13; 1 Thess 5:23-4; Titus 2:14; 1 John 3:3, 9; 5:18), and the wicked will not inherit the kingdom of God (1 Cor 6:9-10; Gal 5:19-21; Eph 5:5), in this life mere human beings, being incapable of ridding themselves of concupiscence, cannot fully satisfy the demands of God's law. "The flesh lusts against the spirit and the spirit against the flesh, for these are contrary to each other so that you do not those things that you desire to do" (Gal 5:17). In this life, even the best of the saints must admit with Paul, "To will is present with me, but to work the good is not" (Rom 4:18b).

SECTION 2.
Sexual Ethics

2.0. Common Statement on Sexual Ethics

Preamble

Catholics and Evangelicals ground the consideration of sexual ethics in God's plan and purpose for the human race, as affirmed by the Scriptures. God created humans in the image and likeness of God, male and female, to live in communion with him. God has made humans with a given nature, following his own design, and they are fulfilled by knowing and embracing this plan as male and female.

Human sexuality, like all aspects of human life, has been affected and damaged by the Fall. Some people are born with sexual developmental anomalies (e.g. intersex); others experience conflict between their given physical sex and their "gender identity" (e.g. gender dysphoria that often leads to transgenderism). Still others experience attraction to those of their own sex (e.g. homosexual desire). As they grow and develop, all human beings experience sexual desires that are not conformed to God's plan.

As Catholics and Evangelicals, as those who have become sons and daughters of God through Christ and in the Spirit, we are called to live faithfully according to God's plan as male and female and to bring our sexuality fully under the lordship of Christ. Thus, in Christ's body and through the Spirit, Christians are called to be transformed and conformed to the image of God's Son.

In response to our surrounding culture, we reaffirm God's beautiful purpose and design for our sexuality as revealed in the Scriptures, and we together approach the following questions concerning sexual ethics with this plan in view.

1. Catholics and Evangelicals affirm that marriage has an integral place in God's plan for all people as part of the created order.

2. Evangelicals and Catholics believe God gives additional blessings to Christian marriage and sets Christ's love for the Church as a model of marital love.
    a. Catholics hold that Jesus Christ raised marriage to the dignity of a sacrament in order to sanctify the couple and give the graces necessary to live out their fidelity, uphold the indissolubility of the marriage, and welcome and educate their children (*CCC* 1641).
    b. Most Evangelicals believe that God sanctifies the marriage union.
    c. Some Evangelicals deny that marriage is a Sacrament instituted by Christ.
    d. Other Evangelicals use sacramental language to describe marriage.

3. Evangelicals and Catholics hold that marriage is only between one male and one female and according to God's plan is the only context for sexual activity. Therefore, Catholics and Evangelicals do not recognize any other claims of marriage (e.g., same sex marriage, polygamy).

4. Catholics and Evangelicals see children as a blessing of marriage. God created the human race as male and female, who in the context of marriage become "one flesh" (union) and fulfill God's command to "be fruitful and multiply" (procreation).
    a. Catholics affirm that every marital union must be open to the conception of a child and hold that every action which separates the unitive and procreative ends of marriage such as direct sterilization or contraception is intrinsically evil.
    b. Most Evangelicals affirm that both the unitive and procreative purposes of marriage are important. Many Evangelicals would not require an expression of the procreative purpose in every individual sexual act and accept non-abortifacient contraceptives.

    c. Some Evangelicals think the use of contraception contravenes God's plan.
    d. Some Evangelicals discourage the use of contraception but do not view it as immoral.

5. Catholics and Evangelicals hold that all human life is sacred, including the unborn.
    a. Catholics and most Evangelicals hold that abortion is the murder of an innocent human life and is always evil.
    b. Some Evangelicals permit abortion under exceptional circumstances. These may include the health of the mother, rape, and incest.

6. Evangelicals and Catholics agree that sexual activities practiced outside of marriage are disordered, such as pre-marital sex, adultery, pornography, and bestiality. Catholics and Evangelicals would agree that certain sexual activities are forbidden, destructive, and damaging both inside and outside of marriage.
    a. Catholics and some Evangelicals would agree that masturbation and oral sex both inside and outside of marriage are forbidden, destructive, and damaging.
    b. Some Evangelicals see masturbation and oral sex as acceptable within marriage by the married couple.

7. Catholics and Evangelicals both value those who hear and respond to the call of a celibate life (1 Cor 7; Matt 19).
    a. Catholics hold that marriage is a great good and that Christ raised marriage to the dignity of a sacrament, nevertheless Catholics see consecrated virginity and celibacy as more excellent than marriage. Catholics see consecrated virginity and celibacy as an imitation of the example of Christ who remained unmarried and a virgin. Catholics also see this as following the counsel of St. Paul who counsels, "Do not seek marriage" (1 Cor 7:27).
    b. Evangelicals recognize the dignity of celibacy [in some evangelical traditions called "singleness"] but do not consider it more excellent than marriage.

c. Some evangelicals consider lifelong promises or vows to celibacy as imprudent.

8. God's intention is for marriage to be life-long. Divorce was permitted under the Mosaic Law, as a concession to human weakness but was contrary to God's original plan. Christ's teaching reaffirms God's original intention.
    Certain impediments can render a real marriage impossible. These include previous marriage, coercion, fraud, and falling within the prohibited degrees of consanguinity.
    a. For Catholics, valid sacramental marriages are indissoluble and can be dissolved only by death. The Church never recognizes divorce as a valid way of ending a marriage. For Catholics, divorce is not the same as annulment. Divorce is a civic act. Annulment is an affirmation by the Church that the conditions for a valid indissoluble marriage were not met at the time of the marriage.
    b. Most Evangelicals allow for divorce in dire pastoral circumstances which may include sexual immorality, infidelity, desertion, and physical abuse.
    d. Some Evangelicals only allow for divorce in circumstances of adultery.
    d. Some Evangelicals also grant annulments.

9. Catholics and Evangelicals affirm that all persons are individuals of sacred worth created in the image of God. We agree that there is an important distinction between same sex attraction and homosexual activity. Evangelicals and Catholics agree that homosexual behavior is revealed in Scripture to be contrary to God's plan for human sexual activity. This biblical teaching reflects God's design in the created order for sexual activity and relationships as male and female.
    a. Catholics and some Evangelicals teach that same sex attraction is disordered but not in itself sinful.
    b. Some Evangelicals teach that same sex attraction is sinful in itself.

2.1. Marriage within the Economy of Salvation: An Introduction to the Catholic Teaching on Marriage

Dr. David P. Fleischacker

Marriage in the Narrative History of Salvation

The Catholic understanding of marriage has its roots in creation, the Fall, and salvation. As all of us have discussed a number of times over the years, all children, men, and women are made in the image of God. Hence, the image is not what differentiates male and female. Rather, that differentiation springs from the way God wants to create first a companion for the man, and second the resulting companionship springs from the way that God wants to create children that are his and theirs.[1]

The implications of this differentiation are significant. God chose to associate us in the work of his creation. That association has its roots in the very nature of how God created man and created woman.[2] They are made to be united in the flesh in the creation of God's

---

1. In Catholic teaching, God alone infuses the spiritual soul into a person. Matter cannot generate spirit. So, mother and father generate the material dimension of the human person, and God is the one who brings about the spiritual dimension. Both are intimately tied together as a whole or composite unity. The body is, as Saint Thomas would say following Aristotle, informed by the spiritual capacities, powers, operations, and acts. The spiritual capacity or powers are realized in and through the sensate activities (phantasm). Hence the reason I say, "his and theirs."

2. CCC 652 and *Gaudium et spes*, §50.1. "God said: 'It is not good that man should be alone,' and 'from the beginning (God) made them male and female'; wishing to associate them in a special way in his own creative work, God blessed man and woman with the

children. And it is not a mere unity of flesh, but one of spirit which one sees when the man exclaims with joy his first encounter with her: "This at last is bone of my bone and flesh of my flesh; she shall be called Woman because she was taken out of Man" (Gen 2:23).[3] This exclamation manifests the divinely ordained relationship through which God wants to create life and more life.

It is important to note 1) that Adam recognizes his equal—another in the image of God. 2) This alone does not explain his exclamation. He can see in any man the image of God but is generally not disposed to make that kind of an exclamation. I think this is at the root of when a young man first sees a young woman with whom he is taken. 3) So, what he does see, even if not able to articulate it, is one who is both in the image of God—hence possessing reason and free will—and one who is "bone of my bone, flesh of my flesh." In her is a completion for which his body and soul yearn, a yearning which also springs to be a co-creator with a loving God. Furthermore, 4) this recognition is that she is the one with whom love in body and soul will bring about their conformance and union with the God who created them out of his love. The man was made to generate with intelligence, freedom, and love. His soul images God in those spiritual powers. Yet, the highest generative act is to generate another like himself, in the image of his Creator. A son. A daughter. But he is not capable of completing that image in his Creator. And he instinctively knows it. His body and soul yearn for the completion, and no other creature could do so, certainly not another man. Only his future bride could be that fulfillment. Children can only come from the two of them.[4] And Scripture manifests this powerful unity between this

---

words: 'Be fruitful and multiply.' Without intending to underestimate the other ends of marriage, it must be said that true married love and the family life which flows from it have this end in view: that the love of the spouses would cooperate generously with the love of the Creator and Savior, who through them will in due time increase and enrich his family." Second Vatican Council, *Gaudium et spes* (December 7, 1965), pp. 163–282 in *Vatican Council II: The Basic Sixteen Documents*, ed. Austin Flannery (Northport, NY: Costello, 1996), §50.1.

3. Biblical citations in this chapter are from the RSVCE.

4. Newer technologies seemingly provide a way around this natural capability given to a man and a woman. At this point, I am just focusing on the created and natural

man and this woman, for she came from his own body—from his rib to tell all of history that she is linked to him in a unique manner. In short, she was created by God from the man's own flesh and bone, as the completion of his being. She completes the man in his creative thirst to be a begetter. She completes the man by being God's bearer of God's children. And for this to be fully in God's image, it must also be in a committed and enduring covenant that lasts until death do them part.

The Gnostic view could never appreciate such a divinely ordained differentiation of creatures and the mystical meaning of their unity. Greeks were good at differentiations of parts. They differentiated the material and the spiritual. But some did more. They not only distinguished but divorced the material and the spiritual by inserting a necessary opposition between the two. The former entraps and enslaves the latter. And if one comes to see the material as a prison of the spiritual, then one will come to see the relationship of man and woman as one of those most powerful and enslaving of all prisons. This is true whether we are talking about ancient Gnosticism or modern. The ancient one tends to think of the need to be liberated from all the material, the modern tends to think of being able to manipulate, especially with modern technology, the material as one pleases (licentiousness). Both cases fail to recognize the unity of the hierarchy of being and how the lower orders provide the conditions for the higher, hence the material for the spiritual. And the higher liberates the lower, hence the spiritual liberating the material. Matter does not imprison in that position. And contrary to the one flesh relationship of man and woman as the greatest of all imprisonments is that it is the most potent locus for liberation. Through their mutual and enduring self-donation, they perfect their bodies, their minds, their wills, and their hearts, but only if following the mind and will of God and listening to the voice of their conscience innate in their souls, and striving with all of their might to live a life of virtue that unites them to their loving Creator, who is lovingly and wisely committed to all of

capabilities of man and woman. It is important to note that the "ways" around this completely ignore the spiritual framework of these creative acts.

his works. He wills and sustains creation out of love. His creation as created is true and good. As associates in creation, the man and the woman must equally commit to each other in order to enter into the likeness to God the committed loving Creator, and thus dwell with him in friendship on the basis of that likeness.

But they do not have to either. God gave them freedom, and an essential element in being in his likeness was to be free as he is free. To love freely. And, as we know, Adam and Eve fell. God wanted to create the human race from the loving, fruitful relationship of this man and woman. He wanted all of his children, their children, to be born in the garden with all of its gifts, and with himself dwelling in the center and essence of their souls. But the serpent tempted Eve with the same sin that cut his life from the kingdom of heaven (*CCC* 392). Pride and envy were Lucifer's rebellious abyss. This great light tempted Eve to drink from the same abyss (*CCC* 398). Her seduction would cut her life off from the tree of life. As we read on in this story, Adam, who was made to embrace in his heart and soul this flesh of his flesh, would be seduced by her offer and then cut off from the same tree. All would fall from beatitude and from life (Gen 3, *CCC* 402–6).

It is worthy of note that Satan's first tactic in taking down the human race was to destroy this primordial companionship etched into the soul and body of Adam and Eve. He wanted slaves who would serve him in his rebellion. What more potent location to begin than in the relationship that God had constituted as an association through which he would continue the rest of his creation and creative work.

The fall of Adam and Eve becomes a stain etched into the fabric of their bodies and souls, especially in that union of flesh that begets and bears forth new life. The stain is concupiscence (*CCC* 406).[5] Their disobedience is the reason for their expulsion from the garden. It is

---

5. To recall from previous dialogues, concupiscence for Catholics is a state of fallenness that every person who is a daughter or son of Adam and Eve inherits. It itself is not personal sin, nor even formally sin, but a disposition to sin that constitutes a crucible in life always warring at our thirst for goodness and being, and hence it causes a kind of fracture in our souls. It does not cause what God has created to be evil as such but puts what God has created into a disordered state that leads away from God and toward death.

the reason why they were forbidden to eat of the tree of life. It would be the cause of the deformity in the essence of each human soul, one which would private the soul of God's love, of God's union, of grace.

Notice one of the immediate effects of this evil. They willfully rebelled against God. Their own bodies and desires rebelled against their own minds and wills (*CCC* 400). Their hearts were now torn and their souls were now fractured. Lust was born. Conflict was born. The woman could no longer love with purity her man; and the man could no longer love her with that initial joy. Lust enslaved his heart.

And the next effects arose naturally from this dialectical deformation. The beauty of their procreative life resulted in pains that would accompany childbirth. Man would have to toil in sweat and blood to find food and to protect his own. Death would be the end of them on earth (Gen 3, *CCC* 400).

This fall was manifested immediately in their actions. They hid from God. They hid from each other. Garments would be necessary for the rest of history. And so they were barred by Cherubim from the garden and her tree of life (Gen 3).

Expelled from the garden, they still had the power to generate children. But righteousness would not be transmitted to their children. God was still free of course to do so as with his acceptance of the sacrifice of Abel (Heb 11:4). But Cain was not so disposed. He was the son of the fallen Adam and Eve. The war in their hearts now generated war in the world starting in this envious and violent son. Cain became the father of the cities of this world, largely built and driven by pride, greed, envy, and lust. His likeness was that of the great fallen light. His father was the father of hell. Neither the husbands nor the wives in these cities flourished. In fact no one flourished.

It is important to note that this fallen state takes its origin from the first man and woman and then continues to be transmitted in its essence and power through their conjugal relationship; henceforth it impacts all human relations, all human institutions, and even the whole of creation. The Fall, in other words, has its transmitting engine in the very heart of the relationship of man and woman. One can see why Satan worked with such devotion upon deforming and maintaining this deformation between the man and the woman. It also reveals why God had to give such unique graces to begin pulling this primordial relationship out of its enslavement to the kingdom of hell.

The depth and stain of the Fall is to remain down through the whole of history but not without a counter. God immediately comes to find Adam and Eve and calls out to them. They are hiding. He calls forth their confession, he makes better garments—they could not even do that right—and then gives to them their penance and punishment, which would put them and their children into a crucible that would prepare the way for a supreme elevation (Gen 3).

God entered fallen history right away. He did not leave it in that state. Why? Love. The same love that was at the root of his creative acts. But he is not going to entirely undo the elements of the fallen state; rather he is going to bring good out of evil by showing the way to return to him via a loving and sacrificial response to evil. Abel's was the right response. Cain's was not. The dialectic between good and evil was to remain until the end of history in the hearts and souls of every man, woman, child. Society would be leavened by this darkness as well. Cities would arise from the way of Cain. But God has his own city. And he wants to gather his faithful together even on earth through the crucible of life.

As history unfolds, God ramps up his economy of salvation. Marriage will be a key ingredient. Male and female will be central. One sees this in Noah, his wife, his sons and their wives, and all the animals that enter the ark two by two, male and female. And then later, Abram does not go it alone. He moves toward the promised land with his beloved bride, Sarai. Divine election is to take place through a man and a woman, and one of the signs of this are that God gives them new names. And then in a miraculous manner, they are given a child in old age. Isaac is to carry God's salvific plan, not just as a verbal carrier, but in his person, as a son. His sonship is central to that salvific plan, and it flows from Abraham as the father of the faith and his mother Sarah. For Catholics, this points to the central import of marriage and family, even in its imperfect state. God gave it a central place in creation, and he also gives it a central place in salvation.

The right relation of man and woman leads to great fruitfulness.

The wrong relation leads to destruction and death. Contrast Sarah and Jezebel for example. Think of how often men were lured to the Baals by women of Baal. At the same time think of Hannah or Naomi or Ruth, and of Judith. Of course, we have a prime example in Eve and Adam, and how the corruption of their marriage led to death in their son. Disobedience leads away from generativity. It is a kind of contraception of life. And it leads to death. It leads the heart to abort the gift of life. At the same time Adam's love for Eve and Eve's for Adam generated Abel and Seth as well. And though the first was not meant to have much of a life let alone a city on earth, the second became the one through whom the fruit of salvation would proceed forth.

At the height of marriage and family were Joseph and the new Eve.[6] But it was prepared with the last great prophet of the old covenant, John the Baptist. And of course, his beginning had its miraculous start as did Isaac's conception. Zechariah and Elizabeth were in their old age. God chose to initiate his final covenant by giving them a son who prepared the way to the messiah through contrition and repentance for sin. His father Zechariah, after he could speak again, gave to us one of the greatest canticles of all time which sprang from the hopes and yearnings of the whole history of Israel. These hopes and yearnings resided in Zechariah's soul, and now he through the inspiration of the Holy Spirit discovers with great joy that God is now fulfilling these hopes and yearnings in his son. And notice how this son is martyred. He dies for the truth of marriage. And then there is his cousin, the messiah. Mary was chosen by our Lord to be his mother. Joseph was chosen to be her spouse and his adoptive father on earth. The holy family was the location of the Incarnation, the point at which the fullness of time began.

One sees the fullness of time prefigured in Adam and Eve. However, it was a long, crooked road between them and the new Adam

---

6. By this title of Mary, I am referring to the development found in Justin Martyr who calls her the New Eve, a title which then endures down through the ages and is before *Theotokos* is officially ratified at Ephesus in AD 431. Though that title is not used in Scripture, one does see its meaning found in the Gospel of Luke, where one finds the parallels of the annunciation by Gabriel to Mary and the suggestions of the serpent to Eve.

and the new Eve. That crooked path was from loving and committed monogamy to everything but loving, committed monogamy. It was deformed by adultery and polygamy. Sodom and Gomorrah became home to all of the deformities conceivable to the human imagination. The patriarchs and the kings had multiple wives, and a multitude of problems ensued. Think of the tension between Sarah and Hagar, or between David's sons Amnon and Absalom. Or the crazy household of Solomon. It was not until after the exile that monogamy had a comeback. And it was not until Jesus that indissolubility was made clear again. "Let no man put asunder what God has united" (Matt 19:6) speaks a truth about marriage for all ages since the beginning of the human race.

Why? We must return to the beginning. Marriage was the locus for the creation of the human race, for the Fall, and for salvation. A right relation between man and woman (marriage) was one of the first gifts given to the human race. It was the key deformation introduced by the Fall. And it will become the way of salvation for all men, women, and children. The New Covenant brings this to supreme clarity.

The New Covenant elevates marriage to a new dignity. It already was central in creation and salvation, but with our Lord, its significance rises to that of a participation in the love God has for us in his Son. Jesus died for his bride, the Church. He died for us to make us into his brothers and sisters. He was born in the loving unity of Joseph and Mary. He chose his mother to be the spotless tabernacle in which he would take on flesh and become one with us. His descent was for our ascent. And the holy family becomes the locus. Joseph the carpenter, the man with the dreams, the man with whom the angel Gabriel speaks, the man who protects the Son of God and his mother as they flee to Egypt, the man who taught his adopted Son to build, God uses this man Joseph to manifest and to bring to us the highest order, that of the love of the Father for his Son, and through his Son, his love for all of us, his adopted sons and daughters. And then there is Mary, Joseph's beloved bride, the woman who said yes to the same angel, the woman who with joy went to visit Elizabeth and then while there gave us her beautiful canticle. She was the one through whom the needs at the wedding taking place in Cana were made known, the simple need for wine, the same need that was fully served by the blood of the Last Supper. She brought this need to her Son. She is the one who then told the world at that wedding to do what her Son tells us. She is the one who stood with the beloved disciple at the foot of the Cross and beheld her Son take on the sin of the world. As that sin crucified her Son before her, her heart was pierced with a sword. This was the mother who suffered her Son's suffering for the redemption of the world. This was the mother given by her Son to the beloved disciple, to be his mother, and hence to all of the beloved brothers and sisters of her Son. The mother's tender love for her child, the mother's sacrifice as her Son on the cross pierces her heart, the mother's fiat of her whole life to the Lord, becomes the location of God's self-donation. That location grows into the entire body of Jesus Christ, the mystical bride of our Lord. The meaning and place that marriage is now given on earth is as a domestic *ecclesia*, a home to our Lord, a tabernacle of the entire Holy Trinity, the place in which the love that Jesus has for his entire Body is brought forth as his sacrament and cherished bride. The holy family on earth now becomes a preparation and the starting point for the "wedding-feast of the Lamb" (Rev 19:7, CCC 1612).

Catholic Teaching Today

FIDELITY BETWEEN THE MAN AND WOMAN

The Catholic way of talking about the right relationship between man and woman today tends to be in terms of the procreative and unitive facets of marriage.[7] In traditional terms it is differentiated into 1) the openness to the creation of children in each and every conjugal act (CCC 1652–54), 2) fidelity as one finds protected by the sixth and ninth Commandments (CCC 1646–51), and 3) indissolubility in the sacramental bond established by God (CCC 1644–45). The

---

7. One can see this in *CCC* 1601: "The matrimonial covenant, by which a man and a woman establish between themselves a partnership of the whole of life, is by its nature ordered toward the good of the spouses and the procreation and education of offspring; this covenant between baptized persons has been raised by Christ the Lord to the dignity of a sacrament."

first directly bears upon the inscription into the human body and soul of the creative power of God. The second informs that inscription with a commitment to this other and only this other both physically and spiritually with regard to one's procreative life and eternal well-being. The third introduces the divine gift by which God takes up into his own heart and being this relationship as a sacred and sanctifying bond both for the good of the husband and wife, and the good of any children they might beget and bear. This third as ratified in God makes it indissoluble.

Only in the union of the man and woman does one find activated and revealed their image in God as the loving committed Creator, especially in God as the Creator of all men, women, and children. This image is also God's instrument of salvation. The man and the woman participate cooperatively in God's sanctification of them and their children, and even others who enter their homes and lives. God the Father begets his Son and together they eternally spirate the Holy Spirit. Because of God's over-abundant generosity, the Father sends his Son and their Holy Spirit to create this world and then, as a result of the Fall, to save it. This mission is at the root of being a husband and father, and being a wife and mother. God chose to accomplish his final and permanent covenant by entering into this world through an act of conception. Mary is chosen to be his mother—Theotokos. She bears forth her Son both into the world and upon the Cross into all of eternity. All natural fathers participate in God the Father's begetting of new life when they beget life. All mothers participate in Mary's fiat to our Lord through Gabriel when they receive life through a covenanted and sacramental bond, when they receive life joyfully. Such a glorious fiat provides the conditions of fruitfulness in actively giving themselves, their bodies, their hearts, their minds, their wombs, and their tender care of love for another.

This participation is one of faithfulness—bodily, mentally, morally—and of the heart. God is the one who creates out of love, who sustains out of love, who promises good things to those who are good, and who even promises to bring good out of evil. This image is brought to life in the man and the woman when wedded in the conjugal relationship only when they unite out of love and indissoluble promise. God is faithful to his people, to the point of giving his own Son for their salvation. Man's faithfulness to his wife and woman's faithfulness to her husband are designed not only to be an image but to participate in God's faithfulness. This is the reality communicated by the wedding feast at Cana. In turn, their graced participation communicates God's faithfulness to the world. This proclamation to the world of God's faithfulness is manifested throughout Scripture; think for example of Adam's faithfulness to Eve and Eve's to Adam, and Abraham's to Sarah and Sarah's to Abraham (God had to help Abraham with this a few times!), and Moses' to Ziapporah and Ziapporah's to Moses, and most potently when Joseph was faithful to Mary and Mary to Joseph. It is through these real, concrete commitments that God's love moves to the world. God made man and woman to be the entry point of his revelation for the world. He made them to be the salvific starting point, the same point at which the Fall entered the human race. That is why the demise of committed faithful husbands and wives has always led to the demise of a city, a nation, an age.

FIDELITY TO THEIR CHILDREN

These kinds of responsibility do not unfold into their full finality unless the man and the woman remain faithful to the creative well-being and eternal life of their children (CCC 1653). And given this identity, their relationship to each other is one of a unique kind of friendship—as even the pagan Aristotle discovered.

The realization of this indissoluble and thus "until-death-do-us-part" promise, one bonded together by the Lord himself, takes place in the highest moment of unity between the man and woman, when with the volitional promises of fidelity, when with the light of God's ratification, they activate the total unity of body-mind-will-soul in the first conjugal act. The sign and reality of this relation, this covenant in the full procreative unity of ensouled bodies, only then realizes the fullness of this covenantal nature of their relationship and the full image of God as the loving and faithful Creator and Savior of the world.

In short, this elevates the relation of the man and woman in the very conjugal act as a locus not only of God's creation but also a locus of God's final stage of salvation. God now associates the man and the woman with his most important act, springing forth from the totality of his being. He associates them in his economy of salvation that now finds its highest apex in Christ crucified and redeems the world in them and through them. They become our Lord's bride as a domestic church or *ecclesia*.

WHY THE CATHOLIC CHURCH SAYS NO

All of the Catholic Church's proscriptions about marriage follow. Every deformity between or in man and woman is a deformity because it privates these goods and gifts that constitute God's creative and salvific acts that he wants to work in and through them. Since these creative and salvific goods regard man and woman as being united in one flesh, there are many points along that unity that can be deformed. There are the goods of fidelity, children, and sacred unity, and thus privations of these are all evils. To provide more detail,

1. The privation can regard the procreative act itself as when one introduces a decision to hinder fertility that accompanies a decision to activate the conjugal act. Fertility is the reality that is in God's image as creator. Contraception is a direct act against this sacred image.

2. The privation can be that of fidelity after the promise and ratification has taken place both
   a. in a deformation of the fullness of the body as in adultery;
   b. in the total commitment of the mind, will, and heart as in actively coveting another's spouse. Pornography is perhaps one of the most frequent violations of this latter sin in today's world.

3. The privation can be of the nature and meaning of the committed and loving conjugal relationship between the man and the woman as in fornication, artificial insemination, or in vitro fertilization. The first privates the loving committed relationship.

The second and third trespass the conjugal act itself. All of these private the kind of relationship and activity through which God wants to generate his children.

4. To the children conceived in such contexts,
   a. it privates the revelation of their lives as a gift coming from a committed and loving God.
   b. It privates the couple and the world of that revelation as well.

5. It can be a privation of the responsibility of educating the children to live well in this world, and/or to live for eternal life.

6. It can be a privation of the friendship constituted between the man and the woman as sacred and faithful, seeking the well-being and eternal life of the one who is at last "bone of my bone and flesh of my flesh."

Catholics who knowingly and freely sin against the basic covenantal relation in the ways mentioned above destroy the sanctification that God has given to them in baptism and through the other sacraments. And even if unknowingly, they still inflict damage and destruction just as if a doctor had provided accidentally a mortal remedy to a patient thinking it would help.

In the case of divorce or remarriage, the Church upholds the gospel injunction that if remarried, then adultery has taken place. Catholics validly married can separate in severe circumstances but not remarry. Reconciliation is always the hope. If they commit adultery or any grave sins, they have separated themselves from Christ, and hence should not follow Judas's pretense of discipleship in the presence of our Lord at the last and eternal banquet. Still, the Church wants to care for them and reunite them with our Lord and bring them back to the full communion of his bride. As Saint John Paul II wrote,

> They should be encouraged to listen to the Word of God, to attend the Sacrifice of the Mass, to persevere in prayer, to contribute to works of charity and to community efforts for justice, to bring up

their children in the Christian faith, to cultivate the spirit and practice of penance and thus implore, day by day, God's grace.[8]

MARRIAGE AS SACRAMENT

> Sacred Scripture begins with the creation of man and woman in the image and likeness of God and concludes with a vision of "the wedding-feast of the Lamb." Scripture speaks throughout of marriage and its "mystery," its institution and the meaning God has given it, its origin and its end, its various realizations throughout the history of salvation, the difficulties arising from sin and its renewal "in the Lord" in the New Covenant of Christ and the Church. (CCC 1602)

The sacramental nature of marriage has its fullness of meaning within the economy of salvation. It is a public act, and thus has witnesses. It is a sacred act, and hence under ordinary circumstances is witnessed by deacons, priests, or bishops.[9] The commitment and the conjugal act that realizes that commitment are central to the marriage covenant. In other words, the full indissoluble promise is made by the man and the woman, flowing from their own hearts and wills into their voices as they proclaim their fidelity until death do them part. Ordinary Catholic marriages take place within a liturgical body, which is the manifestation in a place and time of the mystical Body of Christ, a body that then supports the bride and groom, and a body that becomes the recipient of God's love and gifts through this couple.

As one of the key vehicles on earth by which God associates men and women in his works of creation and salvation, God has communicated to us that special graces are given to married spouses. The grace which God provides is that which helps them to live out their fidelity, uphold the indissolubility of the marriage, and welcome and educate their children (CCC 1641). Jesus especially gives this grace to them from his cross, where the full tenderness, strength, and fidelity of God's love is poured out upon everyone who welcomes him (CCC

---

8. *Familiaris consortio* (November 22, 1981) (Washington, DC: United States Catholic Conference, 1982), §84.

9. In other words, those ordained in the apostolic line springing from Jesus and who are his ordained eyes, ears, and voices on this earth.

1642). If God's love is welcomed as Mary did with her fiat, or Elizabeth did in the presence of her Lord while he was growing in his mother's womb, then we have a real foretaste of the "wedding feast of the Lamb" (CCC 1642).

As these graces build upon the natural, they reveal that even on a natural plane, men and women were made for each other and for their children. One sees this in the joy that mothers throughout Scripture and history take in their unborn and newborn infants. One sees it in the joy of a father's heart who has been awakened to the child growing in his bride's womb. Notice how this is the case many times even in the failures of men and women to commit to each other. And notice as well how one sees the hope for life and love repeatedly in young teenagers before they are clouded over with sin and darkness and the spark and joy of life is extinguished. Their hope is to find someone who makes sense of their lives. The young woman hopes to find the love of her life. The young man deeply yearns for that "bone of his bone and flesh of his flesh." This is a reality inscribed into their bodies and souls. And though we find tsunami damage done to young lives these days, it often is still visible during those first adolescent years.

It is also worth noting how the joy of the man and the woman for a child is found reciprocated. The smile of the mother for the child finds a ready recipient in the smile and joy of the child for both mother and father. One hears of how the mother's smile awakens the trusting heart of the child. But at the same time, children were made to smile and enjoy their mother and their father. The innocents, even when tainted with the stain of original sin, in their need and love for life, call forth life and love from their parents.

All of the proscriptions in Catholic teaching that flow from Scripture say no to acts and actions that cloud and deform these joys of life, both in the mother and father, and in the children.[10]

---

10. I think these truths about marriage can be awakened if we ask a simple question, and then ask people to open their eyes, to look and seek the truth. That question is about whether the unborn, the newborn, the young boy and girl, the young man and woman, are happier, more joyful, more caring, more interested, less dead, less sad, less despairing when their mother and father commit until death do them part to each other, commit through thick and thin, commit to an openness in every conjugal act

THE CHALLENGE OF MIXED MARRIAGES FOR CATHOLICS

This understanding of marriage has something to say about mixed marriages. The general position found in the *Catechism of the Catholic Church* on mixed marriages highlights the difficulty that such marriages encounter over their duration. The Church does not forbid such marriages but makes the point that living the faith, both by and between the spouses and with their children, results in significant challenges. Yet, such challenges do "not constitute an insurmountable obstacle for marriage, when they succeed in placing in common what they have received from their respective communities and learn from each other the way in which each lives in fidelity to Christ" (CCC 1634). In light of this, and in light of the revelatory nature of marriage, the Church sets conditions for such marriages to be valid.[11]

1. For liceity, the couple, if the non-Catholic spouse is Christian, needs the "express permission of the ecclesiastical authority."

2. Both will need to know and not exclude the "essential ends and properties of marriage."

3. The Catholic will need to confirm to "preserve his or her own faith" and make this known to the non-Catholic party.

4. The Catholic will need to promise to baptize and educate their children in the Catholic Church and the non-Catholic will need to know of this obligation. This will include proscriptions against contraception, abortion, in vitro fertilization, artificial insemination, and the use of surrogate mothers.

to God's gifts, commit to the well-being and eternal well-being of each other, commit to the well-being and eternal well-being of each and every child that God brings forth through them. Only the darkest minds and coldest hearts could not at minimum recognize that this would be better than what most have experienced through all societies and all eras of history. Such a commitment brings about not merely life, but a better life, and even opens the heart and mind, and sets one on the path to eternal life, to be a faithful one who says "here I am Lord, your servant is listening" as Jeremiah said. Jeremiah's mother's tears and prayers led both to his conception and to him as a gift to the house of the Lord. In turn, his life became a gift for all of us down through history.

11. These four listed are taken from *CCC* 1635.

These are the conditions mentioned in the *Catechism of the Catholic Church*. The local ordinary and the marriage tribunal could provide further details.

One may think that this requires too much; however if one has been following the discussion above and the meaning of marriage and the responsibilities parents have to each other and to any children they are given, then Catholics want all of the goods of marriage to unite together for the well-being of all members of the family in the loving presence of God and his gifts for them. These minimal conditions set the stage for that light to shine and for the family to be receptive to these gifts and then find the strength to abide in them. In other words, these conditions for mixed marriages really spring from the same source as all other notes, comments, and teachings that the Catholic Church provides to us about marriage. Marriage is the domestic *ecclesia*, the dwelling home of God's love for the human race, a home where Joseph reigns as the great protector of his bride and child. It is the dwelling home of Mary's tender love which reveals her as God's associate of his tender love. God wants his children to be born into such a home. He wants the sacred gifts he gave to the world through his Son to be given to them. These at heart are the sacraments and teachings and commandments of God, all with the aim of bringing his children to his home and kingdom. The spouses' fidelity, their openness in every conjugal act to his children, their promises that God himself unites, are so that every earthly father can live in the heart and die in the arms of his Son and every earthly mother can be pierced with the hope of resurrection. When they do so, they bring this both to their own family and to the world.

The End

I want to conclude with one of the all-time greatest ancient homilies that is found in the Divine Office on Holy Saturday because it brings the beginning and the end together. Catholics and others praying the Divine Office will be well aware of this homily. It highlights everything I have said about a husband and wife. Jesus descends into Sheol, to call forth the dead who sit in darkness and the shadow of death but are not damned for eternity to hell. Our Lord goes to Adam in this homily, and this is what the homilist poetically proclaims.

> At the sight of him Adam, the first man he had created, struck his breast in terror and cried out to everyone: "My Lord be with you all." Christ answered him: And with your spirit." He took him by the hand and raised him up, saying: Awake, O sleeper, and rise from the dead, and Christ will give you light."
>
> I am your God, who for your sake have become your son. Out of love for you and for your descendants I now by my own authority command all who are held in bondage to come forth, all who are in darkness to be enlightened, all who are sleeping to arise. I order, you, O sleeper, to awake. I did not create you to be held a prisoner in hell. Rise from the dead, for I am the life of the dead. Rise up, work of my hands, you who were created in my image, Rise, let us leave this place, for you are in me and I am in you; together we form only one person and we cannot be separated.
>
> For your sake, I your God, became your son; I, the Lord, took the form of a slave; I, whose home is above the heavens, descended to the earth and beneath the earth. For your sake, for the sake of man, I became like a man without help, free among the dead. For the sake of you, who left a garden, I was betrayed to the Jews in a garden, and I was crucified in a garden.
>
> See on my face the spittle I received in order to restore to you the life I once breathed into you. See there the marks of the blows I received in order to refashion your warped nature in my image. On my back see the marks of the scourging I endured to remove the burden of sin that weighs upon your back. See my hands, nailed firmly to a tree, for you who once wickedly stretched out your hand to a tree.
>
> I slept on the cross and a sword pierced my side for you who slept in paradise and brought forth Eve from your side. My side has healed the pain in yours. My sleep will rouse you from your sleep in hell. The sword that pierced me has sheathed the sword that was turned against you.
>
> Rise, let us leave this place. The enemy led you out of the earthly paradise. I will not restore you to that paradise, but I will enthrone you in heaven. I forbade you the tree that was only a symbol of life, but see, I who am life itself am now one with you. I appointed cherubim to guard you as slaves are guarded, but now I make them worship

you as God. The throne formed by cherubim awaits you, its bearers swift and eager. The bridal chamber is adorned, the banquet is ready, the eternal dwelling places are prepared, the treasure houses of all good things lie open. The kingdom of heaven has been prepared for you from all eternity.[12]

Though this homily is not directly revelatory, it does spring at every word and turn from revelation. It is rooted in the starting point of created man and woman, in the image of God, fallen, needing salvation, being made associates in both the creation of the human race and in its salvation. Though Adam and Eve were the cause of the fall of the human race, God does not save the human race without them. And here in death, the Lord comes to them as he did in the garden at the beginning when they fell. The Catholic faith does not proclaim such details about Adam and Holy Saturday as binding. But what is true is that God will raise us as men and women for all of eternity. Even though marriage on earth has a temporal reality, being adopted as sons and daughters of God the Father, as brothers and sisters of Jesus his Son, does not. The throne upon which we all will sit if united with the Son is eternal. This revelation, however, is made crystal clear only through a committed and loving marriage, through a husband becoming a father, and a wife becoming a mother. Through them, God reveals our destiny as his sons and daughters.[13]

I must add one further note. I have focused on the meaning and character of marriage, and its role in bringing out the fullness of the meaning of gender and sexuality. However, one must not think that marriage and family is the only or final locus of God's revelation. Marriage and family is a crucial part or element of God's unfolding revelation to the fullness of time, and then it becomes a crucial part and element of the transmission of revelation through the rest of history. However, God gives us even more. Upon the holy family, he grows his mystical body, with those who follow him in his celibacy,

---

12. "Ancient Homily on Holy Saturday," 1987–89 in *Christian Prayer: The Liturgy of the Hours* (New York: Catholic Book Publishing, 1976).

13. It is important to note that this created and revelatory meaning of marriage and family lays the groundwork for some more profound mysteries of God's activity on earth through the consecrated life and the life of the parish and diocese.

revealing the bridegroom to that mystical bride as his apostles. Upon the holy family, he reveals the profound meaning of being his bride in brides of the Son who consecrate their hearts and souls and minds and wombs for eternity. In other words, upon holy families, God gives to us an even higher revelation of the ultimate destiny of each man and woman as children of the Father in his consecrated virgins and his celibate sons. They reveal that though earthly and sacramental marriage ends on earth, family continues for eternity. Created male and female, he conceived them through the Holy Spirit as brothers and sisters of God the Son, and through the Son as sons and daughters of him, our Father.

2.2. Fruitful Married Love: The Catholic Church's Teaching on Marriage, Abortion, and Contraception

Dr. Christian D. Washburn

For Catholics, God himself is the author of marriage, instituting it in the Garden for the sanctification of men and women. There is a fundamental complementarity between men and women that is part of and informs the structure of the created order. Christ reaffirmed the value and meaning of marriage against the Pharisees: "They are no longer two but one. What therefore God has joined together, let no man put asunder." Paul highlighted marriage's dignity when he compared the marital union to the union of Christ to his bride, the Church. Blessedly, Evangelical ecclesial communities have to a large extent maintained the biblical doctrine of marriage. In more recent times, Evangelicals have often found common cause with Catholics in defending this biblical doctrine. This paper attempts to explain the Catholic Church's teaching on fruitful married love. To this end, this paper will discuss the Catholic Church's doctrine of the sacrament of marriage as a means of grace and its absolute indissolubility. The paper will then discuss the reasons that the Church rejects abortion and contraception, the status of these doctrines, and the natural law arguments against both. Finally, this paper will explain why the Catholic Church holds that Natural Family Planning (NFP) is not contrary to the procreative nature of marriage.

Marriage in the Old Law and in the New Law

The Catholic Church distinguishes two distinct stages of God's establishment of marriage. In the first stage, God himself instituted marriage in the Garden of Eden as part of the law of nature. when he created Eve and gave her to Adam as a companion. In the first creation account, God created humanity as male and female and ordered them to "be fruitful and multiply" (Gen 1:26).[1] In the second creation account, God says, "It is not good that the man should be alone" (Gen 2:18), emphasizing that both sexes are necessary for God's plan.[2] God created Eve as a helpmate (*ezer*), also sometimes translated as a helpmeet, meaning a proper or suitable helper, thereby emphasizing the complementarity between the sexes (Gen 2:18).

Within the Old Law, God tolerated two problematic human reactions to marriage: divorce and polygamy. Although monogamy was clearly God's original plan for marriage (Gen 2:22-24), later God permitted polygamy. The Mosaic Law likewise accommodated the practice of marrying more than one wife, including captured prisoners from foreign conquests (Deut 21:1-17). Several patriarchs and kings had more than one wife; however, polygamy is always presented as causing significant problems. The Mosaic Law also permitted divorce for indecency on the part of the female when the male provided a legal certificate stating his will to divorce her (Deut 24:1-4).

In the second stage, Christ elevated marriage in two important ways. First, in the New Law Jesus Christ raised marriage to the dignity of one of his seven sacraments. The importance of this cannot be overstated. This elevation was designed to give the grace of Christ to spouses so that they may live out this difficult vocation.[3] In the

---

1. All Scripture references are to the *ESV Study Bible* (Wheaton: Crossway, 2008).

2. United States Conference of Catholic Bishops, *Marriage: Love and Life in the Divine Plan* (Washington, DC: United States Conference of Catholic Bishops, 2009), §9.

3. "Si quis dixerit, sacramenta novae Legis non continere gratiam, quam significant, aut gratiam ipsam non ponentibus obicem non conferre [cf *1451], quasi signa tantum externa sint acceptae per fidem gratiae vel iustitiae, et notae quaedam christianae professionis, quibus apud homines discemuntur fideles ab infidelibus: anathema sit." Heinrich Denzinger, Peter Hünermann, Helmut Hoping, Robert L. Fastiggi, and Anne Englund Nash, eds., *Compendium of Creeds, Definitions, and Declarations on Matters of*

natural law and the Old Law, marriage was an occasion of grace, but it did not confer grace. In the New Law, the sacrament of marriage, like the other six sacraments, confers *ex opere operato* both sanctifying grace and actual graces in order to assist the spouses to live out their marriage.⁴ Concerning actual grace the Council of Trent taught: "Christ himself, who instituted the holy sacraments and brought them to perfection, merited for us by his Passion the grace that perfects that natural love, confirms the indissoluble union, and sanctifies the spouses."⁵ These special helps are those that God is ready to grant to spouses in order to carry out their married life. Pius XI refers to this when he says:

> This sacrament . . . also adds particular gifts, dispositions, seeds of grace, by elevating and perfecting the natural powers. By these gifts the parties are assisted not only in understanding, but in knowing intimately, in adhering to firmly, in willing effectively, and in successfully putting into practice, those things which pertain to the marriage state, its aims and duties, giving them in fine right to the actual assistance of grace, whensoever they need it for fulfilling the duties of their state.⁶

Recall that Catholic theology teaches that while unaided man may do some morally good works without grace if no temptations are present, man cannot keep any commandment solely by the force of his nature if temptation is pressing.⁷ It is only by being engrafted into Christ and infused with these graces that man can consistently and habitually live in a way that is pleasing to the Lord.

Faith and Morals, 43rd ed. (San Francisco: Ignatius, 2012) (hereafter DH), 1606. "Si quis dixerit, matrimonium non esse vere et proprie unum ex septem Legis evangelicae sacramentis, a Christo Domino institutum, sed ab hominibus in Ecclesia inventum, neque gratiam conferre: anathema sit." DH 1801.

4. Ludwig Ott, *Fundamentals of Catholic Dogma*, trans. Patrick Lynch, 3rd ed., revised and updated by Robert Fastiggi (Oil City, PA: Baronius Press, 2018), 494.

5. DH 1799.

6. Pius XI, *Casti connubii* (December 31, 1930), pp. 3:391–414 in *The Papal Encyclicals*, 5 vols., ed. Claudia Carlen, IHM (Wilmington, NC: McGrath, 1981), §40.

7. Christian D. Washburn, "*Ex inimico amicus*: Catholic Teaching on Initial Justification," 123–48 in *Justified in Jesus Christ: Evangelicals and Catholics in Dialogue* (Bismarck, ND: University of Mary Press, 2017), 130.

Second, Christ returned marriage to God's original ideal of an indissoluble union between one man and one woman. The Catholic Church, following the example of Christ, forbids all remarriage after divorce for those who are in a "ratified and consummated" (*ratum et consummatum*) marriage.⁸ God had intended from the beginning that marriage be indissoluble, but he permitted divorce as a concession to the hardness of the human heart (Matt 19:8).⁹ Jesus, however, also tells us that "Everyone who divorces his wife and marries another commits adultery, and he who marries a woman divorced from her husband commits adultery" (Luke 16:18). Notice that Christ says "everyone," so there are no exceptions to the divine law. Christ calls all remarriage (while the former spouse is alive) after divorce adultery, regardless of whether it is the husband or the wife who does the divorcing (Mark 10:11–12). Consequently, Christian marriage is both intrinsically indissoluble, i.e., it cannot be dissolved by the couple, and extrinsically indissoluble, i.e., it cannot be dissolved by any other human power such as the Church or the state. The Council of Trent solemnly reconfirmed the truth of this scriptural teaching on the indissolubility of marriage.¹⁰ In the New Law, Christ ensures that the Sixth Commandment, "You shall not commit adultery" (Exod 20:12), retains its full force.¹¹

---

8. Matthew Levering, *The Indissolubility of Marriage: Amoris Laetitia in Context* (San Francisco: Ignatius, 2019).

9. John Corbett, OP, Andrew Hofer, OP, Paul J. Keller, OP, Dominic Langevin, OP, Dominic Legge, OP, Kurt Martens, Thomas Petri, OP, Thomas Joseph White, OP, "Recent Proposals for the Pastoral Care of the Divorced and Remarried: A Theological Assessment," *Nova et Vetera* 12 (2014): 601–30.

10. E. Christian Brugger, *The Indissolubility of Marriage & the Council of Trent* (Washington, DC: Catholic University of America Press, 2017). Christian D. Washburn, Review of *The Indissolubility of Marriage & the Council of Trent*, by E. Christian Brugger, *Nova et Vetera* 18 (2020): 731–40.

11. Civil divorce is permissible in some situations, but remarriage cannot follow divorce while the other spouse is still alive. The *Catechism of the Catholic Church* explains, "there are some situations in which living together becomes practically impossible for a variety of reasons. In such cases the Church permits the physical *separation* of the couple and their living apart. The spouses do not cease to be husband and wife before God and so are not free to contract a new union. In this difficult situation, the best solution would be, if possible, reconciliation. The Christian community is called to help these persons live out their situation in a Christian manner and in fidelity to their marriage bond which remains indissoluble." *CCC* 1649.

The Catholic Church therefore rejects all forms of polygamy, whether simultaneous or successive.[12] In the New Law, Christ reaffirms that marriage is to be between one man and one woman, thus excluding both polygamy and polyandry. Anabaptists, Luther, and Melanchthon, on the other hand, permitted simultaneous polygamy. In response, the Council of Trent solemnly condemned "anyone [who] says that it is lawful for Christians to have several wives at the same time, and that it is not forbidden by any divine law (Matt 19:9f)."[13]

Marriage's Crowning Glory: Children

The *Catechism of the Catholic Church* notes that "by its very nature the institution of marriage and married love is ordered to the procreation and education of the offspring, and it is in them that it finds its crowning glory."[14] This teaching is rooted in Sacred Scripture. God willed that the human race be propagated, and therefore he created both male and female. The truth of this teaching is confirmed in the creation narrative: "Male and female he created them. And God blessed them. And God said to them, 'Be fruitful and multiply and fill the earth'" (Gen 1:27–28). After the destruction of the human race, God repeats this command for Noah: "And God blessed Noah and his sons, and said to them: 'Be fruitful and multiply, and fill the earth'" (Gen 9:1). Thus, the divine will for the human race is to produce children. In the Old Testament children are often presented as a

---

12. Iosepho A. de Aldama, SJ, Richard Franco, SJ, Severino Gonzalez, SJ, Francisco A. P. Sola, SJ, Iosepho F. Sagüés, SJ, *Sacrae Theologiae Summa*, 4th ed. (Madrid: Biblioteca de Autores Cristianos, 1967), 4:755.

13. "Si quis dixerit, licere Christianis plures simul habere uxores, et hoc nulla lege divina esse prohibitum (Mt 19:9 ss): an. sit." DH 1802. See also Robert Fastiggi, "The Ends of Marriage According to the 1917 and the 1983 Codes of Canon Law in Light of Vatican II," *Antiphon* 18.1 (2014): 32–47.

14. (CCC 1652) There are, of course, several ends of marriage including mutual help, affection, spousal friendship, and a remedy to concupiscence, but children have been considered marriage's primary end. Pius XI, *Casti connubii*, §17. *Code of Canon Law* (1917), canon 1013, §1. Ramon Garcia de Haro de Goytisolo, *Marriage and the Family in the Documents of the Magisterium: A Course in the Theology of Marriage*, trans. William E. May, 2nd ed., rev. (San Francisco: Ignatius, 1993), 119. This paper prescinds from the complicated question of the primary end of marriage.

blessing (Gen 24:60). The Psalmist writes, "Behold, children are a heritage from the LORD, the fruit of the womb a reward" (Ps 127:3). On the other hand, barrenness is often presented as a curse or a punishment (Lev 20:20–21; Jer 22:30). Abimelech's wives were punished, for example, with temporary barrenness (Gen 20:17–18). In the New Testament, the importance of childbearing is reconfirmed. Paul teaches that childbearing contributes to the salvation of women: "Yet she will be saved through childbearing—if they continue in faith and love and holiness, with self-control" (1 Tim 2:15).

Catholic doctrine sees the marital act and the *desire* for its fruit, children, as so essential to the sacrament of marriage that, without either, the sacrament does not take place. The Church holds that only a marriage that is "ratified and consummated" is absolutely indissoluble. The good of children is seen as so necessary to marriage that both antecedent and perpetual impotence (but not infertility), whether on the part of the man or the woman, whether absolute or relative, nullifies a marriage by its very nature.[15] Moreover, any marriage in which either of the two spouses wills, during the exchange of vows, not to have children is not a valid sacramental marriage. This is because if either or both of the spouses at the time of the marriage sacrament excludes any essential element of marriage, then they are excluding marriage itself.[16]

The Gift of Consecrated Celibacy

So far, this account shows a fundamental continuity between the Old Law and the New concerning marriage; but there are also several developments that took place in the latter. In the Old Testament,

---

15. *Code of Canon Law*, c. 1084. If a person becomes impotent during his marriage, the marriage remains valid. Second, infertility does not mean that a couple cannot be married. Relative impotence is when a couple are unable to have marital relations with each other, although they would be able to have such relations with other possible spouses.

16. *Code of Canon Law*, c. 1102, §2. This means that if either the bride or groom, or both, had internally willed that they did not want children, it would vitiate matrimonial consent. This would be a simulated consent.

singleness was generally frowned upon. Nonetheless, in the Mosaic Law, having contact with sexual organs resulted in one becoming ritually unclean (Lev 15:4–11). Temporary sexual abstinence was a way to spiritually prepare for important events, such as receiving a message from God. Before going up Mt. Sinai to receive the law, for example, Moses commanded the Israelites to avoid sexual relations for three days (Exod 19:15). Going to war was another important event which required Israelite men to be ritually clean (Deut 23:9–14). As King David fled from Saul, for example, he and his men abstained from sexual relations. This is why they were allowed to eat the Bread of the Presence (1 Sam 21:1–6). Uriah, although not an Israelite, refused to have relations with Bathsheba, to be in union with his men (2 Sam 11). Lastly, sexual abstinence was required for priests while they served in the temple. Eli's sons' violation of this law resulted in their family losing the right to be priests (1 Sam 2:22–24).

One sometimes sees the claim that celibacy was unknown in the Old Testament, but this is not so. God forbade Jeremiah to marry so that he could fulfill his mission: "The word of the Lord came to me: 'You shall not take a wife, nor shall you have sons or daughters in this place'" (Jer 16:1–2). The Essenes also practiced voluntary celibacy.

For Catholics the goodness of the celibate life is a truth deeply rooted in the New Testament in three ways.[17] First and most importantly, Christ did not marry but lived a celibate life. Christ's example of celibacy is of paramount importance since he is the primary exemplar for all Christians.[18] The *Catechism of the Catholic Church* explains it this way:

> Christ is the center of all Christian life. The bond with him takes precedence over all other bonds, familial or social. (Luke 14:26; Matt

---

17. Celibacy is "The state of being unmarried and, in Church usage, of one who has never been married. Catholicism distinguishes between lay and ecclesiastical celibacy, and in both cases a person freely chooses for religious reasons to remain celibate." John Hardon, SJ, *Modern Catholic Dictionary* (Bardstown, KY: Eternal Life, Inc., 2000), 89.

18. Michael J. Dodds, "The Teaching of Thomas Aquinas on the Mysteries of the Life of Christ," 91–116 in Thomas G. Weinandy, Daniel A. Keating, and John P. Yocum, eds., *Aquinas on Doctrine: A Critical Introduction* (London: T&T Clark International, 2004), 109.

10:28–31.) From the very beginning of the Church there have been men and women who have renounced the great good of marriage to follow the Lamb wherever he goes, to be intent on the things of the Lord, to seek to please him, and to go out to meet the Bridegroom who is coming. (Rev 14:4; 1 Cor 7:32; Matt 2:56.) Christ himself has invited certain persons to follow him in this way of life, of which he remains the model.[19]

Second, Christ not only lived a celibate life, but he also taught that celibacy is a good life to live. It is striking that those New Testament texts about marriage (Matt 19:9–12) also often discuss consecrated celibacy. Thus, after Christ teaches that remarriage after divorce is no longer permissible, the disciples exclaim, "If such is the case of a man with his wife, it is better not to marry" (Matt 19:10). Instead of denying this conclusion, Christ affirms it and speaks immediately about celibacy. Christ lists three types:

> For there are eunuchs who have been so from birth, and there are eunuchs who have been made eunuchs by men, and there are eunuchs who have made themselves eunuchs for the sake of the kingdom of heaven. Let the one who is able to receive this receive it (Matt 19:12).

Christ teaches that celibacy is "for the sake of the kingdom" and that if one is given the grace to receive this call to celibacy, one should live accordingly.

Third, Saint Paul holds that it is better to be celibate than to marry. In 1 Corinthians 7, Saint Paul gives instructions concerning marriage. He begins his reflection with "It is good for a man not to have sexual relations with a woman" (1 Cor 7:1). He argues that marriage is in part "because of the temptation to sexual immorality" (1 Cor 7:2). When he turns to give advice to the unmarried, he counsels them to remain unmarried:

> The unmarried man is anxious about the affairs of the Lord, how to please the Lord. 33 But the married man is anxious about worldly things, how to please his wife, 34 and his interests are divided. And the unmarried or betrothed woman is anxious about the things of the

---

19. CCC 1618.

Lord, how to be holy in body and spirit. But the married woman is anxious about worldly things, how to please her husband. 35 I say this for your own benefit, not to lay any restraint upon you, but to promote good order and to secure your undivided devotion to the Lord.

In effect, Paul is arguing that the unmarried can have an undivided heart, while the married will have a divided heart. Paul concludes that while it is good to marry, it is better not to marry (1 Cor 7:38).

Finally, in the New Law, Christ's grace is so transformative that one can live not only temporary sexual abstinence, but also live a life of celibacy in imitation of Our Lord. Consecrated celibacy is an eschatological sign since it points to the nature of the believer's life in heaven where there is, according to Christ, no longer marriage (Matt 22:30).

The Church's Prohibition of Abortion

The Catholic Church considers abortion to be a grave moral evil which denies and works against the good of children. Abortion was a common and accepted practice of birth control in the ancient world. From its foundation by Christ, the Catholic Church has consistently taught that abortion is intrinsically evil. One of the earliest Christian texts, the *Didiache* (also known as *The Teaching of the Twelve Apostles*) (c. 100–150) plainly commands: "Do not kill a fetus by abortion or commit infanticide."[20] The *Epistle of Barnabas* (c. 138) also commands, "Do not kill a fetus by abortion, or commit infanticide."[21] The Fathers of the Church and ecclesiastical writers, including Tertullian (c. 155–240), Minucius Felix (second or third cent.), Athenagoras (d. 177), Saint Cyprian (d. 258), Saint Basil (c. 329–379), and Saint John Chrysostom (347–407) classified abortion as a form of homicide.[22] Athenagoras, for example, writes,

> And when we say that those women who use drugs to bring on abortion commit murder, and will have to give an account to God for the

---

20. *Didache*, 2.2 (trans. James A. Kleist, ACW 6:16).
21. *Epistle of Barnabas*, 19.5 (trans. John J. O'Meara, ACW 6:62).
22. Tertullian, *Apologeticum ad nationes*, 1.15; Minucius Felix, *Octavius* (CSEL 2.43); Cyprian, *Epistle 52* (CSEL 32:619); Basil, *Letter 188* (PG 32:672); John Chrysostom, *Homily 24 on the Epistle to the Romans* (PG 60:626.27).

abortion, on what principle should we commit murder? For it does not belong to the same person to regard the very fœtus in the womb as a created being, and therefore an object of God's care, and when it has passed into life, to kill it; and not to expose an infant, because those who expose them are chargeable with child-murder, and on the other hand, when it has been reared to destroy it.[23]

It must be recalled that most of the Fathers of the Church were bishops and as such were members of the magisterium. We are to receive their teaching "in the name of Christ, and the faithful are to accept their teaching and adhere to it with a religious assent."[24] Moreover, Catholics hold that when Fathers of the Church are morally unanimous in teaching a doctrine, it is normative for Catholics.[25]

Some contemporary authors have suggested that since some Fathers of the Church and medieval theologians, like Augustine and Thomas Aquinas, thought that God infuses a human soul not immediately at conception but at a slightly later time (also called delayed hominization), therefore they did not consider abortion prior to hominization murder or wrong.[26] While it is true that these theologians thought that the ensoulment did not occur until some time after conception, it is false to conclude that they did not think that the destruction of the fertilized egg was gravely evil. The Fathers of the Church and medieval theologians clearly thought that abortion was gravely evil both before and after hominization. Thus, Augustine writes,

> Sometimes, indeed, this lustful cruelty, or, if you please, cruel lust, resorts to such extravagant methods as to use poisonous drugs to secure barrenness; or else, if unsuccessful in this, to destroy (*exstinguat*) the conceived seed by some means previous to birth, preferring

---

23. Athenagoras, *A Plea for the Christians*, 35 (trans. B. P. Pratten, ANF 2:147; PG 6:919).

24. Second Vatican Council, *Lumen gentium* (November 21, 1964), §25 (DH 4149).

25. DH 1507, 3007.

26. See Christian D. Washburn, Review of *A Brief, Liberal, Catholic Defense of Abortion*, by Daniel A. Dombrowski and Robert Deltete, *The Linacre Quarterly* 86 (2019): 145–47. See also Stephen J. Heaney, "Aquinas and the Presence of the Human Rational Soul in the Early Embryo," *The Thomist* 56 (1992): 19–48. D. A. Jones, "Thomas Aquinas, Augustine, and Aristotle on 'Delayed Animation'," *The Thomist* 76 (2012): 1–36.

that its offspring should rather perish than receive vitality; or if it was advancing to life within the womb, should be slain (*occidi*) before it was born.[27]

Augustine here condemns three distinct things: 1. contraception, 2. the killing of a fetus before hominization, 3. the killing of a fetus after hominization. Clearly, Augustine morally distinguishes the acts of producing barrenness, destroying (*exstinguat*), and killing (*occidi*), hence the use of different terms. In any case, what is exceedingly clear is that the Fathers of the Church were unanimous that abortion is gravely and intrinsically evil. Basil was equally clear:

> The hair-splitting difference between formed and unformed makes no difference to us. . . . Whoever deliberately commit abortion are subject to the penalty for homicide.[28]

The papal magisterium has reconfirmed the teaching of the Fathers of the Church, condemning abortion as intrinsically evil. Thus, Popes Stephen V (c. 887), Saint Pius V (1566), Sixtus V (1588), Gregory XIV (1591), Innocent XI (1679), Pius IX (1869), Pius XI (1930), and Pius XII (1944) all condemn abortion in the strongest terms.[29] It is

---

27. "aliquando eo usque pervenit haec libidinosa crudelitas vel libido crudelis, ut etiam sterilitatis venena procuret et si nihil valverit, conceptos fetus aliquo modo intra viscera extinguat ac fundat, volendo suam prolem prius interire quam vivere, aut si in utero iam vivebat, occidi ante quam nasci." Augustine, *On Marriage and Concupiscence*, 1.15.17 (trans. Peter Holmes, NPNF 1/5:271; CSEL 42:229-30).

28. Cited in John T. Noonan, *The Morality of Abortion: Legal and Historical Perspectives* (Cambridge, MA: Harvard University Press, 1970), 17.

29. Pope Stephen V, *Consuluisti de infantibus*, DH 670. St. Pius V promulgated the *Catechism of the Council of Trent*, or as it is correctly known, the *Catechismus Romanus*, which repudiated abortion as evil. See *Catechismus Romanus seu Catechismus ex decreto Concilii Tridentini ad Parochos Pii Quinti Pont. Max. iussu editus*, ed. Petrus Rodríguez et al. (Vatican City: Libreria Editrice Vaticana/Ediciones Univ. de Navarra, 1989), 381. Sixtus V, *Effraenatam* (1588), in *Bullarium Romanum*, V, 1, pp. 25-27; Gregory XIV, *Sedes Apostolicae* (1591), in *Codicis iuris fontes*, I, 330-31; Innocent XI, *Sixty-Five Propositions of the Holy Office* (1679), DH 2134, 2135; Pius IX, *Apostolicae Sedis* (1869); Pius XI, *Casti connubii* (1930), §2; Pius XII, *Allocutio ad Coetum medico-biologicum «S. Lucas»* (November 12, 1944), 181-96 in *Discorsi e Radiomessaggi* 6 (1944-1945), 191; Pius XII, *Allocutio ad Coetum Catholicum Italicum Obstetricum* (October 29, 1951), pp. 835-54 in *Acta Apostolicae Sedis* 43 (1951), §2 (p. 838). See also the CDF, *Declaration on Procured Abortion* (1974), DH 4550-52.

technically true that this teaching is not yet governed by *papal* infallibility, but one cannot conclude from this fact that this teaching is not infallible. The papal magisterium has repeatedly reaffirmed that this teaching is infallible by the ordinary and universal magisterium.[30] Paul VI bluntly stated that the Church's position on abortion "had not changed and was unchangeable."[31] Saint John Paul II (r. 1978–2005) explicitly reaffirmed this position:

> I declare that direct abortion, that is, abortion willed as an end or as a means, *always* constitutes a grave moral disorder, since it is the deliberate killing of an innocent human being. This doctrine is based upon the natural law and upon the written Word of God, is transmitted by the Church's Tradition and taught by the ordinary and universal Magisterium.[32]

Therefore, the Church's teaching on abortion is "irreformable," and its meaning "must be perpetually retained."[33]

Abortion is also considered to be contrary to the natural law, which therefore may be known merely by reason.[34] Man must obtain his ends, both natural and supernatural. In order to obtain these ends man must live, for his life is a means by which he obtains those ends. Therefore, man has a right to life. No man, without a just and proportionate cause, can deprive another man of his right to life. Therefore,

---

30. For an explanation of this designation, please see my previous essay in this volume, "Theological Sources for Morality: Scripture, Tradition, and the Magisterium."

31. Paul VI, *Salutiamo con paterna effusione* (December 9, 1972), pp. 776–79 in *Acta Apostolicae Sedis* 64 (1972), p. 777.

32. "Auctoritate proinde utentes Nos a Christo Beato Petro eiusque Successoribus collata, consentientes cum Episcopis qui abortum crebrius respuerunt quique in superius memorata interrogatione licet per orbem disseminati una mente tamen de hac ipsa concinuerunt doctrina – *declaramus abortum recta via procuratum, sive uti finem intentum seu ut instrumentum, semper gravem prae se ferre ordinis moralis turbationem,* quippe qui deliberata exsistat innocentis hominis occisio. Haec doctrina naturali innititur lege Deique scripto Verbo, transmittitur Ecclesiae Traditione atque ab ordinario et universali Magisterio exponitur (Cfr. *Lumen Gentium*, 25)." John Paul II, *Evangelium vitae* (March 25, 1995), pp. 401–522 in *Acta Apostolicae Sedis* 87 (1995), §62. English text: pp. 792–894 in *The Papal Encyclicals of John Paul II*, ed. J. Michael Miller (Huntington, IN: Our Sunday Visitor, 1996).

33. DH 3020, 3043.

34. CDF, *Declaration on Abortion*, §8.

those acts which are contrary to man's right to life cannot be performed, such as suicide, murder, euthanasia, feticide, and abortion.[35] In *Evangelium vitae*, Pope John Paul II states that the civil law must conform to the natural law to be legitimate. He quotes Saint Thomas: "Every law made by man can be called a law insofar as it derives from the natural law. But if it is somehow opposed to the natural law, then it is not really a law but rather a corruption of the law."[36] For this reason, Catholics work to end the scourge of abortion.

The Church's Prohibition of Contraception

Artificial contraception is hardly new; the practice is testified to in Egyptian, Greek, and Roman sources. There are a number of Egyptian papyri dating between 1900 and 1100 BC with recipes for application to the vulva. One recipe, for example, calls for pulverized crocodile dung in fermented mucilage.[37] The ancient Greeks and Romans had a wide variety of methods similar to our own today, including oral contraceptives, condoms, and even sponges. They do not appear to have had any objection to contraception in principle.

The Catholic Church, in contrast, has always seen contraception as a grave moral evil contrary to the good of children. She bases this first in Sacred Scripture. The Old Testament shows a repeated concern for the preservation of the generative faculties. Deuteronomy 23:1 declares that "No one whose testicles are crushed or whose male organ is cut off shall enter the assembly of the Lord." Deuteronomy

---

35. Austin Fagothey, *Right and Reason: Ethics in Theory and Practice* (Charlotte, NC: TAN Books, 2008), 275–76, 283–87. See also William E. May, *Catholic Bioethics and the Gift of Human Life*, 3rd ed. (Huntington, IN: Our Sunday Visitor Pub. Division, 2018), 159–99; Elio Sgreccia, *Personalist Bioethics*, trans. John A. Di Camillo and Michael J. Miller, with a foreword by John M. Haas (Philadelphia: National Catholic Bioethics Center, 2012), 419–70; James M. Humber, "The Case against Abortion," *The Thomist* 39 (1975): 65–84; D. N. Irving, "Abortion: Correct Application of Natural Law Theory," *The Linacre Quarterly* 67 (2000): 45–55.

36. John Paul II, *Evangelium vitae*, §72.

37. John T. Noonan, *Contraception: A History of Its Treatment by the Catholic Theologians and Canonists* (Cambridge, MA: Belknap Press of Harvard University Press, 1966), 9.

25:11–12 warns that if a wife touches a man's genitals in defense of her husband, her hand must be cut off. The text concludes with the admonition, "Your eye shall have no pity." Moreover, one is not to offer animals as a peace offering to God if they have crushed testicles (Lev 22:20–25).

Historically, however, the most influential text in the life of the Church concerning contraception was Genesis 38:6–10 concerning Tamar and Onan. Onan is told by his father, the Patriarch Judah, to have sex with his dead brother's widow, Tamar, so that his brother's name can be passed on. The Bible records:

> And Judah took a wife for Er his firstborn, and her name was Tamar. But Er, Judah's firstborn, was wicked in the sight of the LORD, and the LORD put him to death. Then Judah said to Onan, "Go in to your brother's wife and perform the duty of a brother-in-law to her, and raise up offspring for your brother." But Onan knew that the offspring would not be his. So whenever he went in to his brother's wife he would waste the semen on the ground, so as not to give offspring to his brother. And what he did was wicked in the sight of the LORD, and he put him to death also (Gen 38:6–10).

Traditionally this passage was used so frequently as the *locus classicus* for condemning contraceptive practices that "onanism" became a synonym for *coitus interruptus* and for all forms of contraception in Catholic moral theology.[38] Indeed the Fathers of the Church, including Cyril of Alexandria, Epiphanius, and Jerome, commonly

---

38. Josef Aertnys, C.Ss.R, and C. A. Damen, C.Ss.R, *Theologia moralis*, 18th ed. (Turin: Marietti, 1968): 1:591; Giuseppe D'Annibale, *Summula Theologiae Moralis*, 5th ed. (Rome: Desclee, Lefebvre Et Soc., 1908), 2:55; A. M. Arregui, SJ, *Summarium theologiae moralis*, 13th ed. (Bilbao: Mesajero del Corazón de Jesus, 1952), 813; H. Jone, OFM Cap., *Moral Theology* (Westminster, MD: Newman, 1945), 540–42; Michel Rosset, *De Sacramento Matrimonii Tractatus Dogmaticus, Moralis, Canonicus, Liturgicus et Judiciarius* (Maurianae: Apud Auctorem, 1895), 5:375; "Instruction des Évêques de Belgique sur l'onanisme," *Nouvelle revue theologique* 41 (1909): 616–22; John A. McHugh and Charles J. Callan, *Moral Theology* (New York: Joseph F. Wagner, 1930), 2:510; Dominicus M. Prummer, *Manuale Theologiae Moralis: Secundum Principia S. Thomae Aquinatis in Usum Scholarum* (Fribourg: Herder, 1928), 3:509–12; A. Sabetti, SJ, *Compendium theologiae moralis*, ed. T. Barrett, SJ, 31st ed. of Gury (New York: Pustet, 1926), 968.

interpreted the passage this way.[39] Augustine writes, for example, "No doubt, even some lawfully named couples do this last mentioned thing; but just the same, when the conception of offspring is precluded, it is wrong and shameful even to sleep with one's lawful wife. Onan, the son of Judah did this, and God killed him for it."[40] Catholic theologians and then Protestant commentators, including Luther, Calvin, and Wesley, also interpreted this passage as such.[41] In

---

39. Epiphanius, *Panarion*, 26.11.11 (GCS 25:290); 63.1.4 (GCS 31:399); Augustine, *Against Faustus*, 22.84 (CSEL 25.1:687); Cyril of Alexandria, *Critical Comments on Genesis* 6 (PG 69:309); Jerome, *Against Jovinian*, 1:19.

40. Augustine, *Adulterous Marriages*, 2.12.12 (CSEL 41:396; trans. Ray Kearney, WSA I/9:175).

41. Martin Luther writes, "Onan must have been a malicious and incorrigible scoundrel. This is a most disgraceful sin. It is far more atrocious than incest and adultery. We call it unchastity, yes, a Sodomitic sin. For Onan goes in to her; that is, he lies with her and copulates, and when it comes to the point of insemination, spills the semen, lest the woman conceive. Surely at such a time the order of nature established by God in procreation should be followed. Accordingly, it was a most disgraceful crime to produce semen and excite the woman, and to frustrate her at that very moment. He was inflamed with the basest spite and hatred. Therefore, he did not allow himself to be compelled to bear that intolerable slavery. Consequently, he deserved to be killed by God. He committed an evil deed. Therefore, God punished him." Luther, *Commentary on Genesis*, trans. Paul D. Pahl, *Luther's Works*, vol. 7 (St. Louis: Concordia, 1965), 20–21. John Calvin writes, "Monstruosa res est voluntaria seminis effusio extra congressum viri & mulieris. A coitu autem se data opera retrahere ut semen in terram decidat, duplex est monstrum: quia hoc est spem generis extinguere, & filium qui sperandus esset, occidere antequam nascatur. Haec maxime impietas damnatur nunc à Spiritu per os Mosis, quod Onam quasi violento abortu fratris sui sobolem ex utero materno avulsam, non minus crudeliter quam foede in terram proiecit. Adde quod hoc modo generis humani partem, quantum in se erat, abolere conatus est. Si qua mulier foetum ex utero medicamentis abigat, inexpiabile censetur crimen: & merito. Eodem piaculi genere se obstrinxit Onam, terram suo semine inficiens, ne Thamar hominem conciperet futurum terrae incolam." Calvin, *Commentarii In Genesin* (Amsterdam: Apud viduam Ioannis Iacobi Schipperi, 1554), 193. Interestingly, this passage is not in the English edition of Calvin's commentary. There is an ellipsis followed by a footnote, which states, "A line or two is here omitted, as well as the comment on the tenth verse." John Calvin, *Commentaries on the First Book of Moses, Called Genesis*, trans. Rev. John King, MA (Grand Rapids: Eerdmans, 1948), 281. John Wesley writes, "Those sins that dishonor the body are very displeasing to God, and the evidence of vile affections. Observe, the thing which he [Onan] did displeased the Lord—And it is to be feared; thousands, especially of single persons, by this very thing, still displease the Lord, and destroy their own

the twentieth century, biblical commentators began to argue that the tradition, whether Catholic or Protestant, did not rightly interpret the passage and that Onan was not killed for performing a type of contraception but rather for merely violating the levirate law.[42]

The traditional interpretation seems at least plausible. It is clear that God was displeased with what Onan "did," and what he did was two intimately connected things, i.e., violation of the levirate law and *coitus interruptus*.[43] Onan, however, is only one of three persons who violated the levirate law in this story. Onan's father, Judah, and his younger brother, Sela, also violated the levirate law. Judah was bound by the law to give Tamar to his third son, Sela, on the death of Onan. Judah even admits his guilt (Gen 38:26), yet he is not killed.

We must ask why Onan was killed, but Judah and Sela were not. Onan differed from the other two only in that he engaged in *coitus interruptus* and the others did not. Perhaps a clue to the severity of Onan's punishment can be found in the fact that sexual sins often required the death penalty, including adultery (Lev 20:10; Deut 22:22), rape (Deut 22:23–29), homosexuality (Lev 20:13), and bestiality (Exod 22:18; Lev 20:15–16). Moreover, it seems unlikely that Onan was punished with death for breaking the levirate law. The book of Deuteronomy specifies a relatively mild punishment (as far as Old Testament punishments go) for this law's violation. According to Deuteronomy, the widow is to bring her brother-in-law before the elders. If he still refuses to do his duty, she could "pull the sandal off his foot and spit in his face. And she shall answer and say, 'So shall it be done to the man who does not build up his brother's house'" (Deut 25:9–10). Thus, while breaking the levirate law was serious,

---

souls." Wesley wrote an entire tract on the subject. John Wesley, *Thoughts on the Sin of Onan* (London: [publisher not identified], 1767).

42. Raymond E. Brown, Augustin Cardinal Bea, Joseph A. Fitzmyer, and Roland E. Murphy, *The Jerome Biblical Commentary* (Englewood Cliffs, NJ: Prentice-Hall, 1968), 39. "Onan's offense is obvious; he selfishly refuses the responsibility of fulfilling his duty to his brother, as the law provided. That is the point of his offense (not what is popularly called onanism today)." Brown, Fitzmyer, Murphy, and Martini, *The Jerome Biblical Commentary*, 38.

43. Manuel Miguens, "Biblical Thoughts on Human Sexuality," 102–19 in *Human Sexuality in Our Time*, ed. George A. Kelly (Boston: St. Paul Editions, 1979), 112–15.

the punishment was little more than humiliating. We would consequently be forced to admit that God punished Onan with severity beyond measure, and in fact beyond the measure of the law which he later gave to Moses.[44]

The Fathers of the Church wrote much against the lax morality of a pagan society. Against this background, the Fathers of the Church vigorously rejected contraception as immoral, including all practices which subverted God's created order. Early pastoral practice, for example, was to exclude unrepentant sexual offenders such as adulterers, pimps, prostitutes, fornicators, homosexuals, and effeminate males (κίναιδος) from the catechumenate itself, and thus to baptism and entry to Christian life.[45] The Fathers generally adopted two approaches to the question: 1. directly condemning contraceptive acts, or 2. affirming that the marital act must be open to life. Clement of Alexandria states, for example, that "to indulge in intercourse without intending children is to outrage nature, whom we should take as our instructor."[46] Epiphanius speaks of some Egyptian heretics who "exercise genital acts, yet prevent the conceiving of children. Not in order to produce offspring, but to satisfy lust, are they eager for corruption."[47] Saint Jerome comments on the Onan story thus: "Onan, who was slain because he grudged his brother seed. Does he imagine that we approve of any sexual intercourse except for the procreation of children?"[48]

In the early Church, however, it was Manicheanism, as opposed to human weakness, that challenged the Church's opposition to

---

44. Johannes B. Schaumberger, "Propter quale peccatum morte punitus est Onan?," *Biblica* 6 (1927): 209–12; C. F. Devine, "The Sin of Onan, Genesis 38:8–10," *Catholic Biblical Quarterly* 4 (1941): 322–40.

45. *Traditio Apostolica*, 16 (SC 11:70–75); *Constitutiones apostolorum*, 8, 32 (Funk 535–37); the Council of Elvira, canons 4, 10, 42 (Hefele 1: 223, 227, 245); Augustine, *De fide et operibus*, 19.34.

46. Clement of Alexandria, *The Instructor of Children*, 2:10:95; trans. Simon P. Wood, *Christ the Educator*, FaCh 23 (Washington, DC: Catholic University of America Press, 1954), 173.

47. Epiphanius, *Panarion*, 26.5.2 (GCS 25:281). English translation from Noonan, *Contraception: A History of Its Treatment by the Catholic Theologians and Canonists*, 97.

48. Jerome, *Against Jovinian*, 1:20 (trans. W. H. Fremantle, NPNF 2/6:361).

contraception at the level of doctrine. Manicheanism began in the third century with a Persian named Mani (c. 215–75). He was considered divinely inspired and gained a large following. In the Manichaean system there are two ultimate sources of creation, the one good and the other evil. God is the creator of all that is good and Satan of all that is evil. Man's spirit is from God, his body is from the devil.[49] In this world, the created light or spirit is imprisoned in the world, and Manichean morality centered around the problem of freeing the light from matter. Manichean morality therefore dictated one should eat the seeds of plants and man in order to liberate the light therein.[50] It also appears that semen was mixed with seeds and ritually eaten as a type of Eucharist.[51] Moreover, any type of procreative sexual activity itself was viewed as evil, since the result was that the light would be imprisoned in an evil body.

There was and is a great deal to object to in the Manichean religion, including their radical dualist view of God, the grotesque mockeries of the true Christian religion, and their belief that matter is bad. Understandably, the Fathers objected to these heresies; just as vigorously they objected to Manichean contraceptive acts and mentality. One of the earliest surviving anti-Manichean writings is by Titus, who wrote a short work, *Against the Manichees,* in which he objects that they "contemptuously vituperate the procreation of children." He seems to ascribe to them a host of non-procreative acts, including abortion.[52] It was Saint Augustine, however, a former Manichean Auditor himself, who became perhaps its most stalwart opponent. Augustine, for our purposes, has two main problems with Manichean morality. First, he repeatedly criticizes them for subverting God's divine command to

---

49. On the Manicheans, see F. Decret, *Aspects du manicheisme dans l'Afrique romaine. Les controverses de Fortunatus, Faustus et Felix avec saint Augustin* (Paris: Études Augustiniennes, 1970); H.-C. Puech, *Le manicheisme, son fondateur, sa doctrine*, BDiff 56 (Paris: Musée Guimet, 1949).

50. Augustine, *The Morals of the Manichees*, 18.66 (PL 32:1373); Augustine, *The Nature of the Good*, 45, 47 (CSEL 252:886–87).

51. Augustine, *Heresies*, 46 (PL 42:36).

52. Noonan, *Contraception: A History of Its Treatment by the Catholic Theologians and Canonists*, 19.

"Be fruitful and multiply and fill the earth."[53] Second, he also maintains that the Manicheans in effect destroy marriage by denying that its purpose or end is procreation.[54] So Augustine repeatedly notes that the Manicheans make the bridal chamber a brothel.[55] This is an important point, for one sometimes gets the distinct impression in contemporary literature on the matter that Augustine's opposition to Manicheanism was that Manicheans *believed* the marital act and procreation were evil, implying that if the Manicheans had believed otherwise, there would have been no issue. It is true that Augustine objected to their belief system, but he also thought that the structure of their sexual acts was contrary to the divine order. This patristic teaching was later taken up by Pope Saint Pius V (r. 1566–1572).[56]

Lastly, in the early twentieth century, the "birth control" movement challenged Christian teaching on the nature of marriage. Initially, Christian churches were uniformly hostile to this challenge. The Anglican bishops, for example, in 1908 and again in 1920 in their Lambeth conferences firmly repeated the traditional prohibition against contraception. By the 1930s, however, decades of secular propaganda had paid off: in 1930 the Church of England broke from Christian tradition. Admirably, the Anglican bishops affirmed that "the primary purpose for which marriage exists is the procreation of children" and "strongly" condemned "the use of any methods of conception-control from motives of selfishness, luxury, or mere convenience." They went on to affirm, however, that a Christian couple may use methods other than complete abstinence.[57]

---

53. Augustine, *Answer to Secundinus, a Manichean*, 21 (trans. Roland J. Teske, WSA 1/19:385).
54. Augustine, *The Morals of the Manichees*, 18.65.
55. Augustine, *Against Faustus*, 15.7 (CSEL 25.1:430).
56. "Atque una etiam haec causa fuit, cur Deus ab initio matrimonium instituerit. quare fit, ut illorum sit scelus gravissimum, qui matrimonio iuncti, medicamentis vel conceptum impediunt, vel partum abigunt. haec enim homicidarum impia conspiratio existimanda est." Pope St. Pius V, *Catechismus Romanus*, 381.
57. Resolution 15, which was passed by a vote of 193 to 67, reads as follows: "Where there is a clearly felt moral obligation to limit or avoid parenthood, the method must be decided on Christian principles. The primary and obvious method is complete abstinence from intercourse (as far as may be necessary) in a life of discipline and self-control

Catholic theologians immediately responded to this decision, and less than four months later so did Pius XI (r. 1922–1939) on the last day of 1930.[58] It was to the Anglican resolution at Lambeth that Pope Pius XI made reference:

> Since, therefore, openly departing from the uninterrupted Christian tradition some recently have judged it possible solemnly to declare another doctrine regarding this question, the Catholic Church, to whom God has entrusted the defense of the integrity and purity of morals, standing erect in the midst of the moral ruin which surrounds her, in order that she may preserve the chastity of the nuptial union from being defiled by this foul stain, raises her voice in token of her divine ambassadorship and through Our mouth proclaims anew: any use whatsoever of matrimony exercised in such a way that the act is deliberately frustrated in its natural power to generate life is an offense against the law of God and of nature, and those who indulge in such are branded with the guilt of a grave sin.[59]

The magisterium has constantly reaffirmed the teaching of the Scriptures and Fathers condemning the use of contraception. Pius XII (r. 1939–1958) condemned unnatural contraception.[60]

In 1960 the first oral contraceptives were approved by the FDA for use. This led some moral theologians to argue for a re-evaluation of

---

lived in the power of the Holy Spirit. Nevertheless, in those cases where there is such a clearly felt moral obligation to limit or avoid parenthood, and where there is a morally sound reason for avoiding complete abstinence, the Conference agrees that other methods may be used, provided that this is done in the light of the same Christian principles. The Conference records its strong condemnation of the use of any methods of conception-control from motives of selfishness, luxury, or mere convenience." Church of England, *Lambeth Conferences 1867–1930: The Reports of the 1920, 1930, and 1948 Conferences, with Selected Resolutions from the Conferences of 1867, 1878, 1888, 1897, and 1908* (London: SPCK, 1930), 166. On the nature and history of the Lambeth conferences, see Paul D. L. Avis and Benjamin Guyer, eds., *The Lambeth Conference: Theology, History, Polity and Purpose* (London: Bloomsbury T&T Clark, 2017).

58. H. Pope, "The Lambeth Report - Resolution 15," *Blackfriars* 11 (1930): 725–40; Reginald Ginns, "The New Morality of Lambeth," *Blackfriars* 11 (1930): 677–83; A. Vermeersch, "La Conference de Lambeth et la morale du marriage," *Nouvelle Revue Théoloqique* 57 (1930): 831–59.

59. Pius XI, *Casti connubii*, §56.

60. Pius XII, *Allocution to Midwives*.

the ban on certain types of contraceptives. In 1963 Pope John XXIII (r. 1958–1963) established a commission of six to study questions of birth control. Pope Paul VI (r. 1963–1978) expanded the commission to fifty-eight members composed of bishops, theologians, and laity;[61] then after receiving its report, he issued *Humanae vitae* on July 25, 1968, reaffirming the traditional position of the Church:

> Equally to be condemned, as the magisterium of the Church has affirmed on many occasions, is direct sterilization, whether of the man or of the woman, whether perpetual or temporary. Similarly excluded is any action which, either before, at the moment of, or after sexual intercourse, is specifically intended to prevent procreation—whether as an end or a means.[62]

This doctrine was reaffirmed by Saint John Paul II (r. 1978–2005) both in *Veritatis splendor* and in the *Catechism of the Catholic Church*: "every action which, whether in anticipation of the conjugal act, or in its accomplishment, or in the development of its natural consequences, proposes, whether as an end or as a means, to render procreation impossible is intrinsically evil."[63] "Legitimate intentions on the part of the spouses do not justify recourse to morally unacceptable means . . . for example, direct sterilization or contraception."[64] In other words, there is no situation in which contraception as contraception can be considered good or even allowable. Later both Benedict XVI (r. 2005–2013) and Pope Francis (r. 2013–) reaffirmed this teaching.[65] These magisterial interventions may seem to appear

---

61. Janet E. Smith, *Humanae Vitae: A Generation Later* (Washington, DC: The Catholic University Press of America, 1991), 11–14. This is the standard work on the subject and should be consulted for the philosophical and theological grounds of the Church's teaching.

62. Paul VI, *Humanae vitae* (July 25, 1968), pp. 4:223–33 in *The Papal Encyclicals*, 5 vols., ed. Claudia Carlen, IHM (Wilmington, NC: McGrath, 1981), §14.

63. CCC 2370.

64. CCC 2399.

65. Pope John Paul II, *Veritatis splendor*, §80; *Compendium – Catechism of the Catholic Church* (Washington, DC: United States Conference of Catholic Bishops, 2006), 143; Pope Benedict XVI, *Message of His Holiness Benedict XVI on the Occasion of the 40th Anniversary of Paul VI's Encyclical Humanae Vitae* (October 2, 2008); Pope Francis, *Amoris laetitia*, §80.

relatively late in the tradition, but as John Henry Newman noted, "no doctrine is defined until it is violated."[66] Moreover, this teaching is commonly understood to be taught infallibly by the ordinary and universal magisterium.[67]

The Argument from Natural Law against Contraception

The Church teaches that we can know the moral law not only through revelation but also through the light of human reason. This is known as the natural moral law, which Paul refers to as the law "written on their hearts" (Rom 2:15). There are a number of natural law arguments against contraception. The argument presented here, sometimes known as the perverted faculty argument, is reduced to its simple syllogistic form:

1. Unnatural acts are wrong.
2. Contraception is an unnatural act.
3. Therefore, contraception is wrong.[68]

It is first necessary to be clear about what is meant by the terms "natural" and "unnatural." We do not mean by the term "natural" simply anything found in the world. There are a great many things that are found in the world that are unnatural. The term "natural" signifies consistency with the ends or final causes inherent in a thing by virtue of its essence.[69] The term "unnatural" signifies inconsistency with

---

66. John Henry Newman, *An Essay on the Development of Christian Doctrine* (London: Pickering, 1878), 151.
67. Pontifical Council for the Family, "Vade mecum for Confessors Concerning Some Aspects of the Morality of Conjugal Life," *Origins* 26 (March 13, 1997): 617–25; John C. Ford and Germain Grisez, "Contraception and the Infallibility of the Ordinary Magisterium," *Theological Studies* 39 (1978): 258–312; Germain Grisez, "Infallibility and Specific Moral Norms: A Review Discussion," *The Thomist* 49 (1985): 248–87; Russel Shaw, "Contraception, Infallibility and the Ordinary Magisterium," *International Review of Natural Family Planning* 2 (1978): 288–98.
68. Smith, *Humanae Vitae: A Generation Later*, 85.
69. Edward Feser explains, "'Natural' for the Aristotelian-Thomistic philosopher does not mean merely 'deeply ingrained,' 'in accordance with the laws of physics,' 'having a genetic basis,' or any other of the readings that a non-teleological view of nature might allow. It has instead to do with the final causes inherent in a thing by virtue of

those ends or final causes that are inherent in a thing by virtue of its essence. Animals and humans have various faculties that they use to accomplish these ends. A faculty is the power of a living substance to exercise a specific life-operation as required by its essence. Take the example of a deer, which has as part of its animality the needs of nutrition and self-preservation. The deer has a faculty of nutrition and a faculty of fear in order to accomplish these two ends.[70] Thus, it is natural and good for a deer to browse boughs in the winter and to escape predators. It is unnatural for the deer to eat only dirt or to lie down before wolves. It would be "unnatural" and bad for the deer to do these latter actions for any reason, were it even CWD (chronic wasting disease) or deer peer pressure, since these two things do not help the deer fulfill its ends.

Regarding rational creatures, the term "natural" means *to will* to do what tends toward the realization of the ends defining what it is for us to flourish as the kind of things we are. The term "unnatural" means *to will* to do what tends toward the frustration of the ends which, given our nature, define what it means for us to flourish as the kind of things we are. Now man has a nature which requires nutrition and generation, and he has faculties to accomplish these two ends. So for a man to flourish, he must act in accord with these ends and order his operations to them. It must be noted that while everyone is required to act in a way that is consistent with his ends, we do not always have to use our operations or always do some particular act that is consistent with our natural ends. Sometimes man will eat, and sometimes he will not eat.

Part of man's nature is to reproduce, and so we have a generative faculty. As bodily organisms, part of man's nature is also to seek pleasure. Consequently, human sexual organs have two purposes, i.e., pleasure and reproduction. Now, what is essential in any act is the achievement of the finality of the operation or faculty. If this is obstructed, the act is unnatural. Various forms of contraception, such

---

its essence, and which it possesses whether or not it ever realizes them or consciously wants to realize them." Edward Feser, "In Defense of the Perverted Faculty Argument," 378–415 in in *Neo-Scholastic Essays* (South Bend, IN: St. Augustine's Press, 2015), 384.

70. A faculty is the power of a living substance to exercise a specific life-operation.

as the condom, the pill, the IUD, etc. produce pleasure but frustrate man's reproductive faculty's operation by preventing the natural course of sperm to egg; they are therefore unnatural. All these things clearly prevent what is by nature supposed to occur, i.e., conception. This is why they are called contraceptives, i.e., against conception. Similarly, we have a nutritive faculty, and nutrition involves two purposes (there are more): taste and absorption of nutrients. It would be unnatural to frustrate the end of our nutritive faculty by eating Styrofoam, even if it tasted like crème brûlée or tarte Tatin. The Styrofoam might taste good and thus fulfill the end of taste, but it would frustrate the nutritive faculty.

Furthermore, by the term "unnatural" we do not mean that which is artificial. Many will argue from analogy that if it is wrong to use contraception, then it is also wrong to use antibiotics to fight infection, to wear glasses to improve sight, or to wear a hearing aid to improve hearing. After all, these things are "unnatural." This objection misses the point since Catholics do not consider antibiotics, glasses, or hearing aids "unnatural." Why, you ask. All organs and operations in the body have a specific end, i.e., a function or purpose. The immune system is to fight off infection, the eyes to see, and the ears to hear. When these are not functioning normally, they need assistance to perform their tasks. Thus, when we use antibiotics, glasses, or hearing aids, we are merely assisting or restoring the natural end or purpose of the immune system, the eyes, and the ears.

Responsible Parenthood and Natural Family Planning

While today the notion of responsible parenthood almost always carries with it the notion of limiting the size of one's family, Pope Paul VI spoke of "responsible parenthood" as exercised by those who "prudently and generously decide to have more children."[71] He also recognized that "responsible parenthood" sometimes involves deciding not to have additional children for either a certain or an indefinite period of time. He thought, however, that this limitation should only be for

---

71. Janet E. Smith, "Conscious Parenthood," *Nova et Vetera* 6 (2008): 927–50.

"serious reasons and with due respect to moral precepts."[72] Pope Paul VI mentioned four kinds of "serious reasons" (*seriis causis*): 1. physical conditions, 2. economic conditions, 3. psychological conditions, 4. social conditions. As we have seen, one cannot limit family size through contraceptives, but Catholics are permitted to use Natural Family Planning (NFP). In NFP, a couple carefully monitors the signs of a woman's fertility and temporarily has intercourse only during the naturally infertile days of her cycle.

Some object that NFP is simply a Catholic form of contraception, but this objection misses the mark. There is an essential difference between contraception and NFP. With contraception, the marital act, as it is being performed, is perverted from its natural purpose and meaning. The procreative aspect is deliberately blocked and divorced from its unitive aspect. With NFP, the act takes place in an entirely natural way. Nature renders a woman periodically infertile, and the couple chooses to have sex temporarily only during these times. There is not an unnatural frustration of the end of the marital act because during periods of abstinence no marital act takes place. It is really observing periods of intermittent continence, an act even espoused in the Scriptures. Priests and Levites, for example, observed temporary continence during their temple ministry (Exod 19:15; Lev 15:16–18; 20:7; 22:4) and during a woman's menstruation (Lev 15:19–24). In the New Testament, Paul says that couples can abstain in order to devote themselves to prayer (1 Cor 7:3–5). In time, of course, nature eventually renders a woman permanently infertile, yet sexual relations continue to be morally permissible.

While NFP does not frustrate the natural end of the action, it must be admitted that it is possible to misuse NFP in such a way that in effect one has a "contraceptive mentality." A married couple could, for example, use NFP with the firm intent of never having children. Or, for example, a couple may want to restrict the number of children in order to live a life of luxury or for other selfish motives. This, I would suggest, is quite rare. First, most Catholics who use NFP do so because they have already rejected contraception on religious

---

72. Paul VI, *Humanae vitae*, §10.

grounds. Second, while NFP is often presented as a way to have sexual relations and avoid pregnancy, NFP is also often used to help the couple have children when they decide it is time. The point is that the very methodology that allows one to avoid pregnancy with a high degree of accuracy can also be used to assist one in getting pregnant. This is why a significant number of Catholic couples who practice NFP are more likely on average to have more children than the 1.87 children of the average US couple and less likely to have an abortion.[73]

Conclusion

The Catholic Church sees marriage not only as a divinely instituted covenant between a male and a female but also as a sacrament which bestows on the recipients the graces necessary for living this covenant. The primary purpose of marriage is the procreation and education of children. The Catholic Church does not reject abortion simply because it is murder but also because it frustrates the procreative end of marriage. Likewise, the Catholic Church's prohibition on contraception flows naturally from her teaching on marriage and sees it as frustrating the procreative end of marriage. Basing her teaching on Scripture, the Fathers of the Church, and natural law, the Catholic Church continues to uphold a vision of marriage and procreative activity that has been espoused from the beginning of the world.

---

73. Andrea M. Bertotti and Sinead M. Christensen, "Comparing Current, Former, and Never Users of Natural Family Planning: An Analysis of Demographic, Socioeconomic, and Attitudinal Variables," *The Linacre Quarterly* 79, no. 4 (2012): 474–86.

2.3. A Catholic Understanding of Homosexual Relations: The Biblical Foundations

Dr. Daniel A. Keating

The Topic

The topic for our dialogue this year is sexual ethics. I was asked to offer the Catholic perspective on homosexual relations and same-sex attraction, with an emphasis on the biblical teaching that grounds this approach. The first part of the title, "A Catholic Understanding of Homosexual Relations," includes far more than I can hope to address here. There are many aspects to a Catholic understanding of this debated topic—and many cognate issues such as same-sex marriage—that only a book-length treatment could begin to cover.

My focus will be on the biblical foundations: What do the Scriptures (Old and New Testament) say about homosexual activity, and how has the Catholic Church evaluated the biblical revelation? It will not be possible to delve deeply into the exegetical "weeds" of the individual biblical texts. This would (once again) require a book-length treatment, as Robert A. Gagnon's lengthy study plainly (and ably) demonstrates.[1] Instead, I will summarize the biblical testimony as received in the Catholic tradition and then show how contemporary exegetes and theologians try to argue that the traditional rejection of homosexual activity does not apply to current expressions of homosexual partnerships (and by extension why the traditional position

---

1. Robert A. Gagnon, *The Bible and Homosexual Practice: Texts and Hermeneutics* (Nashville: Abingdon, 2001).

should be modified to allow for same-sex marriage). To conclude I will state why I believe that these various historical, exegetical, and theological strategies fail.

Before embarking on this biblical investigation, I believe it is important to place in view the wider ideological context that gives rise to our present debates. It is nearly impossible to address any side of this issue without looking at the whole of it, especially given the strong currents in our wider society. The issue of homosexual practice is not a single, stand-alone issue; it is part of a wider cultural reform that seeks to overturn traditional Christian teaching on the human person, marriage, and the family. A brief examination of this ideology and the Catholic response to it provides an important frame for then considering the biblical teaching on the subject. This paper, then, will proceed in three steps: (1) a brief introduction to gender theory; (2) the fundamental teaching on homosexuality in Catholic teaching; and (3) an examination and evaluation of the biblical teaching on homosexual relations.

Gender Theory and the Gender Revolution

The question of homosexual relations—and more broadly homosexual identity—does not arise in a cultural vacuum. Even if we include a wider cluster of topics—same-sex marriage, transgenderism, etc.—we still miss the wider context for the enormous surge in our culture energizing the radical changes proposed for these areas. That wider context has been identified as "gender theory" or "gender ideology," which encompasses a radically new and different view of the human person and of all sexual relations and identities.[2] In my view, one of

---

2. The best overall treatment of the history of gender theory is from Gabriele Kuby, *The Global Sexual Revolution: Destruction of Freedom in the Name of Freedom* (Kettering, OH: LifeSite, 2015). The original German edition, *Die globale sexuelle Revolution: Zerstörung der Freiheit im Namen der Freiheit*, appeared in 2012. The expanded English edition includes a wider treatment of this issue in North America. A recent study by Sr. Prudence Allen also offers an in-depth examination of the rise of gender ideology: "Gender Reality vs. Gender Ideology," 35–88 in *The Complementarity of Women and Men: Philosophy, Theology, Psychology and Art*, ed. Paul C. Vitz (Washington, DC: Catholic University of America Press, 2021).

the best summaries of this new gender ideology comes from Pope Benedict in an address he gave to the Roman clergy in 2012. He goes to the anthropological and metaphysical root of this approach:

> According to this philosophy, sex is no longer a given element of nature, that man has to accept and personally make sense of: it is a social role that we choose for ourselves, while in the past it was chosen for us by society. . . . People dispute the idea that they have a nature, given by their bodily identity, that serves as a defining element of the human being. They deny their nature and decide that it is not something previously given to them, but that they make it for themselves.[3]

Benedict sees in this approach a rejection of our given "nature" in favor of a view of our humanity whereby we become the effective creators of ourselves.

> Man calls his nature into question. From now on he is merely spirit and will. The manipulation of nature, which we deplore today where our environment is concerned, now becomes man's fundamental choice where he himself is concerned. From now on there is only the abstract human being, who chooses for himself what his nature is to be.[4]

We could call this a neo-Gnostic approach to reality, especially to our human reality. Benedict believes that this new gender philosophy not only contradicts Christian revelation but flies in the face of what we can know by natural means:

> The profound falsehood of this theory and of the anthropological revolution contained within it is obvious . . . . According to the biblical creation account, being created by God as male and female pertains to the essence of the human creature. This duality is an essential aspect of what being human is all about, as ordained by God . . . . When the freedom to be creative becomes the freedom to create oneself, then necessarily the Maker himself is denied and ultimately man too is stripped of his dignity as a creature of God, as the image of God at the core of his being.[5]

---

3. Pope Benedict XVI, "Address to the Roman Curia" (December 12, 2012), *L'Osservatore Romano*, English Edition (January 3, 2013): 6.
4. Pope Benedict XVI, "Address to the Roman Curia," 6.
5. Pope Benedict XVI, "Address to the Roman Curia," 6.

In a similar way, Pope Francis has called attention to a gender ideology that undermines the family:

> Yet another challenge is posed by the various forms of an ideology of gender that denies the difference and reciprocity in nature of a man and a woman and envisages a society without sexual differences, thereby eliminating the anthropological basis of the family.

Given Francis's understated approach to hot-button sexual issues in general, his forthright statement on this underlying theory is all the more notable. For Francis,

> It needs to be emphasized that "biological sex and the socio-cultural role of sex (gender) can be distinguished but not separated".... It is one thing to be understanding of human weakness and the complexities of life, and another to accept ideologies that attempt to sunder what are inseparable aspects of reality. Let us not fall into the sin of trying to replace the Creator. We are creatures, and not omnipotent. Creation is prior to us and must be received as a gift.[6]

As Gabriele Kuby has capably demonstrated, one of the main priorities for many Western governments and international agencies is to promote gender theory and practice. Acting through education, media, law, and business, the new gender ideology has brought about a radical rupture with traditional approaches to sex, marriage, and the family. It is within this wider context that questions about homosexual identity and relations arise.

Catholic Teaching on Homosexuality

The most recent and authoritative Catholic teaching on homosexuality appears in three compact paragraphs in the *Catechism of the Catholic Church* (second edition, 1997). The opening paragraph lays down the Church's fundamental convictions about homosexual relations and sexual orientation:

---

6. Pope Francis, *Amoris laetitia* (March 19, 2016), in *Amoris Laetitia: On Love in the Family* (Huntington, IN: Our Sunday Visitor, 2016), §56.

> Homosexuality refers to relations between men or between women who experience an exclusive or predominant sexual attraction toward persons of the same sex. It has taken a great variety of forms through the centuries and in different cultures. Its psychological genesis remains largely unexplained. Basing itself on Sacred Scripture, which presents homosexual acts as acts of grave depravity, tradition has always declared that "homosexual acts are intrinsically disordered." They are contrary to the natural law. They close the sexual act to the gift of life. They do not proceed from a genuine affective and sexual complementarity. Under no circumstances can they be approved.[7]

In this opening statement, homosexuality is defined and circumscribed. It is not the purpose of the *Catechism* to render judgments about different cultural expressions of homosexuality or its root causes (nature and nurture). Crucially, the subject to be evaluated is the category of "homosexual acts," not inclinations or desires. Note that the Church's teaching is explicitly grounded in Sacred Scripture which presents homosexual acts as acts of "grave depravity."

Then citing the document *Persona humana* (1975), the *Catechism* says that the Catholic tradition has *always* declared homosexual acts to be "intrinsically disordered."[8] What this means is further expressed in the following three assertions: (1) such acts are contrary to the natural law; (2) such acts are intrinsically closed to the gift of life; (3) such acts do not proceed from a genuine "affective and sexual complementarity." The conclusion is then stated categorically: Under no circumstances can homosexual acts be approved.

The following two paragraphs, which I will not discuss in detail, proceed to express how those who experience same-sex attraction are to be shown the utmost respect, charity, and sensitivity—there can be no unjust discrimination in their regard. Notably same-sex *inclination* is said to be "objectively disordered." To remove potential misunderstanding on what this might mean, a 2006 document of the US Catholic Bishops' Conference clarifies that a disorder in the inclination does not mean an overall disorder as a person: "It is crucially

---

7. CCC 2357.
8. CDF, *Persona humana*, "Declaration on Certain Questions Concerning Sexual Ethics" (November 7, 1975), §8.

important to understand that saying a person has a particular inclination that is disordered is not to say that the person as a whole is disordered.... While the particular inclination to homosexual acts is disordered, the person retains his or her intrinsic human dignity and value."[9] The *Catechism* concludes, in its third paragraph, by indicating how those with same-sex attraction can pursue holiness through the given means of grace and the activity of the virtues.

In summary, the Catholic Church adopts its position on homosexual activity based on two linked and coordinated authorities: the scriptural testimony and the natural law. Homosexual activity is—in the Church's judgment—clearly and univocally forbidden by divine revelation in Scripture, and it clearly and gravely violates the natural order given in creation for our sexuality as male and female persons.

The Biblical Teaching Reviewed, Questioned, and Reaffirmed

Does the biblical teaching on homosexual relations speak with one voice? What does it say and (more specifically) what is it talking about when it seems to address sexual relations between people of the same sex? Is the traditional reception of scriptural teaching on homosexual activity, accepted by all churches before the mid-twentieth century, justified and does it speak directly to the practice of homosexual relations and unions as understood in contemporary society? This is not just a question (and a problem) for Protestants who hold that the Scripture alone is the final authority in matters of doctrine and practice. The Catholic Church also grounds her teaching in Scripture and on this topic plainly claims that Scripture speaks clearly and decisively. Thus, it is important that we as Catholics and Evangelicals consider the scriptural testimony together.

---

9. United States Conference of Catholic Bishops, *Ministry to Persons with a Homosexual Inclination: Guidelines for Pastoral Care* (November 14, 2006) (Washington, DC: United States Conference of Catholic Bishops, 2006).

A. REVIEW OF THE SCRIPTURAL TEACHING

The primary texts in the Old Testament that address the topic of homosexual relations are Genesis 19 (the story of Abraham and Lot in Sodom) and Leviticus 18:22 and 20:13. The first text is *narrative*, not legal. It describes in turn (1) the renowned dialogue between Abraham and the Lord about saving the city for the sake of a few righteous men, (2) the assault on Lot and his guests, asking that the men be brought out so that the inhabitants might *know* them, (3) the escape of Lot and his family and the destruction of the city. The depravity of the city no doubt encompassed many kinds of evil but the *extent* of it is marked by a desire for same-sex intercourse, men with men. The text has long stood as a cautionary tale of what happens to the wicked but has also served as a marker for the grave wickedness of same-sex activity.

The legal prohibition against homosexual acts is stated in Leviticus 18:22 and 20:13: "You shall not lie with a male as with a woman; it is an abomination," and "If a man lies with a male as with a woman, both of them have committed an abomination." It is important to observe the context for these prohibitions (18:1–5) and the cluster of sexual offenses listed in 18:19–23 and 20:10–16. All the prohibitions concern how people live and act sexually *within the family and within a communal context*, but they also include special offenses (like burning children to false gods). This cluster of specific laws defines and protects the proper sexual relationship between a man and a woman (between husbands and wives) for the good of the people. The passages do not say anything about sexual *desire* or *orientation*, but only forbid certain kinds of sexual activity. But *homosexual practice* in general is clearly forbidden—a man shall not have sexual relations with another man as he does with a woman.

Two further Old Testament texts are sometimes included in the corpus of texts that speak to same-sex activity. The account of the men of Gibeah in Judges 19 parallels the Sodom story: a man finds lodging in the city and the rabble come to the door asking for him so that they might know him. The desire for men to have sexual relations with a man again is viewed as a sign of the overall degradation that has overtaken the city. The second text is the puzzling passage about Noah's son Ham viewing his nakedness (Gen 9:20–27): there seems to be the implication of sexual impropriety that is linked to the further degradation of the children of Ham. But the text is too obscure to shed much light.

The crowning Old Testament witness to the God-given order of marriage as between a man and a woman appears first in Genesis 1:26–27, where the Lord God creates the human race as male and female, both in the image and likeness of God, and then in 2:18–25, where the Lord God forms the woman from man and then brings her to him to be his spouse. These texts are rightly seen as grounding the biblical view of marriage according to God's purpose and are cited by both Jesus (Matt 19:4–6) and Paul (Eph 5:31–33) as laying down the fundamental plan of God for human sexuality.

New Testament references to homosexual activity appear explicitly only in Paul. On two occasions Paul offers lists of activities that bar one from the kingdom of God. In the first (1 Cor 6:9–10), Paul identifies with two words (*malakoi, arsenokoitai*) what appear to be the passive and active partners in a homosexual union. In the second passage (1 Tim 1:9–11), the second term (*arsenokoitai*) is used to identify an activity labelled as godless and unholy. Both texts have been understood specifically to rule out homosexual activity.

The strongest condemnation of homosexual activity, though, appears in Romans 1:24–27. Paul is not directly concerned with sexual activity in the passage: he is offering an account of how human society has darkened itself through idolatry and descended into graver and more wicked activity. Paul specifically names women having sexual relations with other women, and men with men, as a sign that a great darkening has come upon the human race. Here homosexual activity is not directly condemned but is employed as a sign of moral degradation that all would recognize and assent to. Paul is *assuming* in this text the grave disorder of same-sex relations to show the spiraling wickedness of the human race.

When the *Catechism of the Catholic Church* states that Sacred Scripture presents homosexual acts as acts of grave depravity, it identifies in a footnote the primary texts in view (Gen 19:1–29, Rom 1:24–27, 1 Cor 6:10, and 1 Tim 1:10). The story of Sodom and the three Pauline texts receive special mention as indicative of the Bible's view of same-sex activity.[10] In the wider discussion of the biblical teaching found in the *Letter to the Bishops of the Catholic Church on the Pastoral Care of Homosexual Persons* (1986),[11] the Congregation for the Doctrine of the Faith points to the full set of texts we have identified here. Beginning with God's purpose for sexuality found in Genesis 2 (and the fall from this purpose in Genesis 3), the *Letter* proceeds to offer brief commentary on Genesis 19, Leviticus 18 and 20, and the three Pauline texts. We can safely conclude that it is primarily from these texts that the Catholic Church draws her conviction about and moral evaluation of same-sex activity.

B. THE SCRIPTURAL TEACHING QUESTIONED AND CHALLENGED

We are all well aware that the received view—that the Bible univocally and clearly forbids same-sex activity—has been sharply challenged. Rather than attempt a detailed account of this challenge, I will identify the primary strategies used to deflect or reject the traditional approach in favor of acceptance of some forms of same-sex activity and unions. These strategies are by no means internally consistent—some are in direct contradiction to others—but they have a common end and goal: to persuade Christians today that the apparent prohibition against same-sex activity is no longer in force and should be jettisoned. Together they function as a varied arsenal against the received view, attacking the foundations from different positions. There are many ways to organize the strategies used, but I have identified four kinds of arguments used to overturn the received view of the biblical teaching on homosexual relations.

The first is an argument from the incompleteness of the Old Testament revelation for use by Christians. In this view, we simply cannot take laws from Leviticus and assume that they apply directly to

---

10. In the CDF's "Declaration" on sexuality, *Persona humana*, §8, only the three Pauline texts are referenced as indicating serious depravity and the sad consequences of rejecting God.

11. CDF, *Letter to the Bishops of the Catholic Church on the Pastoral Care of Homosexual Persons* (October 1, 1986) (Washington, DC: United States Catholic Conference, 1986).

us today. The sexual prohibitions of Leviticus 18 and 20 contain some laws that we no longer consider to be in force. Therefore, why should we treat the prohibition of same-sex activity as binding on us today? The argument is further refined by the claim that the sexual prohibitions in Leviticus are not really moral laws at all—they are laws regarding ritual purity, and so no longer apply to Christians in the New Covenant.

The second argument contends that the texts cited against same-sex activity simply do not apply to loving same-sex unions today. This is an argument that seeks to make its claim by bracketing off or quarantining the texts at issue. Yes, we are happy to uphold these texts, but they simply are not speaking to this issue. The men of Sodom and Gibeah are guilty of exploitative, coercive sexual designs—but this is not what we are talking about today. Even Paul in Romans and his lists of violations in 1 Corinthians and 1 Timothy is talking mainly about cult prostitution and its excesses. None of this touches loving, committed, voluntary same-sex unions that are being advocated today.

The third argument looks at the Gospels and doesn't find anything in Jesus' words about homosexuality. Jesus never forbade same-sex activity or loving relationships—and he is our primary source of revelation. Therefore, it is at least an open question whether same-sex activity (and unions) are to be allowed and even blessed.

The fourth argument, which recognizes how difficult it is to wriggle around the New Testament prohibitions in Paul, argues that Paul wasn't aware of what homosexuality really is, and so he condemned what he knew but was ignorant of the "natural" givenness of homosexual desire. In other words, Paul *did* condemn this kind of activity, but he was just not aware of what we now know, and we need to move past his prohibitions: "If Paul then could be confronted with the reality of homosexual orientation, consistency would require him to acknowledge the naturalness of homosexual acts for people with a homosexual orientation."[12]

---

12. Dan O. Via, "The Bible, the Church, and Homosexuality," 1–39 in Dan O. Via and Robert A. Gagnon, *Homosexuality and the Bible: Two Views* (Minneapolis: Fortress, 2003), 15.

This argument (along with the third) is normally linked with a further one: that the overall "love ethic" of the New Testament overrides the prohibitions. Doctrine is developing and we see more clearly now than Paul did how loving homosexual relations fulfill the law of love and are consistent with the wider New Testament ethic of love.

When presented not only singly but especially in combination these various exegetical and hermeneutical strategies create a powerful momentum to overturn the received teaching that the Bible forbids same-sex activity. Especially if one is already inclined to accept the legitimacy of same-sex expressions, these arguments about the biblical teaching deliver the "slam-dunk" rationale for fully accepting homosexual sex and unions between same-sex partners.

C. REAFFIRMATION OF THE RECEIVED BIBLICAL UNDERSTANDING

Aware of strategies for revising the received understanding of biblical teaching, the CDF *Letter on the Pastoral Care of Homosexual Persons* offers a critique of

> a new exegesis of Sacred Scripture which claims variously that Scripture has nothing to say on the subject of homosexuality, or that it somehow tacitly approves of it, or that all of its moral injunctions are so culture-bound that they are no longer applicable to contemporary life. These views are gravely erroneous.[13]

What might we say in response to these kinds of strategies that seek to overturn the received and traditional understanding of the biblical teaching on same-sex activity? In response to the first argument, we all agree—in various and different ways—that the Old Testament is incomplete in itself. As Catholics we accept that the Old Testament books "contain some things which are incomplete and temporary,"[14] finding their fulfillment only in Christ. But there are other elements of the Old Testament that have an enduring and authoritative authority, and among these is the moral law framed

---

13. CDF, *Letter on the Pastoral Care of Homosexual Persons*, §4.
14. Second Vatican Council, Constitution on Divine Revelation *Dei verbum* (November 18, 1965), pp. 373–94 in *The Sixteen Documents of Vatican II*, ed. Daughters of St. Paul (Boston: St. Paul Editions, n.d.), §15.

in the Decalogue. We know these remain authoritative—always as interpreted in Christ—because the New Testament itself upholds the moral law as binding upon Christians.[15] We find that the New Testament upholds marriage as between one man and one woman— the truth of this itself grounded in the Old Testament revelation, in what God decreed "in the beginning"—and a re-assertion that various sexual practices cannot be practiced by those who worship the God of Jesus Christ. In fact, Paul specifically names those who engage in homosexual relations as outside the community of faith and salvation. Further, as many exegetes have noted, Paul appears to have coined his own term, *arsenokoitos* (lying-with-a-man), by building it from the language found in Leviticus 18:22 and 20:13 (*arsenos* and *koite*).[16] Paul seems to have the text of Leviticus directly in view. Thus, the argument that we cannot apply the teaching found in Leviticus to life in Christ is not true in this case, because the teaching concerns the moral law and because the New Testament specifically upholds this teaching as applicable to those who are in Christ.[17]

The argument that would bracket off the Old Testament (and New Testament) texts, as not in fact applying to loving same-sex unions, also does not work. The context for the prohibitions in Leviticus is not cult prostitution but the family and everyday life in Israelite society.[18] The same applies to Paul in Romans, 1 Corinthians, and 1 Tim-

---

15. For the agreement by Catholics and Protestants on the binding quality of the moral law (the Decalogue), see my earlier chapter in this volume, "The Role of the Decalogue in Protestant and Catholic Catechisms."

16. For the connection between Paul's terminology and the texts of Leviticus, see Mary Healy, *Scripture, Mercy, and Homosexuality* (El Cajon, CA: Catholic Answers Press, 2016), 65–66, and Jean-Baptiste Edart, "The New Testament and Homosexuality," 73–126 in Innocent Himbaza, Adrien Schenker, and Jean-Baptiste Edart, *The Bible on the Question of Homosexuality*, trans. Benedict M. Guevin (Washington, DC: Catholic University of America Press, 2012), 77–78.

17. The CDF's *Letter on the Pastoral Care of Homosexual Persons*, §6, accepts the teaching of Leviticus as applying to us today: "In Leviticus 18:22 and 20:13, in the course of describing the conditions necessary for belonging to the Chosen People, the author excludes from the People of God those who behave in a homosexual fashion."

18. For the communal and social-family setting of Leviticus 18 and 23, see Innocent Himbaza, "Why Does the Mosaic Law Forbid the Practice of Homosexual Love (Leviticus 18 and 20)," 45–72 in *The Bible on the Question of Homosexuality*, 49–55.

othy: there is nothing in these texts that points to cult prostitution or to coercive sexual acts against boys. In fact, by linking homosexual activity to many other forms of grave sin that were practiced widely in the culture of his day, Paul shows that he is not talking about special cases or environments. What is being forbidden is not a *special* case of homosexual activity linked to structures of oppression but the general practice of same-sex activity within a pagan culture.

The stories of the men of Sodom and Gibeah, while they point to many sins and vices among the inhabitants, underscore their demand to have sexual relations with other males. It is not only the coercive aspect of this act that is condemned in the stories, but also the very desire of men to have sex with other men. The Letter of Jude (v. 7) points to the story of Sodom as an example of those who "indulged in sexual immorality and pursued unnatural desire."[19] The coercive aim is part of the wickedness but the very desire for this kind of sexual union is a sign of deep moral darkness. Innocent Himbaza acknowledges that the narratives of Sodom and Gibeah do not emphasize homosexuality, but he nonetheless concludes that they condemn homosexual acts and that this is "an essential element of the stories."[20] The CDF *Letter* concurs: "In Genesis 19:1-11, the deterioration due to sin continues in the story of the men of Sodom. There can be no doubt of the moral judgement made there against homosexual relations."[21]

The claim that, because Jesus does not specifically condemn homosexuality, he either left it an open question or tacitly approved of it, is an unpersuasive argument from silence. Jesus did not speak directly about many activities—rape, kidnapping, torture—but no one thinks that this silence leaves their moral standing in any doubt. On the one hand, Jesus clearly and with emphasis underlined the purpose of God in marriage as between one man and one woman, and finds the authority for this in the Old Testament. On the other hand,

---

19. The relevant phrase is literally "other flesh," often translated as "unnatural lust" (RSV, NRSV), "unnatural vice" (NAB), or "unnatural desire" (ESV).

20. Innocent Himbaza, "Old Testament Stories and Homosexuality," 5-44 in *The Bible on the Question of Homosexuality*, 22.

21. CDF, *Letter on the Pastoral Care of Homosexual Persons*, §6.

homosexual activity was simply not a controversial issue in Jesus' day within the Jewish community that he was typically addressing. The Jewish position on this issue went against the grain of the dominant societies in which the Jewish communities lived. Homosexual practice was universally condemned and there would have been no obvious reason to speak about it. In the view of Jean-Baptiste Edart, "We have seen that the gospels do not allow us to say that Jesus shows the least approval of homosexual acts . . . . Jesus' silence on this matter can only be interpreted as reflecting agreement with the tradition of Israel on this point."[22] Paul can simply assume this understanding when he makes it an example of moral depravity in Romans 1.

What are we to make of the argument that Paul was simply unaware or ignorant of the reality of homosexuality, and so his clear condemnations of it can be set aside? Paul is plainly aware of disordered desire, sexual and otherwise, as he speaks about this clearly in both Romans 1 and 7. In one sense, this disordered desire is what arises "naturally" in human beings because of the universality of sin. For Paul, however, these and many other desires that are "natural" in one sense are the fruit of Adam's sin and our personal participation in that sin. To the contrary, to live "naturally" and "by nature" means to live according to God's original design "in the beginning"—and this means marriage between one man and one woman according to Genesis. This approach to faulting Paul's clear moral teaching also undermines the inspiration of Scripture. If Paul was ignorant (and therefore in the wrong) on this question, what remains that could not be overturned on the basis of this kind of hermeneutic?

Finally, the appeal to the ethic of love—or a view of doctrinal development—that trumps and overrides specific moral commandments presents a view of scriptural revelation at war with itself. Doctrinal development and the demands of love may lead us to see more deeply into what we have already grasped, but it will always be in continuity with what has come before. This is simply not the case with the overturning of the Bible's condemnation of homosexual activity, and therefore the appeal to these principles in this case fails.

---

22. Edart, "The New Testament and Homosexuality," 114.

It may be useful to document the overall conclusions of several New Testament scholars who have examined these texts in their biblical and historical contexts, with the revisionist arguments on the table before them. The joint conclusion of three Old and New Testament specialists—Innocent Himbaza, Adrien Schenker, and Jean-Baptiste Edart—upholds the judgment of both the *Catechism* and the CDF *Letter*: "It seems difficult to avoid the conclusion that the Bible never approves of homosexual acts: they are against the will of God the Creator."[23] Richard Hays, a renowned New Testament scholar, concludes:

> The biblical witness against homosexual practices is univocal.... Scripture offers no loopholes or exception clauses that might allow for the acceptance of homosexual practices under some circumstances. Despite the efforts of some recent interpreters to explain away the evidence, the Bible remains unambiguous and univocal in its condemnation of homosexual conduct.[24]

Even Dan Via, who argues that the prohibition against homosexuality should be overturned, admits that the biblical teaching is clear in its condemnation:

> Of course, the few biblical texts that deal explicitly with the subject offer no such support [for the moral justifiability of homosexual practice].... If we look at a number of biblical themes in the light of contemporary knowledge and experience, we can justifiably override the unconditional biblical condemnations of homosexual practice.[25]

Conclusion

The questions raised by the societal acceptance of same-sex activity and same-sex unions has required—and continues to require—Christians to re-examine their teaching and pastoral practice in regard to

---

23. Himbaza, Schenker, and Edart, *The Bible on the Question of Homosexuality*, 131.
24. Richard B. Hays, "The Biblical Witness Concerning Homosexuality," 65–84 in *Staying the Course: Supporting the Church's Position on Homosexuality*, ed. Maxie D. Dunnam and H. Newton Malony (Nashville: Abingdon, 2003), 73.
25. Via, "The Bible, the Church, and Homosexuality," 29, 38.

those who experience a homosexual orientation. The response by the Church—and the churches—must be made on many fronts at once: exegetical, theological, and pastoral. In this paper I have examined just one aspect of the question: What does the Bible teach on homosexual activity and relations, and are we justified in overturning the constant teaching of the Church on this issue? The summary statement by the CDF *Letter* capably sums up the response to this question grounded in a close re-examination of the Christian faith as found in the biblical revelation:

> What should be noticed is that, in the presence of such remarkable diversity, there is nevertheless a clear consistency within the Scriptures themselves on the moral issue of homosexual behaviour. The Church's doctrine regarding this issue is thus based, not on isolated phrases for facile theological argument, but on the solid foundation of a constant Biblical testimony. The community of faith today, in unbroken continuity with the Jewish and Christian communities within which the ancient Scriptures were written, continues to be nourished by those same Scriptures and by the Spirit of Truth whose Word they are.[26]

How we are to make this truth known and loved effectively—what strategies to adopt and avoid—is a pressing question for us all. But if we are to remain faithful to our Risen Lord and the way of life he has called us to live and model, Evangelicals and Catholics must remain clear on what the truth of our sexuality is, as grounded in the Bible. We face in fact a heroic call: to stand firm, in charity and mercy, against an avalanche of pressure coming from all quarters, bent on getting us to change our minds about God's purpose for the human person, sexuality, marriage, and the family. We have need of the witness of one another if we are to stand firm and be at the service of our churches and our society.

The closing words of Mary Healy's study, *Scripture, Mercy, and Homosexuality*, provide a thoughtful and heartfelt call to proclaim and live the Gospel teaching on our sexuality:

---

26. CDF, *Letter on the Pastoral Care of Homosexual Persons*, §5.

A Christianity that preaches high standards of sexual morality without imitating Jesus' warm welcome of sinners is hypocritical and unattractive. A Christianity that proclaims mercy toward sinners without calling them to repentance and holiness of life is deceptive, self-deceiving, and anemic. And a Christianity that proclaims mercy and upholds high moral standards without making available the power of healing and transformation is impoverished and burdensome . . . . But a Christianity that proclaims and lives by the full truth of the word of God is an invitation to joy and the fullness of life.[27]

---

27. Mary Healy, *Scripture, Mercy, and Homosexuality*, 76.

2.4. A Quasi Conservative-Progressive Approach to Homosexuality: A Vineyard Approach to Engaging the Biblical, Theological, and Pastoral Issues

Luke T. Geraty, MA, MDiv

Participating in the Evangelical-Catholic Dialogue is a great honor for me and I express my gratitude for the opportunity. I have a strong commitment to ecumenical interaction, especially with those whom I consider to be my sisters and brothers in Christ. I consider engaging with the Roman Catholic tradition and fellow Evangelicals a great joy and responsibility.

To begin, I would like to make several introductory statements. First, I am writing as a Vineyard Church pastor-theologian. I have no ecclesial authority other than ordination within my own denomination and tradition. This paper summarizes my understanding of the Vineyard perspective on the topic of homosexuality and is consistent with other Evangelical traditions.[1]

It has been said that "in all academic writing, authors have their own agendas and influences that determine the nature of their work."[2] For purposes of clarification, my theological method is typical of the Vineyard Church position and follows the Wesleyan

---

1. For a fuller treatment of this subject from a Vineyard USA position, see the position paper "Pastoring LGBT Persons" (August 2014). The paper is unpublished but is available from the denomination's headquarters.

2. Allan Anderson, Michael Bergunder, André Droogers, and Cornelis van der Laan, eds., *Studying Global Pentecostalism* (Berkeley: University of California Press, 2010), 14.

Quadrilateral.³ This method will shape how I engage briefly in three areas, namely the biblical, theological, and pastoral issues.⁴

Defining Homosexuality and Issues of Causation

In order to determine whether or not homosexuality is a sin, what the Church's perspective on homosexuality should be, and how best to engage those who identify as homosexuals, we must first ask what one means by the term.⁵ Are we referring to one's sexual identity, orientation, or behavior?⁶ Preston Sprinkle notes the complications well, writing:

> When we say "homosexuality," what exactly do we mean? Again, we're talking about a diverse group of people, so which person or people are you referring to? Those who are married to someone of the same sex? Someone who is having same-sex intercourse? Someone who is attracted to the same sex? If so, how much attraction on a scale of 1-10 qualifies one to be included in your concept of homosexuality?

---

3. Cf. Luke Geraty, "'Quadrilateraling' in the Vineyard: Creating & Maintaining the Wesleyan Quadrilateral as a Valuable Aspect of Discipleship within the Space of the Local Church," paper presented at the annual meeting for the Society of Vineyard Scholars, Wilmore, KY, June 21, 2018. For a general treatment of the Wesleyan Quadrilateral as theological method, please see Don Thorsen, *The Wesleyan Quadrilateral: Scripture, Tradition, Reason, and Experience as Model of Evangelical Theology* (Lexington, KY: Emeth Press, 2005).

4. I am intentionally avoiding the word "practical" in that I believe all biblical theology is "practical" and serves the Church. This does not assume that all biblical theology should be simplistic but that the complex and challenging topics that biblical scholars and theologians address can and should be helpful to the Church. As Jürgen Moltmann states, "Theology is the business of all God's people," in *Experiences in Theology: Ways and Forms of Christian Theology* (Minneapolis: Fortress, 2000), 11. For a good discussion about the discipline of practical / pastoral theology, see Mark J. Cartledge, *Practical Theology: Charismatic and Empirical Perspectives* (Eugene, OR: Wipf and Stock, 2003), 1–6.

5. Cf. Preston Sprinkle, *People to Be Loved: Why Homosexuality Is Not Just an Issue* (Grand Rapids: Zondervan, 2015), 21–24, on why terminology matters in relation to missiology toward those who self-identify with the term or who are wrestling with their own sexuality.

6. Others suggest five distinct categories: attraction, orientation, identity, behavior, and relationship, cf. Andrew Goddard and Don Horrocks, eds., *Resources for Church Leaders: Biblical and Pastoral Responses to Homosexuality* (London: Evangelical Alliance, 2012), 22–34.

... *Homosexuality*, as you can see, is a broad term that has the potential of erasing the faces of real people with different stories.[7]

In defining homosexuality, the issue of *causation* continues with the debate of *nature vs. nurture* being a central point of contention. Kenneth Ashley's research indicates that "there appears to be some evidence that biological factors play some role in the development of sexual orientation, but at the present time it is not clear to what extent, and what other factors, including psycho-social and post-natal environment, may also play a role,"[8] leading him to conclude that "there are associations/correlations [with one's biology], but no study indicates causation."[9] This is confirmed by a recent study that concludes that "no specific theory of what causes people to be attracted to men, to women, or to both has received enough support to win the backing of all reasonable scientists, most of whom remain open-minded to a large extent."[10]

Therefore, in the Vineyard Church we have suggested that non-specialists, i.e., those untrained in genetics, social sciences, or psychology, take a "humble agnosticism" when it comes to discussions related to causation.[11] This in no way ignores the theological implications of the Fall in Christian doctrine nor the church's statement of faith.[12] Rather, it avoids the complexities of sexual orientation that often shut down conversations in the hopes of continuing the missiological dialogue toward Jesus and the Gospel.

---

7. Sprinkle, *People to Be Loved*, 23.
8. Kenneth B. Ashley MD, "The Science on Sexual Orientation: A Review of the Recent Literature," *Journal Of Gay And Lesbian Mental Health* 17, no. 2 (2013): 175–82, at 180–81.
9. Ashley, "The Science on Sexual Orientation," 179.
10. J. Michael Bailey et al., "Sexual Orientation, Controversy, and Science," *Psychological Science in the Public Interest* 17, no. 2 (2016): 45–101, at 87.
11. Vineyard USA, "Pastoring LGBT Persons," 15.
12. The Vineyard Statement of Faith states, "Through the fall, Satan and his demonic hosts gained access to God's good creation. Creation now experiences the consequences and effects of Adam's original sin. Human beings are born in sin, subject to God's judgment of death, and captive to Satan's kingdom of darkness." Vineyard USA, *Core Statement and Values* (2018), 18.

Biblical, Theological, and Pastoral Issues

When developing a Christian position on homosexuality, we must start by turning to the pages of Sacred Scripture. There are a handful of texts that specifically address homosexual activity which include Genesis 19:4–5, Leviticus 18:22, Leviticus 20:13, Judges 19:20–23, Romans 1:24–32, 1 Corinthians 6:9–11, and 1 Timothy 1:8–11, as well as other texts that we must engage in order to adequately grasp the ancient world's understanding(s) of sexuality.[13] To limit the scope of texts we engage as being only those containing the word "homosexuality" (Greek *arsenokoitai* and the related *malakoi*)[14] is to ignore the Old Testament's influence on the thinking of Jesus and the authors of the New Testament. We must consider all the teachings of Sacred Scripture on sex in order to determine what the church's perspective should be.

It should be noted that Christians affirming the historic and traditional view concerning sexuality are no longer simply engaging unbelievers who reject biblical authority. Rather, there is now debate on whether the Bible does, in fact, oppose all forms of homosexual activity and whether or not there are hermeneutical and/or pastoral reasons to adjust our understandings and application of Scripture.[15]

---

13. E.g., William Loader addresses dozens of texts in *The New Testament on Sexuality* (Grand Rapids: Eerdmans, 2012) as does Richard M. Davidson in *Flame of Yahweh: Sexuality in the Old Testament* (Peabody, MA: Hendrickson, 2007). Scripture addresses numerous issues connected to sexuality, including adultery, celibacy, bestiality, and more.

14. These Greek words describe both the passive and active aspects of homosexuality; cf. Richard B. Hays, *The Moral Vision of the New Testament: Community, Cross, New Creation; A Contemporary Introduction to New Testament Ethics* (San Francisco: HarperOne, 1996), 382.

15. For examples of books taking an affirming position, written by "evangelicals" or those who consider themselves "theologically conservative Christians," see Ken Wilson, *A Letter to My Congregation: An Evangelical Pastor's Path to Embracing People Who Are Gay, Lesbian and Transgender in the Company of Jesus* (Canton, MI: David Crumm Media, 2014), and Matthew Vines, *God and the Gay Christian: The Biblical Case in Support of Same-Sex Relationships* (New York: Convergent Books, 2014). For an example of an esteemed biblical scholar who acknowledges that the Bible condemns homosexual activity, yet holds to an "open and affirming" view because we "should take into account the modern world," see E. P. Sanders, *Paul: The Apostle's Life, Letters and Thought* (Minneapolis: Fortress, 2015), 363–73.

Space and time limitations prevent me from fully engaging every text of Scripture and every hermeneutical issue related to homosexuality,[16] hence, in what follows I would like to address two primary arguments[17] made by those in support of the idea that "Christians who affirm the full authority of Scripture can also affirm committed, monogamous same-sex relationships."[18]

First, did Paul's condemnation of "homosexuality" include committed, monogamous same-sex relationships? At the heart of this argument is the suggestion that Paul knew *nothing* of today's committed, monogamous same-sex relationships and marriages. The type of homosexual activity that the Apostle condemned was connected to temple prostitution, pederasty, or heterosexual men having "unnatural" sex, i.e., not in conformity with their own sexual orientation.[19]

---

16. For works attempting to do so, see Davidson, *Flame of Yahweh*; Loader, *The New Testament on Sexuality*; and Robert A. J. Gagnon, *The Bible and Homosexual Practice: Texts and Hermeneutics* (Nashville: Abingdon, 2001).

17. Vineyard USA, "Pastoring LGBT Persons," 44–45, lists seven arguments made by "affirming" scholars regarding Rom 1:24–27: *1. The heterosexual orientation argument:* Paul describes people with heterosexual orientation who engage in homosexual acts, not people with inborn homosexual orientation; *2. The impure versus sinful argument:* Paul describes same-sex activity as impure (v. 24) or indecent (v. 27). He does not view it as sinful in itself; *3. The not-lesbian argument:* Paul is not describing same-sex relations between women, but unnatural forms of heterosexual sex with women; *4. The misogyny argument:* Paul's context assumed a hierarchical society where the passive partner was necessarily humiliated (made like a woman). This is part of a by-gone world of male dominance, so the text is not relevant today; *5. The exploitation argument:* Paul is condemning pederasty, the abuse of slaves, etc., so the text is not relevant to consenting adults today; *6. The orientation argument:* Paul had no concept of a permanent homosexual orientation, since this has only been "invented" in recent times, so this text is not relevant; *7. The idolatry argument:* Paul is condemning homosexuality within the context of idol worship, so this text is not relevant to modern Western people who are not idol worshippers, and may, in fact, be committed Christians.

18. Vines, *God and the Gay Christian*, 3.

19. Vines and Wilson both build part of their argument on the idea that Paul's prohibitions were related to temple prostitution and pederasty, cf. Wilson, *A Letter to My Congregation*, Kindle Locations 1027–1162, and Vines, *God and the Gay Christian*, 35–36. For an example of those arguing that Romans 1 is addressing those who were heterosexuals participating in homosexual activity, see John Boswell, *Christianity, Social Tolerance, and Homosexuality: Gay People in Western Europe from the Beginning of the Christian Era to the Fourteenth Century* (Chicago: University of Chicago Press, 1980), 111–14. Also see Robin Scroggs, *The New Testament and Homosexuality: Contextual Background*

This argument is what leads John McNeill to state that "nowhere in the Scripture[s] is there a clear condemnation of a loving sexual relationship between two gay persons."[20]

While we can agree that the Apostle Paul clearly condemned homosexuality in connection with temple prostitution and what often amounted to pedophilia,[21] it is misleading to suggest that Paul knew nothing of committed, monogamous same-sex relationships. K. J. Dover's *Greek Homosexuality* "presents evidence . . . to show that Greek homosexuality in both the classical and Hellenistic era consisted of more than pederasty, that it was not always seen as exploitive, and that same-sex relations could include lifelong consensual adult partnerships."[22] In fact, the Roman Emperor Nero, contemporary of the Apostle Paul, is reported to have married Pythagoras in a public ceremony, "plainly visible," that included witnesses, a wedding dower, and nuptial torches.[23] Furthermore, Nero's public marriage to

---

for Contemporary Debate (Philadelphia: Fortress, 1983); Dale B. Martin, *Sex and the Single Savior: Gender and Sexuality in Biblical Interpretation* (Louisville: Westminster John Knox, 2006); James V. Brownson, *Bible, Gender, Sexuality: Reframing the Church's Debate on Same-Sex Relationships* (Grand Rapids: Eerdmans, 2013). For a critical evaluation of these views, see the exegesis of Loader, *The New Testament on Sexuality*, 293–338.

20. John J. McNeill, "Homosexuality: Challenging the Church to Grow," *The Christian Century* (March 11, 1987): 242–46, at 246.

21. In light of pederasty often including young boys, I believe it's important to note that this is an evil and violent act done by *adults* to *children*, regardless of whether the prevailing cultural assumptions consider it dignified. That being said, it is valuable to note that even within the ancient world, these "relationships are sometimes attacked in the texts as eccentric or inappropriate . . . with hostility by certain sources," Thomas K. Hubbard, ed., *Homosexuality in Greece and Rome: A Sourcebook of Basic Documents* (Berkeley: University of California Press, 2003), 5. Not all ancients regarded pederasty in a positive light.

22. Loader, *The New Testament on Sexuality*, 324. Cf. the postscript in K. J. Dover, *Greek Homosexuality*, 2nd ed. (Cambridge, MA: Harvard University Press, 1989), 204. Moreover, Hubbard notes that Aristotle "claims that relationships based on love of character often continued after the loss of the beloved's youthful beauty" and that "in the Hellenistic period, some lovers swore continued attraction even well into their loved one's adulthood," Hubbard, *Homosexuality*, 5.

23. Tacitus, *Annals*, 15.38. This event has been dated during the Roman festival Saturnalia, which took place in December of AD 64. If Paul was martyred in July of AD 64, this matters little; if Paul was martyred in AD 66, it is quite significant given how prominent Nero's life was.

Pythagoras is not the only example of ancient Roman emperors having what appears to be a consenting homosexual relationship. There is historical evidence that Julius Caesar was also part of a consenting homosexual relationship with another ancient ruler, King Nicomedes of Bithynia.[24] Therefore, it is quite misleading to suggest that history reveals an absence of consensual committed homosexual relationships in the ancient Greco-Roman world. Historian Craig Williams notes that though the Romans often looked *down* upon romantic homosexual relationships, "Scattered throughout the Roman sources we find allusions to marriages between males" and "the evidence certainly suggests that some Roman men participated in wedding ceremonies with other men and considered themselves to be married to those men."[25] At the very minimum, Paul would have been aware of homosexual relationships that had similarity to those of today's culture. Suggesting that Paul and the ancient world were ignorant of homosexual relationships outside of pederasty and temple prostitution overlooks the historical data and ignores the contextual implications of Paul's use of *malakoi* and *arsenokoitai* in 1 Corinthians 6:9, which the NET translates as "passive homosexual partners, practicing homosexuals."[26] Though *arsenokoitai* is not found in the ancient literature *prior* to Paul's letter to the Corinthians, scholars[27] who argue that the words *cannot* refer to homosexuality ignore the evidence. As Richard Hays notes,

> The Septuagint (Greek Old Testament) of Leviticus 20:13 reads, "Whoever lies with a man as with a woman [*meta arsenos koitn gynaikos*], they have both done an abomination" (my translation). This is almost

---

24. There is evidence that Julius Caesar and King Nicomedes of Bithynia "were, in modern parlance, two consenting adults," in a homosexual relationship, cf. Marion L. Soards, *Scripture & Homosexuality: Biblical Authority and the Church Today* (Louisville: Westminster John Knox, 1995), 50. This is based on the historian Suetonius's *Lives of the Caesars: "Caesar."*

25. Craig A. Williams, *Roman Homosexuality*, 2nd ed. (New York: Oxford University Press, 2010), Kindle Edition Locations 4332–54.

26. The New English Translation (Nashville: Thomas Nelson Publishers, 2018) includes two extended footnotes indicating why it translates *malakoi* and *arsenokoitai* as describing passive and active homosexual practice.

27. E.g., Boswell, *Christianity, Social Tolerance, and Homosexuality*, 339–41.

certainly the idiom from which the noun *arsenokoitai* was coined. Thus, Paul's use of the term presupposes and reaffirms the holiness code's condemnation of homosexual acts. This is not a controversial point in Paul's argument; the letter gives no evidence that anyone at Corinth was arguing for the acceptance of same-sex erotic activity. Paul simply assumes that his readers will share his conviction that those who indulge in homosexual activity are "wrongdoers"....[28]

These same lexical points lead the esteemed Anglican scholar Anthony Thiselton to note that "No amount of lexicographical manipulation over *malakoi* can avoid the clear meaning of *arsenokoitai* as the activity of males (*arsen*) who have sexual relations with, sleep with (*koites*) other males.... The words more probably reflect 'male with male' in Leviticus 18:22 and Romans 1:27." Thiselton goes on to state that the suggestion that Paul was only aware of homosexuality through the lens of pederasty or temple prostitution "cannot withstand the battery of detailed linguistic arguments brought against it by a number of historical and linguistic specialists."[29] Moreover, if Paul's primary concern was pederasty, as several argue, it is important to note that he does not use the common Greek word for pedophilia in his writings.[30]

Additionally, in relation to *lesbian* same-sex activity, one advocate of an "open and affirming" position states, "Comparatively little is known about the extent or practice of lesbian sex during [the New Testament period]."[31] However, this is a demonstrably false statement in light of the work of Bernadette J. Brooten's *Love Between Women*.[32]

---

28. Hays, *The Moral Vision*, 382–83. Hays builds much of his case on Scroggs's argument that the Septuagint's translation of Lev 18:22 and 20:13 were understood to refer to homosexual intercourse, cf. *The New Testament and Homosexuality*, 106–8.

29. Anthony Thiselton, "Can Hermeneutics Ease the Deadlock? Some Biblical Exegesis and Hermeneutical Models," 145–96 in *The Way Forward?: Christian Voices on Homosexuality and The Church*, ed. Timothy Bradshaw (Grand Rapids: Eerdmans, 2004). For detailed exegesis, see Donald J. Wold, *Out of Order: Homosexuality in the Bible and the Ancient Near East* (San Antonio, TX: Cedar Leaf Press, 1998, 2009), 187–205.

30. *Paiderastía*.

31. Wilson, *A Letter to My Congregation*, Kindle Locations 953–54.

32. Bernadette J. Brooten, *Love Between Women: Early Christian Responses to Female Homoeroticism* (Chicago: University of Chicago Press, 1996).

Brooten's work is helpful in that she (1) provides significant evidence that committed and consensual *female* same-sex relationships existed in the ancient world;³³ (2) that the ancients had a much richer understanding of sexual orientation than some have suggested;³⁴ and (3) agrees that Paul is clearly addressing lesbian sexual relationships in Romans 1:26.³⁵ Brooten's work is valuable for us in that her work cannot be viewed as biased *against* an "open and affirming" position. When it comes to dealing with the implications of Romans 1:26, she simply rejects Paul as authoritative.³⁶

In light of the historical evidence, it is misleading to suggest that the biblical authors were unaware of committed, monogamous same-sex relationships. Not only does this suggestion ignore the historical data from the Greco-Roman sources, it requires exegetical gymnastics to get around the Pauline texts that specifically address the issue.

Second, since Jesus never mentioned "homosexuality," shouldn't we be less dogmatic about same-sex activity? Advocates of this argument inform us that since Jesus is the ultimate revelation of God, we should follow a "new hermeneutic"³⁷ and embrace the way of love, making space for homosexuality within the Christian tradition.³⁸ While we can agree that Jesus is the ultimate revelation of God,³⁹ suggesting that Jesus' omission is evidence for approval significantly overlooks what Jesus *does* say. In the Gospel of Matthew, Jesus gave

---

33. Brooten, *Love Between Women*, 41–71.

34. Brooten, *Love Between Women*, 140.

35. Brooten, *Love Between Women*, 189–302, provides Brooten's engagement with Rom 1:18–32.

36. Brooten writes, "I hope that churches today, being apprised of the history that I have presented, will no longer teach Rom 1:26f as authoritative," *Love Between Women*, 302.

37. Describing her journey into this approach, Vicky Beeching writes, "Could I, someday, dare to be openly gay and Christian? Based on these new ways to understand the biblical texts, perhaps I could," in *Undivided: Coming Out, Becoming Whole, and Living Free from Shame* (London: William Collins, 2018), 68.

38. Cf. J. R. Daniel Kirk, *Jesus Have I Loved, But Paul?: A Narrative Approach to the Problem of Pauline Christianity* (Grand Rapids: Baker Academic, 2011), 175–91. This argument also finds its way in Matthew Vines's *God and the Gay Christian* and is echoed in Vicky Beeching's *Undivided*.

39. Cf. 2 Cor 4:4; Col 1:15; Heb 1:3.

his full affirmation on the authority of the Old Testament (Matt 5:17–18) while also affirming the Creation account of marriage existing in the context of *one* man and *one* woman becoming "one flesh" (Matt 19:4–6). This certainly figures into Jesus' understanding of sexuality.

Yet the most striking statement that Jesus makes concerning the topic of sexuality is in Mark 7:21–23, where Jesus states that "sexual immorality" (*porneia*) is "evil." While the Gospels do not record Jesus specifically addressing homosexuality, Jesus' use of *porneia* "incorporated all the prohibitions of illicit sexual activity in the Levitical Holiness Code, which included incest (Leviticus 18:6–18), adultery (18:20), homosexuality (18:22) and bestiality (18:23)."[40] As J. R. Daniel Kirk notes, "The silence of Jesus on the issue of homosexuality is powerful, because if he had opposed the Jewish law on this point we surely would have heard about it."[41]

Additionally, another relevant text is found in Acts 15 and the corresponding Jerusalem Council. After seeking to discern how the Gentiles were to assimilate into the community of God's kingdom, we can summarize the apostolic invitation as "come as you are, but don't stay as you are." In fact, the Apostle's statement included this clarification: "You [Gentiles] must abstain from . . . sexual immorality (*porneia*)."[42] Surveying the recent scholarship, Thomas Lyons notes that,

> In later Second Temple and Hellenistic Judaism, *porneia* expanded in usage even farther to include virtually any prohibited sexual activity from Torah. Included in this expanded usage are extra-marital intercourse/harlotry, adultery, incest, unnatural vices, sodomy, unlawful marriages, bigamy, exogamy, and same sex activity . . . . The likely background for these [Acts 15] prohibitions is found in Israel's Holiness Code.[43]

40. Vineyard USA, "Pastoring LGBT Persons," 18.
41. Kirk, *Jesus Have I Loved, But Paul?*, 182.
42. Acts 15:28–29 (New Living Translation). Cf. Rev 2:14 and 3:20–22.
43. Thomas Lyons, "On the Road Between Ephesus and Thyatira: An Alternative Model to Ken Wilson's in ALTMC, Part 1," ThinkTheology.org (June 2, 2014), at http://thinktheology.org/2014/06/02/road-ephesus-thyatira-alternative-model-ken-wilsons-part-1/. Also see parts two and three, http://thinktheology.org/2014/06/09/road-ephesus-thyatira-alternative-model-ken-wilsons-altmc-part-2/ and http://thinktheology.org/2014/07/07/road-ephesus-thyatira-alternative-model-ken-wilsons-altmc-part-3/,

This survey of the relevant literature, while brief, indicates that the biblical data condemns *all* forms of homosexual practices, both in the context of the ancient temple worship and pederasty, and committed, monogamous same-sex relationships.

While the biblical data is less ambiguous than some suggest, there are numerous theological questions[44] that arise as we move from same-sex *activity* to homosexual identity and orientation. While, as previously noted, the ancients had a wider understanding of sexual orientation than is often suggested, with the onset of modern psychological and medical studies, questions abound in relation to human ontology. To state it bluntly, though the Church has wrestled with numerous theological topics in the past two millennia, we still fundamentally struggle to understand what it means to be human.[45] Thus, theological anthropology[46] continues to be a challenge and an opportunity for Christian engagement. This leads to several thoughts relevant toward a discussion of the theological issues raised by homosexuality.

First, an inaugurated eschatological[47] approach should inform our

respectively. Lyons's work provides a significant understanding toward the lexical range of and common understanding and usage of *porneia* in the first century amongst Jews and Christians.

44. I am inclined to note that there are many questions in regard to the use of natural law in relation to homosexuality, yet given that there is such diversity amongst Evangelicals and their appropriation of natural law, I refer readers to my Roman Catholic peers. The Catholic tradition makes some of the best arguments for the usefulness of natural law, especially Thomas Aquinas in his *Summa Theologiae*. Evangelicals influenced by Karl Barth have reservations about the usefulness of natural law, which I also find compelling toward chastening a theology that builds entirely on natural law.

45. Conversations about LGBTQ issues tend to reveal a need for Christian theologians to do more work in theological anthropology, as there are numerous questions and challenges raised in regard to identity, ontology, and other subjects tangentially related to the subject.

46. For helpful studies on theological anthropology, see Charles Kraft, *Anthropology for Christian Witness* (Maryknoll, NY: Orbis Books, 1996); Hans Schwarz, *The Human Being: A Theological Anthropology* (Grand Rapids: Eerdmans, 2013); Marc Cortez, *Christological Anthropology in Historical Perspective: Ancient and Contemporary Approaches to Theological Anthropology* (Grand Rapids: Zondervan, 2016). I am indebted to conversations with Dr. Doug Erickson, a Vineyard theologian, for this insight.

47. For an evangelical summary of inaugurated eschatology, see George Eldon Ladd, *The Presence of the Future: The Eschatology of Biblical Realism* (Grand Rapids: Eerdmans, 1974). For the influence of inaugurated eschatology upon the Vineyard, see Douglas R.

theological anthropology to state that "we *are* and *are not yet* what we will be."[48] As the outpouring and indwelling presence of the Spirit is a *down payment, guarantee,* and *pledge* of our realized and enacted eschatological promise,[49] we must remember that this is *consummated* in the future. As there are eschatological tensions at work, we need to think about how this applies to our theological anthropology. This acknowledgement should significantly influence the way in which the very concept of "experience" and "reality" are understood in the life of followers of Jesus, as well as how we understand being human while "working out our salvation."[50] As N. T. Wright states,

> ... a Christian in the present life is a mere shadow of his or her future self, the self that person will be when the body that God has waiting in his heavenly storeroom is brought out, already made to measure, and put on over the present one—or over the self that will still exist after bodily death.[51]

Second, and related to inaugurated eschatology, a sacramental approach to theological anthropology will raise questions about liminal spaces. As liminality interfaces with and informs a robust theological anthropology, questions abound about how one can both have one's identity *in Christ* and yet struggle with issues of sexual identity

---

Erickson, "The Kingdom of God and the Holy Spirit: Eschatology and Pneumatology in the Vineyard" (PhD diss., Marquette University, 2015) or Derek Morphew, *Breakthrough: Discovering the Kingdom* (Cape Town: Vineyard International Publishing, 2006).

48. Cf. Thomas Creedy, "You Are Not Yet What We Will Be: The Relational-Eschatological Turn and Its Contribution for a Vineyard Theological Anthropology," paper presented at the annual meeting for the Society of Vineyard Scholars, Media, PA, April 16, 2015.

49. Cf. 2 Cor 1:21–22; 5:5; Rom 8:23; Eph 1:14. ngentally related to theologicalcf. and the e Letters of Paul iul'ntology, and other subjects tangentially related to theological

50. Phil 2:12.

51. N. T. Wright, *Surprised by Hope: Rethinking Heaven, the Resurrection, and the Mission of the Church* (Grand Rapids: Zondervan, 2008), 154. Wright also powerfully states, "If you are in the Messiah, indwelt by the Spirit, you are at the moment just a shadow of your future self: there is a more glorious, more physical, more REAL 'you' than anything you presently experience, and God intends to create you as this new person in the resurrection," in N. T. Wright, "Ask N. T. Wright: November Q & A." N. T. Wright Author page, Facebook.com. https://www.facebook.com/notes/n-t-wright/ask-n-t-wright-november-q-a/578180515568343 (accessed September 19, 2018).

and orientation. How are we to consider the tension between Luther's doctrine *simul justus et peccator* (simultaneously righteous and sinful) in relation to sexual orientation and identity? Might those who identify as "gay Christians" who also believe that Scripture opposes same-sex activity have more theological legs to stand on than that of which they have often been accused?[58] I realize this raises significant questions about Christian identity and *to whom* Christians belong, but the outright rejection of Wesley Hill and the celibacy-encouraging "spiritual friends" movement, not to mention the constant misrepresentation of their viewpoints,[59] appears to ignore the questions and concerns this orthodox and conservative group of Christians are raising.[60] If salvation is understood as an experiential process whereby individuals who collectively form the Church go from foreknowledge to glorification,[55] how does this shape our understanding of sanctification and discipleship from a theological perspective?

Again, I think we fundamentally struggle to understand and articulate what it means to be human and much of what is currently being discussed in today's cultural milieu is related to this challenge.

Suggestions for Further Pastoral Reflection

As a pastor, I regularly have conversations with church members who want to know what the Bible teaches concerning their family or friends who identify with the LGBTQ community.[56] I often speak

---

58. See, e.g., Wesley Hill, *Washed and Waiting: Reflections on Christian Faithfulness and Homosexuality* (Grand Rapids: Zondervan, 2010); Hill, *Spiritual Friendship: Finding Love in the Church as a Celibate Gay Christian* (Grand Rapids: Brazos, 2015).

59. Cf. Mark Galli, "Revoice's Founder Answers the LGBT Conference's Critics," ChristianityToday.com (July 25, 2018), at https://www.christianitytoday.com/ct/2018/july-web-only/revoices-founder-answers-lgbt-conferences-critics.html.

60. This was the primary issue I had with the Nashville Statement; cf. Luke Geraty, "Nitpicking the #NashvilleStatement (while not being 'liberal' or 'progressive')" (August 31, 2017), at https://lukegeraty.com/2017/08/.

55. Rom 8:29–30's "golden chain of salvation."

56. While this section may be anecdotal, I am convinced that the personal experiences of people, regardless of their viewpoints, needs to be taken into consideration as we engage in the way that people interpret and apply Scripture to their own lives.

with people who say they struggle with same-sex attraction, and I routinely have to think about the cultural challenges we face in the twenty-first century. The "front lines" of the local church have a way of raising their own significant biblical-theological issues. Accordingly, I humbly suggest a number of questions and comments as we move forward.

First, I believe the Church must confirm that all humans are created in the image of God, regardless of ethnicity, social-economic background, religious affiliation, or sexual orientation. The tone of these conversations has often caused the LGBTQ community to feel demeaned and unloved. This is not reflective of the gospel invitation or the way of love that Scripture requires.

Second, if we are going to engage what Scripture teaches and how theologians wrestle with these important topics, we must do so with the people of God in mind, especially those who are wrestling with issues related to sexual orientation, identity, and activity. How might a person who self-identifies as gay understand our views and tone? And how might our views and tone serve as a resource (or a poison) for those in need of biblical-theological reflection that is pastorally sensitive? Again, these are real people with real challenges and real experiences whom God loves.

Third, churches need to think long and hard about how they engage all topics related to what Scripture calls "sexual immorality," i.e., any sex outside of the context of a monogamous covenantal marriage comprised of one male and one female. If a church is willing to baptize or dedicate the children of an unmarried heterosexual couple, why not those of a married homosexual couple? As many local churches have become better described as "missional outposts," due to the onset of postmodernism, "post-postmodernism," and any other secularizing influence, how are we to welcome, not just tolerate, those who are exploring the Christian faith who have yet to surrender their lives, their thoughts, and their identities, to Jesus? What, specifically, is the type of posture and tone that churches should take when homosexual married couples with children enter into the community? How are the children of that couple to be treated, engaged, and included? What type of response do we offer that couple who wants to raise their children in a "Christian environment"?[57] These are complex questions that require thoughtfulness.

Fourth, we need to answer the question of the usefulness of "conversion therapy,"[58] if any. As virtually every secular social scientist rejects this approach,[59] how should local churches approach such a controversial practice? Rosaria Butterfield's powerful testimony of conversion[60] from being a lesbian feminist to a conservative Christian is often celebrated as an example of transformation, but she also states that reparative therapy is a heresy, writing the following:

> This position contends a primary goal of Christianity is to resolve homosexuality through heterosexuality, thus failing to see that repentance and victory over sin are God's gifts and failing to remember that sons and daughters of the King can be full members of Christ's body and still struggle with sexual temptation. This heresy is a modern version of the prosperity gospel. Name it. Claim it. Pray the gay away.[61]

Fifth, how are those who self-identify with the LGBTQ community to participate in the local church? In addition to the baptism question, what about receiving the Eucharist[62] or singing on the

---

57. Current conversations I have been a part of have explored and considered how Western missionaries have dealt with polygamy in cultures that allow such practices. For a discussion about the hermeneutical issues raised by polygamy in relation to homosexuality, see William J. Webb, *Slaves, Women, & Homosexuals: Exploring the Hermeneutics of Cultural Analysis* (Downers Grove, IL: IVP Academic, 2001).

58. This is also known as "reparative therapy."

59. Cf. Human Rights Campaign, "The Lies and Dangers of Efforts to Change Sexual Orientation or Gender Identity," HRC.org, at https://www.hrc.org/resources/the-lies-and-dangers-of-reparative-therapy (accessed October 3, 2018).

60. Cf. Rosaria Champagne Butterfield, *The Secret Thoughts of an Unlikely Convert: An English Professor's Journey in Christian Faith* (Pittsburg, PA: Crown & Covenant Publications, 2012) and her follow up, *Openness Unhindered: Further Thoughts of an Unlikely Convert on Sexual Identity and Union with Christ* (Pittsburg, PA: Crown & Covenant Publications, 2015).

61. Rosaria Butterfield, "You Are What—and How—You Read," The Gospel Coalition (February 13, 2014), at https://www.thegospelcoalition.org/article/you-are-whatand-howyou-read/.

62. In addition to addressing baby dedications and baptism, the Vineyard position paper indicates that the Vineyard *traditionally* holds to an "open communion" perspective, cf. "Pastoring LGBT Persons," 55–58. I argue along these same lines due to a sacramental approach to Vineyard theology, cf. Luke Geraty, "Toward a Vineyard

music team or serving in compassion ministries like feeding the poor? Where is the line between serving and leading? Many of the *ad hoc* decisions local churches make concerning these types of questions often feel arbitrary and, in my experience, inconsistent with how we treat people in other situations.

To be clear, these are simply *some* of the questions that I am currently wrestling with in the context of the local church, in conversations with fellow Vineyard leaders, and in ecumenical dialogue. The Vineyard has identified two "foul lines" in that Vineyard churches "should not ordain someone who is having sex outside of heterosexual marriage" and Vineyard pastors should not perform same-sex marriages.[63] This gives local churches flexibility in how they respond to the other challenges and questions experienced in the local church.

Sexual ethics will continue to be a challenge for the Church in coming generations and we must stop giving five-dollar answers to fifty-dollar questions. While this paper addresses the tip of the iceberg, my prayer is that Evangelicals and Catholics will together faithfully honor the teachings of Jesus, both his radical welcome and his challenging words. I close this paper with wise advice from the Evangelical Alliance:

> . . . we are called to be a people of both grace and truth. This must be evident in our teaching and preaching and also in our relationships and pastoral care. Evangelical churches need, therefore, to be places where, in response to homosexuality, as in all areas of life, people will encounter the welcome, forgiveness and transforming power of Christ whose grace is a costly grace that calls us all to take up our cross and follow him.[64]

Sacramental Theology: The Pneumatic Relationship between the 'Not Yet' and the 'Now'" (MA diss., University of Birmingham, UK, 2015) and Luke Geraty, "'Traditioning' in the Vineyard: A Pastoral Value for Sacramentality," paper presented at the annual meeting for the Society of Vineyard Scholars, New Haven, CT, 2017.

63. Vineyard USA, "Pastoring LGBT Persons," 58–59.

64. Goddard and Horrocks, *Resources for Church Leaders*, 34.

SECTION 3.
Social Ethics

3.0. Common Statement on Social Ethics

Social ethics for both Evangelicals and Catholics flows from our belief in Jesus Christ as our only savior and from how God has ordained the entire created order. We both agree that all people are created in the image of God and this image needs to be continually renewed in Christ so that God's glory shines forth in all aspects of our lives. This is the basis of a Christian social ethics.

A soul united to Jesus in faith is called to sanctification, and in that call we are commanded to love our neighbors as ourselves. This command has ramifications for our life and relations to others in family, economics, politics, health care, culture, and care for the poor. It calls forth from all Christians a responsibility to be just and act justly in faith, hope, and love.

As commissioned agents of justice we work to promote a just ordering of society in a fallen world. Without ceasing to articulate a distinctively Christian perspective on social issues, we strive to work with all—persons, institutions, and governments—who are willing to work with us in promoting a just social order even when they do not share our faith in Jesus Christ. We do this in the hope of the second coming of our Lord who will bring about a "new heavens and a new earth in which righteousness dwells" (2 Pet 3:13).

1. Catholics and Evangelicals agree that scripture provides a divinely revealed and authoritative basis for social ethics.

2. Evangelicals and Catholics hold that some issues in social ethics are discerned through normative sources outside of scripture

such as the traditions of our respective churches and natural law/reason.[1]
   a. Some Evangelicals would identify experience as a normative source.
   b. Catholics and some Evangelicals do not agree that experience is a normative source.

3. Evangelicals and Catholics agree that man is made in the image of God and thereby possesses an inherent dignity. Thus, human dignity is a key principle in discerning and addressing social issues. Affronts to human dignity are contrary to the will of God.
   a. Catholics also speak in terms of three further related principles: The common good, subsidiarity, and solidarity.[2]
   b. Although Evangelicals do not generally use these terms, they would recognize similar principles.

4. Catholics and Evangelicals agree that Christians should be engaged in social issues as citizens, bringing to bear Christian principles where appropriate and possible. The following, among others, are significant social issues about which all Christians should be concerned: education, the morality of war, church-state relations, economics, health care, immigration, the poor, and the death penalty.

5. Evangelicals and Catholics agree that our final hope is not to be placed in the governments of this world. Evangelicals and Catholics typically differ, however, in how they understand the roles of the state and the church in engaging social issues.
   a. Catholics and Evangelicals recognize the church's competence to address social issues and to call on the state to uphold its responsibility in serving the temporal needs of its citizens with justice.

---

1. See 2017 Fall common statements for morality.
2. See Daniel Keating's paper [in this volume], "Catholic Social Teaching: Orientation and Overview."

b. Some Evangelicals are more cautious than Catholics about ecclesiastical pronouncements on matters of public policy and the competence of the state to remedy social problems.

6. Catholics and Evangelicals agree that the state has no competence to obstruct or interfere with the mission of the church.

3.1. Catholic Social Teaching: Orientation and Overview

Dr. Daniel A. Keating

Our topic this year is Christian social ethics. By what principles do we approach this area and how do we evaluate the intricate and complex social issues that face Christians today? How do we bring to bear enduring scriptural truths and traditional norms onto quickly shifting ground in a culture that has largely abandoned its Christian heritage in favor of new forms of post-Christian ideologies?

In this paper, my aim is to offer an orientation to, and overview of, Catholic social teaching (CST) as it has developed in the past 125 years. The aims here are general: I will avoid plunging into any particular social question, remaining at the level of general principles. But grasping the first principles is crucial for understanding how the Catholic Church addresses the many individual issues that confront us all. I offer this overview within a climate in which CST receives both many accolades and sharp criticisms, from those inside and outside the Catholic tradition. Often, it seems to me, both the praise and the critique have more to do with what a given commentator thinks about the concrete issues than with arguments over the general principles. Often, political considerations and allegiances drive these discussions. For this reason, getting a good grip on the general moral principles that lie at the root of CST is essential. I will conclude by identifying certain criticisms lodged against CST and will offer a brief response to each.

The Origins and Development of Catholic Social Teaching

Catholic social teaching, as it has come to be framed and understood in the modern world, originated with the publication of *Rerum novarum* by Pope Leo XIII in 1891. This brief twenty-page encyclical letter did not present a sharp break with past papal teaching—Leo himself refers to other works he has already published on various contemporary issues of the day—but it marked out a new form of commentary on contemporary social concerns that has continued to the present day. The letter first addresses "the misery and wretchedness pressing so unjustly on the majority of the working class," but then quickly takes aim at the socialist solution of banning private ownership.[1] In Leo's view, the contentions of the socialists are "emphatically unjust, for they would rob the lawful possessor, distort the functions of the State, and create utter confusion in the community."[2] Wielding a double-edged sword that cuts in two directions, Leo upholds the right of capital and private property (while castigating greedy industrialists who treat human beings like objects) and defends the rights of the worker and the good of trade unions. In this short letter, the main lines of later Catholic social teaching can be found in seed, and the tradition that followed self-consciously built upon what Leo had inaugurated, several times naming a newly-minted encyclical letter by the year of its anniversary from *Rerum novarum* (see the list of primary documents of CST in the appendix).[3]

It is no easy task to grasp the coherence of this body of teaching given over many years, by numerous popes, in response to various social issues and contexts. To aid in the reception of this body of teaching, a *Compendium of the Social Doctrine of the Church* was

---

1. *Rerum novarum* (May 15, 1891), pp. 2:241–58 in *The Papal Encyclicals*, 5 vols., ed. Claudia Carlen, IHM (Wilmington, NC: McGrath, 1981), §3.

2. *Rerum novarum*, §4.

3. Three social encyclicals are named by the anniversary year from *Rerum novarum* in which they were promulgated: *Quadragesimo anno* (Pius XI, 1931); *Octogesima adveniens* (Paul VI, 1971); *Centesimus annus* (John Paul II, 1991). Two further encyclicals were published on a major anniversary of *Rerum novarum*: *Mater et magistra* (John XXIII, 1961) and *Laborem exercens* (John Paul II, 1981).

published in 2004 under the sponsorship of John Paul II by the Pontifical Council for Justice and Peace. The purpose of the document is announced at the start:

> This document intends to present in a complete and systematic manner, even if by means of an overview, the Church's social teaching, which is the fruit of careful Magisterial reflection and an expression of the Church's constant commitment in fidelity to the grace of salvation wrought in Christ and in loving concern for humanity's destiny. Herein the most relevant theological, philosophical, moral, cultural and pastoral considerations of this teaching are systematically presented as they relate to social questions. In this way, witness is borne to the fruitfulness of the encounter between the Gospel and the problems that mankind encounters on its journey through history.[4]

I will make use of the *Compendium* to describe what Catholic social teaching is and to outline the main principles by which it operates.

What Is Catholic Social Teaching?

The *Compendium* acknowledges that this body of social teaching evolved and became more systematic over time:

> The Church's social doctrine was not initially thought of as an organic system but was formed over the course of time, through the numerous interventions of the Magisterium on social issues. The fact that it came about in this manner makes it understandable that certain changes may have taken place with regard to its nature, method and epistemological structure.[5]

In terms of category, CST "belongs to the field, not of *ideology*, but of *theology* and particularly of moral theology," but "avails itself of contributions from all branches of knowledge, whatever their source, and has an important interdisciplinary dimension."[6] This social teaching is grounded in twin authorities, faith and reason, or more precisely in the revelation of Jesus Christ in the Scriptures and in natural law

---

4. Pontifical Council for Justice and Peace, *Compendium of the Social Doctrine of the Church* (June 29, 2004) (Vatican City: Libreria Editrice Vaticana, 2004), §8 (hereafter *Compendium*).
5. *Compendium*, §72.
6. *Compendium*, §72 (citing *Sollicitudo rei socialis*, §41), §76.

as understood and illuminated in the context of that revelation. The *Compendium* clarifies that revelation is the first and essential foundation for this teaching.

> The Church's social doctrine finds its essential foundation in biblical revelation and in the tradition of the Church. From this source, which comes from above, it draws inspiration and light to understand, judge and guide human experience and history. Before anything else and above everything else is God's plan for the created world and, in particular, for the life and destiny of men and women, called to Trinitarian communion.[7]

Guided by revelation and the narrative of salvation as outlined in the Scriptures, this social doctrine proceeds to address questions that are also capable of being known and understood through natural reason as given in creation.

> Faith and reason represent the two cognitive paths of the Church's social doctrine: Revelation and human nature . . . . The Church's social doctrine is knowledge enlightened by faith, which, as such, is the expression of a greater capacity for knowledge. It explains to all people the truths that it affirms and the duties that it demands; it can be accepted and shared by all.[8]

Consequently, "the Church has the right to be a teacher for mankind, a teacher of the truth of faith: the truth not only of dogmas but also of the morals whose source lies in human nature itself and in the Gospel." The aim is "to make the liberating word of the Gospel resound in the complex worlds of production, labor, business, finance, trade, politics, law, culture, social communications, where men and women live."[9]

Given that CST ranges across all sorts of boundaries, the question arises concerning the *authority* of this teaching for the faithful. Is it to be regarded as the teaching of the faith or merely as useful commentary on current social questions? The answer is complex; the level of authority depends on the nature of the teaching given.

---

7. *Compendium*, §74.
8. *Compendium*, §75.
9. *Compendium*, §70 (citing *Dignitatis humanae*, §14).

> Insofar as it is part of the Church's moral teaching, the Church's social doctrine has the same dignity and authority as her moral teaching. It is authentic Magisterium, which obligates the faithful to adhere to it. The doctrinal weight of the different teachings and the assent required are determined by the nature of the particular teachings, by their level of independence from contingent and variable elements, and by the frequency with which they are invoked.[10]

Because CST presents teaching on both principles and practices, a distinction is made between enduring and permanent moral principles and the prudential application of those principles to given social-historical contexts. "The Church's social doctrine, in fact, offers not only meaning, value and criteria of judgment, but also the norms and directives of action that arise from these. With her social doctrine the Church does not attempt to structure or organize society, but to appeal to, guide and form consciences."[11]

Though it sometimes seems otherwise to many, the aim of CST is not to form concrete social policy but to guide consciences when faced with complex social issues.

> When the Church's Magisterium intervenes in issues concerning social and political life, it does not fail to observe the requirements of a correctly understood autonomy, for "the Church's Magisterium does not wish to exercise political power or eliminate the freedom of opinion of Catholics regarding contingent questions. Instead, it intends—as is its proper function—to instruct and illuminate the consciences of the faithful, particularly those involved in political life, so that their actions may always serve the integral promotion of the human person and the common good. The social doctrine of the Church is not an intrusion into the government of individual countries. It is a question of the lay Catholic's duty to be morally coherent, found within one's conscience, which is one and indivisible."[12]

---

10. *Compendium*, §80.
11. *Compendium*, §81.
12. *Compendium*, §571. The embedded quotation is from the CDF, "Doctrinal Note on Some Questions Regarding the Participation of Catholics in Political Life" (November 24, 2002).

Finally, we should note that CST also finds its place in the wider call for a "new evangelization" today. Social ethics and evangelizing mission are not two distinct fields; the teaching and application of the former serves the good of the latter.

> The Church is aware that she must take "a giant step forward in her evangelization effort, and enter into a new stage of history in her missionary dynamism." The Church's social doctrine is situated within this pastoral vision: "The 'new evangelization', which the modern world urgently needs ... must include among its essential elements a proclamation of the Church's social doctrine."[13]

The Guiding Principles of Catholic Social Teaching

The *Compendium* identifies four foundational principles of Catholic social teaching, the first serving as the foundation for the other three.

> The permanent principles of the Church's social doctrine constitute the very heart of Catholic social teaching. These are the principles of: the dignity of the human person ... which is the foundation of all the other principles and content of the Church's social doctrine; the common good; subsidiarity; and solidarity. These principles, the expression of the whole truth about man known by reason and faith, are born of "the encounter of the Gospel message and of its demands summarized in the supreme commandment of love of God and neighbour in justice with the problems emanating from the life of society."[14]

We will examine each of these briefly in turn.

THE DIGNITY OF THE HUMAN PERSON

The principal foundation, referenced numerous times throughout the corpus of CST, is the dignity of the human person made in the image and likeness of God: "Men and women, in the concrete circumstances of history, represent the heart and soul of Catholic social thought.

---

13. *Compendium*, §523 (citing *Christifideles laici*, §35, and *Centesimus annus*, §5).
14. *Compendium*, §160. The embedded quotation is from the CDF "Instruction," *Libertatis conscientia*, §72.

The whole of the Church's social doctrine, in fact, develops from the principle that affirms the inviolable dignity of the human person."[15] This given dignity of each person can be ascertained through the natural law: "The natural law expresses the dignity of the person and lays the foundations of the person's fundamental duties."[16] But the full measure of human dignity is grounded in divine revelation, and especially in the creation of man and woman in the image and likeness of God.

> The fundamental message of Sacred Scripture proclaims that the human person is a creature of God, and sees in his being in the image of God the element that characterizes and distinguishes him: "God created man in his own image, in the image of God he created him; male and female he created them" (Gen 1:27). Therefore, "being in the image of God the human individual possesses the dignity of a person, who is not just something, but someone. He is capable of self-knowledge, of self-possession and of freely giving himself and entering into communion with other persons. Further, he is called by grace to a covenant with his Creator, to offer him a response of faith and love that no other creature can give in his stead."[17]

Importantly, men and women possess equal dignity but do so distinctly through mutual complementarity: "Man and woman have the same dignity and are of equal value, not only because they are both, in their differences, created in the image of God, but even more profoundly because the dynamic of reciprocity that gives life to the 'we' in the human couple is an image of God."[18]

Further, it is precisely the status of the human being, made in the

---

15. *Compendium*, §107.
16. *Compendium*, §140.
17. *Compendium*, §108 (citing CCC 357).
18. *Compendium*, §111. The *Compendium*, §146, includes a striking statement from John Paul II, *Christifideles laici*, §50, on the distinctness, equality, and mutuality of men and women in Christ: "The condition that will assure the rightful presence of woman in the Church and in society is a more penetrating and accurate consideration of the anthropological foundation for masculinity and femininity with the intent of clarifying woman's personal identity in relation to man, that is, a diversity yet mutual complementarity, not only as it concerns roles to be held and functions to be performed, but also, and more deeply, as it concerns her make-up and meaning as a person."

image and likeness of God and called to community, that grounds a true understanding of freedom:

> Man can turn to good only in freedom, which God has given to him as one of the highest signs of his image: "For God has willed that man remain 'under the control of his own decisions' (Sir 15:14), so that he can seek his Creator spontaneously, and come freely to utter and blissful perfection through loyalty to Him. Hence man's dignity demands that he act according to a knowing and free choice that is personally motivated and prompted from within, neither under blind internal impulse nor by mere external pressure."[19]

Here is a rich vein of wisdom that could be developed, showing how true freedom is freedom *for* excellence and the truth of God, not freedom *from* all external constraint upon the human will. CST acknowledges the goodness of human freedom but also recognizes the impact of Adam's sin that turns human freedom toward evil and separation from God. Thus,

> Human freedom needs therefore to be liberated. Christ, by the power of his Paschal Mystery, frees man from his disordered love of self, which is the source of his contempt for his neighbour and of those relationships marked by domination of others. Christ shows us that freedom attains its fulfilment in the gift of self. By his sacrifice on the cross, Jesus places man once more in communion with God.[20]

THE COMMON GOOD

Three further fundamental principles follow from the foundational truth of the dignity of the human person made in the image and likeness of God. The first is the principle of the common good, which is easily misunderstood in political terms as the priority of the *collective* good over the good of the *individual*, a reading that would not be consistent with the dignity of the human person. The *Compendium* offers the following as a description of the meaning of the common good:

---

19. *Compendium*, §135 (citing *Gaudium et spes*, §17).
20. *Compendium*, §143.

The principle of the common good, to which every aspect of social life must be related if it is to attain its fullest meaning, stems from the dignity, unity and equality of all people. According to its primary and broadly accepted sense, the common good indicates "the sum total of social conditions which allow people, either as groups or as individuals, to reach their fulfilment more fully and more easily."[21]

Plainly, this principle does not yield self-evident applications in the concrete realities of human social conditions; it requires prudence and wisdom to achieve the demands of the common good in specific circumstances. Giving further definition to the meaning of the common good, the *Compendium* identifies the common good as the social and communal dimension of the moral good:

The common good does not consist in the simple sum of the particular goods of each subject of a social entity. Belonging to everyone and to each person, it is and remains "common," because it is indivisible and because only together is it possible to attain it, increase it and safeguard its effectiveness, with regard also to the future. Just as the moral actions of an individual are accomplished in doing what is good, so too the actions of a society attain their full stature when they bring about the common good. The common good, in fact, can be understood as the social and community dimension of the moral good.[22]

One important principle that arises from the common good is the "universal destination of goods," a principle grounded in the act of creation as revealed in the opening chapters of Genesis:

Among the numerous implications of the common good, immediate significance is taken on by the principle of the universal destination of goods: "God destined the earth and all it contains for all men and all peoples so that all created things would be shared fairly by all mankind under the guidance of justice tempered by charity." This principle is based on the fact that "the original source of all that is good is the very act of God, who created both the earth and man, and who gave the earth to man so that he might have dominion over it by his work and enjoy its fruits (Gen 1:28–29). God gave the earth to

---

21. *Compendium*, §164 (citing *Gaudium et spes*, §26).
22. *Compendium*, §164.

the whole human race for the sustenance of all its members, without excluding or favoring anyone."[23]

This principle of the universal destination of human goods appears especially prominent in the writings of John Paul II: "The right to the common use of goods is the 'first principle of the whole ethical and social order' and 'the characteristic principle of Christian social doctrine.'"[24]

How does this principle of the universal destination of human goods comport with the Church's defense of the good and the right of private property, so conspicuous in Pope Leo's *Rerum novarum*? While the right to private property remains an essential element of CST, it functions not as a fundamental end but as an essential means to a just ordering of human social life:

> Private property is an essential element of an authentically social and democratic economic policy, and it is the guarantee of a correct social order.... This principle [the universal destination of goods] is not opposed to the right to private property but indicates the need to regulate it. Private property, in fact, regardless of the concrete forms of the regulations and juridical norms relative to it, is in its essence only an instrument for respecting the principle of the universal destination of goods; in the final analysis, therefore, it is not an end but a means.[25]

SUBSIDIARITY

The principle of subsidiarity, also sometimes mischaracterized in political terms as simply the rejection of big government, follows from the dignity of the human person and the common good. This principle sheds light on the importance of various local social institutions—the family being the first—that give essential shape to human social life. This principle pushes against the extremes of "rugged individualism" on the one hand and the all-encompassing central state collective on the other: for human beings to flourish there must be

---

23. *Compendium*, §171 (citing *Gaudium et spes*, §69, and *Centesimus annus*, §31).
24. *Compendium*, §172 (citing *Laborem exercens*, §19, and *Sollicitudo rei socialis*, §42).
25. *Compendium*, §176, §177.

various intermediate institutions that express and preserve human dignity and freedom.

> Subsidiarity is among the most constant and characteristic directives of the Church's social doctrine and has been present since the first great social encyclical. It is impossible to promote the dignity of the person without showing concern for the family, groups, associations, local territorial realities; in short, for that aggregate of economic, social, cultural, sports-oriented, recreational, professional and political expressions to which people spontaneously give life and which make it possible for them to achieve effective social growth. This is the realm of civil society, understood as the sum of the relationships between individuals and intermediate social groupings.[26]

The principle of subsidiarity does not provide a formula or blueprint for a just society; it cannot determine how the complex realities of social life should function together. But it presents an obligation, such that institutions of a higher order are obliged to serve and provide help for the flourishing of those at a lower order.

> On the basis of this principle, all societies of a superior order must adopt attitudes of help ("subsidium")—therefore of support, promotion, development—with respect to lower-order societies. In this way, intermediate social entities can properly perform the functions that fall to them without being required to hand them over unjustly to other social entities of a higher level, by which they would end up being absorbed and substituted, in the end seeing themselves denied their dignity and essential place.[27]

Along with the requirement that higher entities serve those at a lower level comes an obligation on the part of individuals and the lower institutions to actively participate in and build up the wider society.

> The characteristic implication of subsidiarity is participation, which is expressed essentially in a series of activities by means of which the citizen, either as an individual or in association with others, whether directly or through representation, contributes to the cultural,

---

26. *Compendium*, §185.
27. *Compendium*, §186.

economic, political and social life of the civil community to which he belongs.[28]

SOLIDARITY

The principle of solidarity can be difficult to pin down. The term first appears in the social encyclicals of John XXIII when he speaks specifically about the relations between workers and employers:

> Finally, both workers and employers should regulate their mutual relations in accordance with the principle of human solidarity and Christian brotherhood. Unrestricted competition in the liberal sense, and the Marxist creed of class warfare, are clearly contrary to Christian teaching and the nature of man.[29]

Though employed by Paul VI,[30] the principle of solidarity was given its distinctive shape in the teaching of John Paul II. According to John Paul, solidarity is the firm determination to commit ourselves to the common good of both individuals and peoples:

> When interdependence becomes recognized in this way, the correlative response as a moral and social attitude, as a "virtue," is solidarity. This then is not a feeling of vague compassion or shallow distress at the misfortunes of so many people, both near and far. On the contrary, it is a firm and persevering determination to commit oneself to the common good; that is to say to the good of all and of each individual, because we are all really responsible for all.[31]

In an important sense, solidarity means recognizing the inherent value of the person—and the community of persons—not just as instruments but as sharers in the bounty of God.

> Solidarity helps us to see the "other"—whether a person, people or nation—not just as some kind of instrument, with a work capacity and physical strength to be exploited at low cost and then discarded

---

28. *Compendium*, §189.
29. *Mater et magistra* (May 15, 1961), pp. 5:59–88 in *The Papal Encyclicals*, 5 vols., ed. Claudia Carlen, IHM (Wilmington, NC: McGrath, 1981), §23.
30. See *Populorum progressio*, §17.
31. *Sollicitudo rei socialis* (December 30, 1987), pp. 426–77 in *The Papal Encyclicals of John Paul II*, ed. J. Michael Miller (Huntington, IN: Our Sunday Visitor, 1996), §38.

when no longer useful, but as our "neighbor," a "helper," to be made a sharer, on a par with ourselves, in the banquet of life to which all are equally invited by God.[32]

And though the virtue of solidarity is recognizable and attainable at the human level through reason, it is raised to a specifically Christian virtue when illumined by faith and charity.

> Solidarity is undoubtedly a Christian virtue. In what has been said so far it has been possible to identify many points of contact between solidarity and charity, which is the distinguishing mark of Christ's disciples (cf. Jn 13:35). In the light of faith, solidarity seeks to go beyond itself, to take on the specifically Christian dimension of total gratuity, forgiveness and reconciliation.[33]

For his part, Benedict XVI upholds the principle of solidarity and links it closely with subsidiarity and the common good.

> The principle of subsidiarity must remain closely linked to the principle of solidarity and vice versa, since the former without the latter gives way to social privatism, while the latter without the former gives way to paternalist social assistance that is demeaning to those in need.[34]

This link between solidarity and the other fundamental principles of CST is also underlined by the *Compendium*:

> The message of the Church's social doctrine regarding solidarity clearly shows that there exists an intimate bond between solidarity and the common good, between solidarity and the universal destination of goods, between solidarity and equality among men and peoples, between solidarity and peace in the world.[35]

---

32. *Sollicitudo rei socialis*, §39.
33. *Sollicitudo rei socialis*, §40.
34. *Caritas in veritate* (June 29, 2009) (Washington, DC: United States Conference of Catholic Bishops, 2009), §58 (see also §67).
35. *Compendium*, §194. After laying down these foundational principles for Catholic social teaching, the *Compendium* then addresses the following topics in turn: (1) the family; (2) human work; (3) economic life; (4) the political community; (5) the international community; (6) safeguarding the environment; and (7) the promotion of peace.

Challenges of Application and Interpretation

In this concluding section, my aim is to identify certain criticisms of CST that are often directed against it. One of the obvious strengths of CST is that it provides the Catholic faithful with permanent *principles* by which they can guide their thinking and practice in regard to social questions, thus helping the faithful to avoid being "tossed and turned" by the latest ideas from various ideologies. CST thus provides the faithful with permanent criteria for thinking and acting with respect to concrete social questions. Further, beyond giving these permanent principles, CST offers help to the faithful, in a given time and situation, regarding the specific questions of the day (for example, Leo XIII speaking about workers' issues in the late nineteenth century, and Francis speaking about a Christian ecology in the early twenty-first century). CST, in short, provides clear moral guidance for, and application of truth to, given situations and conditions of the day.

However, this very effort to speak to the concrete needs of the day gives rise to criticisms that CST tries to do too much and so oversteps its bounds. One critique is that CST—despite its disclaimers—sometimes too strongly reflects the terms and conditions of a given time, including the "spirit of the age," and so mixes together timeless truths with very time-bound and questionable premises drawn from the wider culture. An example is the common critique of *Gaudium et spes* (*Constitution on the Church in the Modern World*), that it presents an overly optimistic 1960s view of the world and the world's motives, along with an underestimation of sin and evil. A close reading of *Gaudium et spes*, I would argue, absolves it of this charge in terms of its doctrinal content, but it is more difficult to evaluate the optimistic tone of the document in regard to the world. How much of this should the faithful adopt? Is this "tone and attitude" reflective of a temporary (and questionable) period in the Western world? How much weight should be given to the document's tone and attitude as we face new and even more formidable challenges?

A second related critique is that Catholic social teaching speaks with unwarranted particularity to the specifics of social, economic, and governmental policy, and so intrudes—despite its disclaimers—on the competence of civil government. CST, of course, explicitly denies that it is seeking to govern public policy or dictate to states how they should arrange civil society, but it is not always easy to distinguish "the norms and directives of action" CST offers from improper intervention into the dictating of public policy. As the *Compendium* itself says, recognizing different levels of authority,

> The doctrinal weight of the different teachings and the assent required are determined by the nature of the particular teachings, *by their level of independence from contingent and variable elements*, and by the frequency with which they are invoked.[36]

Insofar as specific directives do get entangled with contingent and variable elements, such teaching would carry less weight. But the question remains as to when and where such entanglement may have occurred.

Finally, there is the criticism that Catholic social teaching sometimes—and even often—presents an overly optimistic view of what is possible to achieve in civil society in this age of the world, and so slides into a form of post-millennial eschatology that speaks as if the kingdom of God can be largely instantiated short of the return of Christ. Obviously, such a claim in a strong form cannot be sustained, but there are texts in the social encyclicals—and in the *Compendium*[37]—that could be read in this direction. Such statements are balanced and qualified by others, however, clarifying that we cannot expect the Messianic kingdom to arrive in the societies of this age.

> In proclaiming the Gospel, the social dimension is an essential and unavoidable but not the only dimension. It is a dimension that must reveal the unlimited possibilities of Christian salvation, even if it is not possible in time to conform social realities perfectly and definitively to the Gospel. No results attained, not even the most spectacular, can escape the limits of human freedom and the eschatological tension of every created reality.[38]

---

36. *Compendium*, §80 (emphasis added).
37. See, e.g., *Compendium*, §82.
38. *Compendium*, §526. For the limits to social progress and perfection that we must recognize in this age of the world, see also *Compendium*, §183.

This statement hardly reflects the theological outlook of the Book of Revelation, but it does uphold the truth, as found in Saint Paul, that the entire created world, including human life and society, is marked by sin and suffers a kind of futility, waiting for its full redemption when Christ returns to bring the fullness of the new creation.

Appendix

CATHOLIC SOCIAL TEACHING (1891–PRESENT)

Rerum novarum (1891)	Leo XIII
Quadragesimo anno (1931)	Pius XI
Mater et magistra (1961)	John XXIII
Pacem in terris (1963)	John XXIII
Dignitatis humanae (1965)	Vatican II
Gaudium et spes (1965)	Vatican II
Populorum progressio (1967)	Paul VI
Humanae vitae (1968)	Paul VI
Octogesima adveniens (1971)	Paul VI
Laborem exercens (1981)	John Paul II
Sollicitudo rei socialis (1987)	John Paul II
Centesimus annus (1991)	John Paul II
Evangelium vitae (1995)	John Paul II
Caritas in veritate (2009)	Benedict XVI
Laudato si' (2015)	Francis

Compendium of the Social Doctrine of the Church (2004)

3.2. "Absurd Equality": The Church's Condemnation of Socialism in *Rerum novarum*

Dr. William B. Stevenson

*R*erum novarum, promulgated in 1891 by Pope Leo XIII, is by all accounts the founding document of what in the twentieth century would come to be known as "Catholic social teaching." Despite the fact that in the nearly 130 years since its appearance, the Church has sought to develop and expand upon its foundational principles, altering and applying them to the varying circumstances of the modern world, it has lost none of its relevance. In particular, its spirited and philosophically sophisticated defense of private property against socialist counter-claims ought to be of especial interest to us at this juncture in contemporary Catholic life and culture. This past summer, for instance, the Jesuit journal *America* published a piece entitled "The Catholic Case for Communism" in which the author attempts, among other marvels, to demonstrate how Christians and communists alike recognize the obvious desirability of a classless society, even as he concedes, with breathtaking callowness, that "Christianity and communism have obviously had a complicated relationship."[1] More wondrously yet, the chancellor of the Pontifical Academy of Social Sciences, Bishop Marcelo Sanchez Sorondo, not long ago declared that "at this moment, those who best realize the social doctrine of the Church are the Chinese."[2] When such pronouncements

---

1. Dean Detloff, "The Catholic Case for Communism," *America* (July 23, 2019), at https://www.americamagazine.org/faith/2019/07/23/catholic-case-communism.
2. "Vatican Official Praises China for Witness to Catholic Social Teaching," *Catholic News Agency* (February 6, 2018), at https://www.catholicnewsagency.com/news/37694

are made without any official follow-up "clarification," one may be permitted to wonder what, if men say such things in the green wood, will be done in the dry? It is unfortunate that many official spokespersons for, and established experts in, Catholic social teaching end up confirming the worst suspicions of its critics, but this surely provides sufficient motive for thoughtful persons to return to its foundational text.

For one whose knowledge of Catholic social thought has been picked up by way of popular presentations of "social justice,"[3] *Rerum novarum* will almost certainly come as a revelation. Throughout, Leo grounds his argument against socialist collectivism largely in the natural law teaching of Saint Thomas Aquinas, whose thought was in the latter half of the nineteenth century enjoying a revival after nearly two hundred years of relative neglect. The encyclical's Thomism, however, is hardly unalloyed. In fact, for reasons which I hope presently to make clear, Leo attempts to harmonize Thomas's account of the natural law with the emphatically modern doctrine of individual natural rights, the definitive—or at least most broadly acceptable—form of which was worked out in the thought of John Locke. But while the Lockean element in *Rerum novarum* is perhaps best regarded as the handmaid of its predominating natural law doctrine, over the course of the last century Catholic social thought has in the main expressed itself more in the language and thought forms

---

/vatican-official-praises-china-for-witness-to-catholic-social-teaching. The bishop went on to marvel that "you do not have shantytowns, you do not have drugs, young people do not have drugs. There is a positive national consciousness." Also, and in the teeth of the evidence, he declared that China, unlike so many Western democracies, "defended the dignity of the human person." None of the one million Uighur Muslims currently in Chinese detention camps was available for comment.

3. This term appears for the first time in Luigi Taparelli d'Azeglio's *Saggio teoretico di dritto naturale appoggiato sul fatto* (Palermo, 1840–1843 and Rome: La Civiltà Cattolica, 1855). Vol. I, bk. 2, ch. 3, for instance, bears the title, "Nozioni del dritto e della giustizia sociale." Although Taparelli was a major figure in the Thomistic revival of the nineteenth century, as well as Leo's former professor, the pope rejected the term for reason of its vagueness and "non-Thomistic pedigree." See Ernest Fortin, "Sacred and Inviolable: *Rerum Novarum* and Natural Rights," 203–33 in *Human Rights, Virtue, and the Common Good: Untimely Meditations on Religion and Politics*, vol. 3 of *Ernest Fortin: Collected Essays*, ed. Brian Benestad (Lanham, MD: Rowman & Littlefield, 1996), 201.

of natural or (since nature is no longer normative) "human" rights than in terms of the natural law.

The significance of this shift lies in the fact that, for all intents and purposes, the teleological view of a normative nature has been abandoned in favor of a non-teleological view of inalienable and imprescriptible individual rights which, according to its originators, was developed in opposition to its classical and premodern alternative. We have ample reason to doubt whether the replacement of the natural law, with its corresponding emphasis on virtue and duty, by natural rights has advanced our understanding of moral phenomena or produced nobler human beings. However that may be, a close and careful reading of *Rerum novarum* effectively prevents whatever blame there may be in the matter from being laid at Leo's door. In this paper, then, I will assess Leo's attack on socialism and his defense of private property as a particular application of Thomas's natural law teaching. But since his argument also depends upon the modern idea of natural rights—an idea wholly foreign to Thomas and to his classical predecessors—I will further examine his use of this notion and venture a provisional explanation for his using it at all.

Socialism and Private Property

While Leo had previously written on political and social matters,[4] *Rerum novarum* is the first Church document which deals explicitly and at length with the conditions of the working classes, *de conditione opificum*, and which seeks to clarify the vexed question of the relation of labor and capital, as well as the "relative rights and mutual duties of the rich and of the poor" (§2).[5] The laissez-faire capitalism engendered by modern liberalism naturally comes under Leo's close and penetrating critical scrutiny inasmuch as it set the conditions for

---

4. See, e.g., Encyclical Letters *Quod apostolici muneris* (1878), *Immortale Dei* (1885), and *Libertas praestantissium* (1888).

5. Leo XIII, *Rerum novarum* (May 15, 1891), pp. 2:241–58 in *The Papal Encyclicals*, 5 vols., ed. Claudia Carlen, IHM (Wilmington, NC: McGrath, 1981), §2. Subsequent references are given parenthetically in the text. Latin text from pp. 640–70 in *Acta Apostolicae Sedis* 23 (1891).

the massive disparity between an impoverished working class and the increasingly affluent middle and upper classes. But whatever its defects, capitalism in fact creates wealth, expands economic opportunity, and in principle allows anyone, regardless of class, to acquire that private property which the encyclical defends as a natural and necessary human good. Even as he criticizes on moral grounds the excesses to which it is given, Leo does not seem to regard capitalism as incorrigible or essentially at odds with the general welfare of mankind. Socialism, on the other hand, which understands itself as the historically necessary solution to the problems created or exacerbated by capitalism, comes under Leo's unqualified condemnation. Indeed, the evil of socialism and "the spirit of revolutionary change which has long been disturbing the nations of the world" (§1) cannot but be opposed to human flourishing, arising as it does out of a reductively materialist anthropology which acknowledges only an "effective truth."[6] This assessment of socialism accounts in part for the encyclical's unprecedented emphasis on private property as a "sacred right," *ius sanctum* (§46).

Leo devotes an entire section (§§4–15) to a philosophical refutation of the socialist claim that "by this transferring property from private individuals to the community, the present mischievous state of things will be set to rights, inasmuch as each citizen will then get his fair share of whatever there is to enjoy" (§4). He begins with the simple observation that the whole reason for a man to engage in remunerative labor is to obtain property which he may hold as his own. He says further that both the remuneration and the "disposal of such remuneration, just as he pleases" is a "right, full and real" (§5).[7] Thus, for instance, if a prudent and frugal worker saves and invests in land, the land is nothing other than his wages under another form. His right to use his land in any way he pleases is as inviolable as his right to the wage by which he purchased it. A thing truly is said to be owned only where there is an accompanying right of disposal. Consequently,

---

6. See Niccolo Machiavelli, *The Prince*, 15.
7. "ideoque ex opera data ius verum perfectumque sibi quaerit non modo exigendae mercedis, *sed collocandae uti velit*" (§5). Emphasis mine.

the "common property of all" sought by the socialists cannot be the actual property of any.

The chief practical implication of the socialist position is that it unjustly prevents human beings from increasing the resources that materially improve their circumstances. But there is in fact a philosophical explanation for why acquisitiveness is actually necessary for human flourishing. This necessity is rooted in the rationality by which the human being is specifically distinguished from other animals. From the point of view of classical and Catholic anthropology, socialists fail to take into account, or rather deny outright, the cardinal difference between man and the beasts. Animals are able to nourish themselves, and to bear and rear offspring, through whatever means are at their immediate disposal. They are directed and moved by sense data alone. Man, on the other hand, provides for these needs by his power of reasoning.

> . . . animal nature, however perfect, is far from representing the human being in his completeness, and is in truth but humanity's humble handmaid, made to serve and obey. It is the mind, or reason, which is the predominant element in us who are human creatures; it is this which renders a human being human, and distinguishes him essentially from the brute. And on this very account—that man alone is endowed with reason—*it must be within his right to possess things not merely for temporary and momentary use, as other living things do, but to have and to hold them in stable and permanent possession; he must have not only things that perish in the use, but those also which, though they have been reduced into use, continue for further use in after time* (§6, emphasis mine).

Man is an animal, but his animal nature is of itself incapable of providing for even his animal needs. The wolf, for example, has a coat which keeps him warm and protects him from the elements, and in this respect his life is more or less untroubled. But the human being, who comes into the world naked, must supply for the deficiencies of his bodily nature through reason and art, fashioning clothing from the materials provided by the world around him—perhaps even by taking the wolf's coat for himself.

Nor is this all. Man's reason is also the ground of his self-

The Church's Condemnation of Socialism in *Rerum novarum*   215

consciousness, that is, his knowledge of himself as a being within a world. But he knows himself precisely as a being in time. Leo observes that,

> Man, fathoming by his faculty of reason matters without number, linking the future with the present, and being master of his own acts, guides his ways under the eternal law and the power of God, whose providence governs all things. Wherefore, it is in his power to exercise the choice not only as to matters that regard his present welfare, but also about those which he deems may be for his advantage in time yet to come. Hence, man not only should possess the fruits of the earth, but also the very soil, inasmuch as from the produce of the earth he has to lay by provision for the future. Man's needs do not die out, but forever recur; although satisfied today, they demand fresh supplies for tomorrow. Nature accordingly must have given to man a source that is stable and remaining always with him, from which he might look to draw continual supplies. And this stable condition of things he finds solely in the earth and its fruits. There is no need to bring in the State. Man precedes the State, and possesses, prior to the formation of any State, the right of providing for the substance of the body (§7).

With the significant exception of the last three sentences—a fact to which I will return later—Leo's argument proceeds along recognizably Thomistic and Aristotelian lines.[8] Man, as a rational animal, is

---

8. See, e.g., Thomas Aquinas, *Summa Theologiae* (hereafter, *ST*) II-II, q. 57, a. 3. It is important to note, however, that Thomas distinguishes in a way that Leo here does not, the right of nations, *ius gentium*, from natural right, *ius naturale*:

> "Ius sive iustum naturale est quod ex sui natura est adaequatum vel commensuratum alteri. Hoc autem potest contingere dupliciter. Uno modo, secundum absolutam sui considerationem, sicut masculus ex sui ratione habet commensurationem ad feminam ut ex ea generet, et parens ad filium ut eum nutriat. Alio modo aliquid est naturaliter alteri commensuratum non secundum absolutam sui rationem, sed secundum aliquid quod ex ipso consequitur, puta proprietas possessionum. Si enim consideretur iste ager absolute, non habet unde magis sit huius quam illius, sed si consideretur quantum ad opportunitatem colendi et ad pacificum usum agri, secundum hoc habet quandam commensurationem ad hoc quod sit unius et non alterius, ut patet per philosophum, in II Polit.
>
> "Absolute autem apprehendere aliquid non solum convenit homini, sed etiam aliis animalibus. Et ideo ius quod dicitur naturale secundum primum modum, commune est nobis et aliis animalibus. A iure autem naturali sic dicto recedit

deeply conscious of himself as a needy being subject to fortune and the caprices of nature. But if his intelligence is the source of this awareness, it is also the power by which he is capable of stabilizing his standing in a world which is not uniformly and predictably generous. In a very real sense, man cannot but give "thought for the morrow." It is a requirement of his nature.

But it is no argument against private ownership to say that the whole earth has been given by God for the use and enjoyment of the entire human race. The earth indeed ministers to the needs of all, but

> ius gentium, ut iurisconsultus dicit, quia illud omnibus animalibus, hoc solum hominibus inter se commune est. Considerare autem aliquid comparando ad id quod ex ipso sequitur, est proprium rationis. Et ideo hoc quidem est naturale homini secundum rationem naturalem, quae hoc dictat. Et ideo dicit Gaius iurisconsultus, quod naturalis ratio inter omnes homines constituit, id apud omnes gentes custoditur, vocaturque ius gentium."
>
> ["the natural right or justice is that which by its very nature is adjusted to or commensurate with another person. Now this may happen in two ways; first, according as it is considered absolutely: thus a male by its very nature is commensurate with the female to beget offspring by her, and a parent is commensurate with the offspring to nourish it. Secondly a thing is naturally commensurate with another person, not according as it is considered absolutely, but according to something resultant from it, for instance the possession of property. For if a particular piece of land be considered absolutely, it contains no reason why it should belong to one man more than to another, but if it be considered in respect of its adaptability to cultivation, and the unmolested use of the land, it has a certain commensuration to be the property of one and not of another man, as the Philosopher shows (Polit. ii, 2).
>
> "Now it belongs not only to man but also to other animals to apprehend a thing absolutely: wherefore the right which we call natural, is common to us and other animals according to the first kind of commensuration. But the right of nations falls short of natural right in this sense, as the jurist [Digest. i, 1; De Just. et Jure i] says because 'the latter is common to all animals, while the former is common to men only.' On the other hand, to consider a thing by comparing it with what results from it, is proper to reason, wherefore this same is natural to man in respect of natural reason which dictates it. Hence the jurist Gaius says (Digest. i, 1; De Just. et Jure i, 9): 'whatever natural reason decrees among all men, is observed by all equally, and is called the right of nations.'"]
>
> English translations of the *Summa Theologiae* throughout this paper are those of the Fathers of the English Dominican Province (New York: Benziger, 1947), which I have occasionally altered for, I hope, greater accuracy and clarity. The Latin text is found in *Sancti Thomae de Aquino Opera Omnia*, vols. 4–12 (Rome: Commissio Leonina, 1888–1906).

it does so precisely by means of private ownership. Anyone can see, for example, that a farm benefits many more than the farmer himself, and with greater abundance than if there were no farmer who owned the land. As Leo points out, "those who do not possess the soil contribute their labor; hence it may truly be said that all subsistence is derived either from labor on one's own land, or from some toil, some calling which is paid for either in produce of the land itself, or in that which is exchanged for what the land brings forth" (§8). All material wealth, therefore, is reduceable to the goods which the earth itself continues to produce of its seemingly infinite fecundity.

In this way, the earth abundantly provides for all of man's material needs, "but not until man has brought it into cultivation and expended upon it his solicitude and skill" (§9). This is the basis for private ownership:

> Now, when man thus turns the activity of his mind and the strength of his body toward procuring the fruits of nature, by such act he makes his own that portion of nature's field which he cultivates—that portion on which he leaves, as it were the impress of his personality; and it cannot but be just that he should possess that portion as his very own, and have a right to hold it without any one being justified in violating that right (§9).
>
> But those who deny these rights do not perceive that they are defrauding man of what his own labor has produced. For the soil which is tilled and cultivated with toil and skill utterly changes its condition; it was wild before, now it is fruitful; was barren, but now brings forth in abundance. That which has thus altered and improved the land becomes so truly part of itself as to be in great measure indistinguishable and inseparable from it. Is it just that the fruit of a man's own sweat and labor should be enjoyed by anyone else? As effects follow their cause, so is it just and right that the results of labor should belong to those who have bestowed their labor (§10).

Labor is as inseparable from private property as a cause from its proper and proximate effect. To the extent that this proximity between cause and effect is diminished, the worker's liberty is curtailed. Thus by this account, the socialists' professed wish to improve the lot of the worker by collectivizing and consolidating all property in the hands of the government entails nothing other than the enslavement of the worker to the state.

Leo is careful to remind us that his argument is drawn from truths knowable and verifiable by the light of unaided reason. These truths are neither recondite nor the special province of a philosophical school. Rather, they represent the "common opinion of mankind" which is vindicated by "the careful study of nature" and "consecrated" by the "practice of all ages" (§11). Moreover, they are the more persuasive when considered in the larger context of man's social obligations and especially the family relations which are "older,"*antiquior*, than the state. The right of private property is in fact all the stronger "in proportion as the human person receives a wider extension in the family group" (§13). Even beyond the basic necessities for which a father is responsible,

> It is natural that he should wish that his children, who carry on, so to speak, and continue his personality, should be by him provided with all that is needful to enable them to keep themselves decently from want and misery amid the uncertainties of this mortal life. Now, in no other way can a father effect this except by the ownership of productive property, which he can transmit to his children by inheritance (§13).

It is important to note that Leo understands the family to be antecedent to the state, and therefore "founded more immediately in nature" than civil society. If, however, political life is still somehow natural to human beings—which Leo affirms to be the case—then the health and validity of a state may be gauged in part by the laws according to which it either upholds and defends the rights of the family or intrudes upon and usurps them. But it is precisely the naturalness of politics that socialism denies on philosophical principle.

In denying the very existence of a normative nature, the socialist state necessarily acts against justice in arrogating to itself the natural rights of paternal authority. In this connection—and invoking Saint Thomas Aquinas by name for the first time (§14)—Leo cites a passage from the *Summa Theologiae* which, interestingly enough, is concerned with the particular question of whether the children of

Jews or unbelievers ought to be baptized against their parents' will. Thomas answers that they should not, partly because to do so would be a violation of natural justice, *quia repugnat iustitiae naturali*: "for a child is by nature part of its father . . . a son, before coming to the use of reason, is under his father's care. Hence it would be contrary to natural justice if a child, before coming to the use of reason, were to be taken away from its parents' custody, or anything done to it against its parents' wish."[9] If even the higher claims concerning man's supernatural end must not violate the norms of natural justice, much less must the lower claims of the state, whose legitimacy is derived from them.

The pronouncements and prescriptions of socialism are derived not from principles naturally knowable and historically verifiable, but rather by way of *a priori* and reductive assumptions about the constitution of the world (or as the socialists prefer, "history") and man's place within it.[10] Because socialism is *contra naturam*, it necessarily

---

9. *ST* II-II, q. 10, a. 12. "Alia vero ratio est quia repugnat iustitiae naturali. Filius enim naturaliter est aliquid patris. Et primo quidem a parentibus non distinguitur secundum corpus, quandiu in matris utero continetur. Postmodum vero, postquam ab utero egreditur, antequam usum liberi arbitrii habeat, continetur sub parentum cura sicut sub quodam spirituali utero. Quandiu enim usum rationis non habet puer, non differt ab animali irrationali. Unde sicut bos vel equus est alicuius ut utatur eo cum voluerit, secundum ius civile, sicut proprio instrumento; ita de iure naturali est quod filius, antequam habeat usum rationis, sit sub cura patris. Unde contra iustitiam naturalem esset si puer, antequam habeat usum rationis, a cura parentum subtrahatur, vel de eo aliquid ordinetur invitis parentibus." ["The other reason is that it is against natural justice. For a child is by nature part of its father: thus, at first, it is not distinct from its parents as to its body, so long as it is enfolded within its mother's womb; and later on after birth, and before it has the use of its free-will, it is enfolded in the care of its parents, which is like a spiritual womb, for so long as man has not the use of reason, he differs not from an irrational animal; so that even as an ox or a horse belongs to someone who, according to the civil law, can use them when he likes, as his own instrument, so, according to the natural law, a son, before coming to the use of reason, is under his father's care. Hence it would be contrary to natural justice, if a child, before coming to the use of reason, were to be taken away from its parents' custody, or anything done to it against its parents' wish."]

10. Hegel, the greatest of whose bastard sons was Karl Marx, remarks in the Preface to his *The Phenomenology of Mind* that "the manner of study in ancient times is distinct from that of modern times, in that the former consisted in the veritable training and perfecting of the natural consciousness. Trying its powers at each part of its life

leads to the destruction of the natural human bonds which allow even the most defective regimes to maintain some good of order. Leo presciently observes that beyond injustice,

> It is only too evident what upset and disturbance there would be in all classes, and to how intolerable and hateful a slavery citizens would be subjected. The door would be thrown open to envy, to mutual invective, and to discord; the sources of wealth themselves would run dry, for no one would have any interest in exerting his talents or his industry; and that ideal equality about which they entertain pleasant dreams would be in reality the levelling down of all to a like condition of misery and degradation. Hence, it is clear that the main tenet of socialism, community of goods, must be utterly rejected, since it only injures those whom it would seem to benefit, is directly contrary to the natural rights of mankind, and would introduce confusion and disorder into the commonweal. *The first and most fundamental principle, therefore, if one would undertake to alleviate the condition of the masses must be the inviolability of private property* (§15, emphasis mine).

The ideal equality of the socialist imagination, insofar as it is imposed on the stubborn realities of human nature, invariably leads to a breakdown of the social fabric, in part because it deprives the citizen of the chief motives for civic virtue.

For the Church, then, socialism is not merely a noble but impractical ideal—somehow desirable, but unrealistic. Far from it. The social levelling it intends is actually an "absurd equality"[11] which must be repugnant to the thoughtful or decent man. In other words, it fails

---

severally, and philosophizing about everything it came across, the natural consciousness transformed itself into a universality of abstract understanding which was active in every matter and in every respect. In modern times, however, the individual finds the abstract form ready-made." *The Phenomenology of Mind*, trans. J. B. Baillie (London: Swan Sonnenschein, 1931), 94. In other words, classical philosophers and their medieval heirs begin with things; modern philosophers begin with concepts.

11. "Nam si ad meliora contendere concessum est non repugnante iustitia, at alteri, quod suum est, detrahere, ac per speciem absurdae cuiusdam aequabilitatis in fortunas alienas involare, iustitia vetat, nec ipsa communis utilitatis ratio sinit" ["for, if all may justly strive to better their condition, neither justice nor the common good allows any individual to seize upon that which belongs to another, or, under the futile and shallow pretext of equality, to lay violent hands on other people's possessions"], §38.

precisely as an ideal. Its utopian aspirations are contrary to the good of the individual and society alike. The unequal distribution amongst men of talents and abilities, to say nothing of the correspondingly unequal merits and rewards which accrue to them, is in fact a boon to society. Human inequality is both natural and necessary:

> It must be first of all recognized that the condition of things inherent in human affairs must be borne with, for it is impossible to reduce civil society to one dead level. Socialists may in that intent do their utmost, but all striving against nature is in vain. There naturally exist among mankind manifold differences of the most important kind; people differ in capacity, skill, health, strength; and unequal fortune is a necessary result of unequal condition. Such inequality is far from being disadvantageous either to individuals or to the community (§17).

Even though, for a variety of reasons, it has become customary since Kant to take as a fundamental axiom the equal and indefectible "dignity"[12] of all human persons, the diverse allocation of gifts, abilities, and excellences is surely the more obvious feature of our common humanity. Society would in any case be the worse for any effort to eliminate, suppress, or otherwise ignore these differences.

Beyond its professed radical egalitarianism, socialism shares with other modern political movements the belief that poverty and human suffering can be eliminated. To this modern faith in unlimited progress, Leo responds simply and directly that suffering and hardship are perduring elements of human life and that "no strength and no artifice will ever succeed in banishing from human life the ills and troubles which beset it" (§18). When the socialists promise freedom from

---

12. The idea of an inalienable "dignity" that belongs to human beings by virtue of their humanity is first formulated by Immanuel Kant in his *Grundlegung zur Metaphysik der Sitten* (1785). Despite its origin in Kant's moral philosophy, and its inextricable connection to the notion of transcendental freedom, it is now a commonplace in contemporary Christian speech. The wish to see it in Christian sources before Kant has led to some astonishingly tendentious readings, especially of Scripture. The *Compendium of the Social Doctrine of the Church* (2004), for example, transforms Gal 3:28, which is specifically about the supernatural grace by which the baptized are united to Christ, into a general statement about the equal dignity of all people (§144). Whatever else may be said for it, there is more than a little irony in an interpretation of Galatians that literally "nullifies the grace of God" (Gal 2:21).

pain and trouble, they delude the credulous and set the conditions for future disaster. "Nothing," counters Leo, "is more useful than to look upon the world as it really is, and at the same time to seek elsewhere, as We have said, for the solace to its troubles" (§18).

The most immediate danger posed by socialism, however, is not its promise of comfortable self-preservation, but "the notion that class is naturally hostile to class" (§19). As long as there are distinctions among classes, says the socialist, there will necessarily be hot-and-cold warfare between them. In so saying, the socialist appeals to the basest passions of the worker, whose otherwise creditable desire for material well-being is disordered by resentment and envy. Leo reminds us that labor and capital, the worker and the wealthy, need each other and moreover that a recognition of their mutually beneficial relation conduces to "the beauty of good order" (§19).

In light of this it is important to note in conclusion that Leo's defense of private ownership as a "natural right of man" (§22) is necessarily coupled with the question of its proper use. His answer is taken directly from *Summa Theologiae* II-II, q. 66, a. 2: "Man should not consider his material possessions as his own, but as common to all, so as to share them without hesitation when others are in need. Whence the Apostle with, 'Command the rich of this world . . . to offer with no stint, to apportion largely.'"[13] At the same time, there is no obligation either to give away what is necessary to support oneself or even what is "reasonably required to keep up becomingly his condition in life."[14] One is responsible, therefore, to give to the poor and

---

13. "Et quantum ad hoc non debet homo habere res exteriores ut proprias, sed ut communes, ut scilicet de facili aliquis ea communicet in necessitates aliorum. Unde apostolus dicit, 1 ad Tim. ult., divitibus huius saeculi praecipe facile tribuere, communicare."

14. See *ST* II-II, q. 32, a. 6: "Alio modo dicitur aliquid esse necessarium sine quo non potest convenienter vita transigi secundum conditionem vel statum personae propriae et aliarum personarum quarum cura ei incumbit. Huius necessarii terminus non est in indivisibili constitutus, sed multis additis, non potest diiudicari esse ultra tale necessarium; et multis subtractis, adhuc remanet unde possit convenienter aliquis vitam transigere secundum proprium statum. De huiusmodi ergo eleemosynam dare est bonum, et non cadit sub praecepto, sed sub consilio. Inordinatum autem esset si aliquis tantum sibi de bonis propriis subtraheret ut aliis largiretur, quod de residuo

indigent out of what remains after the necessities of life and station have been supplied for. This means that the duty to give alms is a matter, not of justice, but of charity. As such, it cannot be enforced by human law. Thus, while it is a mark of the just society to make reasonable provision for its weakest and most vulnerable members, the state oversteps its bounds when care for the poor is regarded solely as a matter of justice. In such a case, almsgiving, which is a species of charity—i.e., the supreme supernatural virtue—is collapsed into a merely natural virtue, the demands of which we may justly doubt can be competently determined by the vast bureaucracy required by the modern state, socialist or otherwise. In fact, justice of this sort is not even a virtue, for social justice is not a habit of soul, but rather a state of affairs in principle achievable by the right sorts of laws and a more or less efficient political administration, irrespective of the goodness or badness of the citizens it superintends.[15]

---

non posset vitam transigere convenienter secundum proprium statum et negotia occurrentia, nullus enim inconvenienter vivere debet." ["In another way, a thing is said to be necessary if a man cannot without it live in keeping with his social station, as regards either himself or those of whom he has charge. The 'necessary' considered thus is not an invariable quantity, for one might add much more to a man's property, and yet not go beyond what he needs in this way, or one might take much from him, and he would still have sufficient for the decencies of life in keeping with his own position. Accordingly it is good to give alms of this kind of 'necessary'; and it is a matter not of precept but of counsel. Yet it would be inordinate to deprive oneself of one's own, in order to give to others to such an extent that the residue would be insufficient for one to live in keeping with one's station and the ordinary occurrences of life: for no man ought to live unbecomingly."]

15. Cf. Immanuel Kant, *Perpetual Peace*: "*The problem of organizing a state, however hard it may seem, can be solved even for a race of devils*, if only they are intelligent. The problem is: 'Given a multitude of rational beings requiring universal laws for their preservation, but each of whom is secretly inclined to exempt himself from them, to establish a constitution in such a way that, although their private intentions conflict, they check each other, with the result that their public conduct is the same as if they had no such intentions.' A problem like this must be capable of solution; *it does not require that we know how to attain the moral improvement of men but only that we should know the mechanism of nature in order to use it on men*, organizing the conflict of the hostile intentions present in a people in such a way that they must compel themselves to submit to coercive laws" (emphasis mine). Taken from Immanuel Kant, *On History*, edited, with an Introduction by Lewis White Beck, trans. Lewis White Beck, Robert E. Anchor, and Emil L. Fackenheim (Indianapolis: Bobbs-Merrill, 1963), 112.

Natural Law and Natural Rights

Rerum novarum seeks to establish the naturalness of private property on solidly Thomistic grounds, but does so in a way that deviates in important ways from Thomas's own natural law doctrine. To better grasp these deviations and their significance it will be useful to look briefly at Aquinas's defense of private property. He gives three reasons why it is good for people to have their own things:

> First, because every man is more careful to procure what is for himself alone than that which is common to many or to all: since each one would shirk the labor and leave to another that which concerns the community.
>
> Secondly, because human affairs are conducted in more orderly fashion if each man is charged with taking care of some particular thing himself, whereas there would be confusion if everyone had to look after any one thing indeterminately.
>
> Thirdly, because a more peaceful state is ensured to man if each one is contented with his own. Hence it is to be observed that quarrels arise more frequently where there is no division of the things possessed.[16]

In other words, the common experience of humanity amply shows the good sense of private ownership. Without it, human industry slackens and the public good is endangered. So far from endangering the peace of the political community, private property harmonizes the otherwise dissonant and conflicting claims of its citizenry.

The licitness of private property will of course mean that some

---

16. *ST* II-II, q. 66, a. 2: "Respondeo dicendum quod circa rem exteriorem duo competunt homini. Quorum unum est potestas procurandi et dispensandi. Et quantum ad hoc licitum est quod homo propria possideat. Et est etiam necessarium ad humanam vitam, propter tria. Primo quidem, quia magis sollicitus est unusquisque ad procurandum aliquid quod sibi soli competit quam aliquid quod est commune omnium vel multorum, quia unusquisque, laborem fugiens, relinquit alteri id quod pertinet ad commune; sicut accidit in multitudine ministrorum. Alio modo, quia ordinatius res humanae tractantur si singulis immineat propria cura alicuius rei procurandae, esset autem confusio si quilibet indistincte quaelibet procuraret. Tertio, quia per hoc magis pacificus status hominum conservatur, dum unusquisque re sua contentus est. Unde videmus quod inter eos qui communiter et ex indiviso aliquid possident, frequentius iurgia oriuntur."

will have more than others, but this is a necessary part of the providential order. Some are granted materially more in this life in order that they might benefit the poor while growing in moral excellence themselves: "Whatever certain people have in superabundance is due, by natural law, to the purpose of aiding the poor."[17] At the same time, however, Thomas teaches that "the distinction of possessions . . . [was] not brought in by nature but devised by human reason for the benefit of human life."[18] As he says in another place,

> For if a particular piece of land be considered absolutely, it contains no reason why it should belong to one man more than to another, but if it be considered in respect of its adaptability to cultivation, and the unmolested use of the land, it has a certain commensuration to be the property of one and not of another man, as the Philosopher shows in the second book of the *Politics*.[19]

So while Thomas teaches that private property is in accord with the natural law and that it makes practical sense in the ordering of human affairs, he does not regard it as a demand or direct precept of the natural law itself. In general terms, his defense of private property makes more moderate claims about its naturalness than does that of Leo.

So precisely what does Thomas teach concerning naturalness of private property, and how does Leo depart from the strict observance of that teaching? As I noted above,[20] Thomas understands the division of property to be assigned by the "right of nations," *ius gentium*, which is that part of the positive law, *ius positivum*, whose principles are derived from the natural law as conclusions from premises.[21] *Rerum novarum*, by contrast, does not include a single reference to the *ius gentium*, despite its crucial importance to Thomas's teaching. The fact is the more noteworthy as the concept figured prominently in the first and third drafts of the encyclical. So what could account for

---

17. *ST* II-II, q. 66, a. 7: "Et ideo res quas aliqui superabundanter habent, ex naturali iure debentur pauperum sustentationi."
18. *ST* I-II, q. 94, a. 5, ad. 3: "distinctio possessionum et servitus non sunt inductee a natura, sed per hominum rationem, ad utilitatem humanae vitae."
19. *ST* II-II, q. 57, a. 4. See footnote 7.
20. *ST* II-II, q. 57, a. 4.
21. See *ST* I-II, q. 95, a. 2.

its omission in the final draft? Fr. Ernest Fortin convincingly argues that the answer may be found in a work by the chief architect of these drafts, the Jesuit Matteo Liberatore.

> A plausible answer is supplied by Liberatore's *Principles of Political Economy*, first published in 1889 and thus very close in time to *Rerum Novarum*. From this work we learn that other contemporary theorists were turning Thomas's categorization of the *ius gentium* as part of positive law into an argument against private property. If the latter is a creation of the civil authority to begin with, it can be abrogated by it. As his spirited response shows, Liberatore was confident that even on Thomas's account of the *ius gentium* a strong case could be made for the naturalness of private property. Thomas's *ius gentium* is not simply a matter of positive law. It stands "midway between natural right and civil right." Its principles are deduced from strict natural law principles and share their necessity. The proof is that for Thomas these principles are binding quite apart from any human enactment.
>
> All well and good, save that the Pope, who participated regularly and actively in the deliberations of the drafting committee, was not about to take any chances.[22]

By eliminating any mention of the *ius gentium*, Leo could remove all doubt about the necessity of private property by rooting it directly in the natural law. There was no absolute requirement to do so, since the bindingness of the *ius gentium* is derived from the natural law, nor was it strictly speaking a distortion of Thomas's doctrine. Nevertheless, for all intents and purposes Leo "built a fence around the law," and thereby exposed the teaching of *Rerum novarum* to the well-attested dangers of so doing.

But Leo's prudential adaptation of Thomas's teaching involves more than the partial reconfiguring of Thomistic principles. *Rerum novarum* goes well beyond the traditional view of private property as practically expedient and preferable to alternative arrangements. Private property is held up as a "sacred right," *ius sanctum* (§46), that is absolutely inviolable and inalienable. The language of "rights," in the plural, is used throughout the encyclical presumably as a way of establishing the just claims of the individual and the family in the

---

22. Fortin, "Sacred and Inviolable," 197–98.

law of nature. But the idea of unconditional rights that inhere in each human being is found neither in Scripture nor in the Christian intellectual tradition before the modern period.[23] In fact, the notion of inalienable and imprescriptible natural rights first appears in the work of such early modern philosophers as Thomas Hobbes and John Locke. This is noteworthy because the non-teleological anthropology of these thinkers and their precursors was developed in opposition to, and as a replacement for, the teleological understanding of the human person embedded in traditional natural law doctrine. It is far from clear that the two accounts are reconcilable and, to date, official pronouncements on Catholic social teaching have shown little awareness of the difficulty.

The contrariety of the two conceptions is not without significance or deep practical importance. To begin with, they regard moral phenomena very differently. Natural law emphasizes the duties or obligations of the moral agent and the salutary habits of soul that result from the observance of these. These duties, moreover, are not derived from a prior "right" of another. The goodness of the Samaritan, for instance, is not reduceable to an inherent entitlement in the injured man. According to the doctrine of natural law, virtue does not stand in need of extrinsic inducements of this sort. The modern view, on the other hand, understands the moral life principally in terms of the sovereign claims of individual rights. That is as may be, but we ought to note two things: first, that existence of such rights is, to say the least, difficult to determine on the basis of unaided reason and, second, that so long as individual rights are sovereign there is no clear principle by which the conflicts which inevitably arise between them may be resolved. We are daily witness to this latter fact as individual rights are multiplied seemingly *ad infinitum*.

It is clear that Leo was as opposed to the individualism fostered by modern liberalism as he was to the collectivism of the socialists. One might argue, however, that his reliance on the moral categories which gave to birth to modern individualism, even if employed for tactical or prudential reasons, ultimately weakens his argument.

---

23. The term *iura*, for instance, is not in the Vulgate.

As it happened, the language of rights carried all before it in Catholic social teaching, relegating the natural law mostly to stalwarts amongst the moral theologians. The result has been that a great deal of contemporary social teaching is left without a firm grounding in nature, which accounts for its oft-noted theoretical weaknesses and limited persuasiveness.

Lastly, and very briefly, I wish to note that the modern view of nature that undergirds the language of rights is evident as well in Leo's occasional statements about the relation of the individual and the family to the political community. Take, for instance, his assertion in paragraph 7:

> Nature accordingly must have given to man a source that is stable and remaining always with him, from which he might look to draw continual supplies. And this stable condition of things he finds solely in the earth and its fruits. *There is no need to bring in the state. Man precedes the State, and possesses, prior to the formation of any State, the right of providing for the substance of the body* (§7, emphasis mine).[24]

One need only compare this with Aristotle's statement in the *Politics* in which he explains why the city is necessarily prior to both the individual and the family—a view with which Saint Thomas is in full agreement:[25]

> And a city is more primary by nature than a household, and more primary than each of us, for the whole is necessarily more primary than its parts. For if the whole is done away with, there will not be a foot or a hand, except in an ambiguous sense, as if one were to speak of a hand made of stone (for once it has been disabled it will be like that); but all things are defined by their work and potency, so when they are no longer of the sort defined they cannot be called the same things except ambiguously. So it is clear both that the city is by nature and that it is more primary than each person, for if each person is not self-sufficient when separate, he will be in a condition similar to that of other parts in relation to the whole, and one who is no part of a city, either from lacking the power to be in an association or from

---

24. "... est enim homo quam respublica, senior: quocirca ius ille suum ad vitam corpusque tuendum habere natura ante debuit quam civitas ulla coisset."

25. See, *Sententia libri politicorum, Sancti Thomae de Aquino Opera Omnia* 48 (Rome: Commissio Leonina, 1971), 79, *ad* 1253a19.

needing nothing on account of self-sufficiency, is for that reason either a beast or a god.[26]

In his efforts to safeguard human freedom from the usurpations of the socialist state, Leo avails himself at strategic points of a certain appeal to nature that has more in common with Hobbes and Locke than with Aristotle or Thomas.

Yet given both the socio-political landscape and the state of the Thomistic revival, which in the late nineteenth century was still finding its footing, Leo's synthetic approach has to be read with a certain hermeneutical generosity. The individual worker was being threatened by political forces which, however opposed they were in other respects, effectively denied the intrinsic value of the worker as a human being, either through laissez-faire economic policies or through the threat of collectivization. Leo formulates a robust response to the competing claims of modern political movements which, despite their differences, share a crudely mechanistic view of man as a being motivated solely by the concern for material security and bodily well-being. Both liberalism and socialism are rooted in philosophical doctrines which deny man a proper *telos*, natural or supernatural. Yet liberalism, for its part, at least seeks to establish and preserve individual liberty, and in so doing makes it possible in principle for the individual to discover and pursue the ends which are perfective of his nature. And while socialism does not altogether dispense with teleology, it more dangerously transfers it from human nature to the realm of history, which is thereby endowed with the force of necessity and inevitability. The evil of socialism is that it makes men the grist for history's mill and denudes them of their humanity by consigning them to the closed and dreary horizon of the modern bureaucratic state. We must read *Rerum novarum* in this light. Leo's daring enlistment of modern rights theory in the cause of reestablishing and asserting the claims of nature against the socialists was, on the foregoing account, a gambit of sorts, yet as such it stands without peer in the magisterial confluence of its theoretical depth, statesmanly prudence, and pastoral charity.

---

26. Aristotle, *Politics*, 1.1253a8–29, trans. Joe Sachs (Newburyport, MA: Focus Publishing, 2012), 5.

3.3. An Evangelical Perspective on Social Ethics

Dr. Glen Menzies

Do not withhold good from those to whom it is due, when it is in your power to do it.
Proverbs 3:27

Before launching into the substance of this essay, a brief roadmap is in order for readers. After a fairly extended introduction and consideration of some preliminary issues, the essay will outline five main approaches to social ethics within Evangelicalism. Following that is a discussion of what John R. Schneider refers to as "moral proximity." Finally, the paper discusses the author's own views, as an example of one Evangelical's thinking, on four important issues in social ethics today. Doubtless, there are many other issues that could be addressed, but I believe these four will be adequate to stimulate dialogue. The presentation is written in the first person as a way of reflecting on the issue that is both authentic to my experience and representative of the nature of the Christian life lived in the world as we have it.

Introduction: Matters of Individual and Social Ethics

Like many Evangelicals, I am uncomfortable discussing social ethics. This has made it difficult to write on the subject at hand, but this discomfort is also characteristic of many Evangelicals, so it is important to admit this at the essay's outset. I also want to make doubly clear that I present a single Evangelical voice. Many Evangelicals would disagree with much that I write below. I recognize that this paper is more of an essay than a traditional theological discourse and is overwhelmingly personal in character and language.

To explain my own thinking about social ethics, perhaps a bit of autobiography will help. While I am an Evangelical, I am also a Pentecostal and I have been my entire life. My parents were both Pentecostals their entire lives and all four of my grandparents chose to become Pentecostals.

Today, most American Pentecostals believe there is such a thing as "just war"; they believe that whether or not to participate in military activity is a matter to be determined by each individual's conscience. However, prior to World War II (the "good" war), most Pentecostals were pacifists. Even today, most Pentecostals in Eastern Europe remain pacifists. Before World War II, the Selective Service recognized the Assemblies of God, my denomination, as a pacifist denomination like the Quakers or Mennonites. For me the matter came to a head in 1973 or 1974, when I was about to turn 18 and I needed to register for the draft. I had my draft card all filled out except for one line: Are you conscientiously opposed to service in the military? This was followed by two checkboxes: one marked "Yes"; and the other marked "No." I held on to that card for weeks, unable to decide if I was a conscientious objector or not. Finally, I ran out of time and sent it in with neither box checked. I thought it was the most honest thing to do. I was not clearly a conscientious objector, and I was not clearly not a conscientious objector. I was still debating the matter. Fortunately, in 1974 there was no longer an active draft; as the Vietnam War wound down, the government was trying to downsize the military, not grow it. Nevertheless, to play it safe, I filed for and received a ministerial student deferment.

Two years later, now a college student, I spent a summer in Belize, in Central America. At that time the Assemblies of God had only one missionary couple in Belize, and they and their children needed to return to the States for the summer to deal with some family matters. So, my college roommate Dale and I were sent to live in the missionaries' home, take care of their dog, and work in the local church. This summer ended up being the most enlightening part of my entire college education.

In 1975, on a percentage basis, Belize had more Mennonites in it than any other country in the world. Part of the reason for this was that Belize only had a population of about 120,000. The other reason was that there were several very conservative Mennonite colonies ("*Alt Kolonier*" and "*Kleine Gemeinde*" colonies) in Belize. The Mennonites in these colonies were the sort who thought electricity in a barn might be okay, but never in a home. They also argued about whether or not rubber tires on tractors were acceptable, or if they should stick to metal tires. There were also some less conservative Mennonites in Belize City, where Dale and I lived, who specialized in disaster recovery and were associated with the Mennonite Central Committee. They were very helpful in explaining all things Mennonite.

I wanted to earn some directed study college credit, so I arranged to research and write about the Mennonites of Belize. This exploration introduced me to a theological and moral world that was eye-opening for this rather inexperienced young man. A central discovery was that Anabaptists think most Christians dismiss the "hard sayings" of Jesus much too easily. What does "turn the other cheek" really mean? Should it impact how one lives his or her life?

I met a Mennonite farmer whose barn was repeatedly burglarized. He wasn't about to buy a gun, but he had considered getting a dog. He thought it would be great if the dog would scare the burglars away, but he wasn't sure if he could live with himself if the dog bit a burglar. I was inspired by this man's moral struggle.

I also became uneasy when I leaned how the Mennonite colonies had ended up in Belize. Originating in central Europe, some had first moved to Russia and others to Canada. Experiencing more government intervention in their lives than they liked, they moved to Belize. The Belizean government had promised not to tax them or to force their children to attend state-run schools. In turn, the Mennonites had to pave their own roads and build and staff their own schools. The clincher was that Belize at that time remained within the British commonwealth, so this small nation was protected from invasion by the British military. This was no idle concern, because at that time, and perhaps still today, Guatemala claimed that Belize was rightly a part of Guatemala. Were the threat of the British military to disappear, the Guatemalan tanks would immediately roll in. While the Mennonites of Belize were pacifists, they also valued security. They very much liked the security provided by the British military even though they were opposed to war.

This "freeriding" troubled me. Was it morally responsible to refuse to fight and instead rely on the protection of others? Did pacifism only work if there were non-pacifists around? Shouldn't a viable ethical system be universally applicable?

Today, I am a pacifist or a near pacifist in terms of individual ethics. If you punch me in the face, I likely will not punch you back. But when it comes to social ethics, my stance is different. Today I am not conscientiously opposed to military service.

This way of thinking requires some rationale for the distinction between individual ethics and social ethics. As I see it, the starting point for ethics is individual ethics. This is made clear in the individualistic orientation of the Ten Commandments. While it is possible to imagine group murder or a group of people engaged in collective idolatry, each of the Ten Commandments can be violated by individuals acting alone. Moreover, the commands to honor one's father and mother, not to commit adultery, not to bear false witness, and not to covet seem exclusively focused on individual behavior.

Social ethics, therefore, is an extension that both presumes and by definition excludes individual ethics. The English word "social," coming through the Old French, is ultimately derived from the Latin *socialis*, which is itself related to both *socium* and *societas*. Each of these words relate, with different nuances, to "partnerships" or "associations." Of course, in normal English usage "social" has come first to mean "relating to society at large," not smaller associations within that larger society.

This suggests that it is important to distinguish between 1) social ethics writ large: i.e., relating to society at large, and 2) social ethics writ small: i.e., social ethics relating to smaller, although not necessarily small, associations. While there is certainly a spiritual dimension to the Church, which transcends other associations, I come from a tradition that understands churches in their concrete expression to be "voluntary cooperative associations." Accordingly, I believe that when congregations, dioceses, denominations, etc. speak or act, they express their social ethics writ small.

There is also the issue of how politics relates to social ethics. I would prefer to avoid using the oxymoron "political ethics," although I suppose it has place in some contexts. But much of what people discuss under the heading of "social ethics" involves matters of political policy.

There is also a difference between government (the State) and society at large. American society is arguably predominately Judeo-Christian, but the government of the United States is not; it is explicitly non-sectarian. Nevertheless, when people wrangle over issues of social ethics writ large, they generally do this in political forums and propose or oppose political policies. So, for the sake of simplicity, I will treat political positions and matters of social ethics writ large as essentially the same thing.

The work of mainline Protestant social ethicist Reinhold Niebuhr speaks to these distinctions. Niebuhr was the twentieth century's most influential Christian ethicist, and while Evangelicalism certainly has many earlier roots, much of its current character stems from the "New Evangelicalism" that commenced in the 1940s. Thus, the New Evangelicalism coalesced during the period of Niebuhr's maximum impact, an impact that was amplified by the great moral issues raised by World War II.

A hallmark of Niebuhr's thought was that social ethics must be distinguished from individual ethics. At the individual level, he believed the New Testament taught an "ethic of love," in which one's personal happiness must often be sacrificed for the happiness of others. To live "Christianly" is to live altruistically. The height of this Christian vision is expressed in the Sermon on the Mount.[1]

---

1. For the classic presentation of Niebuhr's position see both Reinhold Niebuhr, *Moral Man and Immoral Society* (New York: Charles Scribner's Sons, 1932) and the sequel, Reinhold Niebuhr, *Interpretation of Christian Ethics* (New York: Harper and Brothers, 1935).

Unfortunately, the ethic of love is completely impractical in the sphere of society writ large. If you are in need, as an individual I can as an expression of love take what is mine and give it to you. Of course, Christian congregations and other organizations can also act lovingly. But American society, expressed through the agency of the American government, cannot operate this way. The American government is an entity that derives its power and resources from all the citizens of the United States. If certain people are in need, it cannot as an act of love simply take from what it has and give some to them, because for it to give, it first has to extract these resources from others. The government can redistribute property, but this is not unalloyed love. It is not altruistic. Any such redistribution coercively reduces the resources and happiness of some to increase the resources and happiness of others.

As Niebuhr saw it, the highest ideal to which a government might aspire was not "love," but rather the lower standard of "justice." There are, of course, many notions about what constitutes justice in a society, and inevitably different policy options offer differing ethical tradeoffs. This implies a large amount of messiness in social ethics, and Niebuhr felt it was important to acknowledge the inevitability of this messiness, terming his thought "Christian Realism." I do not propose to explore the full complexity of Niebuhr's thinking about justice. His basic distinction between individual and social ethics and the rationale for it will suffice.

Not every Evangelical will agree with Niebuhr's divide between individual and social ethics, but it is fundamental to my own view of the nature of social ethics, so it is important that I highlight this assumption for my readers. I have already acknowledged my discomfort with presenting my views on social ethics. I am not happy that the altruistic ethics Jesus taught seems impractical and an impossible foundation for governmental policy. Perhaps I could be accused of succumbing to the same sort of error I just accused my Mennonite friends of falling into: Shouldn't a viable ethical system be universally applicable?

My defense, however, is based on eschatological or salvation-historical considerations. Human governments are predicated on coercive power. Today, when people disagree about what is to be done, governments use coercive power to override any disagreements. When the kingdom of God has fully come, when God's foes are vanquished and removed, leaving a purified society in which God rules completely, then all disputes will end. It will not be necessary to have resources taken from some against their wills to meet the needs or desires of others. In everything, God's will will be done. After we have passed from this present evil age to the consummated kingdom of God, the ethics Jesus taught will be fully practiced and completely practical.

Five Evangelical Approaches to Social Ethics

Evangelicalism is defined by certain core values. David Bebbington has famously identified the markers of biblicism, crucicentrism, conversionism, and activism (i.e., commitment to evangelism, missions, and sometimes social reform efforts) as the key points, although some Evangelicals insist on other markers as well.[2] Social ethics would fall into the category of activism, but historically the main activist impulse of Evangelicals has been in the areas of evangelism and missions. Consequently, social ethics is an area in which Evangelicals exhibit significant variety. This variety of approaches does not mean that Evangelicals are unserious about social ethics. In fact, Evangelicals have been and remain serious about social ethics. Indeed, over the past few years two African Evangelicals, both Pentecostals, have been named as winners of the Nobel Peace Prize.[3]

---

2. For a complete account, see David W. Bebbington, *Evangelicalism in Modern Britain: A History from the 1730s to the 1930s* (London: Unwin Hyman, 1989). The National Association of Evangelicals endorses Bebbington's markers. See "What Is an Evangelical?," at https://www.nae.net/what-is-an-evangelical/ (accessed October 13, 2019).

3. Just this past week Abiy Ahmed Ali, the Prime Minister of Ethiopia, was announced as the winner of the 2019 Nobel Peace Prize primarily for his work in resolving hostilities between Ethiopia and Eritrea. In 2018 Denis Mukwege and Nadia Murad shared the Nobel Peace Prize "for their efforts to end the use of sexual violence as a weapon of war and armed conflict." The Evangelical Denis Mukwege is a physician who spent much of his life helping the victims of sexual violence in the Democratic Republic of Congo. He is also a pastor. In general, he practices medicine during the week and preaches on

I have identified five approaches to social ethics that I think will facilitate our discussion. There is nothing special about the number five. Others might cogently argue for four or six or seven. And these five approaches sometimes overlap with each other and each itself describes a spectrum rather than a pinpoint. The five approaches are 1) the Reformed, 2) the Wesleyan, 3) the Anabaptist, 4) Sectarian Noninvolvement, and 5) Reluctant Involvement. The last two labels are my own coinage, and I would suggest that my own denomination (the Assemblies of God) at one time took the Sectarian Noninvolvement approach, but now would be better characterized by Reluctant Involvement.[4]

Reformed:[5] Two great symbols of the Reformed approach to social ethics are "Calvin's Geneva" and the Puritan John Winthrop's vision of New England as "a City upon a Hill," which of course echoed the words of Matthew 5:14. While neither completely confounded the church and the state, both believed in Christian government, i.e., that Christian principles should guide every aspect of civil management even in mundane matters. For instance, to vote in the Massachusetts Bay Colony one had to be a registered member of a Puritan church. In Geneva, a consistory composed of Calvinist ministers and

---

Sundays. Ms. Murad is a Yazidi from northern Iraq and a victim of war crimes. She has been outspoken about the widespread rape of Yazidi women and girls as part of military actions in Iraq.

4. A key marker of this transition was the adoption at the General Council of 2005 of a plank adding to the mission of the Assemblies of God: "To respond to human need with ministries of compassion." See "Resolution 12: Ministries of Compassion for Human Need" and the Assemblies of God Constitution, Article III. PREROGATIVES, paragraph e. At the 2017 General Council a resolution to append the words "and actions that promote justice and peacemaking" to this statement was withdrawn by the author after consultation with the denominational leadership, citing "conflict over the resolution" as the reason for this action. This suggests that the label "[social] justice" continues to raise suspicion in the Assemblies of God.

5. I would suggest three examples of Evangelical writing about social ethics from a more Reformed perspective: 1) John R. Schneider, *The Good of Affluence: Seeking God in a Culture of Wealth* (Grand Rapids: Eerdmans, 2002); 2) Craig L. Blomberg, *Neither Poverty nor Riches: A Biblical Theology of Material Possessions* (Grand Rapids: Eerdmans, 1999); and Wayne Grudem and Barry Asmus, *The Poverty of Nations* (Wheaton, IL: Crossway, 2013).

city government officials together regulated the behavior of Geneva's citizens and imposed fines or imprisonment for infractions.[6]

Human character is malleable, and extrinsic factors often impact behavior. Just as children are induced to improve their behavior (and ultimately their character) by punishments and rewards, in general the Reformed tradition has been optimistic about using political means to bring about a better world and prepare the way for the Second Coming of Christ. Despite the widespread caricatures of the Puritans, the Reformed tradition is generally both world-affirming and optimistic in orientation.[7]

The impact of Calvin and the Reformed tradition on Evangelicalism is hard to overestimate. While many Evangelical groups do not fully subscribe to Calvin's theology or have modified it significantly, virtually all have been impacted by it in some way. One of the areas in which Calvin's impact has been less widely sustained is in the area of social ethics, particularly how church and state relate to each other.

Wesleyan: Since my friend Steve Hoskins, who is a good Wesleyan, is also making a presentation on Evangelical approaches to social ethics, I will largely defer to him in describing the Wesleyan tradition. I will simply say that Wesleyans have emphasized the social dimension of the Gospel more than some other strains of Evangelicalism. This is hardly surprising since John Wesley was an heir of the English Reformation and, while there is undeniable originality in his thought, it is grounded in the Reformed tradition and its optimism about the possibility of improving society writ large.

---

6. Frank L. Kidner, Maria Bucur, et al., *Making Europe: People, Politics and Culture Since 1300* (Boston: Houghton Mifflin, 2009), 394.

7. There is a subset within the Reformed tradition that bucks against this optimism. Perhaps best exemplified by John MacArthur, this smaller stream is Premillennial in eschatological orientation rather than embracing Calvin's Amillennialism (or the Postmillennialism that became common in Reformed circles during the nineteenth century). MacArthur believes that a belief in human ability to make the world a better place and to ready it for Christ's return smacks of "works righteousness." As is usual for Premillennialists, MacArthur sees the world going to hell in a handbasket and that only the sovereign intervention of God from outside of human history can bring the complete transformation the world needs. The coming of the kingdom is entirely the work of God.

Anabaptist:[8] While there are a few Mennonites who qualify as Evangelicals, most Anabaptists (Mennonites, Amish, Hutterites) do not fully qualify and do not so identify. Nevertheless, the Anabaptist influence on Evangelical social ethics has been very important. Many Evangelicals identify as Baptists, and many more are "baptistic." While this is not a proper forum for a discussion of the complexities of Baptist history and theology, in very broad terms it is the story of various amalgamations of Reformed and Anabaptist impulses.[9] The most obvious expression of this synthesis is the Baptist adoption of an Anabaptist understanding of the rite of baptism while continuing to embrace many other points of Reformed theology. The characteristic Baptist emphases on conscience and "soul competency" seem to derive more from Anabaptist roots than from Reformed roots.

Sometimes tensions reemerge between these two traditions. For instance, over the past three decades two of the most prominent Converge (formerly Baptist General Conference) pastors in Minnesota, where I live, have been John Piper and Greg Boyd. Piper, who has now retired from his long-time pastorate of Bethlehem Baptist Church in Minneapolis, is the leading light of the movement known as "New Calvinism." In contrast, Greg Boyd, the Senior Pastor of Woodland Hills Church in St. Paul, identifies personally with Anabaptist theology and has promoted stronger ties with historically Anabaptist groups. Although nominally part of the same denomination, they have very publicly disagreed on many issues.

Historically, Anabaptists have been leery of activist governments and hostile to military adventurism. They fear the use of the coercive power of the state, even when deployed for apparently worthy goals.

---

8. The most prominent institutional expressions of Evangelical Anabaptism are Evangelicals for Social Action and Eastern University, both located in St. Davids, PA just outside of Philadelphia. Palmer Seminary (formerly Eastern Baptist Theological Seminary), a seminary embedded within Eastern University, is also part of this constellation. Greg Boyd, the author of *Crucifixion of the Warrior God* and co-author of *Jesus Untangled: Crucifying Our Politics to Pledge Allegiance to the Lamb*, and Ron Sider, author of *Rich Christians in an Age of Hunger*, *Living Like Jesus*, and *Just Politics: A Guide for Christian Engagement*, are prominent Anabaptist Evangelicals.

9. Of course, in America the impact of Roger Williams was also important and perhaps should be considered a third stream of influence.

While there is a strong emphasis on "communal" discipline within the Anabaptist tradition, this discipline happens within the community of faith, not the government or society writ large. In general, Anabaptists fear the state and its programs.

Sectarian Noninvolvement: Many Evangelicals try to avoid entanglements in politics, and for some this posture has itself become a doctrine. Some of this resulted historically from a reaction against the "social gospel" identified most prominently with Walter Rauschenbusch. To many, discussions of political issues or social issues writ large simply distracted from proclamation of the need for individual conversion. To others, the social gospel involved making pronouncements about things that were not clearly taught in Scripture. These pronouncements threw the weight of the church behind political policies based on probabilities of expected outcomes (many of which failed to materialize) and diluted and diminished the authority and impact of the church's teaching of the eternal verities revealed in Scripture. When the National Council of Churches or the U.S. Conference of Catholic Bishops issue statements about the federal budget or housing policy or immigration, many Evangelical eyes begin to roll. This is not to say Evangelicals of this sort do not hold political opinions; they just think the range of matters about which individuals might hold opinions is much larger than the range of matters about which the church ought to teach.

Another reason Evangelicals of this stripe have avoided engagement in political activity is skepticism that it will accomplish much good. "Sectarian Noninvolvement" and Premillennial eschatology usually go hand-in-hand. Premillennial eschatology is essentially an apocalyptic vision. There is nothing humanity can do to ameliorate the problems of "this present evil age." Instead, the only real hope is in the return of the Christ, who will turn the world upside down and right the many wrongs that are so apparent. While there is still opportunity, the Church should encourage nonbelievers to express faith in Christ. This will allow the converts to avoid end-time punishment and participate in eternal blessings and reward. The bottom line is this: evangelism is important and political activity is not.

Despite its wide impact in the past, I believe this approach to Evangelical social ethics is in decline. As the general Judeo-Christian consensus on ethics in the United States has diminished and the culture has coarsened to a degree once unimaginable, many Evangelicals have recognized the need for greater involvement in our nation's dialogue about social issues.

Reluctant Involvement: If "Sectarian Noninvolvement" aims to avoid entanglements in politics entirely, "Reluctant Involvement" aims to limit such entanglements, particularly regarding very narrow policy issues. Nevertheless, it recognizes that some engagement in politics and social ethics is necessary. It does not have the apocalyptic edge which characterizes "Sectarian Noninvolvement"; some societal improvement may be possible and the struggle for improvement is necessary. Evangelicals in this camp would be unlikely to endorse particular numeric targets in the US budget but would support legislation allowing medical practitioners to opt out of performing procedures that violate their consciences. They would condemn racism, but likely would hesitate to endorse specific remedies for America's racist past (e.g., reparations for descendants of slaves).

"Reluctant Involvement" is much less optimistic about the possibilities of social ethics writ large advancing the gospel message than the Reformed or the Wesleyan approaches. It has more in common with the Anabaptist and Sectarian Noninvolvement approaches but differs enough from each to warrant being considered a separate category.

The Principle of Moral Proximity: Issues for Dialogue

Evidence from the New Testament and the early Church suggests that most Christian efforts to alleviate suffering were directed to those within their own communities or those individuals closely associated with specific believers, although there were at least two exceptions to this pattern. Christians ministered to those in prison (who may or may not have been linked to the Christian community), and they rescued exposed children, deserted by their families (and who often were collected to become slaves or sex workers if they did not die or were not rescued first). Nevertheless, the general picture of the early Church is an alternate community that cared for its members. This is part of what outsiders found attractive.

In fact, the lengths to which early Christians went in assisting others in their community was often extraordinary. Note this comment likely written near the end of the first century about the Christian community in Rome: "We know that many among us have had themselves imprisoned, that they might ransom others. Many have sold themselves into slavery, and with the price received for themselves have fed others."[10]

Sometimes the Christian community would care for Christians in other parts of the world. Paul's so-called third missionary journey was dominated by his fundraising efforts among believers in the gentile world to help the impoverished believers in Jerusalem. In contrast, Christians did not try indiscriminately to feed the hungry throughout the world.

John R. Schneider has noted this pattern and suggested a label for the principle behind it: "moral proximity." He explains:

> Now, I believe it is a good thing for Christians to rethink what faith and economic life means in terms of globalism. But I also think that a good many Christian authors are mistaken at a very fundamental place in their biblical reasoning. For they commonly assume (or so it seems) that just to have technical access to a poor person is, for any rich person, sufficient to produce moral obligations. . . .
>
> It seems that the primary norm for close proximity is one's immediate community of faith and, within it, a matter of one's divine calling. In Israel, greatest proximity was found generally in the nuclear family, then in the extended family, the tribe, and finally the nation of fellow Israelites. As the slavery laws make evident, Israelites had obligations to Gentiles, but these were considerably weaker than to fellow Hebrews. The strong suggestion is that what I am calling moral proximity arises from within one's most nearly

---

10. Clement of Rome, *1 Clement*, 28–101 in *The Apostolic Fathers*, ed. and trans. J. B. Lightfoot, J. R. Harmer, Michael W. Holmes, 2nd ed. (Grand Rapids, MI: Baker, 1992), 55.2.

ultimate relationships. The principles are thus not at all messianic, for only the Messiah has undertaken the burden of saving the entire world. They are rather societal, and thus quite personal—the more so, the stronger.[11]

The principle of moral proximity does not prevent an American Christian from feeding starving children in Africa. In fact, it does not remove the obligation incumbent on all Christians to live generously, as God gives them means. But it does remove a sense of endless guilt, so long as a single suffering person anywhere in the world has an unmet need.

As the above illustrates, among the most fraught issues in social ethics are those dealing with economics. The Bible speaks a great deal about possessions and differences in economic status, but it says nothing at all about modern economic theory. The various books of the Bible sketch out a complex, nuanced, and sometimes unclear picture of proper attitudes toward money and possessions. At times wealth is depicted as a blessing from God's hand or as recompense for hard work and a life well lived. At other times wealth is depicted as the fruit of sin and oppression. Of course, both portraits may be true depending on the circumstances. Sometimes wealth results from the accumulation of ill-gotten gain and at other times wealth is the result of commendable prudence and industry.

Throughout the Bible the created world is regarded as good, an extraordinary blessing from God. All material possessions (as well as immaterial blessings) are gifts from God's hand. Nevertheless, possessions are to be held loosely. In many places in both the Old and New Testaments they are depicted as fleeting, subject to rust, spoilage, and loss. One's material standing is always to be judged insignificant in comparison with one's moral or spiritual standing. Also, arrogant elevation of oneself over others on the basis of wealth is uniformly condemned as sinful.

Moreover, generosity is highly esteemed throughout the Bible. Key to the virtue of generosity is that it is voluntary, not mandated. But some within the Christian tradition have argued that Christian

---

11. Schneider, *The Good of Affluence*, 179–80.

morality requires divesting oneself of any accumulation beyond basic necessities. Augustine explains:

> From how much [God] will give you, take from it what is sufficient: the remaining things that are superfluous to you are necessary to others. The extras of the rich are the necessities of the poor. When you keep what is not needed, you usurp the property of others.[12]

While Augustine was an important promoter of this economic theory, he did not invent it; this basic theme can already be observed in the Old Testament and more generally in the literature of the ancient world. Jerry Camery-Hoggatt explains:

> One of the observable norms for the ancient world is called the Law of Limited Goods. Everything's *limited*. The way the ancients saw it, there's a limited amount of water, limited money, limited food. . . . The honorable man doesn't take more of anything than he and his family need. To take more than you need is a form of theft. This means the rich don't just get rich by good management; getting rich is a form of thievery. The honorable person who has a little excess—like the farmer who has a bumper crop in Luke 12:13–21—is supposed to spread it around, share it with the neighbors.[13]

For the past four decades the most prominent figure in Evangelical circles who argues along these lines has been Ron Sider. In the years immediately following the 1977 publication of his *Rich Christians in an Age of Hunger*,[14] Sider spoke repeatedly at Fuller Theological Seminary, where I was a student. I remember well the stir his argument made at this predominately Reformed Evangelical seminary. I remember most vividly a short video he showed about sugar cane harvesters in the Caribbean who did the back-breaking work of chopping

---

12. Augustine, *In Psalmos* 147.12 (PL 37:1922): "Quaere quantum tibi dederit, et ex eo tolle quod sufficit: caetera quae superflua jacent, aliorum sunt necessaria. Superflua divitum, necessaria sunt pauperum. Res alienae possidentur, cum superflua possidentur." English translation by the author.

13. Jerry Camery-Hoggatt, *Reading the Good Book Well* (Nashville: Abingdon, 2007), 123–24.

14. Ronald J. Sider, *Rich Christians in an Age of Hunger* (Downers Grove, IL: InterVarsity Press, 1977).

down tons of sugar cane each day and hauling it onto trucks. This labor paid so little that all their wages for a week could buy each laborer only about a pound of processed, refined sugar. Of course, this meant that these cane-choppers never ate the processed, refined sugar they helped produce. Sider argued that this apparent injustice was structural, an outcome of the capitalist system that concentrated almost all power in the hands of those who held capital, the financial resources necessary to set up the production process that enabled bringing sugar to market. Sider considered this to be as exploitative as the injustice the prophet Amos railed against:

> They sell the righteous for silver, and the needy for a pair of sandals— they who trample the head of the poor into the dust of the earth (Amos 2:6–7).
>
> Hear this word, you cows of Bashan on Mount Samaria, you women who oppress the poor and crush the needy and say to their husbands, "Bring us some drinks!" (Amos 4:1).[15]

And perhaps Sider was right that the sugar cane producers deserved divine condemnation for their exploitative practices. But further investigation of the Caribbean sugar industry revealed that the root cause of the widespread injustice was corrupt government officials who handed out monopolies to industrialist friends. In other words, the oppression was due to a lack of fair free market capitalism, not the capitalist system itself.

Nevertheless, it is hard to deny the significant disparity in wages between well-developed and developing nations. But what does this mean? Should we respond to this disparity by punishing well-developed nations? Isn't there a more serious response? Shouldn't we investigate how developing nations can be made to flourish more and more quickly?

Returning to Camery-Hoggatt's analysis, I would like to point out that the Law of Limited Goods was an observable norm "for the ancient world." In fact, I think this statement probably underplays this law's scope. It was largely in force not just in antiquity, as

---

15. All Scripture references are to the *ESV Study Bible* (Wheaton: Crossway, 2008).

Camery-Hoggatt contends, but was also the controlling pattern up through the Middle Ages as well.

In many places (including Israel) subsistence farming was the norm, even though there were a few tradesmen who earned their livings differently. Subsistence farming doesn't change much even over long stretches of time. Productivity gains are either nonexistent or negligible. This means that subsistence agrarian economies don't grow, and they don't experience inflation. This lack of growth is just another way of articulating the Law of Limited Goods.

The invention of coinage by the Lydians in the sixth century BC signaled a significant development. By the time of the Roman Empire, coins were in widespread use. Unfortunately, the Roman Empire was very, very highly stratified economically, with the senatorial class owning most property and (at least until the second century AD) with half of the population comprised of slaves, most of whom continued as agricultural workers. After the centralized government of the Empire ceased to function effectively (i.e., when Rome "fell"), the subsistence farmers became known as peasants or serfs, (nominally) free people who were attached to the land. Thus, despite apparent advances during the Roman period, the economy of that era and beyond continued to be subject to the Law of Limited Goods.

With the advent of the Early Modern period a new economic dynamic emerged: mercantilism. Hard money, usually in the form of silver and gold bullion, became increasingly important. Every king wanted to take in more silver and gold than he expended. Wealth was viewed as an extractive process. This extraction was augmented by establishing monopolies and governmental control of the economy. Outside of a short-lived and significant increase in the supply of silver from newly discovered mines in the New World (e.g., the "silver mountain" of Potosí), the total supply of precious metal was relatively constant or even decreased as time progressed. The great problem with mercantilism is that it is a zero-sum game. Just as Lake Wobegon's kids can't all be "above average," all countries and kings can't take in more silver and gold than they pay out.

Most accounts of the rise of capitalism point to key developments in the eighteenth century, beginning primarily in the Netherlands.

Chief among these were the creation of the first stock exchange in Amsterdam, a rise in companies owned by shareholders, e.g., the Dutch East India Company, relaxation of medieval prohibitions against Christians charging interest for loans to other Christians and the consequent flourishing of the banking industry, the beginnings of mechanization, and an emerging view that wealth could be created through organization, more efficient use of labor, and the strategic deployment of capital.[16] This new view, of course, implied a repudiation of the Law of Limited Goods.

As modern economies have emerged, modern economic theory takes for granted that wealth can be created; it is not static. This new paradigm raises a hermeneutical challenge for the Christian social ethicist. How are the Bible's moral teachings, which were articulated in economies rooted in subsistence agrarian economies, to be understood today? Capitalism presumes, even requires, that people consume more than the bare necessities of life, and economic growth requires such increased consumption (although within limits). If consuming more than the minimum one needs inures to the greater benefit of society and is not theft, as in Augustine's day, does this not change the modern Christian's moral obligations from the standard that prevailed in the ancient and medieval periods?[17] I think it does. Pope Francis and many mainline Protestants seem less convinced. I contend that Christian generosity linked with robust capitalism provides the best hope for American Christians to ameliorate suffering both in America and around the globe.

Another range of issues for dialogue involves the ethics of violence, war, and the death penalty. I have already discussed my views on violence and war in the Introduction to this essay, and there is no need

---

16. These ideas about wealth creation were articulated most clearly by the Scottish economist Adam Smith in his *An Inquiry into the Nature and Causes of the Wealth of Nations* (London: W. Strahan and T. Cadell, 1776).

17. A particularly beautiful way to be a capitalist Christian is to earn a lot and to "consume" this wealth by giving to others. This spending on others increases the velocity of monetary transactions and thus stimulates the economy, but it is also altruistic. Perhaps this represents a synthesis of pure capitalism and the social ethics Augustine taught.

to replow that ground. The issue of whether the secular state has the right (or even the duty) to execute those guilty of grave crimes, especially murder, is a related but separate issue.

I will restate Niebuhr's premise, which I endorse, that the highest value in social ethics writ large is justice, not love. It would be difficult to conceive of how capital punishment could be a manifestation of the ethic of love.[18] Capital punishment as an act of justice is much more easily imagined. The sentences criminals receive are usually justified on the basis of one or more of the following: rehabilitation, isolation, deterrence, or punishment.

Of course, there is no possibility of rehabilitation with capital punishment, so that justification is excluded. In contrast, capital punishment constitutes the most extreme form of isolation. If locking offenders up lowers the threat of the individual to the general population, killing offenders completely eliminates it on a permanent basis.

It is often argued that the *ius gladii*, the "law of the sword" traditionally wielded by government, deters murder and other very serious crimes because when capital punishment is in play then those crimes very literally become "matters of life and death" for the perpetrators. In some situations, this deterrence probably works. For a prison inmate who is unlikely to be released before he dies a natural death, the death penalty may be the only remaining sanction he fears; this might keep him from murdering a fellow inmate.

The fourth justification often offered for sanctions against criminals is punishment. The two words in the Hebrew Bible that are often translated into English as "justice" are *mishpat* and *tsedeqah* (or its biform *tsedeq*). The most basic meaning of *mishpat* is "judgment" and the most basic meaning of *tsedeqah* is "righteousness." But in many contexts the best way to translate *mishpat* is "sentence" or "punishment." Less commonly, this is also true of *tsedeqah*.[19] In the

---

18. One might suggest that the self-giving execution of our Savior would be a prime demonstration of such love, but this is not quite on point: It demonstrated the love of Jesus, certainly not the love of the state that executed him.

19. An example would be Isa 10:22b–23: "A destruction has been decided, a flowing of punishment (*tsedeqah*). For a complete destruction, one that is decreed, the Lord God of hosts will execute in the midst of the whole land."

Old Testament punishment is often understood to be an essential component of justice.

The LXX (Septuagint) usually uses *krisis* to translate *mishpat*. In the New Testament *krisis* most often refers to "judging" or "judgment," but it also not infrequently refers to "condemnation" or "punishment." Sometimes it also is best translated as "justice" or "righteousness."[20] On the other hand, in the New Testament *dikaiosunē*, the word the LXX normally uses to translate *tsedeqah*, never refers to punishment.

The *lex talionis* ("law of retribution"), summarized in the dictum "an eye for an eye, a tooth for a tooth," is an expression of criminal law as a matter of torts, or wrongs that damage victims and deserve compensation from the perpetrators. In criminal law, the damage comes to be seen as an injury not only to the victim, but also to the whole of the larger society. Punishment is best understood as a way to balance out the inequity to both the victim and to larger society that results from the commission of a wrong. To remove the notion of punishment from the equation risks impairing the balancing act that underpins justice. This is why Christ's atoning work is important in any discussion of the forgiveness of sin. God doesn't just say, "Your sin doesn't matter." Instead, he says, "Your sin matters greatly, but Jesus has paid the penalty for it, so you are free to go."

I understand the reluctance of some who do not want in any way to legitimize capital punishment in the hands of ungodly governments. Clearly capital punishment has been, and continues to be, exercised in horrifically immoral ways. This is an old story, part of the ongoing horror of evil in our world. But it is hard to say, short of the full consummation of God's kingdom, that capital punishment is inconsistent with a government's proper exercise of justice. Even the idealized Law of Moses, which seems to have been too difficult to institute completely in ancient Israel, permits capital punishment. And the New Testament, which judges the crucifixion of Jesus to

---

20. An example is Matt 12:18: "Behold, my servant whom I have chosen, my beloved one with whom my soul is well pleased. I will put my Spirit upon him, and he shall proclaim justice/righteousness [*krisin*] to the Gentiles."

have been the most immoral of executions, never condemns it by suggesting that Rome had no right to execute criminals. Instead, the Bible uniformly presumes that punishment, including capital punishment, is necessary to the proper administration of justice. Like most Evangelicals, I am not in theory opposed to capital punishment. I do believe that this sort of punishment should be exercised with great caution, and only for the most egregious of crimes.

The issue of immigration is another area of social ethics that provides much common ground for dialogue. As in other matters of social ethics, there is no single or standard Evangelical viewpoint on immigration. Many Evangelicals believe that the Bible gives little relevant guidance on this matter and consequently they reach their conclusions based on non-religious assessments. In general, Evangelical denominations have been reluctant to take positions on immigration policy, even though it is an important contemporary issue.

In general, the Old Testament presumes that individuals or family groups are free to move from one land to another, although moving could involve danger. Often this immigration was motivated by economic concerns such as the need to find food in times of famine. The migration of Jacob's family to Egypt is perhaps the most vivid example of such economic migration.

While hospitality was widely regarded as an important virtue in the ancient Near East, native fears of spying, military invasion, and the unknown added elements of danger to immigration. However, the greatest danger was the loss of one's support network comprised of family, friends, and countrymen. The Hebrew Bible often refers to Israelite countrymen as "brothers." Sometimes the word "native" (*'ezrach*) is used. This word literally means "raised up" and is short for the full expression "raised up from the land" (*'ezrach ha'arets*), as may be seen from Exodus 12:19 and 12:48.

Two separate groups of non-Israelites are pictured living in the land. One is spoken of quite warmly, while there is mainly suspicion of the other group. The standard Hebrew word for the first group is *ger*, which is usually translated "sojourner" or "resident alien," and sometimes "proselyte." In contemporary English the words "sojourner" and "proselyte" connote quite different things, and this linguistic tension highlights the modern interpreter's difficulty in describing the status of the *ger*, which seems to have shifted over time. The *ger* is a non-Israelite who lives more-or-less permanently in the land of Israel and raises a family there. Israel retained a consciousness that it too had lived as sojourners in Egypt (Gen 15:13; Exod 2:22; 18:3; 22:21; 23:9, etc.). During that time, it had adopted many, but certainly not all, Egyptian ways. Similarly, the *ger* in Israel was expected to follow much of the legislation that governed conduct among Israelites. Five times the Pentateuch states that "there shall be one law for the native and for the *ger*" (Exod 12:49; Lev 24:22; Num 15:15, 16, 29).

The primary difference between the *ger* and the native Israelite was the right to own land. While it is not clear that the jubilee was ever fully implemented in Israel, the general idea was that land could be leased for up to fifty years, but it could not be permanently sold away from the tribe to which it had been apportioned. The *ger* belonged to no tribe. Therefore, the *ger* was seen as someone marginalized, much like the widow or the orphan. The *ger* was to receive part of the tithe set aside one year in three for such marginalized peoples. The *ger* also had the right, along with widows and orphans, to glean fields and to harvest whatever volunteer crops fields produced during sabbatical years.

The LXX usually translates *ger* with *prosēlutos*, which probably was already well on its way to meaning "religious convert." Certainly the word meant this by the first century AD, as New Testament usage makes clear. The fact that so many duties imposed on native Israelites were also imposed on the *ger* clearly contributed to the sense that the *ger* was adopting Israelite identity. A rather remarkable passage in Ezekiel's vision of eschatological renewal of Israel pictures the territory of an enlarged nation of Israel being reapportioned to its tribes, but now including the *gerim* who live among each tribe (Ezek 47:22). What this implies is made explicit: "They shall be to you [i.e., the people of Israel] as native-born sons of Israel."

The second non-native group found in the land were those who lived there temporarily or who had not committed to living like Israelites. Sometimes these were invading armies. For example, Isaiah 62:8 reads: "The Lord has sworn by his right hand and by his mighty arm: 'I will not again give your grain to be food for your enemies, and foreigners (*benei nekar*) shall not drink your wine for which you have labored....'"

The terms used to designate this group are *zar* ("stranger" or "foreigner") or *ben-nekar* ("a foreigner"; lit. "son of a foreigner"). The LXX never translates these terms with *prosēlutos*, instead using terms like *allogenēs* ("of another ancestry") or *allotrios* ("of another type"). Foreigners were not allowed to eat of the Passover meal as could circumcised *gerim* (Exod 12:43; cf. Exod 12:48). But this exclusion is not to be permanent. In the extraordinary oracle found in Isaiah 56 about the day when the temple will become "a house of prayer for all nations," a new era is pictured in which both eunuchs and "foreigners who join themselves to the Lord" will gain access to the temple and be allowed to minister before the Lord.

The New Testament reflects a situation in which the movement of people from one "country" to another was largely unrestricted, at least in the lands within the Roman Empire. This facilitated the missionary activity of the first-century Church as reflected in both the book of Acts and the letters of Paul.

The Empire contained diasporas of many national groups, which retained their national identities even in foreign environments, with all being subject to Roman law in addition to the laws of their people. Because of their subjection to Rome, neither Israel as God's people nor the tiny first-century Church had any say in formulating immigration policy.

The Old Testament story is largely, although not entirely, about God's interaction with a single people, Israel (or Israel/Judah), an identity combining both ethnic and religious components. In contrast, the New Testament relativizes the special place of Israel as a people. Its story is about God's interaction with all the nations and peoples of the earth. It presents an eschatological vision that the ransomed saints "from every tribe and tongue and people and nation" will become a kingdom and priests, joined together in the worship of the Lord and the sacrificed Lamb (Rev 5:8–13).

So, how should these data affect the social ethics of immigration for the contemporary Christian? A few principles seem relevant for the purposes of dialogue. First, the Bible values the freedom of the individual. Freedom of movement is an element of personal freedom and there should be a bias in favor of such freedom. It would seem very difficult morally to justify a complete ban on immigration or to completely exclude the possibility of granting naturalized citizenship to anyone at all.

On the other hand, the Old Testament places a high value on the rule of law in both the individual and social realms. Both the teaching of Jesus ("Render unto Caesar the things that are Caesar's. . . .") and the larger New Testament recognize the rule of law, even in very imperfect governments. This may suggest that governments have the right to restrict immigration, whether these restrictions are misguided or not. Relatedly, both the repeated declaration of the Pentateuch that "there shall be one law" for both the native-born Israelite and the *ger*/proselyte, and the ethnically, nationally, and linguistically inclusive picture of God's people in the New Testament leave no room for racism or claims of ethnic superiority.

When thinking about the issue of immigration, it is interesting to note that both ancient Israel's pattern of absorbing the *ger*/proselyte into itself and the early Church's missionary activity which aimed at the absorption of new converts into itself regardless of their distinctive backgrounds, suggest that immigration policy should aim to assimilate new citizens into the larger whole (without necessarily erasing distinctive identities). Today, Myanmar is the only nation I know of that does not allow foreigners to become citizens under any circumstances. But I remember when West Germany would not allow anyone without German bloodlines to become a citizen of the country, regardless of how long they had lived in West Germany and regardless of the contributions they had made to the country. Such preoccupation with ethnicity produces an underclass, legal residents without the possibility of citizenship, and is inimical to the inclusive Biblical vision.

Economic factors (e.g., the search for food in times of famine) were commonly the primary motivation for migration in the ancient world and may enlighten dialogue, as well. Unless the conquest of Canaan is pictured in these terms—contrary to the presentation found in the

Old Testament—the Old Testament never pictures such migration as deleterious to a native population. Population density was much lower in the ancient world than it is today, and this perhaps explains why today many modern nations limit immigration to what they consider manageable levels.

If immigration is to be limited, opinions differ as to which considerations ought to govern who gets priority. Hardship in their present circumstances, merit (often calculated in terms of wealth, education, or potential to augment the economy), familial connections with current citizens, and random selection through lottery are each determining factors in some of the various immigration programs currently in use in America. While each of these considerations may have merit, the biblical data lends greatest support to the factor of present hardship. Having some sort of asylum program seems morally important. Currently the American policy on asylum excludes economic hardship as grounds for claiming asylum. The biblical data suggest that perhaps some immigration should be allowed on the basis of economic hardship. Many fear allowing this, seeing it as opening a hole in the dike and inviting the entire immigration system to collapse.

Personally, I support a generous immigration policy, but also one that enforces clear legal standards. I do not believe "open borders" is a viable option at the present time because it precludes the possibility of admitting immigrants in a measured way that allows them to be properly assimilated into American society. I also believe that in some circumstances, deportation is necessary.

I believe that assimilation to certain "American values" should be an explicit expectation of immigrants. It has often been noted that America is based on an idea, not on "blood and soil" as had been the European pattern previous to America's founding. The fundamental idea of America is found in its *Declaration of Independence*, "that all men are created equal, that they are endowed by their Creator with certain unalienable Rights, that among these are Life, Liberty and the pursuit of Happiness." Commitment to this idea is important and should be a prerequisite to legal immigration. I also support requiring a functional knowledge of English as a prerequisite to American citizenship (although not immigration), as this is a practical marker of assimilation.

While I believe that temporary immigration should be allowed for some purposes (e.g., to attend school), I do not believe in granting permanent residency status without the possibility of attaining citizenship. This would facilitate the creation of a two-tiered society composed of 1) citizens and 2) a permanent underclass.

My personal views on immigration draw from many wells, not just biblical and theological wells. I do not expect all Christians, or even all Evangelicals, to agree with me completely on these matters. In so many matters involving social justice, people of good will will disagree.

3.4. Social Issues and Wesleyan Evangelicals

Dr. Steven Hoskins

"The Bible knows nothing of solitary religion."

"The Gospel of Christ knows no religion but social; no holiness but social holiness."

"This doctrine [i.e., scriptural holiness or Christian Perfection] is the grand depositum which God has lodged with the people called Methodists; and for the sake of propagating this chiefly he appears to have raised us up."[1]

John Wesley

John Wesley famously set a high bar in regard to social ethics in making Christian holiness the one goal of his life, and of the Methodist movement that has followed in his wake since the middle of the eighteenth century. Holiness of heart and life as the quotes above indicate was "the aim of his life, the organizing centre of his thought, the spring of all action, his one abiding project."[2] The purpose of the Methodist movement was to "spread scriptural holiness throughout the land." This it did and has done by creating churches, movements, classes, bands, schools, and revivals dedicated to the cause. However, despite Wesley's intentions and best efforts, the social ethics of

---

1. John Wesley, *The Letters of the Rev. John Wesley MA.*, ed. John Telford, 8 vols. (London: Epworth Press, 1931), 3:238.
2. Theodore Jennings, *Good News To The Poor: John Wesley's Evangelical Economics* (Nashville: Abingdon, 1990), 140.

Wesleyan Evangelicals have been, for better or worse, a mixed bag of individualistic approaches often centering upon the interior motives of such folk and the communal and social aspirations of the assemblies to which they belong. As with Wesley, there has been no magisterium to appeal to nor a single-source hypothesis in guiding ethical decisions.

This paper does three things by way of explaining how Wesleyan Evangelicals understand and do social ethics using a simple method: History, Theological Structure, Application. First, it explains what made John Wesley the kind of evangelical he was, especially in regard to method, and what his evangelical followers have followed in the current wave of appeals to his example in figuring out how to do social ethics. Second, the essay explores some of the more productive recent attempts at providing a Wesleyan ethical framework as exemplars toward understanding Wesleyan evangelicals and their ongoing attempts to negotiate the social holiness so dear to John Wesley and his Methodist followers. Third, it provides a foray through some of the positions of Wesleyan Evangelicals in regard to the social issues at stake in our discussion. Given that paper explores the material in this way, it uses the descriptive terms methodist, Wesleyan, and evangelical interchangeably and always in reference to one another.

The Challenge of Following John Wesley

When Mr. Wesley wrote the lines quoted at the beginning of this paper, lines that would go on to inform almost all attempts at Methodist and Wesleyan social ethics, he did not mean to open the floodgates to a diversity of opinions, positions, and approaches to dealing with social issues and ethics for those who would follow in his wake and live in his shadow. Nor did he when he was creating rules of social ethics for his many converts by creating a simple set of rules to follow when making ethical decisions: Do no harm. Do good. Stay in love with God.[3]

Fortunately or unfortunately however, for those evangelicals who

---

3. Reuben Job, *Three Simple Rules: A Wesleyan Way of Living* (Nashville: Abingdon, 2007). Job's book has been through several printings and sold over a million copies in the last decade.

follow Wesley and his Arminian instincts, such simplicity has led to a diversity of opinions both regarding Wesley and in his great army of commentators in the ensuing centuries. Wesley's position has provided both communal (social holiness) *and* individual instruction (inspiring quotes; the three rules). In reflecting on Mr. Wesley, one wishes he had chosen one or the other or simply provided a more systematic body of thinking on the subject that could serve as something of a magisterium. But it is the *and* that proves the difficulty in this or any other paper. Love God and love your neighbor. Do right and believe correctly. Follow God and be a good citizen. Be responsible and be theologically correct. It is the conjunction that makes for the interesting theological grammar in the case of the ethics of Wesleyan evangelicals and that grammar has an interesting history.

Part of this is due to Wesley, who could never be accused of being a systematic theologian or thinker in any regard. Partly, as well, to his recent followers who, following his lead when doing theological work, have taken their cues from a variety of sources (including Wesley) and approaches that fit within the framework of the Wesleyan Quadrilateral made famous by Albert Cook Outler, a construct that has produced quite a wave in modern Wesleyan thought.[4] Tracking Wesley and making great hay within the quadrilateral and mostly from Outler, Wesleyan evangelicals do their work and tell their story differently from each other. For the purposes of this paper, I include some United Methodist evangelicals like Stanley Hauerwas, William Abraham, and D. Stephen Long and their thinking on social issues, particularly in the section below on general approaches to social ethics and issues by Wesleyan evangelicals. They are an interesting part of this conversation and deserve a voice in our dialogue, especially for comparison's sake, but also as they provide a direct link historically and theologically to John Wesley. One could, and I do, make a case for these United Methodists being evangelicals by their membership

---

4. Albert C. Outler, "The Wesleyan Quadrilateral in John Wesley," 75–88 in *Doctrine and Theology in the United Methodist Church*, ed. Thomas A. Langford (Eastbourne, UK: Kingsway Publications, 1991) and the introduction to Albert Cook Outler, *John Wesley* (New York: Oxford University Press, 1964), 3–34, which places the Wesleyan Quadrilateral within the context of Wesley's voluminous works.

in the Wesleyan Theological Society, the largest and only organized body of Wesleyans who identify across denominational and affiliated lines as Wesleyan Evangelicals. As we shall see, when it comes to understanding ethics and determining positions on social issues, these differences are clear and have proved fruitful, though they have not produced a singular or even systematic approach to understanding ethics among Wesleyans. Scripture, Reason, Tradition, and Experience provided the categories that Outler and others have recognized out of which Wesley did his work as an Anglican Evangelical practicing ministry in the long eighteenth century.

Wesley's evangelicalism was linked to a controversy within the Anglican revival of his century (Wesley died in 1791 at the age of 88, coming from a line of long livers) that has been fleshed out most recently by Ryan Danker in his *Wesley and the Anglicans: Political Division in Early Evangelicalism*.[5] Enough ink has been spilled in explaining the controversy.[6] Straightforwardly, some Anglicans wanted a state-church that acted as a way of keeping English political order and the class system in place. Others wanted a church where religion was a matter of personal conversion and grounded in the conviction of holy living, an approach that they themselves characterized as one of evangelical religion. Wesley was squarely within the evangelical camp. That position has come to be characterized by Wesleyans as "the religion of the heart," demanding decisionist conversion and a metanoiac turning away from sin and living unto righteousness in believers after conversion. A summary of Danker's thinking will suffice to explain this: Wesley and the other Anglicans like him were Evangelicals of a certain sort. They distinguished themselves as not Calvinist or determinist in their orienting of the believer toward salvation (at times being called Anti-Calvinists),[7] they were Arminian

---

5. Ryan Danker, *Wesley and the Anglicans: Political Division in Early Evangelicalism* (Downers Grove, IL: InterVarsity Press, 2016), 23–46.

6. See for example the many references to Evangelicals and Methodists in J. C. D. Clark, *English Society, 1688–1832: Ideology, Social Structure and Political Practice in the Ancien Regime* (New York: Cambridge University Press, 1985).

7. For the background of this position in Wesley and others, see Nicholas Tyacke, *Anti-Calvinism: The Rise of Anglican Evangelicals, 1590–1640* (Oxford: Clarendon, 1990).

in affirming free choice for the believer toward God's grace, and they believed that when the human person was converted by God's grace they were also graced with a power to live righteous lives unto the ethical holiness demanded of Jesus' followers. In short, they demanded Christian perfection as a growth in grace for all believers. This demand guided all of Wesley's and, subsequently, Wesley's disciples' attempts at social ethics.

Danker argues that this put Wesley in the position of being misunderstood and criticized (and perhaps rightly so at times) as preaching a "works righteousness" for Christian believers, and being rightly understood as a critic of the Anglican church and its failure to provide an arena for the demand of ethical purity. This meant, says Danker, that what was at stake in Wesley's Methodism was not the Thirty-Nine Articles of Religion but polity—defined as the church's rule-oriented responsibility to demand and provide for the works of Christian holiness (spiritual formation), particularly in regards to social and ethical issues of the day, something Wesley sought to rectify by his creation of the Methodist societies as arenas where such could be practiced.[8] That Wesley was guilty of this is sure and it is easy to historically recount the criticism of Wesley and the Methodists as they foisted their societies onto and within established Anglican parishes.[9]

Perhaps more rightly, what Wesley did was create a "renewing movement" or what some historians have described as an "order" within the Anglican Church that came to be known as Methodism. After the Revolution in America and after Wesley's death in England, Methodism became two functioning churches on two different continents, each with their own distinctives and each with their own histories based on their loyalty to Wesley and their perceptions of how he did his work. With distinctive approaches to ministry and theology drawn from differing sources, they tapestried together their theology and social strategies, mostly out of Wesley's writings and appeals to

---

8. Danker, *Wesley and the Anglicans*, 47–96.
9. See, e.g., David Hempton, *Methodism: Empire of the Spirit* (New Haven: Yale University Press, 2006).

the different parts of the quadrilateral. With no official Methodist ecclesiology and no official magisterium, they did their work in the places where they bloomed taking issues theological and ethical as they arose.

Given the revivalist nature of Methodist history and the willingness of Wesley to differ with established denominations, the history of Methodism broadly considered now includes over one hundred churches, denominations, groups, and revival movements in its fold, with more on the way. In this, it can be argued, the different Methodist churches and different Methodist movements and revivals flourished within their contexts as "Methodist Orders" just as Wesley and his Methodists flourished as an "order" within the Anglican Church of the eighteenth century. In regard to social ethics, some famous, like the Salvation Army, take their cues from Wesley's grand social vision, and some less so, like the Bible Methodists of Oklahoma, center their approach to social ethics on a strict, rule-oriented legalism with those rules bound only by what can be supported via isolating and isolated Scriptural texts.

To bring all of this together, we must note that for Wesley and for his followers, what fueled this revival was an approach to the Christian faith that provided an "Evangelical" approach combining theology and ethics that were rarely, if ever, understood as separate tasks. The rule of faith is the rule of thinking and practice and both are always together for Wesleyan Evangelicals. Intellectually, Wesley made no distinctions between theology and ethics, as many Wesleyan ethicists and theologians have noted. Historically, Wesley was an occasional theologian, rather than a systematic one or even a pastoral one in any modern sense. What all this means, and to put this as succinctly as possible for the purposes of our discussion, for Wesley and Wesleyan Evangelicals there is no practical or theoretical distinction between thinking and acting, between mind and body in the Christian faith. These are not separate things or separable units, because God is joined to us who are Christians by his grace in the way that everyday life is welcomed and created. Stanley Hauerwas and Stephen Long have noted that this dominates Wesley's pathway of discipling his devotees in the subtitle of his fifty-volume Christian

Library (the subscribed reading for the Methodist preachers and societies during his lifetime), calling it "Extracts from the abridgements of the choicest pieces of Practical Divinity."[10] Wesleyan ethics is theologically oriented obedience, the conjoining of holy contemplation and holy living.

What has emerged in the most recent period of Wesley studies is something of a marvel. Just as Wesley distinguished himself as a certain kind of evangelical—orthodox in belief, heart religion in regards to conversion and spirituality almost exclusively within the atmosphere of a religious revival, and openness to emerging or whatever proved modern at the moment approaches to experiential faith—so Wesley's followers did and have done their work. Randy Maddox has provided the genius for understanding this by bringing the two approaches together in his study of Wesley entitled *Responsible Grace*. If Outler began the modern revolution in Wesley studies with his 1964 publication noted earlier, Maddox focused the debate for Wesleyan Evangelicals. Maddox incorporated Outler's quadrilateral within the framework of the history of Wesley's prodigious literary output and the chronological framework of Methodism in Wesley's lifetime and produced a formulaic approach to Wesleyan studies by removing the "and" between theology/ethics.[11]

Maddox's work was bolstered by the English translation of Manfred Marquart's *John Wesley's Social Ethics: Praxis and Principles*, published in 1992, but the German edition underlies much of what Maddox brings together in his work.[12] Responsible grace is the orienting concern of any Wesleyan Evangelical approach to the issues we are discussing in this round of the dialogue, be they a grand social vision

---

10. Stanley Hauerwas and D. Stephen Long, "Theological Ethics," 635–47 in *The Oxford Handbook of Methodist Studies*, ed. James Kirby and William Abraham (New York: Oxford University Press, 2011), 635.

11. Randy Maddox, *Responsible Grace: John Wesley's Practical Theology* (Nashville: Kingswood, 1994), 36–47.

12. Manfred Marquardt, *John Wesley's Social Ethics: Praxis and Principles*, trans. John E. Steely and W. Stephen Gunter (Nashville: Abingdon, 1992). The German edition, *Praxis and prinzipien sozalier Verantwortun. Eine Studie zur Sozialethik John Wesleys*, first appeared as a dissertation for the Theological Faculty of Christian-Albrechts University, Kiel, Germany, in 1975.

or rules-oriented legalism. Combine that with the quote from Wesley on social holiness and Job's Three Rules and one arrives at the recent discussions of Wesleyan Evangelicals on social issues, a continued mixture of both individual motivation and social concern aimed at being socially responsible agents of grace.

Methodist Approaches to Social Ethics

This orienting concern of responsible grace has proven both effective and productive. Denominations, scholars, and schools within the Wesleyan tradition have taken some care to provide structures and outlines in defining social ethics. In this section, I highlight some of those efforts as an attempt to show the broad range of approaches with which Wesleyan Evangelicals think about and press the issues of living out the social dimensions of ethical responsibility.

Denominational Holy Life: Admittedly, this orienting concern and rule-driven approach has proven both effective and productive. Some denominations in the Wesleyan Evangelical tradition have incorporated Wesleyan methodology within their official discipline. In the earlier days of my own denomination, the Church of the Nazarene, the simplicity of the Wesleyan ethical highway and the impetus of being a Wesleyan order produced the Special and General Rules. The General Rules provided edicts for holy living, and principles of organization and government; the Special Rules addressed key issues of contemporary society. For the Church of the Nazarene and other Wesleyan Evangelical denominations, such rules served as close to an ecclesiology as one could find in Wesleyan churches, particularly on this side of the Atlantic. The General Rules provided:

> to be identified with the visible Church is the blessed privilege and sacred duty of all who are saved from their sins and are seeking completeness in Christ Jesus. It is required of all who desire to unite with the Church of the Nazarene, and thus to walk in fellowship with us, that they shall show evidence of salvation from their sins by a godly walk and vital piety; and that they shall be, or earnestly desire to be, cleansed from all indwelling sin. They shall evidence their commitment to God. FIRST. By doing that which is enjoined in the Word of

God, which is our rule of both faith and practice, including: (1) Loving God with all the heart, soul, mind, and strength, and one's neighbor as oneself [Exodus 20:3-6; Leviticus 19:17-18; Deuteronomy 5:7-10; 6:4-5; Mark 12:28-31; Romans 13:8-10]. (2) Pressing upon the attention of the unsaved the claims of the gospel, inviting them to the house of the Lord, and trying to compass their salvation [Matthew 28:19-20; Acts 1:8; Romans 1:14-16; 2 Corinthians 5:18-20]. (3) Being courteous to all men [Ephesians 4:32; Titus 3:2; 1 Peter 2:17; 1 John 3:18]. (4) Being helpful to those who are also of the faith, in love forbearing one another [Romans 12:13; Galatians 6:2, 10; Colossians 3:12-14]. (5) Seeking to do good to the bodies and souls of men; feeding the hungry, clothing the naked, visiting the sick and imprisoned, and ministering to the needy, as opportunity and ability are given [Matthew 25:35-36; 2 Corinthians 9:8-10; Galatians 2:10; James 2:15-16; 1 John 3:17-18]. (6) Contributing to the support of the ministry and the church and its work in tithes and offerings [Malachi 3:10; Luke 6:38; 1 Corinthians 9:14; 16:2; 2 Corinthians 9:6-10; Philippians 4:15-19]. (7) Attending faithfully all the ordinances of God, and the means of grace, including the public worship of God [Hebrews 10:25], the ministry of the Word [Acts 2:42], the sacrament of the Lord's Supper [1 Corinthians 11:23-30]; searching the Scriptures and meditating thereon [Acts 17:11; 2 Timothy 2:15; 3:14-16]; family and private devotions [Deuteronomy 6:6-7; Matthew 6:6]. SECOND. By avoiding evil of every kind, including: (1) Taking the name of God in vain [Exodus 20:7; Leviticus 19:12; James 5:12]. (2) Profaning of the Lord's Day by participation in unnecessary secular activities, thereby indulging in practices which deny its sanctity [Exodus 20:8-11; Isaiah 58:13-14; Mark 2:27-28; Acts 20:7; Revelation 1:10]. (3) Sexual immorality, such as premarital or extramarital relations, perversion in any form, or looseness and impropriety of conduct [Exodus 20:14; Matthew 5:27-32; 1 Corinthians 6:9-11; Galatians 5:19; 1 Thessalonians 4:3-7]. (4) Habits or practices known to be destructive of physical and mental well-being. Christians are to regard themselves as temples of the Holy Spirit [Proverbs 20:1; 23:1-3; 1 Corinthians 6:17-20; 2 Corinthians 7:1; Ephesians 5:18]. (5) Quarreling, returning evil for evil, gossiping, slandering, spreading surmises injurious to the good names of others [2 Corinthians 12:20; Galatians 5:15; Ephesians 4:30-32; James 3:5-18; 1 Peter 3:9-10]. (6) Dishonesty, taking advantage in buying and selling, bearing false witness, and like works of darkness [Leviticus 19:10-11; Romans 12:17; 1 Corinthians 6:7-10]. (7) The indulging of pride in dress or behavior. Our people are to dress with the Christian simplicity and modesty that become holiness [Proverbs 29:23; 1 Timothy 2:8-10; James 4:6; 1 Peter 3:3-4; 1 John 2:15-17]. (8) Music, literature, and entertainments that dishonor God [1 Corinthians 10:31; 2 Corinthians 6:14-17; James 4:4]. THIRD. By abiding in hearty fellowship with the church, not inveighing against but wholly committed to its doctrines and usages and actively involved in its continuing witness and outreach [Ephesians 2:18-22; 4:1-3, 11-16; Philippians 2:1-8; 1 Peter 2:9-10].[13]

One could just as easily have inserted quotes from Wesley where the scriptural citations exist and perhaps to similar effect.

The Special Rules outlined, generally in a more negative fashion, the concerns of the day. Since the denomination's beginning in 1908, we have abstained from alcohol. We have avoided, at times, the Hollywood lifestyle, the circus, the ballpark, and the movies. In more recent times we have taken stances more modern and a mixture of prohibition and construction: marriage between a man and a woman, a stance against the practice of homosexual sex and sex outside of marriage, education as a moral construct to fight society's ills, a preferential option for taking care of the poor spelled out in denominational institutions like orphanages, hospitals, and schools, and positions on the treatment of LGBTQ persons and on the intersection of science and religion. No matter the denomination, such obligations reflect the both/and approach to ethics either implicitly or explicitly. The rules are for individuals and for social behaviors at the same time within the boundaries of church membership.[14]

Manfred Marquart—Wesley as Model: Manfred Marquart's *John Wesley's Social Ethics: Praxis and Principles* is written as prescription through historical analysis.[15] Wesley insisted that any social ethic is based on loving God as loving neighbor; his theologically based

---

13. *Manual*, Church of the Nazarene (Kansas City, MO: Nazarene Publishing House, 1989), 20-21.
14. See, e.g., *Manual*, Church of the Nazarene (1989), 36-37.
15. Marquardt, *John Wesley's Social Ethics: Praxis and Principles*, 15-16.

prescriptive was a revivalist slogan. "Each person is someone for whom Christ died" provides the motivation for social change rather than a guideline for changing the social structures. Noting that there was a change in Wesley's approach to social ethics after his Aldersgate experience of assurance in 1738, Marquart helps us to understand the lack of distinction between theology and ethics for Wesleyan Evangelicals. Prior to 1738, Wesley emphasized good works as a preparation for conversion, but after 1738, he demanded good works from the Methodists as a result of their conversion. Such a perspective led Wesley to take a stand against slavery, create aid societies that gave money to aid to the poor, enact prison reform, and provide education to the illiterate and orphans. For Marquart the ideal is that Wesley's followers today would take up the same causes, thus providing a consistent model of social ethics through a direct historical appeal to Wesley. To the earlier point, this means that Wesleyan Evangelicals today would remove any "and" between history and theology/ethics.

D. Stephen Long—Wesley's Moral Vision for Social Ethics: In his book *John Wesley's Moral Theology: The Quest for God and Goodness*, D. Stephen Long, a United Methodist and a Wesleyan Evangelical, seeks to disconnect Methodism from doing ethics on the trajectory of Kantian liberalism (something implied in Outler's formation of the quadrilateral) in favor of an approach more akin to the recent Radical Orthodoxy project. In Long's approach, Wesley's understanding of social ethics is removed from being individualistic with the rational capacity for ethical decision making to being a communal participation in a holy and happy life.[16] Using both the ethical vision of Aquinas and a metaphysics of theology/ethics as participation in God and God's life, Long argues that Wesleyan social ethics is best understood when beginning, as does Thomas, with a "shared particular propensity in starting with Scripture in moral theology, particularly with 2 Peter 1:4–5 and the Sermon on the Mount." As a result, notes Long, Wesleyans share a moral vision of the Christian life with Aquinas.

---

16. D. Stephen Long, *John Wesley's Moral Theology: The Quest for God and Goodness*, (Nashville: Kingswood, 2005), 117–18.

"Our ultimate happiness is only found in our participation in God as disclosed in 2 Peter 1:4. To participate in the divine nature is the end for which all humanity aims."[17]

Decidedly this has less to do with ethics than moral theology, but is nonetheless a useful perspective when considering the broad range of Wesleyan approaches to social ethics. Long does make the connection between the force of Methodism in Wesley's lifetime and the poor aid societies, anti-slavery movement, and the moral formation of Methodist communities which lobbied their members to give up alcohol (mostly as an economic issue) and to use Scripture as the foundation for social relationships inside of Methodism. He also uses Wesley's moral vision as an impetus for Wesleyan Evangelicals to think about their social witness in light of current social issues.

H. Ray Dunning—Reflecting the Divine Image: Addressing the issue of ethics within the Holiness wing of Evangelical Wesleyans, Ray Dunning's *Reflecting the Divine Image* makes the case for an ethics based on an interplay between an orienting concern of Wesley's, the restoration of the *imago dei* in each believer at their conversion, and the quadrilateral where Scripture is the reigning and informing source of Reason, Tradition, and Experience.[18] Dunning's book is full of exegetical work highlighting the weight of the books of Genesis, Deuteronomy, and James as prescriptive norms for Christian ethics and what should be a decided turn to righteous living in the life of the sanctified believer. God's sanctifying grace means the renewal of the image of God in the human person which was totally lost in the Fall, and that renewal is the means by which freedom and love (reflecting the Divine Image) are achieved in the holy life. This is for Dunning a freedom from a duty-based ethic to live toward a teleology of (at least) reflecting God's activity in loving one's neighbor. Reserving much for the renewed or sanctified common sense in each individual believer, Dunning's book is more about ethics as the inspiration for a holy life than it is about ethics. He does give one paragraph to Wesley's stance

---

17. Long, *John Wesley's Moral Theology*, 197.
18. H. Ray Dunning, *Reflecting the Divine Image: Biblical Ethics in a Wesleyan Perspective*, (Downers Grove, IL: InterVarsity Press, 1998), 7–8.

against slavery as an example of how this could be lived out, but does not touch on the issues of Wesley's work with the poor, the prisoner, or other current social issues.

This book is reflective of much that is true about the way many Evangelical Wesleyans do ethics. Believing that Christians are spirit-filled and have the mind of Christ is more about individualistic judgment than any grand social vision. Dunning's reserved goal-oriented not goal-achieving approach is seen by some as a corrective to the more deontological duty-filled approach to Christian ethics of a previous era in the American Holiness Movement and is appealing to conservatives like those in the Church of the Nazarene, of which he is a member as we shall see below.

Stanley Hauerwas—Ethics as Prayer: In *The Blackwell Companion to Christian Ethics*, which he edits with Sam Wells, Stanley Hauerwas explores one of the more underutilized sources for doing ethics in the Wesleyan arsenal, Christian worship.[19] Criticizing the Kantian tradition and the deadlock on seemingly intractable ethical issues within Christianity at large, Hauerwas and the other authors of this volume see Christian worship as God's guidance for a vigorous ethical life. In what might be a genuine paradigm shift in the field, Hauerwas et al. want to restore the critical edge of theological thinking about virtues and vices by examining the way that liturgy can turn into critical prescriptions for ethical issues that range from economics to living with the disabled. Following the Post-Liberal school, the Evangelicals (Wesleyan, Anglican, Catholic, United Methodist) in this volume seek yet another way to do Christian ethics and achieve Wesley's vision of the Church and its individual members as the sanctified carriers of divine action. A fully theological ethic, as Rowan Williams notes in commenting on Hauerwas's thought, is to be "transformed into one who enacts Christ's action" through practices guided by communal praying.[20] While not all of the essays are written by those within

---

19. Stanley Hauerwas and Sam Wells, "Christian Ethics as Informed Prayer," 3–13 in *The Blackwell Companion to Christian Ethics*, eds. Stanley Hauerwas and Sam Wells (Malden, MA: Blackwell, 2011).

20. Rowan Williams, "Afterword," 495–498 in *The Blackwell Companion to Christian Ethics*, eds. Stanley Hauerwas and Sam Wells (Malden, MA: Blackwell, 2011), 497.

traditions that would strictly identify with Evangelicals, it is Hauerwas's Wesleyan vision that undergirds this volume.

Social Issues in Wesleyan Evangelical Churches as a Way into Dialogue

Before proceeding to a comparison of social issues and ethics in three distinct Wesleyan evangelical churches, it is fitting to say a word or two about Wesleyan Evangelicals and their stances on social issues/ethics. The three churches discussed in this section—the Church of the Nazarene, the Free Methodist Church, and the Salvation Army—are all a vital part of our dialogue and members of those churches are present for this discussion. My friends Bruce Cromwell, a Superintendent in the Free Methodist Church, and Bill Ury, who serves as the National Ambassador for Holiness in the Salvation Army, are both well-credentialed and both represent their respective communions with distinction. I am a lifelong Nazarene, having been born into that holiness tribe in 1963. While I will let Bruce and Bill speak for themselves, I am fairly sure that, like me, they will discuss these issues with the candor that comes from being well-conditioned from lengthy and spirited discussions on these issues where a variety of approaches and understandings of our Wesleyan heritage and method and the vital piety of believers have framed the discussions.

Further, the descriptions below are not as complete as they could be and reflect research that is part of the ongoing life of dynamic denominations. Some of the social issues we are discussing have no official position within these denominations. Yet officialdom is not always a defining category for Wesleyan Evangelicals. Each of these churches holds that their positions on social ethics are "guidelines" for their members and while serious are not absolutely binding. Positions change, are changing, and remain open to the revision of ongoing discovery and the witness to God's enlightening grace by those involved in their creation. That is to say, I am hesitant to isolate positions on particulars in these matters. Such an approach can be misleading, so we must remember that the discussions below reflect the discussion above. The positions on these social issues for Wesleyan

Evangelicals in these distinct communions reflect the occasional theological methodology of Wesley and the ever-present orienting concern of responsible grace. The influences of denominational structures of polity and doctrines are ever-present. Overarching concerns for evangelism and the instructions of John Wesley to do good to the bodies and souls of all people are ever-present, as well, and perhaps more persuasive in the discussions regarding social ethics among us. There is a great deal of "and" grammar in the construction of the positions below and that will, I think, be evident as we consider these positions "and" in the discussion to follow.

It is also important to note that behind these statements are the positions and thinking of many practicing Wesleyan academics in the arenas of both systematic theology and Bible who received their training in ethics, something most evident in section two above. My first systematic theology professor, H. Ray Dunning, did his PhD in ethics at Vanderbilt with Nels Ferre. Most evangelical seminary or university theology departments in the Wesleyan tradition have an ethicist on their faculty. At Garrett Divinity School in Chicago, where several Nazarenes have studied, the "and" approach applies to anyone who wishes to achieve a PhD. The degree always has an "and" inserted between two disciplines of study and almost all of the evangelicals at Garrett have an ethics tag on one of the two ends of the conjunction. So the modern studies of ethics, often Kantian in orientation and with a tendency to isolate ethical issues from their history and the ministry contexts of churches, provides yet another shadow in the room. The movement beyond isolation is, as Wesley noted in his statement on social holiness which was directed against the danger of living the Christian life as "holy solitaries," the pathway to social holiness and Christian perfection.[21]

As to my own testimony, I am both comfortable discussing these issues and remain uncomfortable speaking for my denomination and other Wesleyan Evangelicals. I have no magisterium to appeal to and

---

21. John Wesley, *The Bicentennial Works of John Wesley*, ed. Frank Baker et al. (Nashville: Abingdon, 1984ff), 7:36–40. Wesley's statement on social holiness was set in the preface to *Sacred Hymns and Poems* (1739), published with his brother, Charles.

find Experience to be the least dependable of the categories foisted upon me in the quadrilateral. I live in the "and" of my own convictions and a denomination that is constantly revising such statements to better reflect a more correct Wesleyan understanding—every four years at our General Assembly—and, at times, too great a silence on issues vital to the public and evangelistic witness of my church. I remain in such discussions dependent, as do all Wesleyan Evangelicals, on the Holy Spirit of God to speak to me and to my church. I am also confident of the Spirit's witness among us in this dialogue. I have learned in the years of this dialogue, fourteen now for me, that the Spirit speaks to the churches and through people like you who are my friends gathered here. Herein, I am convinced, is God's perfecting grace among us. That is why ecumenical discussions, across both time and space, are both vital and necessary. They are the fruit of holy friendship, perhaps the greatest of the Spirit's gifts to the saints. I am open to the criticism and revision of these statements as the Spirit leads us.[22]

Capital Punishment: The positions of Wesleyan Evangelicals regarding capital punishment reflect the dynamics of Wesleyanism. While clearly recognizing that Scripture has been used to both reject and defend capital punishment, Wesleyan Evangelicals have been reticent to take official stands against such. The Salvation Army allows its different international territories to make statements in regards to capital punishment.[23] The Army is generally against capital punishment or its revival in world areas where it has been outlawed. Yet it "acknowledges the need of society to be protected from wrongdoers, especially those willing to use violence, but recognizes also the responsibility placed upon society so to regulate itself that the dignity

---

22. I admit that the presentations of the positions of the churches discussed here are somewhat abbreviated. This is done for the sake of the discussion with that hopes that some clarity will emerge and the positions stated will be sufficient for dialogue. Liberty has been taken to shorten what would be a most extended discussion by giving preference at varying points below to the denomination whose position on a particular area of social ethics I find to be the most exemplary position for Wesleyan evangelicals.

23. Positions regarding capital punishment are available from the administrative offices of every international territory of the Salvation Army and those positions always respect the rights of governments to form their own laws.

and worth of all persons are made paramount and that the lowest instincts of men and women are not incited or inflamed."[24] It does acknowledge there are Salvationists who uphold the state's right to execute in certain circumstances and yet balances that view with statements acknowledging the possibility of redemption of even the most wretched of individuals who commit violent criminal acts.

The positions of the Free Methodist Church and the Church of the Nazarene regarding capital punishment are not so clear. The Free Methodists have attempted to introduce the following statement regarding capital punishment into their Discipline:

> The Free Methodist Church is deeply grieved when any life is taken in murder or homicide. We believe that persons who commit these or other horrendous crimes should be justly punished by just laws. Nevertheless, we believe that all human life is sacred, created by God, and therefore we must see all human life as significant and valuable. When governments implement the death penalty (capital punishment), then the life of the convicted person is devalued and all possibility of change in that person's life ends. Its use denies the power of Christ to redeem, restore, and transform all human beings, regardless of previous attitudes or actions. For these reasons, we oppose the death penalty (capital punishment) and urge its elimination from all criminal codes.[25]

The proposed statement has been tabled by the denomination for further consideration as there is the acknowledgement, as with the Salvation Army, that there are some Free Methodists who sincerely support the right of the state to capital punishment. The Church of the Nazarene has no official statement on capital punishment. There is some research into Nazarene attitudes toward the issue that reflects that a majority of its clergy support capital punishment. In *Pulpit and Politics*, Corwin Smidt notes that according to his survey, seventy-two

---

24. The Salvation Army United Kingdom Territory Positional Statement, "Capital Punishment," at https://www.salvationarmy.org.uk/files/capitalpunishmentpdf/download?token=yvf7VsuP (accessed October 1, 2019).

25. This statement was written by Bruce Cromwell, Free Methodist Bishop of the Great Plains Conference and a member of this dialogue. Permission to use the statement has been given by him.

percent of Nazarene clergy support capital punishment and do so in their preaching.[26]

The official positions of these bodies reflect underlying concerns related to them and are indicative of the "and" grammar of much of Wesleyanism. The positions are usually thoughtful and are also often read in the context of other denominational positions on social ethics. The recognition of positions on the right to life, euthanasia, and assisted suicide are, at times, present in the discussions regarding capital punishment. The overarching pastoral concern for evangelism and individual conversion is also attentively present in the positions of these discussions, as are the concerns of sovereign governments to allow the continued presence of the churches in world areas to do both evangelism and social ministry.

Church-State Relations: Each of the three churches discussed for the purposes of our dialogue, promotes peace among the nations, good relations with governing authorities, and a willingness toward subsidiarity, the permission of local church authorities to negotiate and participate with local and national governing bodies where possible. Each of the three appeals to Scripture as an ultimate authority when describing their best intentions and hopes for church-state relations. While there are many interesting and promising conversations and statements on church-state relations among these groups, the best discussion comes from our friend, Bruce Cromwell. In his discussion on the matter for the Free Methodist Conversations dialogue and website that provides a forum for the discussion of social ethics related to their Study on Doctrine commission, Cromwell invites ecumenical voices into the Wesleyan discussion with Reformed and Roman Catholic thought in his presentation.[27] He maintains a distinction for the Church as representative of the "Kingdom of God" separate from the State and its actions and as a witness for peace and justice where it ministers.

26. James Guth, John Green, Corwin Smidt, and Lyman Kellstedt, *The Bully Pulpit: The Politics of Protestant Clergy* (Lawrence, KS: University of Kansas Press, 1997), 194.

27. Bruce Cromwell, "Church-State Relations," Free Methodist Conversations (October 15, 2018), at https://freemethodistconversations.com/relationship-between-church-and-state/.

In the longest and most recent of its positions regarding social ethics, the Church of the Nazarene has officially stated the following:

> **Affirmation and Declaration of Human Freedom.** Whereas, as Nazarenes, we embrace the divine call to a life of holiness, wholeness, and restorative living where all things and all peoples are reconciled to God. In response, the Holy Spirit brings freedom to the marginalized, oppressed, broken, and hurting, and justice to right injustices and cease selfish influence caused by sin, until all things are restored in God's reign.
>
> Consistent with our Wesleyan-holiness heritage and character, we confront the contemporary scourge of modern slavery, illegal or forced labor, and the trafficking of human beings and bodies.[28]

Following this declaration is a long list that promotes justice in the future, repentance for past actions, fighting against slavery and human trafficking, advocacy for the marginalized and a number of other like concerns. There is no mention of church-state relations but there is an activist position in the midst of national governance and any issues of unjust action by them without mentioning political relations.

The Salvation Army's International Positional Statement is distinct and direct and reflects the concern of Wesleyan Evangelicals for Scriptural authority, the orienting concern of responsible theology and ministry in world areas and the cause of evangelism.

> The Salvation Army is politically nonpartisan. Although it seeks to influence governmental and public affairs, it will not promote or endorse specific candidates or political parties. In working with any State and its agencies, The Salvation Army seeks to promote Biblical values, including justice, truth, mercy, equity, human rights and peace, as part of its religious convictions and practice.[29]

Education: Each of the three denominations has a commitment to education wherever it is present around the globe and in history. The

---

28. *Manual*, Church of the Nazarene (Kansas City: MO: Nazarene Publishing House, 2017), paragraph 920.

29. The Salvation Army International Positional Statements, 2011, at https://s3.amazonaws.com/cache.salvationarmy.org/412b2aec-575d-4510-8591-d04ecbd20810_English+The+Salvation+Army+and+the+State+IPS.pdf (accessed October 1, 2019).

history of the Salvation Army and its beginnings in England provides a strong connection to the Sunday School movement of the nineteenth century. The Free Methodist Church and the Church of the Nazarene provide for a number of institutions of higher education in the United States and internationally. The *Manual* of the Church of the Nazarene serves as an example and gives insight as to the relationship between social ethics and education for Wesleyan Evangelicals, noting that education is a means to the end of social improvement in that it points to the "value and the dignity of human life and the need for providing an environment in which people can be redeemed and enriched spiritually, intellectually, and physically."[30] Education is one of the redemptive ministries that the local and general church provides for. An interesting point here is the connection of education as social ethic done within the "philosophical and theological framework" of the church. Such pointedness in regard to social and theological significance is maintained by both the Salvation Army and the Free Methodist Churches.

The poor and economics: John Wesley's famous "preferential option for the poor" in Wesleyan circles has proven both an organizing principle and a galvanizing center for Evangelicals in regards to social ethics. While the Church of the Nazarene and the Free Methodist Church maintain strong statements of commitment and ministries to the poor, the commitment of the Salvation Army is the "gold standard" among those churches and provides a witness for all churches to emulate. The witness of the Salvationists to the "least of these" reflects John Wesley's social holiness vision and provides current reflections that guide such ministries. Capitalizing on the Wesleyan theological commitment that all people are created in God's image, the statement on ministering to the poor and those who live in poverty from the International Headquarters of the Army is exemplary:

> The Salvation Army is committed to the alleviation of poverty through humanitarian aid and long-term development in those parts of the world in which it is present. It acknowledges its responsibilities towards others and the need for good stewardship. The Salvation

---

30. *Manual*, Church of the Nazarene (2017), paragraph 400.

Army is committed to addressing the needs of people living in poverty and stands in solidarity with the poor by: defending the right of people living in poverty to play a full part in their communities; advocating that poorer nations should have the opportunity to participate fully in political and economic activity and debate on an international level; speaking out for the needs of the poor when government and corporate policies could cause greater poverty, and also recognising and encouraging positive initiatives; supporting activities that can alleviate the economic burden for people living on a low income; recognising and responding to the particular needs of ethnic and other minority groups who are particularly affected by social and economic disadvantage; implementing and encouraging the provision of education and vocational training, empowering the poor to help themselves out of the poverty trap; listening to, learning from and building relationships with vulnerable groups to ensure people are not stigmatised by their circumstances, but are assisted holistically.

The Salvation Army recognises that it has a corporate responsibility to live out the gospel and Christ's call to care for the poor, and it encourages individual Salvationists to share in the discharge of that responsibility according to their means.[31]

Ethnic relations: The positions on ethnic relations among the Wesleyan Evangelicals, particularly in the United States, in many ways mirrors American history. The Free Methodist Church was founded as an abolitionist church in the decade before the Civil War and championed the freeing of enslaved people in the United States. All three churches have struggled toward integration and equality among the races in both social services and local churches during the Civil Rights movement and beyond. The recounting of those histories, often filled with stories of disappointment, are the stuff of dissertations and history books and are well worth reading as cautionary tales and reminders of denominational failures in regards to race and ethnic relations.[32]

---

31. The Salvation Army Positional Statement, "Poverty," https://www.salvationarmy.org.uk/files/povertypdf/download?token=ZlhStWP2 (accessed October 1, 2019).

32. For the difficult history of race relations in the Church of the Nazarene see Charles Perabeau, "The Church of the Nazarene in the U.S.: Race, Gender, and Class in the Struggle with Pentecostalism and Aspirations Toward Respectability, 1895–1985" (Ph.D. diss., Drew University, 2011).

The current positions of the three denominations all affirm the dignity of all persons and the imperative to promote racial understanding and harmony.[33] The Salvation Army's statement on ethnic and cultural diversity is, perhaps, the most forward thinking of those positions. Beyond being a statement that is clearly informed by Wesleyan theological commitments, it has also created a policy in regards to the treatment of all persons the church serves.

> In response to the gospel, The Salvation Army is committed to upholding and respecting the dignity of each person. We seek to empower each person to celebrate their uniqueness in Christ. In our worship, our community work and our social service we are challenged to welcome, embrace and discover innovative ways to develop and draw upon the rich variety of experience and gifts which ethnic and cultural diversity brings to the body of Christ. We recognise that when this happens in practice, our worshipping community is enriched, our community and social endeavour is strengthened and the values of the Kingdom of God are demonstrated. The Salvation Army opposes any attitude or discriminatory practice which denies the God-given value of any person. We strive to uphold justice for every person and will take positive action to combat stereotyping, prejudice, marginalisation, unjust discrimination, racism, exploitation, and oppression. The Salvation Army has in place an Equality, Diversity and Human Rights Policy and Procedure. This is designed to provide a framework for monitoring the delivery of our services to ensure that these are consistently relevant and accessible to the diverse needs of the people we are seeking to serve or whom we employ.[34]

It is important to note that the crafting of these statements and their implementation reflects national and local governmental requirements in the countries where Wesleyan Evangelicals serve.

There is no holiness but social holiness. The grammatical construction of that sentence has no "and" and includes a larger conjunction that brings with it greater responsibility as the promise of

---

33. See, e.g., *Manual*, Church of the Nazarene (2017), paragraph 915.
34. The Salvation Army Positional Statement, "Ethnic and Cultural Diversity," 2015, https://www.salvationarmy.org.uk/files/ethnicandculturaldiversitypdf/download?token=-3h1wR8V (accessed October 1, 2019).

consideration. The consideration of our ethical responsibility for Wesleyan Evangelicals means the combined weight of theological commitments (really imperatives) even in denominational structures, histories well-marked and judgmental, and the insights of our academics as a mark of our faithfulness to God who is perfecting us by his grace. May this dialogue be a considerate and responsible testimony to that work.

SECTION 4.
Moral Life and Eschatology

4.0. Common Statement on the Moral Life and Eschatology

1. Catholics and Evangelicals affirm that the moral life has as its goal conformity to the image of Christ, communion with the Triune God, and final beatitude to the praise of His glory (Romans 8:29).

2. Evangelicals and Catholics affirm that our life in Christ will be characterized by good works and the fruit of the Spirit (Galatians 5:22–24, Ephesians 2:10). We are to live lives of holiness without which no one will see the Lord (Hebrews 12:14).

3. Evangelicals and Catholics affirm that our sinful works can lead to hell and eternal separation from God (1 Corinthians 6:9, Galatians 5:21).
    i. Catholics affirm those who die in personal "mortal sin" enter hell. However, there is some sin that does not lead to hell which Catholics call "venial sin" (1 John 5:17).
    ii. Evangelicals reject the language of mortal and venial sin.
        i. Some Evangelicals believe that there are some sins for those who are in Christ that do not lead to hell.
        ii. Some Evangelicals hold that all sins merit hell.

4. Catholics and Evangelicals affirm that immediately after death, a divine judgment takes place that immutably decides each person's eternal destiny to either heaven or hell (Hebrews 9:27).

5. Evangelicals and Catholics affirm that at the final judgment, consistent with the judgment immediately after death, each person

shall be judged according to the works done in this life (Romans 2:6, 2 Corinthians 5:10).

6. Catholics and Evangelicals agree that the final judgment is according to works, but they differ in their understanding of how works do or do not contribute to eternal destiny.
    i. Catholics affirm that the justified individual is able to cooperate with the grace of God in such a way that she or he is able to "merit" eternal life.
    ii. Evangelicals hold that good works of the justified do not "merit" eternal life.

7. Evangelicals and Catholics agree that all the saved receive glory and reward in eternal life, and that the degree of glory and reward in eternal life is apportioned according to each one's good works enabled by God's grace (Matthew 25:15–23, Revelation 22:12).

8. Evangelicals and Catholics affirm that the secrets of all people will be revealed on the last day (Mark 4:22) and their works tested as by fire (1 Corinthians 3:12–15).

9. Catholics and Evangelicals affirm that before entering eternal glory the faithful must be cleansed of all unrighteousness (Revelation 21:27).
    i. Catholics affirm that the justified who at the moment of death have either venial sin and/or temporal punishment due to sin enter purgatory. The justified souls in purgatory are certain of their salvation and when their period of purgation is completed they will attain beatitude.
    ii. Some Evangelicals affirm that the doctrine of purgatory is contrary to Scripture; others affirm that it is not found in Scripture.

Catholics and Evangelicals, walking together with Christ, spur one another toward love and good works as we look toward the return of Christ in Glory (Hebrews 10:24).

4.1. "What must I do to be saved?": The Power of Grace, the Moral Life, and Eschatology in Catholic Doctrine and Theology

Dr. Christian D. Washburn

In the Gospel of Matthew, Jesus is asked by the rich young man, "Teacher, what good deed must I do to have eternal life?" (Matt 19:16).[1] The Catholic Church teaches that grace is so powerful and transformative that Jesus' answer, "Keep the commandments," is in fact possible for him who is justified by the grace of God. This chapter will discuss the power of grace, which for the Catholic is such that it can expel sin and transform the believer into a new creation who, with the help of grace, can observe the commandments and merit eternal life. To this end, the chapter will first explain the Catholic Church's teaching on the grace of the first man, original sin, and the power of unaided fallen man to know and to do good. The chapter will next treat of the Catholic Church's doctrine of the justification of the sinner as a transition from the state of sin to the state of justice, emphasizing its twofold dimension as both the forgiveness of sin and the internal renovation of man. This renovation is such that once man is engrafted into Christ, he can keep the commandments and live a life in conformity with the will of God. Next, the chapter will discuss the Catholic Church's doctrine on the justified man's ability to merit grace and eternal life. Finally it will discuss the eschatological consequences of not fulfilling the law.

---

1. All Scripture references are to the *ESV Study Bible* (Wheaton: Crossway, 2008).

The Powers of the Fallen Intellect and Will without Grace

Man was originally "constituted" in a state of friendship with God. In this state, God bestowed on man several supernatural and preternatural gifts. Man, however, disobeyed God and lost his friendship with him, along with the corresponding supernatural and preternatural gifts. What are the powers of the fallen intellect and will without grace? Concerning the powers of the unaided intellect, the magisterium has maintained that man can know some moral truth without the assistance of grace. In *Unigenitus Dei Filius* (1713), Clement XI rejected the Jansenist proposition that without faith we are in total darkness.[2] Later, Vatican I defined against both Traditionalism and atheism that the one true God, our Creator and Lord, can "be known with certainty with the natural light of reason through the things that are created."[3] These natural moral and religious truths, however, are difficult to discover without the gift of grace. Catholic theologians generally hold that only a few, after arduous intellectual work, and with an admixture of error, would discover these truths.[4] Theologians generally hold that "in the state of fallen nature the light of practical reason was not so extinguished" in man that he could not know some moral truths with only the general help of God, although he is often mistaken when divine guidance is absent.[5]

Concerning the powers of the unaided will, Trent began its canons on justification, like its canons on original sin, with a condemnation

---

2. Heinrich Denzinger, Peter Hünermann, Helmut Hoping, Robert L. Fastiggi, and Anne Englund Nash, eds., *Compendium of Creeds, Definitions, and Declarations on Matters of Faith and Morals*, 43rd ed. (San Francisco: Ignatius, 2012) (hereafter DH), 2448, 2441.

3. DH 3026.

4. Thomas Aquinas, *Summa Theologiae* (hereafter, *ST*) I, q. 1, a. 1. English translations of the *ST* in this chapter are taken from *Summa Theologica*, 3 vols., trans. Fathers of the English Dominican Province (New York: Benziger, 1947).

5. Robert Bellarmine, SJ, *Disputationes Roberti Bellarmini Politiani Societatis Jesu, de Controversiis Christianae Fidei, adversus hujus temporis Haereticos* (Paris: Triadelphorum, 1613), 15.1.5.2, vol. 4, col. 586; 15.1.5.9, vol. 4, col. 605. Domingo de Soto, *De natura & gratia. Quod opus ab ipso authore denuo recognitum est, nonnullisque in locis emendatum, & apologia contra reverendum episcopum Catharinum auctum* (Paris: Apud Ioannem Foucher et excudebat Ioannes Gemet, 1549), 10.

of Pelagianism. Trent anathematized anyone who claims that "man can be justified before God by his own works, whether done by his own natural powers or through the teaching of the law, without divine grace through Jesus Christ."[6] The council went on to condemn those who say that "divine grace through Christ Jesus is given for this only, that man may be able more easily to live justly and to merit eternal life, as if by free will without grace he is able to do both, though with hardship and difficulty."[7] Finally, in canon 3, the council condemned those who say "that without the predisposing inspiration of the Holy Ghost and without His help, man can believe, hope, love, or be repentant as he ought, so that the grace of justification may be bestowed upon him."[8] What is clear from Trent's condemnation is that both Semi-Pelagianism and Pelagianism are formally excluded and that divine grace then is not merely a help but a *sine qua non* for living a properly ordered Christian life.

Catholic theologians have specified some types of ungraced acts as completely beyond man's capacity *per se*. For example, one cannot believe God's word or the mysteries of faith.[9] Nor can an unbeliever, by his own powers of natural reason alone, believe as he ought to believe, even if he understands the value of the evidence concerning the Christian religion.[10] Concerning supernatural acts, Catholic theologians deny that man, by the power of the human will and without the special grace of God, is able to desire or to do anything affecting his salvation.[11] Nor is man able by his own strength to dispose himself to receive grace or to do something on account of which God would confer grace.[12] Man is not able to love God either perfectly or imperfectly as the author of nature without the special grace of God.[13] Finally, while man may do some morally good works without

---

6. DH 1551.
7. DH 1552.
8. DH 1553.
9. Bellarmine, *De Controversiis*, 15.1.4.1, vol. 4, col. 547.
10. Bellarmine, *De Controversiis*, 15.1.6.2, vol. 4, col. 677; 15.1.6.3, vol. 4, col. 681.
11. Bellarmine, *De Controversiis*, 15.1.6.4, vol. 4, col. 683.
12. Bellarmine, *De Controversiis*, 15.1.6.5, vol. 4, col. 686.
13. This was a contested issue in the sixteenth century. Normally in the scholastic period, the issue was whether one could love God *super omnia* without grace, but the

grace if no temptations are present, man cannot keep any commandment solely by the forces of his nature if temptation is pressing.[14] Before initial justification, man remains "under the power of the devil" and is a "child of wrath."[15]

In addition to being a "child of wrath", one in the state of original sin is also "under the power of death," according to the Council of Trent. By death the council does not mean biological death but rather eternal death.[16] The point is that if one dies in the state of original sin, then one descends immediately to the hell of the damned. Trent here is simply reaffirming what was taught infallibly by other ecumenical councils. The Council of Florence (1439) taught,

> As for the souls of those who die in actual mortal sin or *with original sin only* [emphasis mine], they go down immediately to hell, to be punished, however, with different punishments.[17]

The Second Council of Lyons (1274) solemnly taught,

> As for the souls of those who die in mortal sin or *with original sin only* [emphasis mine], they go down immediately to hell, to be punished, however, with different punishments.[18]

According to three ecumenical councils, one does not even have to commit a single mortal sin in order to go to hell. It is sufficient to die in the state of original sin alone to be damned. This is the dire state of the unregenerate souls, according to Catholic doctrine.

---

second question, whether one could love God with a perfect act of natural love, was not always denied. Aquinas denied that man can love God above all things in the state of fallen nature without the grace of God (*gratia sanans*). ST I-II, q. 109, a. 3. See also Domingo Báñez, *Scholastica commentaria in secundam secundae angelici doctoris S. Thomae. Quibus, quae ad fidem, spem, & charitatem spectant; clarissimè explicantur* (Douai: Ex typographia Petri Borremans, 1615), 3:345; Soto, *De natura & gratia*, 88. Bellarmine, *De Controversiis*, 15.1.6.7, vol. 4, col. 691.

14. Bellarmine, *De Controversiis*, 15.1.5.7, vol. 4, col. 600; 15.1.5.9, vol. 4, col. 605.
15. DH 1521.
16. DH 1512.
17. DH 1306.
18. DH 858, cf. 926.

The Absolutely Gratuitous Nature of Man's Initial Justification

Catholics can agree with Evangelicals that the grace of initial justification is entirely gratuitous. According to Catholic doctrine, man is unable by either the observance of the law or through the powers of his own nature to turn to God and merit his own initial justification.[19] The Council of Trent states that "nothing that precedes justification, neither faith nor works, merits the grace of justification."[20] The Council of Trent defines that man's initial justification is:

> not only the remission of sins but the sanctification and renewal of the interior man through the voluntary reception of grace and of the gifts, whereby from unjust, man becomes just, and from enemy a friend, that he may be "an heir in hope of eternal life" [Tit 3:7].[21]

There are two aspects to this initial justification: 1. the remission of sins, and 2. sanctification or "the renewal of the interior man through the voluntary reception of grace and of the gifts."[22] The remission of sins is such that "all that is sin in the true and proper sense" is taken away by the grace conferred in baptism and that in justification man is made "innocent, immaculate, pure, guiltless and beloved sons of God."[23] The remission of sins is not merely a non-imputation of sin to the sinner. Furthermore, the interior renewal of man is such that it is not the mere imputation of righteousness to the justified, but rather

---

19. DH 1521.
20. DH 1532.
21. DH 1528.
22. Bellarmine, *De Controversiis*, 15.2.2.6, vol. 4, col. 818.
23. DH 1515. See also the Council of Trent: "Si quis per Iesu Christi Domini nostri gratiam, quæ in baptismate confertur, reatum originalis peccati remitti negat; aut etiam asserit, non tolli totum id, quod veram et propriam peccati rationem habet, sed illud dicit tantum radi aut non imputari: anathema sit." DH 1515. The ongoing presence of sin in the justified is perhaps one of the most contentious issues and one not fundamentally resolved with respect to the *Joint Declaration on the Doctrine of Justification*. It is difficult to see, in light of the clear and infallible teaching of the magisterium, how this issue does not still remain a church-dividing issue. See Pontifical Council for Promoting Christian Unity, *Response of the Catholic Church to the Joint Declaration of the Catholic Church and the Lutheran World Federation on the Doctrine of Justification*, 1; Cardinal Avery Dulles, SJ, "Justification: The Joint Declaration," *Josephinum* 9 (2002): 113.

grace is "poured forth in their hearts by the Holy Ghost and remains in them."[24] This is why Trent frequently speaks of grace "inhering" in the soul of the justified. One can immediately see the fundamental difference in the doctrine of grace between some Protestant theologies of justification and the Catholic Church's. The Catholic Church is close to many Protestant ecclesial communities with respect to what can be accomplished before man's initial justification, i.e., man is incapable of turning himself toward God without grace. In one's initial justification, however, there is a kind of elevation of man that takes place in being transformed from an enemy of God to his friend and by being engrafted into Christ.[25]

The Good Works of the Justified and the Catholic Concept of Merit

What is the consequence of this doctrine of initial justification? Man can fulfill the law in Christ Jesus. Trent is clear that "nothing further is wanting to the justified for them to be regarded as having entirely fulfilled the divine law."[26] Trent adds that "for, while we can do nothing of ourselves as of ourselves, we can do everything with the cooperation of him who strengthens us [cf. Phil 4:13]."[27] We can see the power of grace in the Catholic doctrine of merit.

Trent speaks of eternal life both as a grace mercifully promised to the sons of God in their initial justification through Christ Jesus and as a reward promised by God for the good works and merits of the justified.[28] Thus one has a kind of twofold claim on heaven which is due to the justice of God, who is faithful to his divine promise,

---

24. DH 1561.
25. DH 1530.
26. DH 1546.
27. DH 1691. Some contemporary Catholics have called for a new pastoral solution concerning "the problem of the divorced and remarried" in the Catholic Church. This new solution involves the partners in a second marriage not living as brother and sister but instead continuing to engage in the marital act. One of the basic assumptions of this new proposal is the assumption that chastity is not possible for those who find themselves in such a situation. Trent makes it clear that chastity is possible. As Trent teaches: "God does not command the impossible." DH 1536.
28. DH 1545.

which he has extended to man in initial justification, and to what he has bound himself (irrevocably agreed to) in relation to man's works. Thus, it is a matter not only of justice, but ultimately and principally, the justice of God.

Lutheran theologians argued that merit, understood as a right to a reward, presupposes that man can make a claim on God in justice, but God is not a debtor to any person.[29] In response, the Council of Trent defined that:

> If anyone shall say that the good works of the man justified are in such a way the gifts of God that they are not also the good merits of him who is justified, or that the one justified by the good works, which are done by him through the grace of God and the merit of Jesus Christ (whose living member he is), does not truly merit increase of grace, eternal life, and the attainment of that eternal life (if he should die in grace), and also an increase of glory: let him be anathema.[30]

It will be helpful to break this canon down into its constituent pieces to understand what the council intended.[31]

First, the subject of the canon is the "justified man" who, by his justification, has become a member of Christ. Trent rejected any view

---

29. "We cannot, by our best works, merit pardon of sin, or eternal life at the hand of God, by reason of the great disproportion that is between them and the glory to come, and the infinite distance that is between us and God, whom by them we can neither profit, nor satisfy for the debt of our former sins; but when we have done all we can, we have done but our duty, and are unprofitable servants; and because, as they are good, they proceed from his Spirit; and as they are wrought by us, they are defiled, and mixed with so much weakness and imperfection that they cannot endure the severity of God's judgment." *Westminster Confession*, 16.5 (pp. 600–673 in *The Creeds of Christendom*, ed. Philip Schaff, vol. 3 [New York: Harper & Brothers, 1877], at 634–35). Strikingly, Calvin held that not even Christ's humanity had the capacity to merit, since there "cannot be found in man a worth which could make God a debtor." Calvin, *Institutes*, 2.17.1 (trans. Henry Beveridge [Peabody, MA: Hendrickson, 2008]).

30. "Si quis dixerit hominis iustifati bona opera ita esse dona Dei, ut non sint etiam bona ipsius iustificati merita, aut ipsum iustificatum bonis operibus, quae ab eo per Dei gratiam et Iesu Christi meritum (cuius vivum membrum est) fiunt, non vere mereri augmentum gratiae, vitam aeternam et ipsius vitae aeternae (si tamen in gratia decesserit) consecutionem, atque etiam gloriae augmentum: a.s." DH 1582.

31. On the historical development of canon 32 at the council, see Christian D. Washburn, "Transformative Power of Grace and Condign Merit at the Council of Trent," *The Thomist* 79 (2015): 173–212.

that simply reduces our justice to the justice of Christ; however, the council was clear that "our justice" is not "considered as coming from us."[32] It is precisely the infusion of sanctifying grace and the engrafting into Christ which makes one able to merit. Moreover, the decree makes it clear that, aside from sanctifying grace, Christ's influence always "precedes, accompanies, and follows" the good actions of a justified man.[33]

Second, the council fathers anathematized those who say that merits are understood merely as the gift of God. They deliberately phrased this canon in Augustinian terminology.[34] Both Luther and Seripando had suggested that merits were not properly the merits of the one justified but rather were imputed to him from Christ. Canon 32 is quite clear that each merit is truly and properly "the good merits of him who is justified" and thus the result of the activity of the agent. This teaching is a corollary to chapter 16's assertion that even the justice one receives in justification is not only "called ours" but is "our own personal justice" since it inheres in us.[35]

Third, one should note the use of the phrase "truly merit," *vere mereri*. The fathers of Trent almost without exception were convinced

---

32. DH 1547.

33. DH 1546.

34. *Dictionnaire de théologie catholique* (Paris: Letouzey et Ané, 1899–1950), s.v. "mérite," 759. Augustine on this point is frequently abused for several statements, usually taken out of context, particularly from his Letter 194. Augustine wrote: "When God crowns our merits, He crowns His own gifts." "Quod est ergo meritum hominis ante gratiam, quo merito percipiat gratiam, cum omne bonum meritum nostrum non in nobis faciat nisi gratia et cum Deus coronat merita nostra, nihil aliud coronet quam munera sua?" (Letter 194, 5.19; CSEL 57.176–214). Some argue that Augustine was quite clear that merit is reducible to grace, citing the following passage: "For, if eternal life is given in return for good works, . . . how is eternal life a grace since grace is not repayment for works, . . . It seems to me, then, that this question can only be resolved if we understand that our good works themselves, for which eternal life is our recompense, also pertain to the grace of God. . . ." (trans. Roland J. Teske, WSA 1/26:83). Augustine also wrote, "If they understood our merits so that they recognized that they were also gifts of God, this view would not have to be rejected." *On Grace and Free Choice*, 6.15 (trans. Teske, WSA 1/26:81). Here Augustine was really describing the dual agency that takes place in merit. By affirming that "our merits" are "also" the gifts of God, he did not say that they are exclusively the "gifts of God."

35. "propria nostra iustitia" and "iustitia nostra dicitur." DH 1547.

that the merit inherent in good works is a true *meritum*, based upon divine justice. They purposely employed the term *vere* to exclude the *quasi* merit which, in the technical terminology of the Schools, is called *meritum de congruo*. This phrase is even more significant when one realizes that it was used prior to the Reformation against the Scotists, whose "*mereri* was not *vere mereri*."[36]

Catholic theologians generally enumerate seven conditions necessary to accomplish a meritorious work. Four of these have reference to the meritorious work itself, two to the agent who performs it, and one to God who gives the reward.[37] The first four are obvious and universally admitted by Catholic theologians: the work must be 1. morally good, 2. done with a free will, 3. done to honor and serve God, and 4. accompanied by actual grace. I will discuss each of these individually.

For an act to be morally good, the following three conditions must obtain. First, the object of the act must be good.[38] Second, the end or the intention of the agent must be good. Third, its circumstances must be good. For an action to be good, it must be good in every respect, and if any of these three are evil, the act as such is evil, thus the expression, "A thing to be good must be wholly so; it is vitiated by any defect" (*Bonum ex integra causa, malum ex quocumque defectu*).

---

36. C. Feckes, *Die Rechtfertigungslehre des Gabriel Biel und ihre Stellung innerhalb der nominalistischen Schule* (Münster i.W.: Verlag der Aschendorffschen Verlagsbuchh, 1925), 84, note 251, cited in Hubert Jedin, *Papal Legate at the Council of Trent, Cardinal Seripando*, trans. Frederic Eckhoff (St. Louis: B. Herder Book Co., 1947), 364.

37. Joseph Pohle, *Grace: Actual and Habitual: A Dogmatic Treatise*, ed. Arthur Preuss (St. Louis: B. Herder Book Co., 1929), 410.

38. John Paul II affirmed the fundamental importance of the object of the act when he wrote, "The morality of the human act depends primarily and fundamentally on the 'object' rationally chosen by the deliberate will, as is borne out by the insightful analysis, still valid today, made by Saint Thomas. . . . And Saint Thomas observes that 'it often happens that man acts with a good intention, but without spiritual gain, because he lacks a good will. Let us say that someone robs in order to feed the poor: in this case, even though the intention is good, the uprightness of the will is lacking. Consequently, no evil done with a good intention can be excused. "There are those who say: And why not do evil that good may come? Their condemnation is just" (*Rom* 3:8).'" John Paul II, *Veritatis splendor*, pp. 674–771 in *The Papal Encyclicals of John Paul II*, ed. J. Michael Miller (Huntington, IN: Our Sunday Visitor, 1996), §78.

Thus some acts are always intrinsically evil, and these include abortion, homosexual acts, contraceptive acts, adultery, fornication, lying, and drunkenness.[39] Neither a good intention nor a good set of circumstances can ever render these intrinsically evil acts good, and as such there is no set of circumstances under which they would be meritorious before God. These acts always

> remain "irremediably" evil acts; per se and in themselves they are not capable of being ordered to God and to the good of the person. . . . Consequently, circumstances or intentions can never transform an act intrinsically evil by virtue of its object into an act 'subjectively' good or defensible as a choice.[40]

So, too, a bad intention or bad circumstance always renders evil even an intrinsically good act.

Second, the act must be a human act (*actus humanus*) done with free will. The act must be free from natural necessity arising from an intrinsic principle or from an extrinsic principle. If an act is done without a free will, then it cannot be described as a moral act. That free will is necessary for a reward is clear from biblical texts regarding merit, which assume that works do not have to be done and are therefore voluntary.[41] For example, many things such as the sun, vineyards, gardens, and beasts of burden all actively provide goods to man; yet none of these merits a reward from man because they act without freedom. So too an act of man that is not a human act, such as digesting or breathing, cannot be meritorious because one does not usually choose to breathe or digest food. Equally, evil acts, if they are done without freedom, deserve no punishment, since they would not be morally evil acts; for the same reason, good works done without freedom do not deserve a reward.[42]

---

39. Catholics consider the acts listed by Paul in 1 Cor 6:9–10 as all intrinsically evil: "Or do you not know that the unrighteous will not inherit the kingdom of God? Do not be deceived; neither the sexually immoral, nor idolaters, nor adulterers, nor men who practice homosexuality, nor thieves, nor the greedy, nor drunkards, nor revilers, nor swindlers will inherit the kingdom of God."
40. John Paul II, *Veritatis splendor*, §81.
41. Bellarmine, *De Controversiis*, 15.2.5.10, vol. 4, col. 993.
42. Bellarmine, *De Controversiis*, 15.2.5.10, vol. 4, col. 994.

Third, the meritorious act must not only be done with a morally good intention but must be done with the intention to honor and serve God. Fourth, the work must be accomplished with the help of actual grace.[43] Actual grace is simply a transient divine assistance that enlightens the mind or strengthens the will to perform supernaturally good works that lead to heaven. This grace must precede, accompany, and follow a good work for it to be a meritorious work.

There are two conditions for merit that pertain to the agent who performs it. First, the act must be accomplished by a man who is a wayfarer. Catholic doctrine is clear in teaching that death is the end of the probationary period in which one can either merit or demerit, since the human soul undergoes judgment immediately after death.[44] Second, Catholics understand that being in the state of grace is absolutely necessary for merit. By this, Catholics mean that only those who are justified may merit. This was affirmed dogmatically at Trent and, as we saw above, is based on scriptural texts, such as: "As the branch cannot bear fruit by itself, unless it abides in the vine, neither can you unless you abide in me. I am the vine; you are the branches. Whoever abides in me and I in him, he it is that bears much fruit, for

---

43. Bellarmine, *De Controversiis*, 15.2.5.10, vol. 4, col. 993.

44. Franc. X. De Abarzuza, OFM Cap., *Manuale Theologiae Dogmaticae*, 2nd ed. (Madrid: Ediciones Studium, 1956), 2:401; Louis Billot, *Quaestiones de novissimis* (Rome: Gregorian University Press, 1946), 9. Garrigou-Lagrange noted, "This common doctrine has not been solemnly defined, but is based on Scripture and tradition." Reginald Garrigou-Lagrange, OP, *Life Everlasting*, trans. Patrick Cummins, OSB (St. Louis: B. Herder, 1952), 62; J. M. Hervé, *Manuale Theologiae Dogmaticae*, 16th ed. (Westminster, MD: The Newman Bookshop, 1943), 4:553; Sylvester Joseph Hunter, SJ, *Outlines of Dogmatic Theology* (London: Longmans, Green and Co., 1896), 3:427; Bernhard Jungmann, *Tractatus de novissimis* (Ratisbonæ: F. Pustet, 1874), 8; Heinrich Lennerz, *De novissimis* (Rome: Universitas Gregoriana, 1950), 100; Ludwig Ott, *Fundamentals of Catholic Dogma*, ed. James Canon Bastible, trans. Patrick Lynch (St. Louis: B. Herder Book Company, 1958), 474–75; Christian Pesch, *Praelectiones Dogmaticae*, 3rd ed. (Freiburg im Breisgau: B. Herder, 1911), 9:278–80; Joseph Pohle, *Eschatology or the Catholic Doctrine of the Last Things: A Dogmatic Treatise*, adapt. and ed. Arthur Preuss (St. Louis: B. Herder Book Co., 1929), 13–17; Iosepho F. Sagüés, SJ, "De novissimis hominis," 4:827–1030 in Iosepho A. de Aldama, SJ, Richardo Franco, SJ, Severino Gonzalez, SJ, Francisco A. P. Sola, SJ, Iosepho F. Sagüés, SJ, *Sacrae Theologiae Summa*, 4th ed. (Madrid: Biblioteca de Autores Cristianos, 1967), 4:839; Adolphe Tanquerey, *Synopsis Theologiae Dogmaticae*, 27th ed. (Paris: Desclée et Socii, 1953), 3:769.

apart from me you can do nothing" (John 15:4-5). This engrafting into Christ is considered the *sine qua non* of merit.

Lastly, and most importantly, there must be a promise from God to accept good acts done in a state of grace as worthy of heaven. The Council of Trent described eternal life "as a reward promised by God Himself."[45] Saint Pius V explicitly condemned Baius's proposition which denied that a special promise of God was necessary for the works of the righteous to deserve eternal life. For Baius, "Just as an evil work by its nature is deserving of eternal death, so a good work by its own nature is meritorious of eternal life."[46] In the Scriptures God often promises man an eternal reward for his works and eternal punishment for his mortal sins. Moreover, good works, if we consider only their nature, have no proportion to supernatural beatitude. As Saint Thomas Aquinas explained, "If it is considered as regards the substance of the work, and inasmuch as it springs from the free-will, there can be no condignity because of the very great inequality."[47] This beatitude cannot therefore be due in justice to morally good works. God has no need of our works, and all good works are due to him by virtue of his right of creation. He is not therefore obliged to grant one a reward.[48] Nonetheless, God can and does bind himself to his own promises.

The Object of Merit for the Justified

The question remains, what can and cannot be merited? According to canon 32, there are four objects of merit. First, one may merit an increase in grace; second, one may merit eternal life; third, one may merit the attainment of eternal life; and finally, one may merit an increase in glory.[49] Catholic theologians often look to biblical pas-

---

45. DH 1545/809.
46. DH 1902/1002.
47. Thomas Aquinas, *ST* I-II, q. 114, a. 3.
48. Bellarmine, *De Controversiis*, 15.5.14, vol. 4, cols. 1002-3.
49. Otto Hermann Pesch, "The Canons of the Tridentine Decree on Justification," 175-216 in *Justification by Faith: Do the Sixteenth-Century Condemnations Still Apply?*, ed. Karl Lehmann (New York: Continuum, 1997), 190f.

sages to support this understanding, such as Paul's claim that "I have fought the good fight, I have finished the race, I have kept the faith. Henceforth there is laid up for me the crown of righteousness, which the Lord, the righteous judge, will award to me on that day, and not only to me but also to all who have loved his appearing" (2 Tim 4:7–8). Here we see the actual eschatological significance of merit, which has as its end not merely a good work but a good work which is ordered to attaining eternal beatitude. It must be recalled that according to Catholic doctrine, one may not merit the initial actual grace, initial justification, restoration from a fall due to mortal sin, or final perseverance. God's activity always precedes that of man.

Even though we can merit heaven when we are in a state of grace, the spiritual disposition of properly formed Catholics is not to rely on our merits. In the sixteenth century, Saint Robert Bellarmine, SJ, one of the greatest defenders of the Catholic doctrine of merit, wrote in his will: "First, therefore, I desire with all my heart to have my soul commended into the hands of God, whom from my youth I have desired to serve. And I beseech Him, not as the valuer of merit, but as a giver of pardon, to admit me among his Saints and Elect."[50] In the face of God's judgment and God's grace, we stand as persons dependent on God's mercy and gifts. We hope not in ourselves but in God, who is surely faithful to his promises.

The Reward for Good Works Performed: Heaven

According to Catholic doctrine, immediately after death the soul is subject to the particular judgment, in which God judges the soul and immutably determines the soul's eternal destiny.[51] This is seen in Sacred Scripture, for example, when Lazarus is immediately after death taken into the bosom of Abraham and the rich man is

---

50. James Brodrick, *The Life and Work of Blessed Robert Francis Cardinal Bellarmine, S. J., 1542–1621* (London: Longmans, Green, 1950), 2:441. Cited in *The Hope of Eternal Life: Common Statement of the Eleventh Round of the U.S. Lutheran-Catholic Dialogue*, ed. Lowell G. Almen and Richard J. Sklba (Minneapolis: Lutheran University Press, 2011), 119.

51. DH 1000–1002.

immediately sent to hell (Luke 16:22ff). Another example is when Christ on the cross says to Dismas, the penitent thief, that "today you will be with me in paradise" (Luke 23:43). Justification is the root of salvation so that in the Scriptures the justified on earth are said to have eternal life now (John 3:16) and the guarantee of an inheritance (2 Cor 1:22; 5:5). According to the Council of Florence the souls of the justified, who at the moment of death are free from all guilt of either mortal or venial sin and of the punishment due to sin "are received immediately into heaven and see clearly God himself."[52] This beatific vision of man is that clear and intuitive, but not comprehensive, knowledge of God as he is in himself.

The Council of Florence also teaches that the souls of those who attain beatitude see God "though some more perfectly than others, according to the diversity of merits."[53] The Catholic Church sees this teaching as grounded in the Sacred Scriptures, where heaven is presented as a reward that corresponds to one's work: "each will receive his wages according to his labor" (1 Cor 3:8), and "whoever sows sparingly will also reap sparingly, and whoever sows bountifully will also reap bountifully" (2 Cor 9:6:), and "For the Son of Man is going to come with his angels in the glory of his Father, and then he will repay each person according to what he has done" (Matt 16:27). Moreover, this inequality in heaven is based in part on the scriptural teaching of 1 Corinthians 15:40–41. Here Saint Paul speaks of the difference between celestial bodies and terrestrial bodies. Thus, Saint Paul writes, "There is one glory of the sun, and another glory of the moon, and another glory of the stars; for star differs from star in glory" (1 Cor 15:41).

This beatitude can be divided into essential and accidental happiness. Essential beatitude consists in the vision of God, the love of God, and the joy of God. This essential beatitude is unequal not with respect to the object of that beatitude but with respect to one's participation in that vision.[54] Man's intellect is naturally incapable of

---

52. DH 1305.
53. DH 1305.
54. Sagüés, *Sacrae Theologiae Summa*, 4:893.

having this vision, and so a new supernatural faculty, *lumen gloriae*, is bestowed on man to allow him to have this vision of God. Man's will now loves God perfectly, which ultimately involves a freedom from evil, either physical or moral.[55]

In addition to this essential beatitude, there is also the accidental happiness of beatitude, which proceeds from the natural knowledge and love of created things.[56] Accidental beatitude is also unequal, corresponding to the graced good acts that one has done in this life. Part of accidental beatitude is the three classes of *aureolae*, i.e., little golden crowns bestowed on the blessed. These are to be contrasted with the great crown, which is beatitude itself. These little crowns are not to be understood as actual crowns, but rather as a special joy in the perfection of saints' works on earth as pleasing to God. These *aureolae* are granted as a reward for an exceptional special conformity to Christ:[57] the martyrs for their victory over the world, the virgins for their victory over the flesh, and the teachers of the faith for their victory over the devil, who is the father of all lies.[58] This ordering of the *aureolae* is a matter of excellence so that one accidental gift of beatitude is greater than another. Thus, the death of the martyr most closely conforms him to Christ, while the subduing of the flesh of the virgin has a certain likeness to martyrdom that is greater than that of the teacher of the faith.[59] In addition to these *aureolae* are the "fruits." These are special joys bestowed on virgins, widowed persons, and faithful spouses for the practice of continence in this life.

The Punishment for Evil Works: Purgatory

Purgatory is based in part on two biblical doctrines: 1. there are non-mortal sins and temporal punishment due to sin which require expiation, and 2. only the clean can enter heaven. Mortal sins break

---

55. Thomas Aquinas, *Summa contra gentiles*, 4.92.
56. Ludwig Ott, *Fundamentals of Catholic Dogma*, 3rd ed. revised and updated by Robert Fastiggi, trans. Patrick Lynch (London: Baronius Press, 2018), 506.
57. Thomas Aquinas, *ST*, Suppl, q. 96, a. 11.
58. Thomas Aquinas, *ST*, Suppl, q. 96, a. 1.
59. Thomas Aquinas, *ST*, Suppl, q. 96, a. 12.

one's relationship with God, but venial sins do not. Venial sins are those sins in which the matter is not grave. The distinction between mortal and venial sins is based on Scripture passages such as "there is sin that does not lead to death" (1 John 5:17). The biblical doctrine that "nothing unclean will ever enter [heaven]" (Rev 21:27) requires that the justified who dies without expiating his venial sin or temporal punishment due to sin must be cleansed before entering heaven. This expiation takes place in purgatory.

There are only two *doctrines* that have been solemnly defined by the magisterium concerning purgatory.[60] First, the magisterium has defined that purgatory (*purgatorium*) exists as the place or the state in which the souls of the just who die with venial sin or the temporal punishment due to sin are purged of this sin and their attachment to sin. Second, the souls therein can be assisted by the faithful on earth. Both of these teachings have been repeatedly and definitively defined at the Second Council of Lyons (1274), the Council of Florence (1431–1449), and the Council of Trent (1563).[61]

Once in purgatory, souls are deprived of the ability to engage in works of satisfaction since their probationary period is over. They can no longer lovingly seek out the cross, uniting their wills with that of Christ's. They are only left with voluntarily accepting and enduring the sufferings offered to them, which theologians call satispassion (*satispassio*). What makes this satispassion effective is the same thing that makes satisfaction effective: union with Christ in divine love.[62] In any case, this suffering unites the souls in purgatory more closely to Christ. Just as satisfaction in the present life not only pays a debt in full but also leads Christians to live a life according to God's will, so too it is with satispassion, for not only is the debt paid through

---

60. Saint Catherine of Genoa, *Purgation and Purgatory; The Spiritual Dialogue*, trans. Serge Hughes (New York: Paulist, 1979).

61. DH 856, 1304, 1820.

62. While satispassion suffices for the remission of temporal punishment (*reatus poenae*), the theologians following Saint Thomas hold that those in purgatory must not just endure suffering but also must perform an act of contrition since in the present economy this is required for the forgiveness of sin (*reatus culpae*). Sagüés, *Sacrae Theologiae Summa*, 4:978, 980.

satispassion, but also the poor souls who undergo this voluntary suffering become more virtuous, and the attachments of the world burn away.

The Punishment for Evil Works: Hell

In Catholic theology the term "hell" (*infernus*) refers to those "secret dwellings in which are detained the souls that are not included in the happiness of Heaven."[63] The term "hell" can refer to four distinct things. First it can refer to the "Bosom of Abraham" or *limbus patrum* in which the souls of the just who died before the death of Christ awaited their liberation and triumphal procession to heaven. Catholics understand that this is the meaning signified in the Apostles' Creed when it is said that Christ "descended to hell" (*descendit ad inferos*). Catholics reject the view of some of the Protestant reformers that Christ descended to the hell of the damned.[64] Second, the term hell can refer to the limbo of the infants (*limbus parvulorum*) in which the children who die with original sin alone suffer natural punishments. Third, the term hell can refer to purgatory, whose sufferings are similar.

Fourth, the term hell can signify the state and place of punishment for the damned.[65] It is this fourth meaning that is considered hell in

---

63. *Catechismus Romanus seu Catechismus ex decreto Concilii Tridentini ad Paraochos Pii Quinti Pont. Max. iussu editus*, ed. Petrus Rodríguez et al. (Vatican City: Libreria Editrice Vaticana/Ediciones Univ. de Navarra, 1989), 70.

64. Bellarmine, *De Controversiis*, 2.4.10, vol. 1, col. 417. On the *Book of Concord*, Bellarmine notes, "Sextus error est, quod totus Christus, Deus & homo, ad inferos descenderit." *Judicium de Libro Concordiae* (Ingolstadt: David Sartorius, 1586), 4:1196. Or as Gregorio de Valencia writes, "Caeterum sententia Ecclesiae Catholicae CERTA & indubitata est, Christum secundum animam vere ac proprie & substantialiter descendisse ad illum saltem locum infernum, qui fuit *limbus* sanctorum Patrum, non minus quam vere etiam ac proprie & substantialiter secundum corpus fuit positus in sepulchro." Gregorio de Valencia, *Commentariorum Theologicorum Tomus Quartus complectens materias Tertiae Partis ac supplementi D. Thomae* (Ingolstadt: David Sartorius, 1592–1597), 4:578. On this issue in the Fathers, see Jared Wicks, SJ, "Christ's Saving Descent to the Dead: Early Witnesses from Ignatius of Antioch to Origen," *Pro Ecclesia* 17 (2008): 281–309.

65. Compare the manuals on this point to *Catechismus Romanus seu Catechismus ex decreto Concilii Tridentini ad Paraochos Pii Quinti Pont. Max. iussu editus*, 70–71.

the strict sense and to which we now turn. According to Catholic doctrine, man may break his friendship with God through mortal sin, thereby losing his justification. Mortal sin is

> the act by which man freely and consciously rejects God, his law, the covenant of love that God offers, preferring to turn in on himself or to some created and finite reality, something contrary to the divine will (*conversio ad creaturam*). This can occur in a direct and formal way, in the sins of idolatry, apostasy and atheism; or in an equivalent way, as in every act of disobedience to God's commandments in a grave matter.[66]

In every mortal sin, man rejects God, substituting the creature for the creator. There are three basic conditions necessary for a mortal sin to occur: 1. grave matter; 2. sufficient reflection; 3. full consent of the will. For the Catholic Church not every sin is mortal, and any sin not meeting these three conditions is merely a venial sin, not a mortal sin.

The consequence of committing a mortal sin and dying in that state is the eternal punishment of hell. Pope Benedict XII (1336) defined that

> According to the general disposition of God, the souls of those who die in actual mortal sin go down into hell immediately after death and there suffer the pains of hell.[67]

This teaching was also taught by two ecumenical councils: the Second Council of Lyons (1274) and the Council of Florence (1447).[68] Of course, one who has committed a mortal sin may, while he still lives, be returned to a state of grace through the sacrament of reconciliation.

There are two essential properties of the punishments of hell. The first of these is that they last for all eternity. This teaching on the eternity of hell and its punishments was repeatedly affirmed by the magisterium both explicitly and implicitly. The Fourth Lateran Council (1215) states that they who have done evil works will receive

---

66. John Paul II, *Reconciliatio et paenitentia* (December 2, 1984) (Washington, DC: United States Catholic Conference, 1984), §17.

67. DH 1002.

68. DH 858, 1306.

"perpetual punishment with the devil," and the Council of Trent repeatedly refers to perpetual punishment, eternal punishment, and eternal damnation.[69] This teaching is based on Sacred Scripture, which frequently describes this punishment as an "eternal fire" (Matt 18:8; 25:41) and an "eternal destruction" (2 Thess 1:9). In the Gospel of Matthew, the "everlasting punishment" of hell is contrasted with "eternal life" that is heaven (Matt 25:46).

The second property of hell is that the punishments of the damned are different from one another and proportioned to each of the damned's demerits. The Second Council of Lyons and the Council of Florence both declare that the souls of the damned are punished with "different (*disparibus*) punishments."[70] Christ teaches that the punishment inflicted on the unbelieving inhabitants of Chorazin and Bethsaida will be worse than the punishment of Tyre and Sidon on the Day of Judgment (Matt 11:22). Saint John says of the corrupt city of Babylon: "Pay her back as she herself has paid back others, and repay her double for her deeds; mix a double portion for her in the cup she mixed. As she glorified herself and lived in luxury, so give her a like measure of torment and mourning" (Rev 18:6–7).

Catholic doctrine asserts that the nature of the punishment of hell for the unjustified is twofold: the pain of loss (*poena damni*) and the pain of sense (*poena sensus*). The pain of loss consists in the exclusion from the beatific vision. This pain of loss is based on biblical passages such as "Depart from me, you cursed!" (Matt 25:41) and "I know you not!" (Matt 25:12). The pain of sense (*poena sensus*), on the other hand, is the suffering caused by material things and is amply testified to in Sacred Scripture, particularly by the use of the term "fire" for this punishment (Matt 13:30–50; Matt 18:8; Mark 9:42ff; Heb 10:27; Rev 18:8). The Catholic Church has understood the term "fire" to refer to real fire in the proper sense as opposed to a metaphorical sense.

Why are these two different types of punishments in hell? There are two explanations for this. First, sins are not performed by disembodied intellects. In some cases, a sin may be entirely interior to

---

69. DH 801, 1575, 1580, 1705.
70. DH 858, 1306; see also DH 926.

the man. In most cases, however, there is an interior act of the intellect and will followed by acts of the body.[71] Second, the types of punishment are proportionate to different aspects of sin. Saint Thomas explains that

> Punishment is proportionate to sin. Now sin comprises two things. First, there is the turning away from the immutable good, which is infinite, wherefore, in this respect, sin is infinite. Secondly, there is the inordinate turning to mutable good. In this respect sin is finite, both because the mutable good itself is finite, and because the movement of turning towards it is finite, since the acts of a creature cannot be infinite. Accordingly, in so far as sin consists in turning away from something, its corresponding punishment is the "pain of loss," which also is infinite, because it is the loss of the infinite good, i.e., God. But in so far as sin turns inordinately to something, its corresponding punishment is the "pain of sense," which is also finite.[72]

Thomas's point is that these two aspects of sin require two different, proportionate, and concomitant types of punishment. Having said this, many Catholic theologians generally teach that God punishes less than what individuals deserve.[73]

Conclusion

According to Catholic doctrine, fallen man is unable, either through the use of the law or the power of nature, to merit initial justification. In the fallen state, man can do a natural morally good work but is completely unable to merit either grace or salvation. Neither faith nor works prior to justification can merit the grace of justification. In the initial justification of the sinner, God gratuitously both forgives sins and transforms the sinner interiorly. Once his sins are forgiven, man becomes a "new creation" who is now "innocent, unstained, pure, and guiltless." In his interior reform, man is not just imputed or called just but is "truly just." Man, now engrafted into Christ, can fulfill the

---

71. Thomas Aquinas, *Summa contra gentiles*, 4.89.
72. Thomas Aquinas, *ST* I-II, q. 87, a. 4.
73. Thomas Aquinas, *ST* I-II, q. 87, a. 3, ad. 3.

law with the grace Christ provides and therefore merit an increase in grace, eternal life, and a higher place in heaven. If he dies in the state of justification and free from all sin, he ascends to heaven. In heaven the faithful will contemplate God face to face. If man dies in the state of grace but still has attachment to sin, he will go to purgatory, where he will be purged of this attachment. If man commits mortal sin and dies in this state, he is unable to obtain beatitude but will descend to the place of the damned.

4.2. Our Moral Life Determines Our After Life: Catholic Notes on the Relationship of the Moral Life to the Last Things

Dr. David P. Fleischacker

I want to start by saying the title is not Pelagian though it may sound so. Making possible the significance of the moral life for eternal life is the life of grace.[1] Hopefully that became clear over the last couple of years in how the Catholic Tradition formulates merit. So, in the light of grace, what I want to articulate is the direct link that God has created between our moral life and the destination he has paved for us into the inner heart of the Holy Trinity and the entire kingdom of God. One alternative way of stating this is that our life has ultimate significance because God has given us the status of pilgrims on earth, and he has made us actors in our own salvation and even that of others. The denial of this fact can help to make this point clear. If we are not actors in any fashion in our salvation or our damnation, then life here on earth has no real significance. And then one is left puzzled by a God who has made anything that is pointless, especially regarding human existence on earth. One further note as well. I deliberately choose to write this from the angle of belief rather than as a third-party account of a position. This is to highlight something that is sometimes forgotten through third-party accounts, namely

---

1. CCC 2007: "With regard to God, there is no strict right to any merit on the part of man. Between God and us there is an immeasurable inequality, for we have received everything from him, our Creator."

that Catholics do not hold these teachings as simply another position among other possible positions but as true. So I apologize if this sounds like a sermon. It is not, in my mind, nor is it meant to be. But it is meant to be an account of a position that is true so that others can know that Catholics hold these truths with certitude. At the same time, I write as a layman, not as a magisterial teacher, and so my own authority is limited to something less than the teaching magisterium upon which I am basing my beliefs and theological positions. Thus, I extensively reference that magisterium but cannot claim the authority of that magisterium.

Recalling the End with an Eye to the Moral Life

What I will do in the next couple of pages with an eye to our moral life in Christ is to recall the main features of Catholic teaching on the end of all things. Those last things include our private judgment at our own death,[2] purgatory,[3] heaven,[4] hell,[5] the final apostasy and passion of the Church,[6] the resurrection of the dead,[7] the return of Israel to faith,[8] the Final Judgment,[9] and Jesus' handing us over as the new heavens and the new earth to his Father.[10]

Let us start with one's own death. The destiny of every human being will be determined and privately revealed at the moment of death.[11] At that moment when one's soul and body are separated, it is the body that dies and the soul that lives on. So one never really dies.[12]

---

2. *CCC* 1021–22.
3. *CCC* 1030–32.
4. *CCC* 1023–29.
5. *CCC* 1033–37.
6. *CCC* 675–77.
7. *CCC* 1038–41.
8. *CCC* 674.
9. *CCC* 678–679, 1038–41.
10. *CCC* 1042–50.
11. *CCC* 1022: "Each man receives his eternal retribution in his immortal soul at the very moment of his death, in a particular judgment that refers his life to Christ: either entrance into the blessedness of heaven—through a purification or immediately—or immediate and everlasting damnation."
12. *CCC* 997.

Now if one's heart at that moment is stony, if it is empty of sanctity, of love of God and neighbor, one will know that one's life has been sealed for eternity with Satan as one's most hateful father. Suffering of the most immense kind awaits one without end. There is no "death do you part." One's mass and momentum for all of eternity will be hatred of all that is good. It will be an eternal dying with no death, as Saint Augustine speculates.[13] And just wait until your body rejoins you so that your damnation can reach its plenitude of suffering, darkness, and hatred.

At the same time, if you still have a spark of holiness in you, a heart that loves God and neighbor at the moment of death, you will know your destiny for heaven as well. As Catholics, we know that it does not guarantee an instant abode in heaven. You might be escorted off to become purified so that you can be perfect like your Father in heaven in order to be with him for all eternity. So, you will need to suffer in purgatory. Your sentence will begin at that moment of death. You will be there until every last penny is paid back. But it is not without hope. True hope. The virtue of hope. Certitude and trust and love in the promise from our Lord that you will be with him for all eternity gives you more happiness than you ever had as a pilgrim. This is true even though you will be in a place that mimics the flames of hell.

But for some who have run the race to the end, whose purging was completed, whose heart was aflame until one's dying breath, and whose life set the world on fire with God's immense love, our Lord will be there with all the saints and angels to greet him as a faithful and trustworthy servant, a brother or sister to him through whom all things were made. He will say, "My kingdom is your inheritance." And this eternal joy begins at death.

That beginning though still awaits the completion that will take place when Jesus hands over a new heaven and a new earth to his Father. In large part, this handing over, this gift of the Son, will be all of his brothers and sisters for whom he prayed and whom he held close to his heart, asking his Father constantly never to lose them. And so he prayed continuously that they not be tempted, that they

---

13. Augustine, Sermon 169, 11.13 (PL 38:923).

be delivered from evil. And now in this final gift, the Father receives them as he receives his own Son.

Between one's death and the final gift are the final days of fallen history. We know that our dead bodies will rise, both of the damned and of those in heaven.[14] We know that Israel will return to the faith. And before these two events, the Church will undergo a passion that is like her Lord's.[15] This persecution is the horrendous end game of Satan and his anti-Christ, the real anti-Christ, who thus far has only been prefigured by such figures as Antiochus IV and Frederick II, and arguably by Hitler and others of his ilk. In short, however, the anti-Christ will lead the parade into the final apostasy and passion of the Church.

That final passion and crucifixion of the Bride of Christ will be a first step that begins to call our Lord to set in motion the procession which leads to his second coming. The passion of the Church is followed by a comprehensive resurrection of all the dead. I am sure that the resurrection of the dead will be most spectacular to those who are still living. Speculation would place that resurrection before the return of Israel because if Abraham, Moses, and King David are walking among us again, all pointing to Jesus as the authentic messiah, what good Israelite would not listen?

The resurrection of the dead is a gathering not to a wedding feast but to a final trial and judgment. And that judgment itself is the light of Truth revealing all things, all hearts, every detail of every moment of every choice and whether that choice was for life or death.[16] It will reveal the full plan of providence and the sinister plan of Satan. It will reveal in the end who has embraced for eternity the Tree of Life and who has refused that gift. Nothing of any heart will remain hidden.[17]

---

14. CCC 998.
15. CCC 677: "The Church will enter the glory of the kingdom only through this final Passover, when she will follow her Lord in His death and resurrection. The kingdom will be fulfilled, then, not by a historic triumph of the Church through a progressive ascendancy, but only by God's victory over the final unleashing of evil, which will cause His Bride to come down from heaven. God's triumph over the revolt of evil will take the form of the Last Judgment after the final cosmic upheaval of this passing world."
16. CCC 1039.
17. CCC 678, 1039.

One imagines, for those standing in love with our Father, the great joy they will experience for being forgiven, a forgiveness that will be vastly magnified in them because their merciful Father has shed forgiveness upon all of their brothers and sisters. One also imagines the intense hatred that will well up in those who swept all sanctity from the core of their souls, including if they hung themselves on a tree in despair because of a failed attempt to undo their sins themselves. Their shame now turns to an eternal hatred for the loving light that shines upon them.

The Moral Life in Relation to the Last Things

So how are we actors in sealing our fate at death, in bringing forth the final persecution, in the passion of the Bride of Christ, in the revelation of our entire existence and history under the Final Judgment, and in the handing of us over to an eternal kingdom (heaven or hell)? The answer is in our freedom. All of our good acts have God as their ultimate cause. But all of our evil acts, our sins, stop with us as cause. God only permits but does not cause sin. This is why sin is ultimately unintelligible. Our good acts are the choosing of life. Our sinful acts are the choosing of death. This is what makes us actors in our salvation. Even when we do evil and God's mercy rains upon us, he still leaves us free to accept that mercy and to be restored in his grace.

MORTAL SIN AND A LIFE ENSLAVED IN HELL

Eternally, every mortal sin is a choice to join the kingdom of hell. And every venial sin is a bow in that direction.[18] And these mortal sins do not need to be outright rejections of God or of the desire for eternal happiness. They can be, of course. One can deliberately refuse to love God with one's whole heart, mind, and soul.[19] But it can consist in not

---

18. CCC 1854–64.

19. Just to recall, all of the Ten Commandments identify acts which are grave, and thus mortal if committed with "full knowledge and deliberate consent" (*CCC* 1857). "Grave matter is specified by the Ten Commandments, corresponding to the answer of Jesus to the rich young man: 'Do not kill, Do not commit adultery, Do not steal,

trusting in him, not having faith in him. It can be in despair against the hope of his promises. It can be an explicit abuse of the sacred name of our God. Taking his name in vain proclaims one's allegiance to Satan. The same with sacred time, that new Sabbath on the day of his resurrection and its celebration in the holy Mass.

Mortal sins can be against one's neighbor. On this front, one must remember that three of the Ten Commandments deal with marriage and family. Not honoring your father and mother, infidelity to your spouse in mind or body all result in your allegiance to Lucifer. To die doing nothing more than trying to fix the damage you have done leaves you no better than Judas. You cannot save yourself and break the just chains that Satan has fixed upon your soul. The same is true, of course, with murder, whether it is a child in a mother's womb or an elderly uncle who is suffering. And even if it is not as obvious as murder, stealing and perjury merit a permanent place with the fallen angels and the men who join them.

One could also review the seven deadly sins and the world of vice to see where each of these leaves you at your death. The bottom line is the same. Our forgiveness requires God's mercy. To be freed, we must choose to be contrite, we must ask for forgiveness with a sincere heart, even if it is just running from hell. The life of moral virtue cannot reconcile, and it cannot restore faith, hope, and love. But even one mortal sin can merit eternal damnation.

THE LIFE OF VIRTUE BINDS US MORE INTIMATELY TO GOD

Nevertheless, the life of virtue does impact us at death. Committing or avoiding mortal sin is not the sole way that we are actors in our salvation. Once God liberates us from our sin, even if by imperfect contrition, the liberation of our hearts can move forward and higher through a purgation that rises into an illumination and is consummated in a unification with our Father. We can grow more deeply as

---

Do not bear false witness, Do not defraud, Honor your father and your mother.' The gravity of sins is more or less great: murder is graver than theft. One must also take into account who is wronged: violence against parents is in itself graver than violence against a stranger" (CCC 1858).

sons and daughters by the Holy Spirit, who binds us to our Brother.[20] And this growth in likeness will result in higher places within the entire kingdom of heaven, higher because one is more intimately united with the Holy Trinity.[21]

As we love our neighbor as ourself; as we reverence God in his Mass on Holy Days; as we cherish his name; as we love him every day with our whole heart, mind, and soul; as our faith, hope, and love grow in prayer and in sacrament; as we grow in honoring our father and mother; as we protect the life of everyone, especially the most vulnerable; as we proclaim the truth even if our livelihood is destroyed or our life is taken; as we respect the goods of others in thought and deed; as we grow in courage, prudence, justice, and temperance; as we grow in understanding, knowledge and wisdom, we become increasingly like him. In this growing likeness, the Holy Spirit will flow more fully and perfectly through us, binding us with greater intimacy to Jesus so that our hands and feet, our minds and will then more perfectly and vigorously beat with his. The greater this intimacy, the greater love with which he will raise us to his Father from his cross.

In other words, those who have grown most like him, washed in baptism, forgiven of sin, fed with his Body and Blood in the Eucharist, healed with his anointing oil, elevated in one's vocation, confirmed in the light of Pentecost, these will be the least on earth, nearly as overlooked and forgotten as the blessed mother who stands in tears and silence at the Cross, and yet the greatest in heaven. They will be elevated to the highest places, the nearest to Jesus, the most intimate friends within the infinite exchange of the Holy Trinity. At their death, Jesus will embrace them more fully, the more fully he abides in them. They will be brought closest to him so that they can lean into his breast with abundant affection flowing from a more complete sharing in his brotherhood. They who hang with him on the Cross, they whose blood is spilt in love for their enemies, will be those who

---

20. *CCC* 2016: "The children of our holy mother the Church rightly hope for the grace of final perseverance and the recompense of God their Father for the good works accomplished with His grace in communion with Jesus."

21. There is also a differentiation of places as well.

receive in the most direct and intimate way the ancient kiss of the Father for his own Son.

At our death, we will know either the depths to which we will descend into the abyss or the heights to which we will ascend into the light and love of the Holy Trinity. The depths and heights of this descent or ascent are conditioned on our moral merits. At the Last Judgment this will be manifested to all.

As well, we will know at that Last Judgment how our moral acts as good or as evil contributed to the procession of good and the parade of evil down through history, including how our sins crucified our Lord. We will see how our sins sent our Lord's bride to her passion on earth at the final apostasy. And because our bodies will be restored, we will feel these contributions to the depths of our bones.

And if we were forgiven, if we were contrite at that last moment of our natural life, we will be thankful that God has forgiven us even of our role in the crucifixion of Jesus and the passion of mother Church. And to the degree that God's goodness can rise up in us to self-sacrificing love, we will be grateful to God for all those he saves through us. He created us without us, but he saves us with us, as Saint Augustine notes. And the more we participate in his salvific plan, the more others come to him through us, the higher he will bring us to himself.

Because our life has ultimate significance, our moral life merits an ultimate destiny. And the power of this moral life has its wellspring in something of greater importance, namely in a decision of faith, a decision to receive his love like Mary did while standing before the Angel Gabriel. Our fiat is the key wellspring that makes us into actors in the salvation of our own lives and in that of others.

If we persevere in our fiat to our end, Jesus then, as his final and last act, will hand us over to his Father. Then the new heavens and the new earth begin. All things will be made new. Every tear and every sorrow will be gone. Death will be no more. Joy will be eternal. The light of the Holy Trinity will be ours, and we will be theirs.

4.3. The Way to Heaven: Wesleyan Ecclesial Ethics and Eschatology

Rev. Bruce Cromwell, PhD and Dr. Steven Hoskins

"I want to know one thing, the way to heaven—how to land safe on that happy shore. God himself has condescended to teach the way: for this very end he came from heaven."
John Wesley, Preface to Sermons on Several Occasions, 1746.[1]

Eighteenth-century England was rife with ecclesiological struggle. If one wanted to vote, attend university, hold any public office, or simply participate in the civil life of the country, one had to subscribe to the Thirty-Nine Articles of Religion of the Church of England. However, John Wesley (1703-1791), raised in an Anglican parsonage and himself an Anglican Divine, had no such list of beliefs required of the people called Methodists as they sought to join his movement. Rather, all that people had to profess in order to join a Methodist society was "a desire to flee from the wrath to come and to be saved from their sins."

While this simple indication was enough for membership in the societies, remaining a member within a Methodist society was a different matter. Members had to exhibit their desire for salvation by following three general rules. First, they must avoid evil in every kind. Second, they must do good in every possible way to every possible person they might encounter. And third, whenever possible they must attend to all the ordinances of God, all the means of grace

---

1. John Wesley, *Sermons on Several Occasions* (London: John Mason, 1838), 12.

presented to them.² Wesley was clear and consistent in saying that true religion entailed more than simply being a good person, going to church, avoiding evil, and the like. But he also was clear and consistent in saying that such actions ought to be at least the minimal marks of any person who is striving to follow Christ. True religion, in other words, must entail more than simply attending to the ordinances of God, being an ethical person, and having good works, but it certainly cannot exist without.³

Wesley's Via Salutis *as Ecclesial Ethics*

In communicating his understanding of true religion to individual followers of Christ, Wesley followed the ethical teaching that dominated the English church of his day conveying the Christian life through the pattern of an *ordo salutis* or a pattern of salvation. For Wesley this was a patterned *via salutis* or way of being saved by God's grace that showed the clear movement in the Christian life from prevenient grace, an awakening that involved knowledge of one's sinfulness and the conviction of judgment, to saving or justifying grace, being justified or forgiven of sins as well as regeneration and the restoration of the image of God in the believer, to sanctifying grace. Together prevenient, saving, and sanctifying grace were the grand drama of what he termed "full salvation" and which Randy Maddox has reminted in his idea of Wesley's "orienting concern" as

---

2. John Wesley, "General Rules of the Methodist Societies," in *The Bicentennial Works of John Wesley:* ed. Frank Baker, et al. (Nashville: Abingdon, 1984ff), 9:69–75. References to Wesley's works all come from the *Bicentennial Edition* unless otherwise noted and will be referred to hereafter simply as *Works*.

3. A few good resources to consider on the general topic of Wesleyan ethics and eschatology include William J. Abraham and James E. Kirby, eds., *The Oxford Handbook of Methodist Studies* (Oxford: Oxford University Press, 2009); Robert Wallace Burtner, *John Wesley's Theology* (Nashville: Abingdon, 1982); Kenneth J. Collins, *The Theology of John Wesley* (Nashville: Abingdon, 2007); S. T. Kimbrough, ed., *Orthodox and Wesleyan Ecclesiology* (Crestwood, NY: St. Vladimir's Seminary Press, 2007); Randy L. Maddox, *Responsible Grace* (Nashville: Kingswood, 1994); and Colin Williams, *John Wesley's Theology Today* (New York: Abingdon, 1960).

"responsible grace" in the life of every believer.[4] Salvation, for him, was greater than a mere momentary experience but, rather, involved a gradual dynamic of growth that extended from awakening until glorification and life in heaven with God. This was evidenced by many of his sermon titles. In 1746, near the beginning of the Methodist revival, he preached "The Way to the Kingdom." In 1765, with the revival in full flower, "The Scripture Way of Salvation" explained the journey. Twenty-two years later, with Methodism already reaching to at least ten countries and approximately one million followers and Wesley being just four years from death, he preached a sermon on "The More Excellent Way."[5] Multiple other examples exist as well. The point is clear: a doctrinal test was not the litmus for whether one could join and remain within the Methodist societies. Rather, it was whether one had an eschatological focus with present implications as one walked with Christ throughout life. To make it to heaven and to do so while bringing heaven to earth was more than just a mantra.

The soteriological intent had specific expectations of the believer and growth in grace was expected even unto the afterlife. Wesley himself spelled this out in his statement in the *Large Minutes* of 1763. When asked, "What was the purpose of God in raising up the Methodist preachers?" he responded, in a well-known and oft-repeated phrase within Methodism around the world, "To reform the nation, especially the Church; and spread scriptural holiness across the land."[6]

This ideal has remained as the goal of Wesley's co-laborers and is echoed in the many denominations that take their theological cues from him. A good example of this can be found in the writings of Benjamin Titus Roberts, the "founder" of the Free Methodist Church. He frequently repeated the heart of Wesley's response, saying that

---

4. Randy Maddox, "Responsible Grace: The Systematic Perspective of Wesleyan Theology," *The Wesleyan Theological Journal* 19, no. 1 (1984): 7–22, at 12–14.

5. These sermons and more on the topic can be found in John Wesley, *John Wesley's Sermons: An Anthology*, eds. Albert Outler and Richard Heitzenrater (Nashville: Abingdon, 1991), 123f., 371f., and 531f. respectively.

6. John Wesley, "The Methodist Societies: The Minutes of the Conference," *Works*, 10:105–6.

the purpose of a Free Methodist was to "spread scriptural holiness across the land and to preach the gospel to the poor."[7] Indeed, the Free Methodist Church, consistent with other inheritors of Wesley's Methodism, continues to profess that "Free Methodist maintain a life of daily devotion to Christ that springs from inward holiness and separates the Christian from the world, even while he/she lives in the world. They believe the best way to keep worldliness from invading the church is for the church to invade the world with redemptive purpose."[8]

Reforming the nation and the Church was certainly ambitious and making it to heaven made this doubly so. For Wesley, these ideals were driven by a very specific method. "You have nothing to do but to save souls," Wesley counseled his preachers. "Therefore, spend and be spent in this work. And go always, not only to those who want you, but to those who want you most."[9] Call people to repentance. Teach them how to walk in the ways of Christ. Release them to go and do likewise. Works, for Wesley, were never the basis of one's salvation. But one could hardly claim to be saved if one didn't have them.

This was what it meant to be holy, to be sanctified. Wesley's *ordo* method as employed meant that such a life of love could only come "from a conviction wrought in us by the Holy Ghost of the pardoning love of God."[10] This theme of love of others springing from the love of God and birthed in us by the love of God is central to Wesleyan theology. "The Character of a Methodist,"[11] "The Principles of a Methodist,"[12] and his "An Earnest Appeal to Men and Reason and Religion"[13] all speak to this, as do Wesley's sermons "The Witness of

---

7. For a biography of B. T. Roberts, see Howard Snyder, *Populist Saints: B. T. and Ellen Roberts and the First Free Methodists* (Grand Rapids: Eerdmans, 2006).
8. *Free Methodist Book of Discipline*, 2020 (Indianapolis, IN: Light and Life Publishing, 2020), 7.
9. John Wesley, *Works*, 10:106. In this eleventh of his twelve "Rules for Helpers" by using "want" Wesley was more properly referring to those who "need" spiritual guidance.
10. John Wesley, "Letter to Mr. John Smith," December 30, 1745, *Works*, 26:183.
11. John Wesley, *Works*, 9:35, 39.
12. John Wesley, *Works*, 9:53.
13. John Wesley, *Works*, 11:70.

the Spirit,"[14] "The Law Established through Faith,"[15] and "The Unity of the Divine Being,"[16] to name but a few. Wesley further added that God ought to be loved simply for God's sake, even though we can love God only in response to our awareness of God's saving love for all humankind.[17]

Faith, then, the evidence and acceptance of God's pardoning love for us, is the motivating power behind one's growth in holiness. It is the impetus behind one's Christ-like actions and ethic. This connection between faith and sanctification is vitally important to note. Wesley did not consider faith the epitome of the Christian religion, as many other Protestants claimed and continue to claim today. Rather, for Wesley faith is always "the handmaid of love."[18]

Preaching on 1 Corinthians 13:1–3, he devoted an entire sermon to the thought that love is "the greatest of these," a more excellent way than either faith or hope. As he wrote,

> The sum of all that has been observed is this: whatever I speak, whatever I know, whatever I believe, whatever I do, whatever I suffer; if I have not the faith that worketh by love, that produces love to God and all mankind, I am not in the narrow way which leadeth to life (eternal), but in the broad road that leadeth to destruction.[19]

For Wesley, the way of love doesn't compel the Christian to follow God's commands as much as finding the Christian who loves God rejoicing to do so.[20] This gets to the heart of the matter of the role of works and ethical decisions and one's eternal life, as explained by Randy Maddox:

> Protestants have constantly worried that Roman Catholics elevate good works at the expense of faith, while Roman Catholics have feared that the Protestant emphasis on "faith alone" undercuts good

---

14. John Wesley, "The Witness of the Spirit, I," *Works*, 1:274.
15. John Wesley, *Works*, 2:41–42.
16. John Wesley, "The Unity of the Divine Being," *Works*, 4:67.
17. John Wesley, "Letter to Dr. John Robertson," September 24, 1753, *Works*, 26:518.
18. John Wesley, "The Law Established through Faith, II," *Works*, 2:38.
19. John Wesley, "On Charity," *Works*, 3:306.
20. John Wesley, "The Witness of the Spirit, I, " *Works*, 1:280.

works rather than being productive of them. Wesley's mature comments touching on this issue reflect sensitivity to the concerns of both groups.[21]

Keeping these ideals vibrant and alive in the dynamic tension of his methodology is woven by Wesley throughout his long ministry. In his sermon "The Law Established through Faith," Wesley proclaimed that the truth lies between both. We are, doubtless, "justified by faith." This is the cornerstone of the whole Christian building. "We are justified without the works of the law" as any previous condition of justification. Good works for Wesley, then, are an immediate fruit of that faith whereby we are justified. So that if good works do not follow our faith, even all inward and outward holiness, it is plain our faith is worth nothing; we are yet in our sins. Therefore we are "justified by faith," even by "faith without works." There is no ground for "making void the law through faith"; or for imagining that faith is a dispensation from any kind or degree of holiness.[22]

Such a message was not new for Wesley. In 1750, the same year he preached "The Law Established through Faith," he preached his thirteenth homily on the Sermon on the Mount. Within it, he cried:

> Lord! Increase my faith, if I now believe! Else, give me faith though but as a grain of mustard seed! But "what doth it profit if a man say he hath faith, and have not works? Can" *that* "faith save him?" O no! That faith which hath not works, which does not produce both inward and outward holiness, which does not stamp the whole image of God on the heart, and purify us as he is pure; that faith which does not produce the whole of the religion described in the foregoing chapters, is not the faith of the gospel, not the Christian faith, not the faith which leads to glory. O beware of this, above all other snares of the devil, of resting on unholy, unsaving faith![23]

Wesley's favorite text to preach on regarding faith and good works was Galatians 5:6, "Being circumcised or not being circumcised

---

21. Maddox, *Responsible Grace*, 175.
22. John Wesley, "The Law Established through Faith, 1," *Works*, 2:27–28.
23. John Wesley, "Sermon on the Mount, XIII," *Works*, 1:695–96. The emphasis on the italicized word is present in Wesley's text.

doesn't matter in Christ Jesus, but faith working through love does matter."²⁴ For Wesley this is a matter of faith working through love. Again, Randy Maddox's commentary on Wesley is helpful here. He claims that "Roman Catholic theology continued the majority practice of the Early Church in translating *energumen* as a passive participle, with the implication that our faith is generated (worked) through our repeated acts of love or virtue."²⁵ Protestants, however, stressed the active voice of the participle, insisting that Saint Paul was claiming that faith is the power behind any real acts of love. Wesley integrated both of these approaches. "On the one hand, he affirmed that Christian faith (understood subjectively) is evoked in us by an act of love; though it was God's ultimate act of love for us, not our acts of love," Maddox writes. "On the other hand, [Wesley] was equally convinced that faith (understood "objectively" as the Witness of the Spirit) is the energizing source of our disposition and acts of love for God and others."²⁶

In simplest terms, Wesley believed that faith works by love and is worked by love in the life of the believer all the way to heaven. The biblical counsels of James and Paul are not at odds with one another in Wesley's thought. Instead, the faith which Paul affirms is one that truly effects new lives of love. The faith which James condemns is one that does not.²⁷ God's grace brings about faith in us. Our co-operant responsibility then expresses itself in loving, ethical works throughout the Christian life as one advances in faith shown through works and progresses in life toward the goal of making it to heaven.

Such an emphasis on the partnership of faith in God and works of love can be seen in the counsel Wesley gave to his preachers. Do they have gifts, graces, and fruits necessary for the work? Being theologically sound was not enough. John and his younger brother Charles disagreed as to which marks were most important among those called to ministry. John leaned toward whether or not a preacher exhibited the grace of God in their life. For Charles, he was much more concerned

---

24. Biblical citations in this chapter are from the Common English Bible.
25. Maddox, *Responsible Grace*, 175.
26. Maddox, *Responsible Grace*, 175.
27. John Wesley, "A Letter to the Rev. Mr. Horne," 1761, *Works*, 11:456.

that the potential preacher had natural gifts and talents. Both, however, were convinced that the person should be able to exhibit the fruit of their calling through the lives of those entrusted to their care, lives which had been changed by the Holy Spirit through their ministry.[28]

The heavenly ideal was for all. Laypersons were similarly called to such a balance of faith and works. Within his pamphlet "The Character of a Methodist," Wesley asks what the defining mark of a Methodist might be. What distinguishes the Methodist from other followers of Christ? He then runs through a list of several obvious possibilities. Is it their view of the Trinity? Their view of the Scriptures? Their view of Jesus? Their view of worship? The answer to all of these is no. But Wesley then answers his own question by saying that the Methodist is one who loves God and neighbor. Anticipating the response of the reader that all Christians are called to such a standard, Wesley concedes this, saying that this is his point exactly. The true and genuine Methodist is simply a true and genuine Christian. She or he obeys the Great Commandment. She or he truly loves God and loves their neighbor. A Methodist is one who actually does this in practice.[29]

For a Methodist holiness is seen in love of God and love of neighbor. By defining a Methodist in this way, and by stressing the need to spread scriptural holiness across the land, Wesley argued that Methodism was simply trying to fulfill its role in renewing the Church by calling it to holiness itself, the heart of true religion. This is our joy, he claimed, constantly equating holiness with the goal of the happiness of the heavenly (eschatological) life.

To illustrate this, Wesley uses the analogy of a house. Repentance, he says, is the porch. We confess our sins and denounce evil. Faith is the door. We walk through it, exercising our belief, but it is a belief that requires a response. Receiving the Lord's Supper, for example, would be but one example of our response to our faith. But holy living is the house itself. Once inside, we continue to live a holy life. It is true religion and in it is the formative playground of Christian ethics lived with those who also are occupants of the house.

---

28. John Wesley, "Address to the Clergy," *Works*, 10:480–500.
29. John Wesley, "The Character of a Methodist," *Works*, 9:31–46.

Such love of God and neighbor became evident in the life of the Church through works of piety, such as worship and devotion, and works of mercy, such as social concern for justice. These were far more than simply individual characteristics. Sometimes Methodism is misconstrued as promoting a focus on individual piety, on individual holiness, though that is not the case. Wesley's understanding of a vital personal piety lived in the constant dynamic of the *via salutis* claimed there was no such thing as solitary religion, as solitary holiness. In fact, he coined the term "social holiness" to counteract such misunderstanding. When confronted with an unnamed "serious man," Wesley was reminded that the Bible knows nothing of solitary holiness:

> Solitary religion is not to be found there. "Holy Solitaries" is a phrase no more consistent with the gospel than Holy Adulterers. The gospel of Christ knows of no religion, but social; no holiness but social holiness. Faith working by love, is the length and breadth and depth and height of Christian perfection. "This commandment we have from Christ, that he who loves God should love his brother also;" and that we manifest our love "by doing good unto all men, especially to them that are of the household of faith."[30]

This is the heart of Wesleyan ecclesiological practice and informs all of his work on Christian ethics.

It is in Wesley's understanding of social holiness that his work on ethics, much of which has been explored in other papers during this round of the dialogue, flourished. Wesley, like so many others, touched on many areas of ethical concern as he went: economics, race relations, family structure, slavery, etc. It was his *ordo* and his understanding of the "way to heaven" that gave eschatological focus to the salvific implications of the present life and the dilemmas of living together in the household of God. While the *ordo* brought meaning and purpose to Christian living, Wesley also gave much attention to matters of eschatology and its attending concerns: dying well, death itself, the afterlife, and even what heaven would be like.

---

30. Wesley, *Hymns and Sacred Poems* (London: William Strahan, 1739), Preface.

Ethics and Eschatology

That any study of the ethics of John Wesley and the Methodist movement that has coalesced around him (and his continuing presence with us) would be rife with enough material to fit under the qualifier "eschatological" to be its own significant subset within Wesleyan academic circles is no surprise to anyone who has read Wesley and the many and generous accounts of his life and ministry.[31] To say that John Wesley was obsessed with death and dying and so are Methodists would, further, be an understatement of the highest order. For Wesley and his followers, "eschatological ethics" is not just fascination; it is an essential and guiding theological template in which the riches of the Christian faith past and present, the intellectual workings of Christian theology, and Christian instruction on the holy life coalesce as a roadmap to eternity and our ultimate future with God.

Wesley's (and Wesleyanism's) fascination with death and dying and the beyond began early in the legend. Wesley and Wesleyans are fond of telling the "brand plucked from the burning" story from Wesley's childhood, how a human ladder was dramatically formed by his father and the people of the Epworth parish to pull the ten-year-old Jackie Wesley from the second story of the burning parsonage and certain death in Epworth where his father was the Anglican curate. Early Methodism and its development of holiness theology and technique (Wesley's *via salutis* as argued above), during the Holy Club days at Oxford in the 1720s, found in the *Ars moriendi* movement (still popular in the 1720s after almost 300 years) and the seventeenth century publication(s) of Jeremy Taylor's *Rules and Exercises for Holy Living and Holy Dying* (published 1650 and 1651 respectively) that was the fresh expression of that movement for the Wesley brothers and the Holy Club, a contributing source within its intellectual

---

31. See, e.g. Randy Maddox, "The Triumph of Responsible Grace," Chapter 9 in *Responsible Grace* (1994); Kenneth Collins, "Eschatology and Glorification: The Triumph of Holy Love," Chapter 9 in *The Theology of John Wesley* (2007); and Joseph McPherson, *Our People Die Well: Glorious Accounts of Early Methodists at Death's Door* (Bloomington, IN: AuthorHouse, 2008) which charts the numerous death scenes of Methodists in John Wesley's *Arminian Magazine* and weighs in at 420 pages.

domain.³² The Wesleys made that text standard reading for Methodists in their holiness/theological/character training for both ministers and laity, a tradition that continues today. The Wesleys' own thinking about death emerges first in the journal accounts of their missionary sojourn to the colony of Georgia (1735-1736) where they encountered "the insect fever" that accompanied daily life among the swampy bogs of the southeastern coast of the United States and the terrors of performing exorcisms for the first time, being shot at, rushed by mobs, imprisoned, and run out of the colony because of the strict holiness demands they placed on the unruly colonists there through their attempts at "primitive Christianity."³³

Their fascination with things eschatological continued and grew throughout their long ministry and vast writings, beginning with their first collection of hymns in 1738-1739 and John's first publication of his *Sermons on Several Occasions* in 1744 as noted above. Eventually the "standard" hymnal for Methodists included a section entitled "Describing Death."³⁴ Most of John's published sermons included some mention of the subject and references to death, dying, and the afterlife often found their way into their titles ("Death and Deliverance," "On Mourning the Dead," "On Eternity"). Death, dying, judgment, the intermediate subjects of hades and paradise (the former

---

32. See Sister Mary Catherine O'Connell, *The Art of Dying Well: The Development of the Ars moriendi* (New York: AMS Press, 1966). The *Ars moriendi* was published in Germany, ca. 1415, complete with texts for those who could read and with explicit pictures of death and the afterlife for those who could not. By 1450 it had been quickly translated into several languages, including English. It was a manual for Christians on how to die well, written during the Black Plague. The publication of the book began a tradition in European Christianity. As to Jeremy Taylor, *Rules and Exercises for Holy Living* (London: William Royston, 1650) and his *Rules and Exercises for Holy Dying* (London: William Royston, 1650), given Anglican history and its affinity for the killing of kings, nonconformists, and Puritans alike, one can easily see the reason for the popularity of Taylor.

33. See Geordan Hammond, *John Wesley in America* (New York: Oxford University Press, 2014), Chapter 2, and Steven Hoskins, "Insects, Energumens, and Illicit Affairs: Oh My!: The Role of the New Birth in Charles Wesley's Georgia Experience," *Proceedings of the Charles Wesley Society* 22, no. 1 (2017): 69-83.

34. John Wesley, *A Collection of Hymns, for the Use of the People Called Methodists* (London: J. Paramore, 1780).

the dwelling place of all the dead and the second the subset of hades for those who die in the Lord with the eventual promise of heaven), hell, and heavenly eternal existence found many attributions in the sermons, hymns, letters, and other writings.

As Methodists preserved the writings of the Wesleys and contributed their own theological literatures to it throughout the nineteenth century, Eschatology became one of the "standard" subsets of Methodist theology along with Salvation, Sanctification, and Sin, and of the substance of the "official" teachings of the movement with "Standard" versions of the works that included such writings from those who formed their theological, ecclesiastical, and ministerial legacy.[35] There are also the publication of hundreds of "death scenes" of Methodists with their emphasis on confession, worship, and passing from this existence to the next recorded in the pages of *The Arminian Magazine*, first published by Wesley in 1787 and continuing after his death by the Methodists in some form up until today.[36] John's staging of his own death scene at least five times (most of which were recorded in *The Arminian Magazine*) which included the final one ("Best of All, God is with us") found their way into the canon. Add to all of this the casual remark of Charles Wesley's physician that Methodists were tough people who died well, something that became a slogan ("Our People Die Well") for the Wesleys and was repeated by Francis Asbury as the founder of Methodism in America; the insistence (at least by John) of the presence of the ghosts of the dead with us in this realm; and an evolving and maturing theology of eschatology in

---

35. Maddox, *Responsible Grace*, Chapter 9.

36. For the complete run of *The Arminian Magazine* during John Wesley's life see John Wesley, *The Arminian Magazine* (London: J. Fry, 1794). *The Arminian Magazine* was created by John Wesley in 1781 to combat the Calvinist influence in the Methodist movement after the death of Whitefield who was himself a Calvinist. *The Arminian Magazine* was significant because it gave Wesley a weekly platform to write short takes on heavy theological subjects and give reports on the spiritual lives of Methodists—with women as significant as their male counterparts. The scandal columns and gossip it included on everything from private sin to national issues made it engrossing and essential reading for the followers of Wesley. The magazine has persisted among Methodists since then in one form or another and continues to be published by The Fundamental Wesleyan Society at https://fwponline.cc/the-arminian-magazine-2/.

John's writings, and you get the picture. Methodists and Methodist theology have a long fascination with the subject.

The twentieth century saw the gentrification of the movement. Church splits and reunions (many aimed at growing a larger footprint on American culture to keep up with the burgeoning Baptist denominations), the creation of new Methodist denominations (including my own Church of the Nazarene), and the desire for social and academic credibility, saw the waning of the fascination with things eschatological. Ethics, eschatological and otherwise, became a generic title for Methodist theology in general. Biography became the standard of human interest rather than "the way to heaven" and a fascination with death scenes. The dynamic of doing theology with Wesley's categories and fascination with the totality of humanity and creation bound up in the engrossing narrative of salvation history was replaced by systematic theology, scholastic and mostly arid on the one hand, and the recasting of eschatology with the rage of "end times" marks of the beast thinking that flourished in the 1970s and 1980s, on the other.[37] It was, indeed, the dark ages of Methodism.

Fascinatingly, it was the creation of the newly minted United Methodist Church in 1968 and the head of their first committee on doctrine, the historical theologian Albert Cook Outler (Southern

---

37. For an accounting of this, see Robert Chiles, *Theological Transition in American Methodism* (Nashville: Abingdon, 1965) and James Heidinger, *The Rise of Theological Liberalism and the Decline of American Methodism* (Nashville: Seedbed Press, 2017). During the aftermath of World War II, many Methodist academics began attending the "best" theological and divinity schools to gain respectability and recognition and eventually created their own bastions of respectability at places like Duke, Emory, and Northwestern University. Some of those theologians simply did degrees in ethics and took up the work of systematics. Northwestern University combined the efforts to create doctoral degrees in joint studies like ethics and the Bible, ethics and theology, etc., a tradition that continues. For proof that systematics replaced ethics and its dynamic, one need look no further than my own denomination, the Church of the Nazarene, which has three official systematic theologies, all replete with extended sections on Christian ethics: H. Orton Wiley, *Christian Theology*, 3 vols. (Kansas City, MO: Nazarene Publishing House, 1940), H. Ray Dunning, *Grace, Faith, and Holiness* (Kansas City, MO: The Nazarene Publishing House, 1987), and J. Kenneth Grider, *A Wesleyan-Holiness Theology* (Kansas City, MO: Nazarene Publishing House, 1994). A fourth "officially commissioned" systematic theology from the denomination is under contract with Thomas Noble.

Methodist University), which brought Wesleyan theology and its concerns with holy living and dying back to Wesley and the dynamics of his theological interests. Outler edited the new "standard" book of the essential writings of John Wesley for Oxford University Press's *The Library of Protestant Thought* in 1964 and with it created the famed "Wesleyan Quadrilateral" of Scripture, Tradition, Reason, and Experience as the way back into Wesley's theological dynamic. The works which followed Outler's lead by Ted Runyon, Mildred Wynkoop, Randy Maddox, and Ken Collins cemented the re-turn to Wesley as theological guide and mentor.[38] The re-setting of Wesleyan theology with Wesley's own "orienting concern" of "Responsible Grace" as Maddox so eloquently put things (or as Wesley would have put it, "Reasonable Christianity") has recreated Wesleyan theology and Wesleyan Christians in the image of Wesley, and he has become (again) the guide and mentor of the movement.

Eschatological Ethics and Ecumenical Dialogue

So, what does this offer for our consideration in this ecumenical dialogue? It is clear that Wesley and Wesleyan thinking has contributed to our discussions over the past decades concerning Church, salvation, atonement, holiness, and the many topics we have discussed. In this round of the dialogue concerning ethics and this session exploring dialogue about the eschatological character of ethics, there are a few things that may help us.

First, the Wesleyan fascination with death, eternal life in heaven, and all things "eschatological," marked a real turn in eighteenth-century theology, a turn that continues to mark much discussion and debate today. As Randy Maddox notes, the eschatological emphasis in Wesley was an attempt to return to a more medieval understanding of eschatology as "a biblical hope for a future new life in the new heavens and new earth."[39] The prevailing view among Protestants in

---

38. See Ted Runyon, *The New Creation* (Nashville: Abingdon, 1998), along with Mildred Wynkoop, *A Theology of Love*, Randy Maddox, *Responsible Grace*, and Ken Collins, *The Theology of John Wesley*, noted above.

39. Maddox, *Responsible Grace*, 395.

general and Wesley's contemporaries had fixed on the "aspiration of immediate translation at death to a transcendent heaven."[40] Charles Wesley's hymns followed suit and consistently treated death as a simple transition to eternal life with God and glory. For the Wesleys this meant that eschatology is not simply a future state (something modern Wesleyans are recovering from the systematicians), but that it is a dynamic, creative part of our present reality, something we could even "experience" here below in the worship and Christian fellowship of Christ's Holy Church.[41] Charles Wesley's hymn "Head of The Church Triumphant" (1745) poetically stated the dynamically joined states or realms of Christianity found so often throughout Wesleyan thought:

> The church triumphant in Thy love
> Their mighty joys we show;
> They sing the Lamb in hymns above,
> And we in hymns below.
> Thee in Thy glorious realm they praise,
> And bow before Thy throne;
> We in the kingdom of Thy grace,
> The kingdoms are but one.[42]

Second, the renewed medieval eschatological vision freed Wesleyan theology and worship (including funerals) from the dread of death, the idea of soul sleep with a "future" resurrection of the dead, and any concerns about the annihilation of the soul. Any Wesleyan eschatology affirms that we should welcome death, find theological curiosity in watching God's working as his saints die, and take our theological cues, even speculative ones, from what we learn about and from God as we die.[43] Death and the idea of death becomes a potent and powerful means to the working of God's grace, a

---

40. Maddox, *Responsible Grace*, 395.
41. Steven Hoskins, "Eucharist and Eschatology in the Writings of the Wesleys," *Wesleyan Theological Journal* 29, nos. 1 and 2 (1994): 63–81.
42. Charles Wesley, "Head of the Church Triumphant," *Hymns for the Time of Trouble* (London: 1745).
43. See, e.g., Charles Wesley's hymn, "Ah, lovely appearance of death. No sight on earth is so fair," *Funeral Hymns* (London: 1746).

meaningful theological contributor to Wesley's vision of responsible grace (or reasonable Christianity) and sharing what we understand about eschatology and its various theological manifestations should provide fruitful dialogue for any ecumenical effort.

Third, for Wesley's thinking, dying and the state of death gave much to think about and much to connect to the broader emphasis of reasonable Christianity as a life lived on the continuum or *ordo* that joins us and our present state to the life that is eternal. For Wesley, death is an intermediate state between our present and the fullness of the final consummation of all things throughout eternity which includes the bodily resurrection from the dead (though Wesley admits he was unsure of just what this body it would be, it would obviously be a better and more reasonable one).[44] As such, it represents a point on the continuum of life and follows reasonably the dictates of a part of God's creation. While Wesley struggles to find language to keep this intermediate state as dynamic as the present and the eternal future fullness of heaven with its activities of worship, praise, and living for God, in the last sermon he preached in January of 1791, Wesley speculated that if we believe that faith is the dynamic working of God in us and life and death are but two states on the continuum of creation, that God's work will continue in death and souls in the state of death will "ripen" for heaven becoming "holier and happier."[45] Eventually at the final resurrection, the intermediate state will be replaced with a physical state—a "new creation," even better than the original one with Adam and Eve.[46] Based on the ultimate goodness of God, the new creation will restore to us the ultimacy of salvation, a place where we who follow Christ will be holiest and happiest, even more so than we were in the original creation. In his "Further Thoughts upon Christian Perfection," Wesley remarked that the given nature of

---

44. Wesley borrows much of his thinking on the intermediate state of death from the Non-juror Archibald Campbell's work *The Doctrines of a Middle State between Death and Resurrection* (1721). Wesley thought so much of the work that he refers to it in his Sermon "On Faith" (noted below) and had the book read to him during the final month of his life, see Maddox, *Responsible Grace*, 411, note 133.

45. John Wesley, "On Faith," *Works*, 4:194.

46. John Wesley, "On the General Spread of the Gospel," *Works*, 2:494.

God's work in humans will be so pervasive in the new creation (ultimate heaven) that those who are "perfect" will continue to grow in grace through all eternity, a remark that pushes even the outer limits of any state bound by the language of an "-est" ending.[47] Whatever else Wesleyan eschatological ethics gives to think about (and there is much there), let us be clear that Wesleyan thinking on the subject is shaped around the orienting concern of responsible grace and that (eventually) to the "nth" degree, the perfecting grace of God will work to include all the saints (and for Wesley the entire creation) and it will be truly responsible, allowing for the continual growth of the creation in God, both responsively and transformationally.[48]

To end this paper, let us consider two things. The first is this: Wesleyan eschatology means ethics and the attending questions and answers that make it a dynamic consideration for ethical/theological thinking. Given that this is a Methodist take on the subject, it must be admitted that much of Wesley's work was speculative and much was about biblical interpretation and that of a Protestant variety. Further, we must remember that Wesley's take on "justification by faith alone" was tempered by his orienting concern of "responsible grace," the role that our responsible appropriation of God's grace plays in our salvation. Wesleyan eschatology declares eternal salvation is based on faith alone and ultimate damnation unto hell (*Gehena*) is a real and necessarily alternative possibility.[49]

However, given what Wesley believed about the new creation and about the continual working of God's holiness in us throughout eternity, Wesleyan eschatology allows that there are still some things to work out about "faith and works" and Wesley gives us a perspective to add to the discussion. If holiness and happiness increase in the intermediate state of death and we grow in reasonable grace throughout heaven, then Wesley speculates, works, our active response to God's

---

47. John Wesley, "Further Thoughts upon Christian Perfection," *Works*, 13:44–45.
48. Maddox, *Responsible Grace*, 392, 398. It should be noted that Wesley eventually and finally believed that the entire creation would be renewed, including animals and plants.
49. John Wesley, "Of Hell," *Works*, 3:17–26.

working grace, matter and can even increase in some ways.⁵⁰ What becomes apparent if one peers deeply into any ecumenical discussion on ethics between Evangelicals and Catholics is that it matters to us how we live and die. There is even more to consider if we allow that the two parts are but a single explanation of human existence in God that extends beyond those two categories to include life in heaven in a serious discussion of ethics and the eschatological implications of the character of our life with God.

Second, Wesley, Outler, and their current like are all ecumenicists. Wesley's *Letter to a Roman Catholic* ("If thy heart is as my heart, give me thine hand . . .") published in 1749 still holds a galvanizing place in the "standard" theology of the movement.⁵¹ Outler was the lone "official" Methodist observer at Vatican II, though a few others with evangelical sympathies like George Lindbeck were present as well. The post-liberal followers of Outler and Lindbeck and other Wesleyans continue to catch the ecumenical bug and have formed "Ecumenical Studies" sections which are a regular and recurrent part of the meetings of the Wesleyan Theological Society and the Society for Pentecostal Studies (I have presented several papers to both groups). Ecumenism is proof of much and lends itself to as much discussion as theology—grace and how we act toward one another. There is much for us to agree on and much to dispute, though admittedly much of it is speculative in nature and much of it has to do with "how" we read and perform Scripture. Ethical considerations of eschatology point toward some fruitfulness, it seems. Let us admit we have an orienting concern in this (and perhaps every) round of our dialogue together, one which Wesley stated so well: We want to know one thing—and that together—the way to heaven.

---

50. John Wesley, *Explanatory Notes upon the New Testament* (London: Bowyer, 1755), cf. Rom 9:21 and 1 Cor 3:8.
51. John Wesley, "Letter to a Roman Catholic," *Works*, 14:163–75.

Contributors

Catholic Contributing Authors

DR. DAVID P. FLEISCHACKER, PHD is Adjunct Professor of Theology at the University of Mary, Bismarck, North Dakota. Dr. Fleischacker's publications can be found in the *Newman Studies Journal, The Thomist, Logos: A Journal of Catholic Thought and Culture, Logos: A Journal of Eastern Christian Studies,* and *Divyadaan: Journal of Philosophy and Education.*

DR. DANIEL A. KEATING, PHD is Professor of Theology at Sacred Heart Major Seminary in Detroit, Michigan, where he teaches on Scripture, the Church Fathers, ecumenism, and the New Evangelization. He is the author of *The Appropriation of Divine Life in Cyril of Alexandria* (2004), *Deification and Grace* (2007), *First and Second Peter, Jude* (2011), and co-author of *James, First, Second and Third John* (2017).

DR. WILLIAM B. STEVENSON, PHD is Associate Professor of Dogmatic Theology at the Saint Paul Seminary School of Divinity at the University of St. Thomas in St. Paul, Minnesota. He has published articles on philosophy and theology in *The Thomist, New Blackfriars, Moreana,* and *Logos: A Journal of Catholic Thought and Culture.*

DR. CHRISTIAN D. WASHBURN, PHD is Professor of Dogmatic Theology at the Saint Paul Seminary School of Divinity at the University of St. Thomas in St. Paul, Minnesota. His articles have appeared in journals such as *Pro Ecclesia, Annuarium Historiae Conciliorum, The Thomist, Nova et Vetera,* and *Gregorianum.* He has also served as a member of the National Reformed–Catholic Dialogue,

National Lutheran–Roman Catholic Dialogue, and the International Lutheran–Roman Catholic Commission on Unity.

Evangelical Contributing Authors

REV. BRUCE CROMWELL, PHD is the District Superintendent of the Great Plains and Mid-America Conferences of the Free Methodist Church, McPherson, Kansas. He is a member of the Free Methodist Church's Study Commission on Doctrine and was the leader of the Justice and Social Witness focus group at the General Conference in 2019. Dr. Cromwell is the author of *Loving From Where We Stand: A Call to Biblically Faithful Ministry with the LGBTQ+ Community* (2021).

LUKE T. GERATY, MA, MDIV is the Co-Lead Pastor of Red Bluff Vineyard Church in Red Bluff, California. He has given papers at a number of Vineyard conferences on theology and is an active participant in Vineyard efforts at ecumenical dialogue.

DR. STEVEN HOSKINS, PHD is Associate Professor of Religion at Trevecca Nazarene University in Nashville, Tennessee. An ordained elder in his denomination, he serves as the Promotional Secretary for the Wesleyan Theological Society and on the Executive Board of the Wesleyan Holiness Connection. His articles have appeared in the academic journals *Wesleyan Theological Journal* and *Gottesdienst*, and he has a number of books published by The Foundry, the publishing concern of the Church of the Nazarene. He is the co-editor and contributing author to the books *Wesleyan Theological Society: The 50th Anniversary History* (2015) and *A Year with Rabbi Jesus*, Vols. I and II (2021, 2022).

DR. DENNIS W. JOWERS, PHD is Professor of Theology and Apologetics at the Faith International Seminary in Tacoma, Washington. Dr. Jowers is the author and co-editor of several books, including *The Trinitarian Axiom of Karl Rahner: "The Economic Trinity is the Immanent Trinity and Vice Versa"* (Lewiston, NY: Edwin Mellen Press, 2006).

His articles have appeared in many journals, including *The Reformed Theological Review*, *Scottish Journal of Theology*, *The Thomist*, and *Journal of the Evangelical Theology Society*.

DR. GLEN MENZIES, PHD is a minister in the Assemblies of God and (Retired) Professor of New Testament and Early Christianity at North Central University in Minneapolis, Minnesota, where he was Dean of the School of Religion and Philosophy. He has also served as a Research Projects Coordinator for the Museum of the Bible.

Index of Names

Abel, 113, 114, 115
Abraham (Abram), 88, 97, 114, 119, 161, 258, 295, 299
Abraham, William, 258, 262
Absalom, 116
Adam, 87, 110, 112–15, 119, 126, 127, 130, 168, 174, 201, 247, 327
Alcidamas, 41
Ali, Abiy Ahmed, 236
Amnon, 116
Amos, 88, 245
Anabaptists, 13, 133, 232, 237, 239–41
Antiochus IV, 307
Aquinas, Thomas, 17, 39, 40, 41, 45–47, 51, 135, 138, 182, 211, 215, 218, 224, 266, 284, 286, 294, 297, 302
Aristotle, 39, 41, 42, 45–46, 109, 119, 177, 229
Ashley, Kenneth, 174
Athanagoras, 137, 138
Augustine, 39, 40, 42, 44–47, 50, 61, 63, 65, 138, 139, 143, 145–47, 244, 247, 290, 306, 311

Baal, 115
Baius, 294
Barth, Karl, 37, 182
Basil, 73, 137, 139
Bebbington, David, 236
Bellarmine, Robert, 10–11, 13, 19, 27, 28, 33, 34, 35, 36, 284, 285, 286, 287, 292, 293, 294, 295, 299
Boyd, Greg, 239

Boyer, Charles, 8
Brooten, Bernadette J., 179–80
Bullinger, Heinrich, 52
Butterfield, Rosaria, 186

Cain, 113, 114
Calvin, John, 72, 84, 89, 143, 237, 238, 289
Camery-Hoggatt, Jerry, 244–46
Campbell, Ted, 73, 327
Chrysostom, 73, 137
Cicero, 42–45
Clement of Alexandria, 73, 145
Collins, Ken, 69, 313, 321, 325
Cromwell, Bruce, xiii, xiv, 269, 272, 273, 332
Cyprian, 73, 137

Danker, Ryan, 259–60
David, King, 92, 98, 116, 135, 307
Dismas, 296
Dover, K. J., 177
Dunning, H. Ray, 68, 76, 267, 268, 270, 324

Édart, Jean-Baptiste, 168–69
Elizabeth, 115, 116, 123
Empedocles, 41
Ephrem Syrus, 73
Essenes, 135
Eusebius, 18
Euthyphro, 86
Eve, 87, 110, 112–15, 119, 127, 130, 327
Ezekiel, 251

335

INDEX OF NAMES

Ferre, Nels, 270
Fleischacker, David, xiii, 331
Fortin, Ernest, 38, 40, 226
Frederick II, 307
Frederick III, 56

Gabriel, 115, 116, 118, 311
Gasser, Vincent, 25
Geiselmann, Joseph, 8
Geraty, Luke, xiii, 173, 184, 186, 187, 332
Gunter, Stephen, 72, 262

Hannah, 115
Hauerwas, Stanley, 258
Hays, Richard, 169, 178-79
Hegel, 219
Himbaza, Innocent, 166, 167-69
Hitler, Adolph, 307
Hobbes, Thomas, 227, 229
Hoskins, Steven, xii, xiii, 238, 322, 326, 332

Isaac, 97, 114, 115
Isaiah, 92, 93, 97, 251, 252, 264

Jacob, 97, 250
Jacobatius, Dominico, 16
Jerome, 142, 145
Jezebel, 115
John, Apostle, ix, 301
Joseph (husband of Mary), 115, 116, 119, 125
Jowers, Dennis, xiii, 332
Judas, 121, 309
Judith, 115
Julius Caesar, 178
Justin Martyr, 74, 115

Kant, Immanuel, 221, 223
Keating, Daniel, xiii, 135, 192, 331
Kirk, J. R. Daniel, 181

Lactantius, 18, 43
Laelius, 43

Lazarus, 295
Lennerz, Heinrich, 8, 293
Liberatore, Matteo, 226
Lindbeck, George, 329
Locke, John, 211, 227, 229
Long, D. Stephen, 76, 258, 261, 262, 266
Lot, 161
Lucifer, 112, 309
Luther, Martin, 13, 49, 50, 54-56, 58, 61, 72, 133, 143, 184, 290

MacArthur, John, 238
Maddox, Randy, 68, 76, 262, 313, 314, 316, 317, 318, 321, 323, 325, 326, 327, 328
Marquart, Manfred, 262, 264, 266
Marx, Karl, 219
Mary, Blessed Virgin, 115-19, 123, 125, 311
Matthew, Apostle, 21, 88, 91, 180, 237, 264, 283, 301
Melanchthon, 13, 133
Melchizedek, 92
Menzies, Glen, xiii, 333
Miles, Rebekah, 76
Minucius Felix, 137
Moses, 52, 53, 57, 61, 88, 92, 95, 119, 135, 145, 249, 307
Mukwege, Denis, 236
Murad, Nadia, 236

Naomi, 115
Nero, 177
Newman, John Henry, 13, 21, 150
Niebuhr, Reinhold, 234-35, 248
Noah, 87, 114, 133, 162
Noll, Mark, 52, 55, 56, 57, 58

Onan, 142-145
Origen, 18, 73
Outler, Albert, xiv, 68, 69, 70, 71, 76, 258, 259, 262, 266, 314, 324, 325, 329

Paul, Apostle, xiv, 8, 9, 51, 68, 88-91, 100-102, 107, 129, 134, 137, 150, 153,

INDEX OF NAMES

162, 164–68, 176–80, 209, 242, 252, 292, 295, 296, 318
Peter, Apostle, 6, 15, 17, 21, 31, 91
Pharisees, 85, 129
Philus, 42–43
Pigge, Albert, 27
Piper, John, 239
Plato, 40, 41, 42, 45
Polanus, Amandus, 84
Polycarp, 73
Pope Benedict XII, 300
Pope Benedict XVI, 18, 149, 157, 206, 209
Pope Clement XI, 284
Pope Francis, 149, 158, 207, 209, 247
Pope Gregory XIV, 139
Pope Innocent III, 27
Pope Innocent IV, 27
Pope Innocent XI, 139
Pope John XXIII, 149, 205, 209
Pope John Paul II, 12, 14, 16, 22, 24, 28, 31, 35, 121, 140, 141, 149, 195, 196, 200, 203, 205, 209, 291, 292, 300
Pope Leo XIII, 7, 19, 22, 30, 195, 203, 207, 209, 210–215, 217–18, 220–22, 225–29
Pope Paul IV, 27
Pope Paul VI, 12, 14, 22, 35, 140, 149, 152–53, 195, 205, 209
Pope Pius V, 12, 61, 139, 147, 294
Pope Pius IX, 24, 139
Pope Pius X, 6, 33, 34
Pope Pius XI, 13, 23, 24, 131, 139, 148, 209
Pope Pius XII, 9, 21, 87, 139, 148
Pope Sixtus V, 139
Pope Stephen V, 139

Ratzinger, Joseph, 29, 35, 36
Rauschenbusch, Walter, 240
Roberts, Benjamin Titus, 314, 315
Runyon, Ted, 325
Ruth, 115

Sanchez Sorondo, Marcelo, 210
Sarah (Sarai), 114, 115, 116, 119

Satan, 112, 113, 146, 174, 306–10
Saul, King, 135
Schenker, Adrien, 169
Schneider, John R., 230, 242
Scipio, 43
Seripando, 290
Seth, 115
Sider, Ron, 244–45
Smidt, Corwin, 272
Smith, Adam, 247
Socrates, 40, 74
Solomon, 38, 116
Sophocles, 41
Sprinkle, Preston, 173, 174
Stevenson, William, xiii, 331
Sullivan, Francis, SJ, 14, 16, 26, 27, 30, 34

Tamar, 142–44
Taylor, Jeremy, 321, 322
Tertullian, 18, 38, 48, 73, 137
Thiselton, Anthony, 179
Thorsen, Don, 70

Ury, Bill, 269

Via, Dan, 169
Vincent of Lerins, 33

Washburn, Christian D., xiii, 8, 10, 11, 27, 28, 131, 132, 138, 289, 331
Wesley, Charles, 318, 323, 326
Wesley, John, 53, 68–81, 143, 144, 172, 184, 238, 256–68, 270, 275, 312–29
Williams, Craig, 178
Williams, Roger, 239
Winthrop, John, 237
Wynkoop, Mildred, 68, 325

Yahweh, 93–94, 97–100

Zechariah, 97, 115
Zephaniah, 97
Ziapporah, 119

Index of Subjects

Abortion, xiii, 12, 31, 54, 65, 107, 124, 129, 137–41, 146, 154, 292
Adultery, 53, 54, 56, 57, 59, 60, 62, 64, 107, 108, 116, 120, 121, 132, 143, 144, 175, 181, 233, 292, 308

Baptism, 18, 63, 69, 88, 121, 145, 186, 239, 287, 310

Capitalism, 212–13, 245–47
Celibacy, 107–8, 127–28, 134–37, 175, 184
Children, ix, 73, 75, 90, 100, 106, 109, 110–28, 133–34, 137, 141, 145, 146, 147, 152–54, 161–62, 177, 185, 186, 218, 231, 232, 238, 241, 243, 299, 310
Common good, 192, 198, 199, 201–3, 205–6, 211, 220
Communism, 24, 210
Concupiscence, 101–2, 112, 133, 139
Contraception, xiii, 12, 13, 20, 21, 30, 54, 65, 106–7, 115, 120, 124, 129, 139, 141–54
Council, Ecumenical, xii, xvii, xviii, 6–19, 21, 23, 24–27, 30, 31, 33–36, 49, 50, 58, 61, 63, 64, 87, 91, 110, 131, 132, 133, 138, 139, 145, 150, 165, 181, 196, 237, 240, 285, 286, 287, 289, 290, 294, 296, 298, 300, 301

Death, 5, 6, 71, 88, 100, 108, 111, 112, 113, 115, 119, 122, 123, 125, 127, 142, 144, 174, 183, 192, 247, 248, 260, 272, 281, 286, 293–300, 305–11, 314, 320, 321–28, 329
Divorce, 12

Economics, 191
Eucharist, 88, 146, 186, 310

Fall of Adam and Eve, 53, 87, 105, 109, 112–14, 116, 118, 119, 127, 163, 174, 267
Fathers of the Church, 7, 18–19, 24, 39, 137–39, 142, 145, 146, 148, 154, 242, 299, 331
Fornication, 31, 60, 120, 292

Grace, 46, 58, 60, 63, 65, 66, 67, 78, 80, 90, 97, 106, 113, 114, 119, 122, 123, 129–131, 137, 154, 160, 187, 196, 200, 221, 260–64, 267, 269–71, 278

Heaven, 3, 85, 91, 112, 126, 127, 136–37, 183, 191, 281, 288, 293–99, 301, 303, 305–8, 310, 312, 314–20, 323–29
Hell, 14, 113, 114, 126, 238, 281, 286, 296, 299–301, 306, 308–9, 323, 328
Heterosexual, 176, 185, 186, 187
Homosexual, xiii, 31, 105, 108, 144, 145, 155–171, 172–87, 265, 292
Hymn, 270, 320, 322, 323, 326

Infallibility, 4, 10, 13, 14, 21, 24–37, 140, 150, 286, 287

339

Justice, 37–40, 42–44, 63, 88, 93, 121, 191, 192, 196, 199, 202, 211, 216, 218–20, 223, 235, 237, 248–50, 255, 273, 274, 277, 283, 288–91, 294, 310, 320, 332
Justification, ix, xii, 63, 71, 85, 89, 131, 248, 283–90, 294–96, 300, 302–3, 317, 328
Labor, 195, 197, 203, 209, 212, 213, 217, 222, 224, 245, 247, 252, 274, 296, 314
Law, Divine (Mosaic), 13, 30, 48, 88, 91–92, 95, 108, 130, 132, 133, 135, 166, 288
    Natural, xiii, 3, 4, 14, 21, 22, 24, 29–31, 37–47, 53, 85, 87, 88, 100, 129, 131, 140, 141, 150, 159, 160, 182, 192, 196, 200, 211, 212, 219, 224–28
Lord's Supper, 69, 78, 264, 319

Magisterium, xiii, 4, 5–36, 133, 138–40, 148–50, 196, 198, 229, 257, 258, 261, 270, 284, 287, 298, 300, 304
Marriage, xiii, 12, 13, 59, 60, 101, 106–8, 109–10, 114–17, 119–25, 127–28, 129–34, 136–37, 139, 143, 147, 148, 154, 155–58, 170, 176–78, 181, 185, 187, 265, 288
Merit, 14, 42, 44, 101, 131, 143, 221, 254, 281–82, 283, 285, 287–89, 291–304, 309, 311
Moral proximity, 230, 241–43

Natural family planning, 12, 129, 153–54

Penance, 114
Poverty, 67, 221, 237, 275–76
Private property, 195, 203, 210, 121, 212–13, 217, 218, 220, 224–26
Purgatory, 282, 297–99, 303, 305, 306
Redemption, 117, 209, 303
Rerum novarum, 195–96, 203, 209, 210–29

Sacrament, 20, 35, 36, 55, 58, 61, 65, 69, 106–8, 117, 118, 121–22, 128, 129–31, 134, 142, 154, 264, 300, 310
Sanctification, 66, 69, 118, 121, 129, 184, 191, 287, 316, 323
Sin, 3, 13, 44, 46, 53, 58, 59, 60, 63–65, 73, 77, 78, 85, 90, 93, 95, 96, 101, 108, 112, 115, 117, 120, 121, 122, 123, 143, 144, 145, 148, 158, 167, 168, 171, 173, 176, 184, 186, 201, 207, 209, 243, 249, 259, 263, 274, 286–87, 289, 294–305, 308–13, 317, 319, 325
    Mortal, 281, 286, 294, 295, 297, 300, 308, 309
    Original, 69, 123, 174, 283, 284, 285, 286, 299
    Venial, 281, 282, 296, 298, 300, 308
Socialism, xiii, 24, 210, 212–13, 218–22, 229
Solidarity, 205–6
Subsidiarity, 203–5

Quadrilateral, Wesleyan, 67–72, 82, 173, 258, 261, 262, 266, 267, 271, 325